Trade and Climate Change

A report by the United Nations Environment Programme and the World Trade Organization

Ludivine Tamiotti

Robert Teh

Vesile Kulaçoğlu

Anne Olhoff

Benjamin Simmons

Hussein Abaza

Disclaimers

For the WTO:

Any opinions reflected in this publication are the sole responsibility of the World Trade Organization (WTO) Secretariat. They do not purport to reflect the opinions or views of Members of the WTO.

For UNEP:

The designations employed and the presentation of the material in this publication do not imply the expression of any opinion whatsoever on the part of the United Nations Environment Programme concerning the legal status of any country, territory, city or area or of its authorities, or concerning delimitation of its frontiers or boundaries. Moreover, the views expressed do not necessarily represent the decision or the stated policy of the United Nations Environment Programme, nor does citing of trade names or commercial processes constitute endorsement.

WTO ISBN: 978-92-870-3522-6

UNEP ISBN: 978-92-807-3038-8 - Job number: DTI/1188/GE

Also available in French and Spanish:

French title ISBN: 978-92-870-3523-3

Spanish title ISBN: 978-92-870-3524-0

WTO publications can be obtained through major booksellers or from:

WTO Publications
World Trade Organization
154, rue de Lausanne
CH-1211 Geneva 21
Tel: (41 22) 739 52 08
Fax: (41 22) 739 54 58
Email: publications@wto.org

WTO online bookshop: http://onlinebookshop.wto.org
WTO website: http://www.wto.org
UNEP website: http://www.unep.org

Printed by WTO Secretariat, Switzerland, 2009

Contents

Part I

Part II

Part III

Part IV

Acknowledgments

The Report is the product of a joint and collaborative effort by the WTO Secretariat and UNEP.

From the WTO, Ludivine Tamiotti and Vesile Kulaçoğlu are the authors of Section III.B on "Multilateral Work related to Climate Change: Trade negotiations" and Part IV on "National Policies to Mitigate, and Adapt to, Climate Change and their Trade Implications", and Robert Teh is the author of Part II on "Trade and Climate Change: Theory and Evidence". The Report also benefited from the valuable comments and research assistance of a number of colleagues and consultants in the WTO.

From UNEP, Anne Olhoff and Ulrich E. Hansen from the UNEP Risoe Centre on Energy, Climate and Sustainable Development are the authors of Part I on "Climate Change: The Current State of Knowledge", and Benjamin Simmons from UNEP, and Xianli Zhu, John M. Christensen, John M. Callaway from the UNEP Risoe Centre are the authors of Section III.A on "Multilateral Work related to Climate Change: Multilateral action to reduce greenhouse gas emissions". Hussein Abaza, Chief of the UNEP Economics and Trade Branch, managed the preparation of UNEP's contribution. UNEP would also like to thank for their comments and assistance Ezra Clark, James S. Curlin, Kirsten Halsnaes, Blaise Horisberger, Adrian Lema, Anja von Moltke, Gaylor Montmasson-Clair, Gerald Mutisya, Mark Radka, John Scanlon, Megumi Seki, Rajendra Shende, Fulai Sheng, Lutz Weischer and Kaveh Zahedi.

The authors also wish to thank the following individuals from outside UNEP and the WTO Secretariat who took the time to review and comment on the earlier versions of the different parts of the Report: Niranjali Amerasinghe (Center for International Environmental Law), Richard Bradley (International Energy Agency), Adrian Macey (New Zealand's Climate Change Ambassador), Joost Pauwelyn (Graduate Institute of International Studies, Geneva), Stephen Porter (Center for International Environmental Law), Julia Reinaud (ClimateWorks Foundation) and Dave Sawyer (International Institute for Sustainable Development).

Vesile Kulaçoğlu, Director of the WTO Trade and Environment Division, led the overall preparation of the Report.

The production of the Report was managed by Anthony Martin and Serge Marin-Pache of the WTO Information and External Relations Division. Gratitude is also due to the WTO Language Services and Documentation Division for their hard work.

Foreword

Climate change is one of the greatest challenges facing the international community. Mitigating global warming and adapting to its consequences will require major economic investment and, above all, unequivocal determination on the part of policy-makers. With a challenge of this magnitude, multilateral cooperation is crucial, and a successful conclusion to the ongoing global negotiations on climate change would be the first step towards achieving sustainable development for future generations. As we march towards Copenhagen, we all have a responsibility to make a success of these negotiations. Climate change is not a problem that can afford to wait. It is a threat to future development, peace and prosperity that must be tackled with the greatest sense of urgency by the entire community of nations.

The WTO and UNEP are partners in the pursuit of sustainable development. As the principal UN agency for the protection of the environment, UNEP has years of experience in the field of climate change. The WTO has also launched its first ever trade and environment negotiation under the Doha Development Agenda. Certain climate change mitigation measures intersect with existing WTO rules and recent discussions in various fora have brought to the fore the importance of better understanding the various linkages between trade and climate change.

This report is the outcome of collaborative research between the WTO Secretariat and UNEP. It reviews how trade and climate change policies interact and how they can be mutually supportive. The aim is to promote greater understanding of this interaction and to assist policy-makers in this complex policy area. The report uniquely examines the intersection between trade and climate change from four different but correlated perspectives: the science of climate change; trade theory; multilateral efforts to tackle climate change; and national climate change policies and their effect on trade. The report underlines that, as a critical first step, governments must urgently seal a scientifically-credible and equitable deal in Copenhagen: one that addresses the need for both significant emission reductions and adaptation for vulnerable economies and communities. Moreover, it highlights that there is considerable scope and flexibility under WTO rules for addressing climate change at the national level, and that mitigation measures should be designed and implemented in a manner that ensures that trade and climate policies are mutually supportive.

With these findings in mind, we are pleased to present this report. It is an illustration of fruitful and increasing cooperation between our two organizations on issues of common interest.

Pascal Lamy
Director General
WTO

Achim Steiner
Executive Director
UNEP

Executive summary

This Report provides an overview of the key linkages between trade and climate change based on a review of available literature and a survey of relevant national policies. It begins with a summary of the current state of scientific knowledge on existing and projected climate change; on the impacts associated with climate change; and on the available options for responding, through mitigation and adaptation, to the challenges posed by climate change (Part I).

The scientific review is followed by an analysis on the economic aspects of the link between trade and climate change (Part II), and these two parts set the context for the subsequent discussion in the Report, which reviews in greater detail trade and climate change policies at both the international and national level.

Part III on international policy responses to climate change describes multilateral efforts at reducing greenhouse gas (GHG) emissions and adapting to the risks posed by climate change, and also discusses the role of the current trade and environment negotiations in promoting trade in climate mitigation technologies.

The final part of the Report gives an overview of a range of national policies and measures that have been used in a number of countries to reduce greenhouse gas emissions and to increase energy efficiency (Part IV). It presents key features in the design and implementation of these policies, in order to draw a clearer picture of their overall effect and potential impact on environmental protection, sustainable development and trade. It also gives, where appropriate, an overview of the WTO rules that may be relevant to such measures.

Climate change: the current state of knowledge

Climate change trends

The scientific evidence regarding climate change is compelling. Based on a review of thousands of scientific publications, the Intergovernmental Panel on Climate Change (IPCC) has concluded that the warming of the Earth's climate system is "unequivocal", and that human activities are "very likely" the cause of this warming. It is estimated that, over the last century, the global average surface temperature has increased by about 0.74° C.

Moreover, many greenhouse gases remain in the atmosphere for long periods of time, and as a result global warming will continue to affect the natural systems of the planet for several hundred years, even if emissions were reduced substantially or halted today. When greenhouse gases emitted in the past are included in the calculations, it has been shown that we are likely to be already committed to global warming of between 1.8° and 2.0° C.

Most worrying, however, is that global greenhouse gas emission levels are still growing, and are projected to continue growing over the coming decades unless there are significant changes to current laws, policies and actions. The International Energy Agency has reported that global greenhouse gas emissions have roughly doubled since the beginning of the 1970s. Current estimates indicate that these emissions will increase by between 25 and 90 per cent in the period from 2000 to 2030, with the proportion of greenhouse gases emitted by developing countries becoming significantly larger in the coming decades.

Over the last half century greenhouse gas emissions per person in industrialized countries have been around four times higher than emissions per person in developing countries, and for the least-developed countries the difference is even greater. The member countries of the Organisation for Economic Co-operation and Development (OECD), which are the world's most industrialized countries, are responsible for an estimated 77 per cent of the total greenhouse gases which were emitted in the past. The emissions from developing countries, however, are becoming increasingly significant: it is estimated that two-thirds of new emissions to the atmosphere are from non-OECD countries. Moreover, between 2005 and 2030, the greenhouse gas emission levels from non-OECD countries are expected to increase by an average of 2.5 per cent each year, whereas the projected average annual increase for OECD countries is 0.5 per cent.

The result of these increased emissions will be a further rise in temperatures. Current estimates of climate change have calculated that global average temperatures will increase by 1.4° to 6.4° C between 1990 and 2100. This is significant, as a 2°-3° C increase in temperature is often cited as a threshold limit, beyond which it may be impossible to avoid dangerous interference with the global climate system.

Climate change impacts

As greenhouse gas emissions and temperatures increase, the impacts from climate change are expected to become more widespread and to intensify. For example, even with small increases in average temperature, the type, frequency and intensity of extreme weather – such as hurricanes, typhoons, floods, droughts, and storms – are projected to increase. The distribution of these weather events, however, is expected to vary considerably among regions and countries, and impacts will depend to a large extent on the vulnerability of populations or ecosystems.

Developing countries, and particularly the poorest and most marginalized populations within these countries, will generally be both the most adversely affected by the impacts of future climate change and the most vulnerable to its effects, because they are less able to adapt than developed countries and populations. In addition, climate change risks compound the other challenges which are already faced by these countries, including tackling poverty, improving health care, increasing food security and improving access to sources of energy. For instance, climate change is projected to lead to hundreds of millions of people having limited access to water supplies or facing inadequate water quality, which will, in turn, lead to greater health problems.

Although the impacts of climate change are specific to location and to the level of development, most sectors of the global economy are expected to be affected and these impacts will often have implications for trade. For example, three trade-related areas are considered to be particularly vulnerable to climate change.

Agriculture is considered to be one of the sectors most vulnerable to climate change, and also represents a key sector for international trade. In low-latitude regions, where most developing countries are located, reductions of about 5 to 10 per cent in the yields of major cereal crops are projected even in the case of small temperature increases of around 1° C. Although it is expected that local temperature increases of between 1° C and 3° C would have beneficial impacts on agricultural outputs in mid- to high-latitude regions, warming beyond this range will most likely result in increasingly negative impacts for these regions also. According to some studies, crop yields in some African countries could fall by up to 50 per cent by 2020, with net revenues from crops falling by as much as 90 per cent by 2100. Depending on the location, agriculture will also be prone to water scarcity due to loss of glacial meltwater and reduced rainfall or droughts.

Tourism is another industry that may be particularly vulnerable to climate change, for example, through changes in snow cover, coastal degradation and extreme weather. Both the fisheries and forestry sectors also risk being adversely impacted by climate change. Likewise, there are expected to be major impacts on coastal ecosystems, including the disappearance of coral and the loss of marine biodiversity.

Finally, one of the clearest impacts will be on *trade infrastructure and routes*. The IPCC has identified port facilities, as well as buildings, roads, railways, airports and bridges, as being dangerously at risk of damage from rising sea levels and the increased occurrence of instances of extreme weather, such as flooding and hurricanes. Moreover, it is projected that changes in sea ice, particularly in the Arctic, will lead to the availability of new shipping routes.

Climate change mitigation and adaptation

The projections of future climate change and its associated impacts amply illustrate the need for increased efforts focused on climate change mitigation and adaptation. Mitigation refers to policies and options aimed at reducing greenhouse gas emissions or at enhancing the "sinks" (such as oceans or forests) which absorb carbon or carbon dioxide from the atmosphere. Adaptation, on the other hand, refers to responses to diminish the negative impacts of climate change or to exploit its potential benefits. In other words, mitigation reduces the rate and magnitude of climate change and its associated impacts, whereas adaptation reduces the consequences of those impacts by increasing the ability of humans or ecosystems to cope with the changes.

Mitigation and adaptation also differ in terms of timescales and geographical location. Although the costs of emission reductions are often specific to the location where the reduction scheme is brought into action, the benefits are long term and worldwide, since emission reductions contribute to decreasing overall atmospheric concentrations of greenhouse gases. Adaptation, by contrast, is characterized by benefits in the short to medium term, and both the costs and the benefits are primarily local. Despite these differences, there are important linkages between mitigation and adaptation. Action in one area can have important implications for the other, particularly in terms of ecosystem management, carbon sequestration and soil and land management. For instance, reforestation can serve both to mitigate climate change by acting as a carbon sink and can help to adapt to climate change by slowing land degradation.

Most international action has been focused on mitigation. The emphasis on mitigation reflects a belief – widely held until the end of the 1990s – that an internationally coordinated effort to reduce greenhouse gas emissions would be sufficient to avoid the most significant climate change impacts. As a result, mitigation efforts are relatively well-defined and there is considerable information available on the opportunities and costs associated with achieving a given reduction of greenhouse gas emissions.

Greenhouse gas emissions arise from almost all the economic activities and day-to-day functions of society and the range of practices and technologies that are potentially available for achieving emission reductions are equally broad and diverse. Most studies addressing mitigation opportunities have, however, largely converged around a few key areas that have the potential to deliver significant reductions in emission levels. These include using energy more efficiently in transport, buildings and industry; switching to zero- or low-carbon energy technologies; reducing deforestation and improving land and farming management practices; and improving waste management.

Several studies have concluded that even ambitious emission targets can be achieved through the use of existing technologies and practices in the areas identified above. For instance, a study by the International Energy Agency demonstrates how employing technologies that already exist or that are currently being developed could bring global energy-related carbon dioxide (CO_2) emissions back to their 2005 levels by 2050.

The extent to which these opportunities are fulfilled depends on the policies that are set up to promote mitigation activities. Multilateral agreement on a target for greenhouse gas stabilization in the atmosphere, as well as firm and binding commitments on the level of global greenhouse gas emission reductions that will be required to achieve this stabilization target, will be instrumental in the large-scale deployment of emission-reduction technologies and practices. Policies and measures at the national level are also essential for creating incentives for consumers and enterprises to demand and adopt climate-friendly products and technologies.

Financing, technology transfer and cooperation between developing and industrialized countries is another key factor in achieving emission reductions. In particular, bringing the potential of global mitigation to fruition will also depend on the ability of developing countries to manufacture, diffuse and maintain low-carbon technologies, and this can be facilitated through trade and technology transfer. The costs of the technological solutions will have implications for the relative emphasis given to various mitigation sectors and technologies. Technological development and reductions in the cost of existing technologies and of technologies yet to be commercialized will also have a significant role to play in overall mitigation.

Scientific analyses and multilateral debate on the costs of greenhouse gas emission reductions have, to a large extent, focused on two specific stabilization scenarios and targets. The first target, to limit global warming to 2° C, has been put forward by a number of countries. The second target of 550 parts per million (ppm) of CO_2-equivalent (CO_2-eq) would lead to a scenario where the CO_2 concentration in the atmosphere would be stabilized at around twice its pre-industrial level, which would correspond to a temperature increase of around 3° C. This scenario has been most extensively studied by the IPCC, since it is considered to be the upper limit for avoiding dangerous human interference with the climate system.

The two stabilization targets would have very different implications for the estimated macro-economic costs at the global level. Whereas the IPCC estimates that a stabilization target of around 550 ppm CO_2-eq would result in an annual reduction of global gross domestic product (GDP) of 0.2 to 2.5 per cent, a stabilization target of 2° C would imply an annual reduction in global GDP of more than 3 per cent. In terms of "carbon pricing" (i.e. charging polluters a set price according to the amount of greenhouse gases emitted), the IPCC estimates that carbon prices of US$ 20-80/tonne of CO_2-eq would be required by 2030 to put the world on track to achieving stabilization of emissions at around 550 ppm CO_2-eq by 2100.

Activities focused on adapting to climate change are more difficult to define and measure than mitigation activities. The potential for adaptation depends on the "adaptive capacity" or the ability of people or ecological systems to respond successfully to climate variability and change. Contrary to mitigation, which can be measured in terms of reduced greenhouse gas emissions, adaptation cannot be assessed by any one single indicator. Moreover, its success depends on a large number of factors that are related to overall development issues, such as political stability, market development, and education, as well as income and poverty levels.

A range of responses to climate change are possible, covering a wide array of practices and technologies. Many of these are well-known and have been adopted and refined over the centuries to cope with climate variability, such as changing levels of rainfall. Studies focused on adaptation have noted that action is rarely based only on a response to climate change. Instead, in most cases, adaptation measures are undertaken as part of larger sectoral and national initiatives related to, for example, planning and policy development, improvements to the water sector and integrated coastal zone management, or as a response to current climate variability and its implications, such as flooding and droughts.

It is generally recognized that technological innovation, together with the financing, transfer and widespread implementation of technologies, will be central to global efforts to adapt to climate change. Adaptation technologies may be applied in a variety of ways, and may include, for example, infrastructure construction (dykes, sea walls, harbours, railways, etc.); building design and structure; and research into, development and deployment of drought-resistant crops.

The costs of these technologies and of other adaptation activities may be considerable. However, very few adaptation cost estimates have been made available to date, and they differ considerably (with estimates varying from US$ 4 billion to US$ 86 billion for annual adaptation costs in developing countries, for example). Nonetheless, there is broad agreement in the literature that the benefits of adaptation will outweigh the costs.

As previously stated, technological innovation, as well as the transfer and widespread implementation of technologies, will be central to global efforts to address climate change mitigation and adaptation. International transfer of technologies may broadly be understood as involving two aspects. One concerns the transfer of technologies which are physically embodied in tangible assets or capital goods, such as industrial plant and equipment, machinery, components, and devices. Another aspect of technology transfer relates to the intangible knowledge and information associated with the technology or technological system in question. Since it is predominantly private companies that retain ownership of various technologies, it is relevant to identify ways within the private sector, such as foreign direct investment, licence or royalty agreements and different forms of cooperation arrangements, which can facilitate technology transfer. Moreover, bilateral and multilateral technical assistance programmes can play a key role in technology transfer.

A continuing debate within political discussions and among academia has been whether the protection of intellectual property rights – such as copyrights, patents or trade secrets – impedes or facilitates the transfer of technologies to developing countries. One key rationale for the protection of intellectual property rights, and in particular patents, is to encourage innovation: patent protection ensures that innovators can reap the benefits and recoup the costs of their research and development (R&D) investments. On the other hand, it has also been argued that, in some cases, stronger protection of intellectual property rights might act as an impediment to the acquisition of new technologies and innovations in developing countries. While strong patent laws provide the legal security for technology-related transactions to occur, firms in developing countries may not have the necessary financial means to purchase expensive patented technologies.

The importance of intellectual property rights needs to be set in a relevant context. In fact, many of the technologies which are relevant to addressing climate change, such as better energy management or building insulation, may not be protected by patents or other intellectual property rights. Moreover, even where technologies and products benefit from intellectual property protection, the likelihood of competing technologies and substitute products being available is thought to be high. Further studies in this area would be useful.

Trade and climate change: theory and evidence

The 60 years prior to 2008 have been marked by an unprecedented expansion of international trade. In terms of volume, world trade is nearly 32 times greater now than it was in 1950, and the share of global GDP it represents rose from 5.5 per cent in 1950 to 21 per cent in 2007. This enormous expansion in world trade has been made possible by technological changes which have dramatically reduced the cost of transportation and communications, and by the adoption of more open trade and investment policies. The number of countries participating in international trade has increased: developing countries, for instance, now account for 34 per cent of merchandise trade – about double their share in the early 1960s.

This expansion in trade raises questions such as: "Will trade opening lead to more greenhouse gas emissions?" and "How much does trade change greenhouse gas emissions?" Trade opening can affect the amount of emissions in three principal ways, which are typically referred to as the scale, composition and technique effects.

The *scale effect* refers to the expansion of economic activity arising from trade opening, and its effect on greenhouse gas emissions. This increased level of economic activity will require greater energy use and will therefore lead to higher levels of greenhouse gas emissions.

The *composition effect* describes the way that trade opening changes the structure of a country's production in response to changes in relative prices, and the consequences of this on emission levels. Changes in the structure of a liberalizing country's production will depend on where the country's "comparative advantage" lies. The effect on a country's greenhouse gas emissions will depend on whether a country has a comparative advantage in emission-intensive sectors and whether these sectors are expanding or contracting. The composition of production in an economy that is opening its markets to trade may also be a response to differences in environmental regulations between countries (resulting in the "pollution haven hypothesis", which suggests that high-emission industries may relocate to countries with less stringent emission regulation policies).

Finally, the *technique effect* refers to improvements in the methods by which goods and services are produced, so that the emission intensity of output is reduced. This is the principal way in which trade opening can help mitigate climate change. A decline in greenhouse gas emission intensity can come about in two ways. First, more open trade can increase the availability, and lower the cost of, climate-friendly goods and services. This will help meet the demand in countries whose domestic industries do not produce these climate-friendly goods and services in sufficient quantities or at affordable prices. Such potential benefits of more open trade highlight the importance of the WTO's current trade negotiations under the Doha Round, which aim to open markets for environmental goods and services.

Second, as income levels rise because of trade opening, populations may demand lower greenhouse gas emissions. For rising income to lead to environmental improvement, governments must supply the appropriate tax and regulatory measures to meet the public's demand. Only if such measures are put in place will firms adopt cleaner production technologies, so that a given level of output can be produced with fewer greenhouse gas emissions.

It has been pointed out, however, that the positive link between per capita income and environmental quality may not necessarily apply to climate change. Since greenhouse gas emissions are released into the atmosphere, and since part of the cost is borne by populations in other countries, there may not be a strong incentive for any given nation to take action to reduce such emissions, even if its citizens' incomes are improving.

Since the scale and technique effects tend to work in opposite directions, and the composition effect depends on the comparative advantage of countries and on differences in regulations between countries, the overall impact of trade on greenhouse gas emissions cannot be determined *a priori*. The net impact of greenhouse gas emissions will depend on the magnitude or strength of each of the three effects, and ascertaining this requires detailed empirical analyses.

Three aspects of the empirical literature on trade opening and emission levels have been reviewed: econometric or statistical studies of the effects of trade opening on emissions; estimates of the "environmental Kuznets curve" for greenhouse gases (which describes the relationship between higher per capita incomes and lower greenhouse gas emissions); and assessments – carried out by the parties to various trade agreements – of the environmental impact of these agreements.

Most of the statistical studies reviewed indicate that more open trade will most likely lead to increased CO_2 emissions, and suggest that the scale effect tends to offset the technique and composition effects. Some studies indicate, however, that there may be differences in outcomes between developed and developing countries, with environmental improvement being observed in OECD countries and environmental deterioration in developing countries.

The empirical literature on the environmental Kuznets curve for greenhouse gas emissions has produced inconsistent results, although the more recent studies tend to show that there is no relationship between higher income and lower CO_2 emissions. Studies that differentiate between OECD and non-OECD countries tend to find evidence of an environmental Kuznets curve for the first group of countries but not for the second.

Although many developed countries now require environmental assessments of trade agreements that they enter into, these assessments tend to be focused on national rather than cross-border or global pollutants. A few of these assessments have raised concerns about the possible increase in greenhouse gas emissions from increased transport activity, although none have attempted a detailed quantitative analysis of these effects. Some assessments have alluded to the potential of mitigation measures to reduce the effects of increased emissions from transport.

Trade involves a process of exchange requiring that goods be transported from the place of production to the place of consumption. Consequently, international trade expansion is likely to lead to increased use of transportation services. Merchandise trade can be transported by air, road, rail and water. Maritime transport accounts for the bulk of international trade by volume and for a significant share by value. Recent studies indicate that, excluding trade within the European Union, seaborne cargo accounted for 89.6 per cent of world trade by volume and 70.1 per cent of global trade by value in 2006.

International maritime shipping, however, accounted for only 11.8 per cent of the transport sector's total contribution to CO_2 emissions. Aviation represents an 11.2 per cent share of CO_2 emissions, rail transport constitutes another 2 per cent share and road transport has the biggest share, at 72.6 per cent of the total CO_2 emissions from transport. Among the different modes of transport, shipping is the most carbon-emission efficient, and this should be taken into account when assessing the contribution of trade to transport-related emissions.

International trade can serve as a channel for spreading technologies that mitigate climate change. The spread of technological knowledge made possible by trade provides one mechanism by which developing countries can benefit from developed countries' innovations in climate change technology. There are several ways in which this transmission of technology can occur. One is through the import of intermediate and capital goods which a country could not have produced on its own. Second, trade may increase communication opportunities between countries, allowing developing countries to learn about production methods and design from developed countries. Third, international trade can increase the available opportunities for adapting foreign technologies to meet local conditions. Finally, the learning process made possible by international economic relations reduces the cost of future innovation and imitation.

Beyond offering opportunities for mitigation, trade can also play a valuable role in helping humankind adapt to a warmer future. Climate change threatens to alter geographical patterns of production, with food and agricultural products likely to be the most affected. Trade can provide a means to bridge differences in demand and supply, so that countries where climate change creates scarcity are able to meet their needs by importing from countries where these goods and services continue to be available.

A number of economic studies have simulated how trade can help reduce the cost of adapting to climate change in the agricultural or food sectors. However, some of these studies also suggest that the extent to which international trade can contribute to adaptation depends on how agricultural prices – which are the signals of economic scarcity or abundance – are transmitted across markets. Where these price signals are distorted by the use of certain trade measures (such as subsidies), the contribution that trade can make to adaptation to climate change may be significantly reduced.

Finally, climate change can affect the pattern and volume of international trade flows. It may alter the comparative advantage of countries and lead to shifts in the pattern of international trade. This effect will be stronger in those countries whose comparative advantage stems from climatic or geophysical sources. Moreover, climate change can also increase the vulnerability of the supply, transport and distribution chains upon which international trade depends. Any disruptions to these chains will raise the costs of engaging in international trade.

Multilateral work related to climate change

Multilateral action to reduce greenhouse gas emissions

International policy responses

Although scientific discussions regarding climate change date back more than a century, it was not until the 1980s that policy-makers started to actively focus on the issue. The IPCC was launched in 1988 by UNEP and the World Meteorological Organization (WMO) to undertake the first authoritative assessment of the scientific literature on climate change. In its first report in 1990, the IPCC confirmed that climate change represents a serious threat and, more importantly, called for a global treaty to address the challenge.

The IPCC report catalyzed government support for international negotiations on climate change, which formally commenced in 1991, and concluded with the adoption of the UNFCCC in 1992 at the Earth Summit. The Convention, which seeks the stabilization of greenhouse gases in the atmosphere at a level that would prevent dangerous human interference with the climate system, was groundbreaking, as it represented the first global effort to address climate change.

The Convention elaborates a number of principles to guide its parties in reaching this objective, including the principle of "common but differentiated responsibility" first articulated in the 1992 Earth Summit Rio Declaration, which recognizes that, even though all countries bear a responsibility to address climate change, countries have not all contributed equally to causing the problem, nor are they all equally equipped to address it.

Although the Convention sets out the general framework for international climate change action, it did not create mandatory emission limits and commitments. However, as scientific consensus and alarm regarding climate change grew in the years following the Earth Summit, there were increased calls for the conclusion of a supplementary agreement with legally binding commitments for reducing greenhouse gas emissions. This increased political momentum ultimately led to the signing of the Kyoto Protocol in 1997. The Protocol establishes specific and binding emission reduction commitments for industrialized countries, and represents a significant step forward in a multilateral response to climate change.

The Kyoto Protocol builds on the UNFCCC principle of "common but differentiated responsibility" by creating different obligations for developing and industrialized countries based on responsibility for past emissions and level of development.

Developing countries (non-Annex I parties), for example, have no binding emission reduction obligations. In contrast, industrialized countries and economies in transition (Annex I parties) must meet agreed levels of emission reductions over an initial commitment period that runs from 2008 to 2012. The exact amount of emission reduction commitments varies among the industrialized countries, but the overall total commitment represents a reduction of greenhouse gas emissions to at least 5 per cent less than 1990 emission levels.

In addition to establishing binding emission reduction commitments, in order to ensure compliance the Protocol also includes requirements for Annex I parties to monitor and report their greenhouse gas emissions. Annex I parties are also required to provide financial and technological support to developing countries to assist in their efforts to mitigate climate change.

The Kyoto Protocol includes three "flexibility mechanisms" (emission trading, Joint Implementation, and the Clean Development Mechanism (CDM)) to help parties meet their obligations and achieve their emission reduction commitments in a more cost-efficient manner. Emission trading allows parties to buy emission credits from other parties. These emission credits may be the unused emission allowances from other Annex I parties or they may be derived from Joint Implementation or CDM climate-mitigation projects.

Joint Implementation allows an Annex I party to invest in emission-reduction projects in the territory of another Annex I party, and so earn emission reduction units that can be used to meet its own emission target. In a similar manner, the CDM allows an Annex I party to meet its obligations by earning emission reduction units from projects implemented in a developing country. However, given that developing countries do not have binding emission reduction targets, the CDM requires evidence that the emission reductions achieved through such projects are "additional" in the sense that they would not have occurred without the CDM financing.

As the first commitment period of the Kyoto Protocol has just begun, it is too early to determine the ultimate effectiveness of its provisions. Nonetheless, it appears that most industrialized countries will not be able to meet their targets by the end of the commitment period. Moreover, global greenhouse gas emissions have increased by approximately 24 per cent since 1990, despite action taken under the UNFCCC and Kyoto Protocol.

Climate change negotiations

The challenge now facing climate change negotiators is to agree on a multilateral response to climate change after the Kyoto Protocol's first commitment period has expired (i.e. in the "post-2012" period). At the 13th UNFCCC Conference of the Parties meeting in Bali, Indonesia, in 2007, parties agreed on a "Bali Action Plan" with the aim of realizing long-term cooperative action on climate change. It was also agreed that the negotiations already under way on the post-2012 commitments of Kyoto Protocol Annex I parties would continue as a separate negotiating track.

While the two negotiating tracks are not formally linked, the negotiations around them are closely intertwined. Both negotiating efforts aim at reaching agreement at the 15th Conference of the Parties to the UNFCCC meeting in December 2009 in Copenhagen, Denmark.

The Bali Action Plan calls for measurable, reportable and verifiable emission reduction commitments on the part of developed countries. Significantly, it also considers, for the first time, the involvement of developing countries in mitigation efforts through non-binding "nationally appropriate mitigation actions", which must be supported by financing, capacity-building and technology transfer from developed countries.

Under the separate negotiating track focused on post-2012 commitments for Kyoto Protocol Annex I countries, parties appear to be in general agreement that the Protocol's cap-and-trade approach (i.e. limiting or capping emission levels and allowing carbon trading among countries) should be retained, but that specific mechanisms for achieving emission reductions require refinement based on the lessons learned so far during implementation. However, no conclusions have been reached on the range of emission reductions to be undertaken by developed countries after 2012.

Montreal Protocol

While the UNFCCC and the Kyoto Protocol represent the principal agreements addressing climate change, the Montreal Protocol on Substances that Deplete the Ozone Layer has emerged as another important mechanism for mitigating climate change. The Montreal Protocol was established in 1987 in response to stratospheric ozone destruction caused by chlorofluorocarbons (CFCs) and other ozone-depleting substances (ODS). The Protocol is focused on phasing-out the consumption and production of nearly 100 ODS chemicals. These chemicals are deliberately not addressed under the UNFCCC or the Kyoto Protocol, although many are potent greenhouse gases which are used on a global scale.

The Montreal Protocol has been extremely effective in reducing the use of ODS. It is estimated that the Protocol will have decreased the contribution of ODS emissions to climate change by 135 $GtCO_2$-eq over the 1990 to 2010 period. To put this into perspective, this means that the Montreal Protocol has achieved four to five times greater levels of climate mitigation than the target contemplated by the first commitment period under the Kyoto Protocol.

The Montreal Protocol recently had another breakthrough that will further contribute to reducing greenhouse gas emissions. In 2007, the parties decided to accelerate the phase-out of hydrochlorofluorocarbons (HCFCs), which were developed as transitional replacements for CFCs. According to various estimates, phasing out HCFCs could result in an additional emission reduction of 17.5 to 25.5 $GtCO_2$-eq over the period from 2010 to 2050.

WTO trade and environment negotiations

In the Marrakesh Agreement establishing the WTO, members highlighted a clear link between sustainable development and trade opening – in order to ensure that market opening goes hand in hand with environmental and social objectives. In the ongoing Doha Round of negotiations, members went further in their pledge to pursue a sustainable development path by launching the first-ever multilateral trade and environment negotiations.

One issue addressed in the Doha Round is the relationship between the WTO and multilateral environmental agreements (MEAs), such as the UNFCCC. In this area of negotiations, WTO members have focused on opportunities for further strengthening cooperation between the WTO and MEA secretariats, as well as promoting coherence and mutual supportiveness between the international trade and environment regimes.

While, to date, there have been no WTO legal disputes directly involving MEAs, a successful outcome to the Doha negotiations will nevertheless contribute to reinforcing the relationship between the trade and environmental regimes. The negotiators have drawn from experiences in the negotiation and implementation of MEAs at the national level, and are seeking ways to improve national coordination and cooperation between trade and environment policies.

Also in the context of the Doha Round, ministers have singled out environmental goods and services for liberalization. The negotiations call for "the reduction, or as appropriate, elimination of tariff and non-tariff barriers to environmental goods and services". The objective is to improve access to more efficient, diverse and less expensive environmental goods and services on the global market, including goods and services that contribute to climate change mitigation and adaptation.

Climate-friendly technologies can be employed to mitigate and adapt to climate change in diverse sectors. Many of these technologies involve products currently being discussed in the Doha negotiations, such as wind and hydropower turbines, solar water heaters, photovoltaic cells, tanks for the production of biogas, and landfill liners for methane collection. In this context, the WTO environmental goods and services negotiations have a role to play in improving access to climate-friendly goods and technologies.

There are two key rationales for reducing tariffs and other trade-distorting measures in climate-friendly goods and technologies. First, reducing or eliminating import tariffs and non-tariff barriers in these types of products should reduce their price and therefore facilitate their deployment. The access to lower-cost and more energy-efficient technologies may be particularly important for industries that must comply with climate change mitigation policies (see Part IV).

Second, liberalization of trade in climate-friendly goods could provide incentives and domestic expertise for producers to expand the production and export of these goods. Trade in climate-friendly goods has seen a considerable increase in the past few years, including exports from a number of developing countries.

National policies to mitigate, and adapt to, climate change, and their trade implications

A number of policy measures have been used or are available at the national level to mitigate climate change. They are typically distinguished as either regulatory measures (i.e. regulations and standards) or economic incentives (e.g. taxes, tradable permits, and subsidies).

The range of climate policy measures that are in place or that are currently being considered are described according to their key objectives: internalization of the environmental costs of greenhouse gas emissions;

regulation of the use of climate-friendly goods and technologies; or the development and deployment of such goods. These distinctions also provide a useful framework for considering the potential relevance of trade rules.

Price and market mechanisms to internalize environmental costs of GHG emissions

A key environmental policy measure, often used by regulators to induce change in behaviour, is to put a price on pollution. This Report describes two types of pricing mechanism that have been used to reduce greenhouse gas emissions: taxes and cap-and-trade systems. Such pricing tools aim at internalizing the environmental externality (i.e. climate change) by setting a price on the carbon content of energy consumed or on the CO_2 emissions generated in the production and/or consumption of goods.

Paying a price for carbon involves an additional cost for producers and/or consumers, and acts as an incentive to limit their use of carbon-intensive fuels and products, to abate emissions and to shift to less carbon-intensive energy sources and products. Moreover, taxes and emission trading schemes (in particular schemes featuring auctioning) may be a significant source of public revenue, which can then be "recycled" to the industries that are most affected by these pricing mechanisms. For instance, the revenue may be used to fund programmes that help industries switch to less carbon-intensive methods of production or to reduce the burden imposed by some other taxes.

The approach taken by a number of countries over the last two decades has been to put a price on the introduction of CO_2 into the atmosphere by imposing taxes on the consumption of fossil fuels according to their level of carbon content. In contrast, a number of other countries opted not to adopt an explicit "carbon tax", but instead have introduced general taxes on the consumption of energy, which are aimed at promoting energy efficiency and energy savings, and which in turn have an effect on CO_2 emissions. Furthermore, governments often use a combination of tax on CO_2 emissions and tax on energy use.

In theory, in order to be fully efficient, a carbon tax should be set at a level that internalizes the costs of environmental damage, so that prices reflect the real environmental costs of pollution (this is known as a "Pigouvian tax"). However, experience shows that genuine Pigouvian carbon taxes have rarely been used by policy-makers because of the difficulties in evaluating the cost of damage associated with, in this case, greenhouse gas emissions. Instead, countries have followed a more pragmatic "Baumol-Oates" approach, in which the tax is set at a rate which should influence taxpayers' behaviour in order to achieve a given environmental objective.

Another approach to setting a carbon price is to fix a cap on total emissions, translate this into allowances to cover those emissions, and create a market to trade these allowances at a price determined by the market. At the national level, the first and most wide-ranging trading scheme for greenhouse gas emissions, the EU Emission Trading Scheme, was introduced in 2005. A number of other mandatory or voluntary emission trading schemes have been put in place at state and regional levels in developed countries. Currently, important proposals for establishing emission trading schemes at the national level in several developed countries are also being discussed.

The emission trading schemes share a number of design characteristics that are important, as they determine the costs for participants, and may influence the overall trade implications of the schemes. Such characteristics include: the type of emission target (a general cap on the total emissions that regulated sources can emit or an emission benchmark for each individual source); the number of participants and the range of sectors covered; the types of gases covered by the policy; the method used by the regulator to distribute emission allowances (free allocation or auctioning); the linkages with other emission trading schemes; and the existence of flexibility mechanisms, such as banking or borrowing of emission allowances.

Whether the regulator chooses a carbon tax or an emission trading scheme may be influenced by the fact that the price of the carbon tax is determined in advance, whereas there is uncertainty about the costs of achieving a desired level of emission reduction. A carbon tax may therefore be more appropriate than an emission trading scheme, especially when there is no particular risk of passing a critical threshold level for emissions.

On the other hand, an emission trading scheme may be preferable in situations where greater environmental certainty is needed, a typical case being when the concentration of greenhouse gases in the atmosphere in the longer term is in danger of passing a certain threshold beyond which the likelihood of unwanted environmental consequences increases to unacceptable levels. In such a case, stabilization of emissions below this threshold concentration is essential.

Most of the studies undertaken in the early 1990s on carbon taxes show that these have small but positive effects on CO_2 emissions in specific sectors, such as heating, and in the industrial and housing sectors. Existing emission trading schemes have not long been in operation, and most schemes, until now, have had limited scope and thus limited range for curbing emissions. Longer periods of implementation are needed to gather the necessary information for an environmental evaluation of the effectiveness of emission trading schemes.

The development of the emission trading scheme in Europe, and proposals for the introduction of mandatory emission trading schemes in other developed economies has given rise to a considerable amount of debate on how to design an instrument that would impose minimal costs for the economy, and yet effectively contribute to mitigating climate change. Of particular concern has been the extent to which the international competitiveness of energy-intensive industrial sectors will be affected by carbon-constraining domestic policies.

Related to the potential impact on competitiveness, the issue of "carbon leakage" (in other words, the risk that energy-intensive industries will simply relocate to countries without climate regulations) has also recently received a great deal of attention. Indeed, in their legislation on emission trading schemes, some countries are debating or have already introduced criteria – such as the carbon or energy intensity of production processes or the trade exposure of the industry concerned – to identify sectors that would be at risk of carbon leakage.

It should be noted, however, that studies to date find generally that the cost of compliance with an emission trading scheme is a relatively minor component of a firm's overall costs, which include exchange-rate fluctuations, transportation costs, energy prices and differences across countries in the cost of labour. Of course, the carbon constraint in future emission trading schemes (for example, in Phase III of the EU-ETS) is expected to be more stringent, with a lower capped limit and fewer free allowances. This may therefore increase the potential impact of carbon costs on the competitiveness of a number of industrial sectors.

In this context, a number of emission trading scheme design features have been discussed, which may reduce the cost of compliance for some energy-intensive and trade exposed industries. These design features include free allocation of emission allowances, exemptions for particularly sensitive industries, or the use of certain flexibility mechanisms, such as borrowing or banking of emission allowances.

However, alleviations and exemptions may not be sufficient and the question that then arises is whether concerns over carbon leakage and competitiveness can justify governmental measures that impose similar costs on foreign producers, through the use of border adjustment measures. Such adjustments could, for example, take the form of a requirement for importers of a given product to acquire and submit emission allowances in cases where carbon leakage is occurring in the competing domestic sector.

There are two main challenges in implementing border measures: providing a clear rationale for border measures (i.e. accurately assessing carbon leakage and competitiveness losses); and determining a "fair" price to be imposed on imported products to bring their prices into line with the domestic cost of compliance with an emission trading scheme. Discussions of such measures so far have highlighted the difficulty in implementing a border adjustment mechanism that responds to the concerns of domestic industries while still contributing to the wider goal of global climate change mitigation.

A number of WTO rules may be relevant to carbon taxes and cap-and-trade systems and related border measures, including core trade disciplines, such as the non discrimination principle. The provisions of the Agreement on Subsidies and Countervailing Measures (SCM) may also be relevant to emission trading schemes, for instance if allowances are allocated free of charge. Moreover, detailed rules on border tax adjustments (BTAs) exist in the General Agreement on Tariffs and Trade (GATT) and the WTO SCM Agreement. These rules permit, under certain conditions, the use of BTAs on imported and exported products. Indeed, border adjustments on internal taxes are a commonly used measure with respect to domestic indirect taxes on the sale and consumption of goods, such as cigarettes or alcohol. The objective of a border tax adjustment is to level the playing field between taxed domestic industries and untaxed foreign competition by ensuring that internal taxes on products are trade neutral.

In the context of climate change, the debate has mainly focused on two aspects: the extent to which domestic carbon/energy taxes (which are imposed on inputs, such as energy) are eligible for border tax adjustments; and the extent to which BTAs may be limited to inputs which are physically incorporated into the final products.

The general approach under WTO rules has been to acknowledge that some degree of trade restriction may be necessary to achieve certain policy objectives, as long as a number of carefully crafted conditions are respected. WTO case law has confirmed that WTO rules do not trump environmental requirements. If, for instance, a border measure related to climate change was found to be inconsistent with one of the core provisions of the GATT, justification might nonetheless be sought under the general exceptions to the GATT (i.e. Article XX), provided that two key conditions are met.

First, the measure must fall under at least one of the GATT exceptions, and a connection must be established between the stated goal of the climate change policy and the border measure at issue. It should be noted in this regard that WTO members' autonomy to determine their own environmental objectives has been reaffirmed by the WTO's Dispute Settlement Body on a number of occasions (for example, in the *US - Gasoline* and the *Brazil - Retreaded Tyres* cases). Although no policies aimed at climate change mitigation have been discussed in the dispute settlement system of the WTO, it has been argued that policies aimed at reducing CO_2 emissions could fall under the GATT exceptions, as they are intended to protect human beings from the negative consequences of climate change; and to conserve not only the planet's climate, but also certain plant and animal species that may disappear as a result of global warming.

Second, the manner in which the measure in question will be applied is important: in particular, the measure must not constitute a "means of arbitrary or unjustifiable discrimination" or a "disguised restriction on international trade". GATT case law has shown that the implementation of a measure in a way that does not amount to arbitrary or unjustifiable discrimination or to a disguised restriction on international trade has often been the most challenging aspect of the use of GATT exceptions.

Financial mechanisms to promote the development and deployment of climate-friendly goods and technologies

Government funding to encourage the deployment and utilization of new climate-friendly technologies and renewable energy is another type of economic incentive which is commonly used in climate change mitigation policies. This Report introduces and gives examples of the wide range of governmental policies that are being discussed, or are already in place, to facilitate innovation or to address the additional costs related to the use of climate-friendly goods and technologies, and thus encourage their development and deployment.

Numerous mitigation technologies are currently commercially available or are expected to be commercialized soon. However, the development and deployment of new technologies, including renewable and/or cleaner energy technologies, may be occurring at a slower pace than is environmentally desirable, and may therefore need support through domestic policies. Although the private sector plays the major role in the development and diffusion of technology, it is generally considered that closer collaboration between government and industry can further stimulate the development of a broad portfolio of low-carbon technologies and reduce their costs.

A number of countries, mainly developed countries, have set up funding programmes at the national level to support both mitigation and adaptation policies. Funding projects are either targeted at consumers or at producers. Consumer-based policies are designed to increase the demand for mitigation technologies by reducing their cost for end-users, and are mainly used in the energy, transport and building sectors. Producer-based policies aim at providing entrepreneurs with incentives to invent, adopt and deploy mitigation technologies. Such production support programmes are mainly used in the energy sector (especially in renewable energy production) and in the transport sector.

Usually, government financing in the context of climate change focuses on three areas: (i) increased use of renewable and/or cleaner energy; (ii) development and deployment of energy-efficient and/or low-carbon goods and technologies; and (iii) development and deployment of carbon sequestration technologies. These financial incentives may be applied at different stages in the technology innovation process. For example, incentives may be aimed at fostering research and development of climate-friendly goods and technologies (mainly through grants and awards), or at increasing the deployment (including first commercialization and diffusion) through financial incentives that reduce the cost of production or use of climate-friendly goods and services.

There are three types of financial incentives for deployment which are currently used or are being discussed by governments in the context of climate change: fiscal instruments; price support measures, such as feed-in tariffs (i.e. a regulated minimum guaranteed price); and investment support policies, which aim to reduce the capital cost of installing and deploying renewable energy technologies. Concrete examples of these incentives are provided in Section IV.B.

Governmental financing for the development and deployment of renewable energy and low-carbon goods and technologies may have an impact on the price and production of such goods. From an international trade perspective, such policies lower the producers costs, leading to lower product prices. In turn, lower prices may reduce exporting countries' access to the market of the subsidizing country, or may result in increased exports from the subsidizing country.

Moreover, some countries may provide domestic energy-consuming industries with subsidies to offset the costs of installing emission-reducing technologies and thus maintain their international competitiveness. Since the sector of renewable energy and low-carbon technologies is significantly open to international trade, the WTO rules on subsidies (as contained in the SCM Agreement) may become relevant for certain financing policies.

The SCM Agreement aims at striking a balance between the concern that a country's industries should not be put at an unfair disadvantage by competition from imported goods that benefit from government subsidies, and the concern that measures taken to offset those subsidies should not themselves be obstacles to fair trade. The rules of the SCM Agreement define the concept of "subsidy", establish the conditions under which WTO members may not employ subsidies and regulate the countervailing duties that may be taken against subsidized imports.

The SCM Agreement also contains surveillance provisions, which require each WTO member to notify the WTO of all the specific subsidies it provides and which call for the Committee on Subsidies and Countervailing Measures to review these notifications.

Technical requirements to promote the use of climate-friendly goods and technologies

In addition to economic incentives, governments have also used traditional regulatory tools in their climate change mitigation strategies. The Report reviews the range of technical requirements for products and production methods aimed at reducing greenhouse gas emissions and energy consumption, and gives concrete examples of these requirements.

Climate change related technical requirements may take the form of maximum levels of emissions or of energy consumption, or they may specify standards for energy efficiency for both products and production methods. Such requirements are accompanied by implementation and enforcement measures, such as labelling requirements and procedures to assess conformity.

Technical requirements to promote energy efficiency, such as labelling to indicate the energy efficiency of a product, have been adopted at the national level by most developed countries, and by a growing number of developing countries. It is estimated that energy-efficiency improvements have resulted in reductions in energy consumption of more than 50 per cent over the last 30 years. A number of studies show that regulations and standards in OECD countries have the potential to increase the energy efficiency of specific products, particularly electrical equipment, such as household appliances. However, a significant energy-efficiency potential remains untapped in various sectors, such as buildings, transport and industry.

Standards that aim at enhancing energy efficiency have also been developed internationally. Such international standards are often used as a basis for regulations at the national level. Currently, examples of areas where international standards may assist in the application of climate-related regulations include standards on measurement and methodology for quantifying energy efficiency and greenhouse gas emissions, and standards related to the development and use of new energy-efficient technologies and renewable energy sources, such as solar power.

The type of technical requirement that is chosen depends on the desired environmental outcome. Product-related requirements may achieve indirect results depending on whether consumers choose to purchase energy-efficient products and how they use these products. On the other hand, requirements targeting production methods may result in direct environmental benefits, such as a reduction in emissions, during the production process. Moreover, standards and regulations, whether related to products or to processes, can be based either on design characteristics, or in terms of performance.

Requirements based on design characteristics determine the specific features of a product, or, with regard to production methods, set out the specific actions to be taken, goods to be used, or technologies to be installed. Regulations based on design standards are often used when there are few options available to the polluter for controlling emissions; in this case, the regulator is able to specify the technological steps that a firm must take to limit pollution.

In contrast, performance-based requirements prescribe the specific environmental outcomes which should be achieved by products or production methods, without defining how the outcomes are to be delivered. Such requirements may be established, for instance, in terms of maximum CO_2 emission levels, maximum energy consumption levels, minimum fuel economy for cars or minimum energy performance standards for lighting products. Performance-based requirements often provide more flexibility than design-based requirements, and their costs may be lower, as firms may decide how best to meet the environmental target.

Energy labelling schemes are intended to provide consumers with data on a product's energy performance (such as its energy use, efficiency, or energy cost) and/or its related greenhouse gas emissions. Labelling schemes may also provide information on a product's entire life cycle, including its production, use and disposal. Labelling schemes have also been used by some private companies to declare the origin of an agricultural product, how many "food miles" it has travelled from where it was grown to where it will be consumed, and the emissions generated during transport.

Labelling schemes, such as energy labelling, help consumers make informed decisions that take into account the relative energy efficiency of a product compared to other similar products. Another key objective of energy labelling is to encourage manufacturers to develop and market the most efficient products. By increasing the visibility of energy costs and measuring them against an energy benchmark, labelling schemes also aim to stimulate innovation in energy-efficient products, transforming these more energy-efficient products from "niche markets" to market leaders.

In the context of the climate-related regulations and voluntary standards discussed above, assessment procedures (e.g. testing and inspection) are often used to ensure conformity with the relevant energy-efficiency and CO_2 emission reduction requirements. Conformity assessment serves to give consumers confidence in the integrity of products, and add value to manufacturers' marketing claims.

Finally, measures have been taken by governments to restrict the sale or prohibit the import of certain products which are not energy-efficient, or to ban the use of certain greenhouse gases in the composition of products. It is common for governments to restrict the use of certain substances for environmental and health reasons. However, since bans and prohibitions have a direct impact on trade (by removing or reducing trade opportunities), governments commonly seek to apply such measures while taking into account such factors as the availability of viable alternatives, technical feasibility and cost-effectiveness.

The Technical Barriers to Trade (TBT) Agreement is the key WTO mechanism for governing technical regulations, standards and conformity assessment procedures, including those on climate change mitigation objectives, although other GATT rules may also be relevant, particularly in cases where the measure in question prohibits the import of certain substances or products. The TBT Agreement applies the core non-discrimination principle of the GATT 1994 to mandatory technical regulations, voluntary standards and conformity assessment procedures. The TBT Agreement also sets out detailed rules on avoiding unnecessary barriers to trade, ensuring the harmonization of regulations and standards and on transparency.

Part I

Climate Change: the Current State of Knowledge

The scientific evidence on climate change and its impacts is compelling and continues to evolve. The Fourth Assessment Report by the Intergovernmental Panel on Climate Change (IPCC 2007a) states that our planet's climate is indisputably warming, and the Stern Review (2006) on the economics of climate change concludes that climate change presents very serious global risks and demands an urgent global response.

This part provides an overview of the current knowledge on existing and projected climate change and its associated impacts, and discusses the available options for responding to the challenges of climate change through mitigation and adaptation. While specific analyses of the linkages between climate change and trade are not covered in this part, any aspects which are pertinent from a trade perspective will, to the extent possible, be highlighted, in order to provide a background to, and frame of reference for, the subsequent parts.

Part I is structured around two main sections. The first section covers the current knowledge on climate change and its associated impacts. It begins with a brief introduction to the linkages between greenhouse gas emissions and climate change, followed by a discussion on past, current and future trends for the emissions of greenhouse gases and how various regions and activities contribute to total emissions. Projections of greenhouse gas emissions and the associated scenarios for future climate change are subsequently addressed, including observed and projected temperature and precipitation changes, sea level rise and changes in snow, ice and frozen ground, as well as changes in climate variability and extreme weather events. This section concludes with an overview and discussion of findings related to the projected impacts on various sectors (such as agriculture or health) and on specific regions, introducing issues that are of relevance to adapting to climate change.

The two main approaches for responding to climate change and climate change impacts – mitigation and adaptation – are reviewed in Section I.B. In the past few years there has been increasing effort from both scientists and policy-makers to relate these two approaches. The characteristics of mitigation and adaptation are compared, and the ways and degree to which they are related are discussed. This is followed by a review of mitigation and adaptation opportunities, with specific emphasis on technology and the development of technology know-how given its links to trade.

The Intergovernmental Panel on Climate Change (IPCC), which was set up by the World Meteorological Organization and the United Nations Environment Programme, is widely recognized as the principal authority for objective information on climate change, its potential impacts, and possible responses to these. This part makes frequent reference to IPCC reports,[1] and uses the IPCC definition of climate change. According to this definition, climate change "… refers to a change in the state of the climate that can be identified (e.g. using statistical tests) by changes in the mean and/or the variability of its properties, and that persists for an extended period, typically decades or longer. It refers to any change in climate over time, whether due to natural variability or as a result of human activity" (IPCC 2007a).[2]

A. Current knowledge on climate change and its impacts

1. Greenhouse gas (GHG) emissions and climate change

a) Greenhouse gases and the climate system

Since the onset of industrialization, there have been large increases in the levels of greenhouse gas (GHG) emissions caused by human activities (known as "anthropogenic" GHGs), and as a result their concentration in the atmosphere has also increased. In simplified terms, higher concentrations of greenhouse gases in the atmosphere cause the sun's heat (which would otherwise be radiated back into space) to be retained in the earth's atmosphere, thereby contributing to the greenhouse effect that causes global warming and climate change.[3]

Figures 1 and 2 illustrate this trend of increasing emission levels for the case of carbon dioxide (CO_2). Figure 1 indicates the increase in global carbon dioxide emissions resulting from consumption of fossil fuels during the past 250 years, while Figure 2 shows the increase in the concentration of carbon dioxide in the atmosphere for the past 50 years.

Atmospheric concentrations of CO_2 – and of greenhouse gases in general – are measured in parts per million (ppm), referring to the number of greenhouse gas molecules per million molecules of dry air. In 2005, the global average atmospheric concentration for CO_2 was 379 ppm, indicating that there were 379 molecules of CO_2 per million molecules of dry air. In comparison, pre-industrial levels of CO_2 concentration in the atmosphere were around 275 ppm (Forster et al., 2007), indicating that the atmospheric concentration of CO_2 has increased globally by about 36 per cent over the last 250 years. As Figure 2 illustrates, most of the increase in the atmospheric concentration of CO_2 has occurred during the last 50 years.

Besides carbon dioxide, the major anthropogenic greenhouse gases are ozone, methane, nitrous oxide, halocarbons and other industrial gases (Forster et al., 2007). All of these gases occur naturally in the atmosphere, with the exception of industrial gases, such as halocarbons. Carbon dioxide emissions currently account for 77 per cent of the anthropogenic, or "enhanced", greenhouse effect[4] and mainly result from the burning of fossil fuels and from deforestation (Baumert et al., 2005). Changes in agriculture and land use are the main causes of increased emissions of methane and nitrous oxide, with methane emissions accounting for 14 per cent of the enhanced greenhouse effect. The remaining approximately 9 per cent consists of nitrous oxide emissions, ozone emissions from vehicle exhaust fumes and other sources, and emissions of halocarbons and other gases from industrial processes.

In the literature on this subject, it is now generally agreed that human activities have been a major cause of the accelerating pace of climate change (this accelerating effect is called "anthropogenic forcing") (IPCC, 2007a). The general consensus on anthropogenic forcing, and an increased scientific understanding of climate change, are the result of improved analyses of temperature records, coupled with the use of new computer models to estimate variability and climate system responses to both natural and man-made causes. This increased understanding of climate processes has made it possible to incorporate more detailed information (for example on sea-ice dynamics, ocean heat transport and water vapour) into the climate models, which has resulted in a greater certainty that the links observed between warming and its impacts are reliable (Levin and Pershing, 2008, and IPCC, 2007a). Based on an assessment of thousands of peer-reviewed scientific publications, the IPCC (2007a) concluded that the warming of the climate system is "unequivocal", and that there is a very high level of confidence, defined as more than 90 per

FIGURE 1. Global carbon dioxide emissions from fossil fuels, 1751-2004

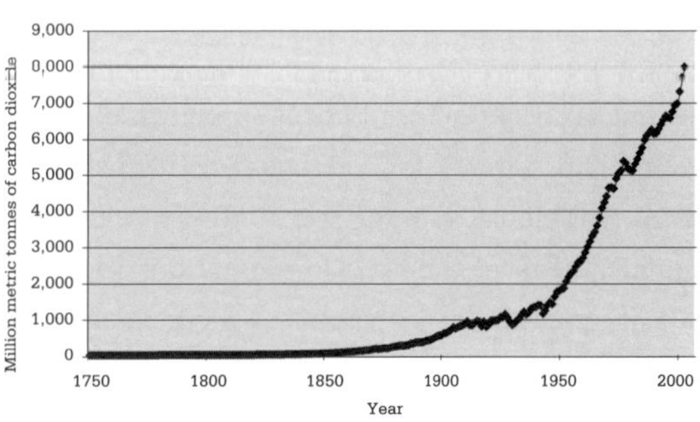

Source: Calculations based on data from http://cdiac.ornl.gov.

FIGURE 2. Atmospheric carbon dioxide concentrations, 1957-2007

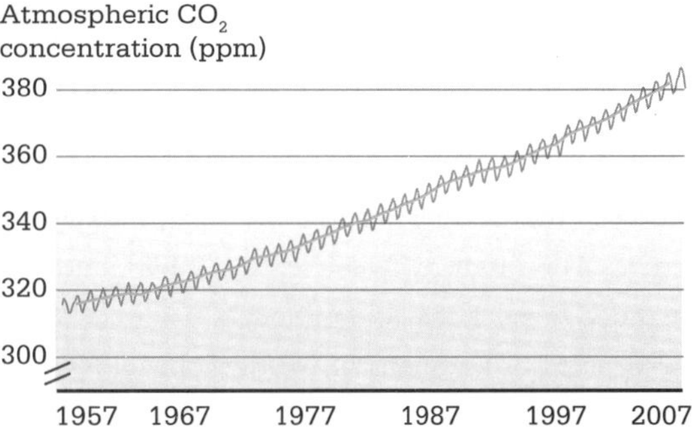

Source: UNEP/GRID-Arendal (2008) based on data from NOAA Earth System Research Laboratory (2007). Monthly mean atmospheric carbon dioxide at Mauna Loa Observatory, Hawaii. www.esrl.noaa.gov (accessed 8 November 2007).

cent likelihood, that the global average net effect of human activities is climate warming.

Moreover, the fact that several greenhouse gases remain in the atmosphere for very long periods, combined with the time lag between the moment of their emission and the climate system's final response and rebalancing, means that global warming will continue to affect the natural systems of the earth for several hundred years, even if greenhouse gas emissions were substantially reduced or ceased altogether today. In other words, global warming is a concentration problem as well as an emission problem. The World Bank (2008a) estimates that, taking account of past GHG emissions, a global warming of around 2° C is probably already unavoidable. The corresponding best estimate from the IPCC scenarios is 1.8° C (IPCC, 2007c).

Thus, the remaining uncertainties relate mainly to determining the exact response of the climate system to any given increase of the levels of greenhouse gases emitted and of their concentration in the atmosphere; and to the modelling of the complex interactions between the various components of the climate system. For instance, Webb et al. (2006) find that in the General Circulation Models (GCMs), which use detailed observations of weather phenomena and other factors to study past, present and future climate patterns, the manner in which feedback mechanisms are specified has much larger implications for the range of climate change predictions than differences in concentrations of various greenhouse gases.[5, 6] It is important to keep this in mind with respect to the global and regional projections of climate change and the associated impacts – the subjects of the following subsections.

b) Greenhouse gas emission trends and structure

Despite national and international efforts to establish measures to stabilize greenhouse gas concentrations in the atmosphere (discussed further in Part IV), GHG emissions continue to grow. The IPCC (2007a) notes that, between 1970 and 2004, global anthropogenic greenhouse gas emissions increased by 70 per cent, from 28.7 to 49 Giga tonnes of CO_2-equivalent ($GtCO_2$-eq).[7] The International Energy Agency (IEA) and the Organisation for Economic Co-operation and Development (OECD) report that global GHG emissions have roughly doubled from the beginning of the 1970s to 2005 (IEA, 2008 and OECD, 2008).

As noted above, carbon dioxide is the most prevalent greenhouse gas, and has the fastest growing emission levels. Carbon dioxide represented 77 per cent of total GHG emissions in 2004, its emission levels having increased by 80 per cent between 1970 and 2004 (IPCC, 2007a). Furthermore, the growth rate of carbon dioxide emissions from fossil fuel use and industrial processes increased from 1.1 per cent per year during the 1990s to more than 3 per cent per year from 2000 to 2004 (EIA, 2008, Raupach et al., 2007, and the CDIAC 2009). These figures indicate that, unless there is a significant improvement in current climate change mitigation policies and related sustainable development practices, global greenhouse gas emissions will continue to grow over the coming decades (IPCC, 2007a). IEA (2008b) has noted that without such a change in policies, i.e. in a "business as usual" scenario, GHG emissions could increase by more than 70 per cent between 2008 and 2050.[8] Figure 3 shows these trends, and further illustrates how the regional structure (i.e. how much each region contributes to total emissions) of greenhouse gas emissions is expected to change.

Historically, industrialized countries have produced large amounts of energy-related emissions of carbon dioxide, and their share of responsibility for the present atmospheric concentration of GHGs also includes their accumulated past emissions (Raupach et al., 2007, IEA, 2008, and World Bank, 2008a). The cumulative emissions of carbon dioxide from the consumption of fossil fuels and from cement production in industrialized countries have, until now, exceeded developing countries' emissions by a factor of roughly three (World Bank, 2008a, and Raupach et al., 2007). By contrast, agriculture and forestry activities, which generate emissions of methane and nitrous oxide, and deforestation, which reduces "carbon sinks" (i.e. forests that absorb CO_2 from the atmosphere) are more extensive in developing countries (Nyong, 2008). Emissions from these sectors have historically been twice as high in developing countries as in industrialized countries (World Bank, 2008a).[9]

Since the 1950s, emissions per capita in industrialized countries have been, on average, around four times higher than in developing countries, and the difference is even greater between industrialized countries and the least developed countries (EIA, 2007). However, the CO_2 intensity of developing countries (i.e. the tonnes of carbon dioxide (equivalent) emitted per unit of gross domestic product (GDP), or, in other words, a measure of emission levels in relation to production levels) exceeds industrialized country CO_2 intensity. This is illustrated in Figure 4. The figure also reveals that the amount of difference in CO_2 intensities between various regions of the world depends significantly on whether emissions from land use are included or excluded in the estimates.

Today, however, and as indicated in Figure 3, annual energy-related carbon dioxide emissions from non-OECD countries surpass emissions from OECD countries. In 2005, CO_2 emissions from non-OECD countries exceeded OECD-country emissions by 7 per cent (EIA, 2008). The total annual amount of greenhouse gas emissions of both industrialized countries and developing countries are now roughly the same, and of the 20 countries with the largest greenhouse gas emission levels, eight are developing countries (WRI, 2009).[10] In fact, developing countries outside the OECD account for roughly two-thirds of the flow of new emissions into the atmosphere (EIA, 2008). This corresponds quite closely to the estimate by Raupach et al. (2007), who note that 73 per cent of the growth in emissions in 2004 was attributed to developing nations. They also note that the emission growth rate reflects not only developing countries' dependence on fossil fuels, but also their growing use of industrial processes. The average annual increase in emissions for 2005 to 2030 is projected to be 2.5 per cent for non-OECD countries, whereas the projected average annual increase is 0.5 per cent for OECD

FIGURE 3. Projected increase in global GHG emissions in a "business as usual" scenario

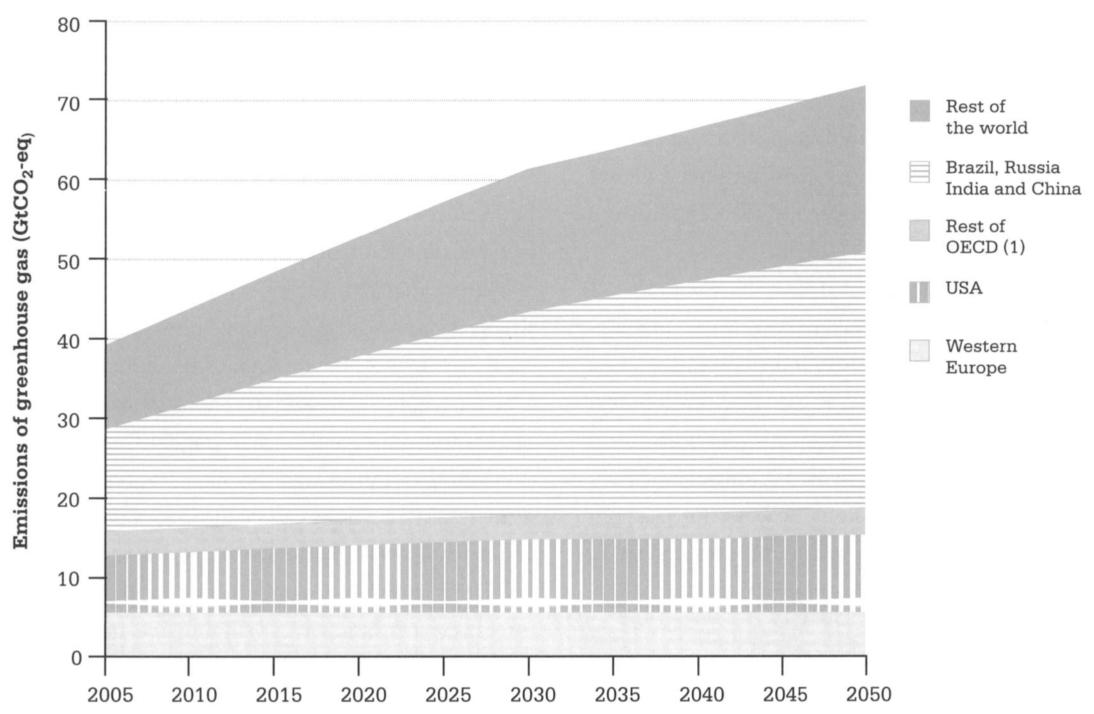

Source: Adapted from Figure 1, OECD (2008). Note: (1) Rest of OECD does not include Korea, Mexico and Turkey, which are aggregated in Rest of the world.

FIGURE 4. CO_2 and GHG intensity by region

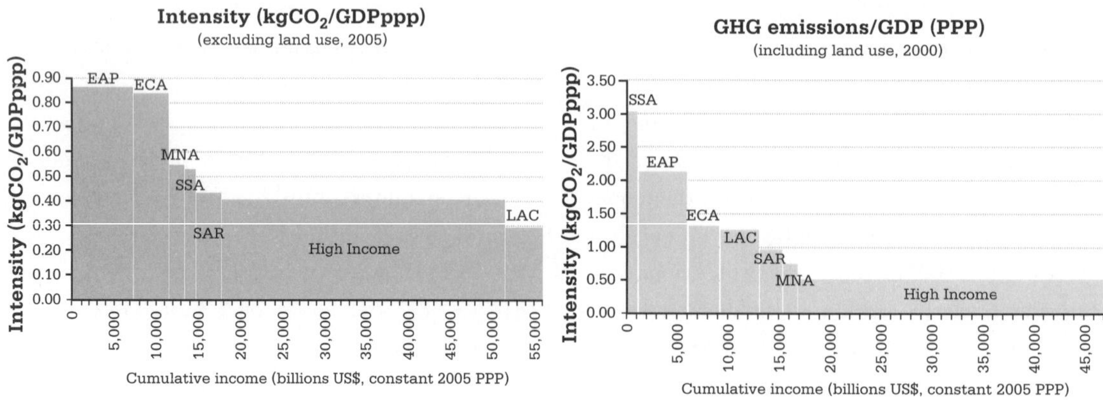

Source: World Bank, 2008a, Figure A1:2.

Notes: The charts show significant variations in the intensity of energy-related CO_2 emissions and the intensity of greenhouse gas emissions between regions and between levels of GDP. There is also a significant difference in the overall ranking of regions, depending on whether the measurements are of emissions carbon dioxide or emissions of total greenhouse gases. The ECA region has the highest energy-related CO_2 emission intensity per unit of GDP, while the LAC region has the lowest. High-income countries generate by far the largest volume of CO_2 emissions. However, if all greenhouse gas emissions were taken into account (including those arising from land use, land use change and forestry), the emission intensity levels and the total contribution to global greenhouse gas emissions would tend to increase for the SSA, EAP and LAC regions, since land degradation and deforestation have been proceeding at a rapid rate in these regions.

SSA refers to Sub-Saharan Africa; EAP to the East Asia and Pacific region; LAC to Latin America and the Caribbean region; ECA to Europe and Central Asia region; SAR to South Asia region; and MENA to Middle East and North Africa region.

Source: CO_2 emissions (emissions from energy use) from EIA website (as of 18 September 2007); GDP, PPP (constant US$) from World Development Indicators; GHG emissions from Climate Analysis Indicators Tool (CAIT) Version 5.0. (World Resources Institute, 2008). Comprehensive emission data (for as many countries and as many greenhouse gases as possible) are only available up to 2000.

countries. Taken together, this means that, unless there is a change in greenhouse gas emission policies, non-OECD carbon emissions will exceed OECD emissions by 72 per cent in 2030 (EIA, 2008).

To summarize, levels of global greenhouse gas emissions are increasing, and unless there is a significant change in current laws, policies and sustainable development practices, they will continue to grow over the next decades. Activities in industrialized countries have been the main cause of past emissions, and therefore account for the current concentration in the atmosphere of greenhouse gases due to human activities.

Today, the total energy-related carbon dioxide emissions from developing countries slightly surpass the total emissions from industrialized countries, and since the annual rate of growth of carbon dioxide emissions is five times higher in non-OECD countries than it is in OECD countries, the difference in total emissions between these countries is projected to increase. If no new emission reduction policies are brought into force, it is likely that non-OECD carbon dioxide emissions will be 72 per cent higher than emissions from OECD countries by 2030. It should be noted, however, that per capita emissions in industrialized countries remain four times higher on average than emissions in developing countries, and that only around 23 per cent of total past emissions can be attributed to developing countries (World Bank, 2008a and Raupach et al., 2007). In addition, it is important to take account of the differences between developing and industrialized countries in terms of carbon dioxide intensity, as such differences may indicate, for example, where there is a potential for increased efficiency in reducing carbon dioxide emissions.

c) Projections of future greenhouse gas emissions and climate change scenarios

In order to predict future climate change and assess its likely impacts, it is necessary to estimate how greenhouse gas emissions might increase in the future, and what impacts, such as changes in earth-surface temperature, will be associated with these emissions. Greenhouse gas emission projections are available from several sources, but the most commonly used and referenced baselines for climate change projections are the scenarios provided in the Special Report on Emission Scenarios (SRES), published by the IPCC in 2000. Based on four different storylines of how the future situation might evolve, the SRES scenarios provide a wide range of possible future emissions up to 2100, which can be used as baselines for modelling and analysing climate change.[11] As shown in Figure 5, each storyline and corresponding scenario has different assumptions about which technologies and energy sources are used, as well as about the rate of economic growth and governance structures.

Figure 5. Characteristics of the four SRES scenarios

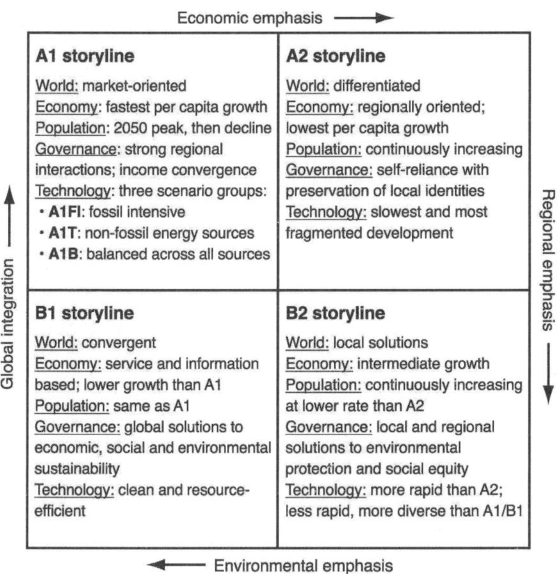

Source: Parry et al., 2007, Figure TS.2.

In the A1 storyline shown in Figure 5, the future world is characterized by very rapid economic growth, by a population that peaks in mid-century and declines thereafter, and by three different assumptions on technology development that each have substantially different implications for future GHG emissions: the highest emission levels are associated with the intensive fossil fuel scenario (A1FI); technologies using a balanced mix of energy sources (A1B) result in medium levels of emissions; while technologies which use non-fossil fuel energy sources (A1T) result in the lowest GHG emissions under the A1 storyline). Under the B1 storyline, the assumptions on population growth are similar to the A1 storyline, but the B1 storyline assumes a rapid transition towards cleaner and less carbon-intensive economic activities based on services and information, with a somewhat lower economic growth rate compared to the A1 situation. The A2 storyline describes a future world where population continues to increase, economic development trends are regional rather than global, and per-capita economic growth and technological change are slower and more fragmented, i.e. do not penetrate the entire economy. Finally, the B2 storyline emphasizes local and regional solutions to sustainability, with a slowly but steadily growing population and medium economic development.

It is important to note that the SRES scenarios do not include additional climate initiatives such as international agreements, and thus none of the scenarios explicitly assume that the emission targets of the Kyoto Protocol (see Section III.A) will be implemented. However, as indicated above, some of the scenarios assume an increased use of energy-efficient technologies and decarbonization policies, resulting in lower reliance on fossil fuels than at present. Such assumptions have the same implications for the reduction of greenhouse gas emissions as emission targets do. In particular, the "B1" reference scenario shown in Figure 5 includes wide-ranging policies to limit total global warming to about 2° C. The SRES scenarios have been extensively used as the basis for scientific climate change modelling and for economic analysis of climate change impacts and mitigation in different regions and countries (IPCC, 2001a, 2007a).

Figure 6, from the IPCC (2007a), shows the wide range of possible future greenhouse gas emission levels based on the SRES scenarios, and the corresponding estimates of increases in surface temperature calculated using climate models.

As illustrated in the figure, depending on which scenario is used, global greenhouse gas emissions, measured in Giga tonnes of CO_2-equivalent, are projected to increase by between 25 and 90 per cent in the period 2000-2030. Warming of about 0.2° C per decade is projected up to around 2020 for a range of SRES emission scenarios. After this point, temperature projections increasingly depend on which specific emission scenario is used, and climate models estimate that the global average temperature will rise by 1.4 to 6.4° C between 1990 and 2100. A comparison of 153 SRES and pre-SRES, i.e. scenarios produced before the SRES report, scenarios with 133 more recent scenarios which, like the SRES scenarios, assume no additional emission mitigation measures shows projected results that are of a comparable range (Fisher et al., 2007).

In the SRES report, all scenarios are assigned equal likelihood, but independent analyses which use these scenarios may select a particular scenario as being more likely or plausible as a baseline. In practice there seems to have been a tendency so far to emphasize the lower and middle-range GHG emission scenarios (see Pachauri, 2007).

By contrast, some recent studies (including, for example, the Garnaut Climate Change Review for Australia (Garnaut, 2008)), having made a number of observations on the actual levels of emissions and of

Figure 6. Scenarios for GHG emissions from 2000 to 2100 (assuming no additional climate policies are brought into effect) and estimates of corresponding surface temperatures

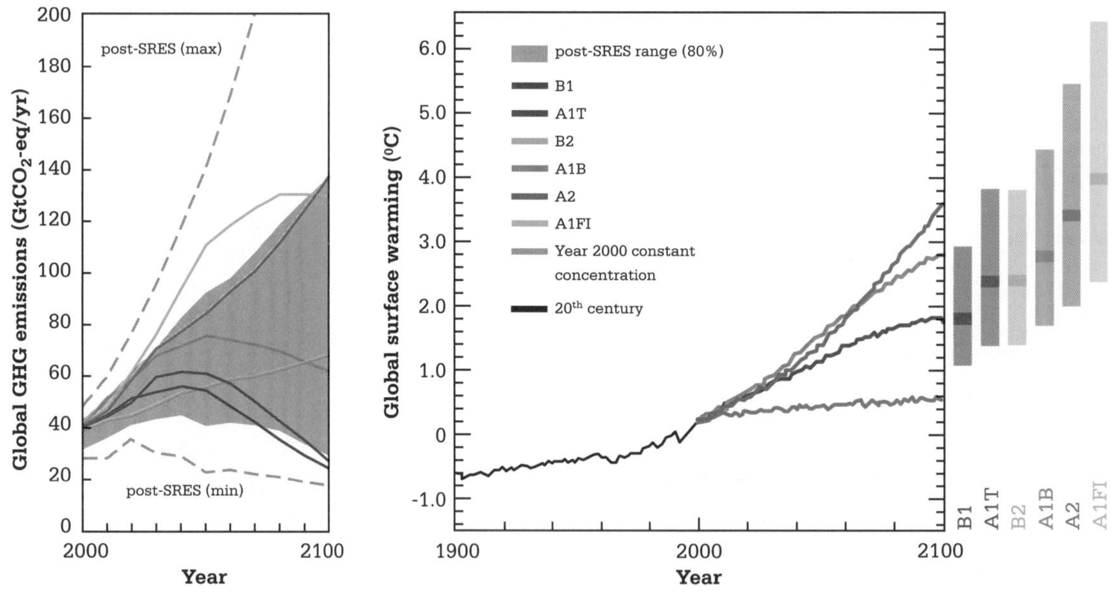

Left panel: Global GHG emissions (in $GtCO_2$-eq per year) in the absence of additional climate policies, showing six illustrative SRES scenarios (coloured lines) and the grey shaded area indicating the 80th percentile range of projections of recent scenarios published since SRES (i.e. post-SRES). Dashed lines show the full range of post-SRES scenarios. The emissions considered include carbon dioxide (CO_2), methane (CH_4), nitrous oxide (N_2O) and the fluoride gases sulphur hexafluoride (SF_6), hydrofluorocarbons (HFCs), and perfluorocarbons (PFCs).

Right panel: The solid lines depict the global averages (calculated using several climate models) of surface warming for scenarios A2, A1B and B1, shown as continuations of the 20th-century emission levels. These projections also take into account emissions of short-lived GHGs and aerosols. The pink line is not a scenario, but represents the simulations of the Atmosphere-Ocean General Circulation Model (AOGCM), with atmospheric concentrations held constant at year 2000 values. The coloured bars at the right of the figure indicate the best estimate (shown as a darker band within each bar) within the full best-case to worst-case range of likely temperature increases assessed for the six SRES scenarios at 2090-2099. All temperatures are relative to the baseline temperature from the period 1980-1999.

Source: IPCC (2007a), figure SPM.5.

economic growth, have focused most intensely on the high SRES scenario, i.e. the A1F1 scenario, to estimate future impacts. For instance, Garnaut (2008) points out that the actual economic growth rates, as well as the growth in carbon dioxide emissions since 2000, have been significantly larger than was assumed under even the highest SRES scenario, i.e. the A1F1 scenario.

More generally, the SRES scenarios have been criticized for being too optimistic in their baseline assumptions regarding the progress towards realizing lower GHG emissions from economic activities on both the demand and the supply side of the energy sector, resulting in an underestimation of the challenges as well as of the costs of reducing global warming (see Pielke et al., 2008). This is in line with the key points from the previous section on the trends and structure of GHG emissions: if the rates of decline in energy intensity and carbon intensity per unit of GDP are slowing down – or are even being reversed, as indicated by, for example, IEA (2008b) and Raupach et al. (2007) – then the SRES scenarios that implicitly or explicitly assume the opposite may represent overly conservative estimates of future climate change and its associated impacts.

Richels et al. (2008) argue that a more serious constraint of the SRES approach is that it fails to incorporate the dynamic nature of the decision problem into the analysis of climate change policies. They argue that an iterative risk management approach where uncertain long-term goals are used to develop short-term emission targets would be more adequate, since it focuses on the short-term policy analysis and advice that decision-makers need. Based on the latest available information, moreover, the analysis should incorporate uncertainty and should incorporate new information and data as they become available. An additional strength of this approach, it is argued, is that it would facilitate distinctions between autonomous trends, i.e. changes that do not result from deliberate climate change policies, and policy-induced developments.

2. Observed and projected climate change and its impacts

a) Temperature and precipitation

One of the strongest observed climate change trends is the warming of our planet. Time series observations (i.e. data collected over successive periods of time) for the past 150 years not only show an increase in global average temperatures, but also show that the rate of change in average temperatures is increasing. Between 1906 and 2005, the global average earth-surface temperature increased by about 0.74° C and the warming trend per decade has been almost twice as high for the last 50 years compared to the trend for the past 100 years (IPCC, 2007a). Furthermore, for the 30 year period from 1976 to 2007, the rate of temperature change was three times higher than the rate for the past 100 years, according to the National Climate Data Center (NCDC) under National Oceanic and Atmospheric Administration (NOAA, 2007). Analyses of measurements from weather balloons and satellites indicate that warming rates in the atmospheric temperature are similar to those observed in surface temperature (Meehl et al., 2007).

The increase in temperature is prevalent all over the globe, but there are significant regional variations compared to the global average. Observations show that temperature increases are greater at higher northern latitudes, where average Arctic temperatures, for example, have increased at almost twice the average global rate in the past 100 years (Meehl et al., 2007). In addition, both Asia and Africa have experienced warming above the average global temperature increase. South America, Australia and New Zealand have experienced less warming than the global average, whereas the warming experienced in Europe and North America is comparable to the global average increase in temperature (Trenberth et al., 2007).

Several effects of temperature increases on people, plant and animal species, and a range of human-managed systems have already been verified in the literature. Among such effects are an increase in mortality due to extreme heat in Europe; changes in how infectious diseases are transmitted in parts of Europe; and earlier and increased seasonal production of allergenic pollen in the Northern Hemisphere's high and mid-latitudes. Agricultural and forestry management, particularly in the higher latitudes of the Northern Hemisphere, have also reportedly been affected, mainly through earlier spring planting of crops and changes related to fires and pests affecting forests.

In addition, rising temperatures strongly affect terrestrial biological systems, resulting in, for example, earlier leaf-unfolding, bird migration and egg-laying, and pole-ward and upward shifts in the ranges of plant and animal species (Rosenzweig et al., 2007, Rosenzweig et al., 2008). It should be noted, however, that particularly for northern Europe, small temperature increases are also expected to have beneficial impacts, mainly in relation to agriculture (see later subsection on agriculture).

Regional variations in temperature changes are expected to persist throughout the century. Figure 7 shows the projected surface temperature changes for the early and late 21st century relative to the surface temperatures during the period 1980-1999, based on average climate-model projections for the high, middle and low SRES scenarios.

Figure 7. Climate model projections of surface warming (early and late 21st century)

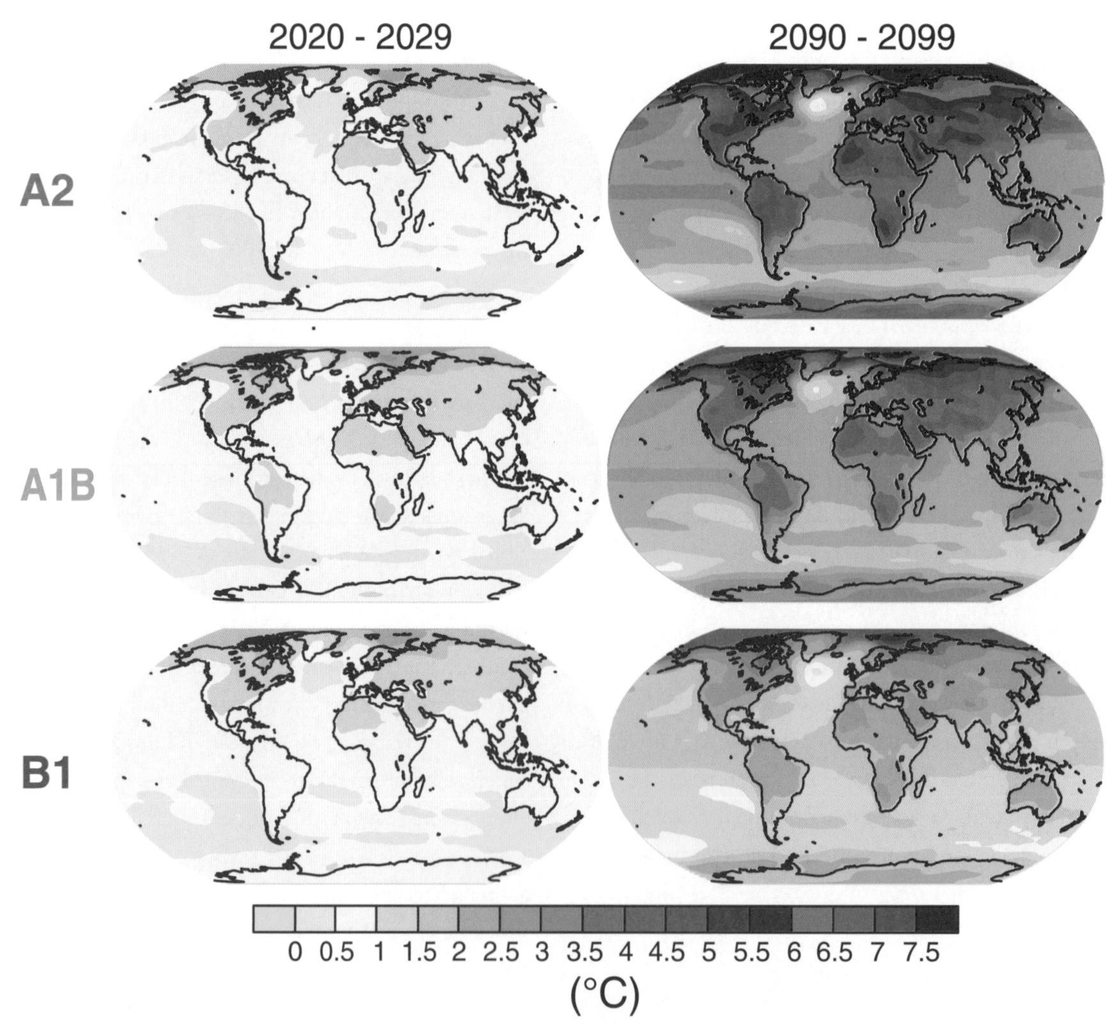

Source: IPCC (2007a), Fig. 3-2. The panels show the multi-Atmosphere-Ocean General Circulation Model (AOGCM) average projections for the A2 (top), A1B (middle) and B1 (bottom) SRES scenarios averaged over the decades 2020-2029 (left) and 2090-2099 (right).

Figure 7 illustrates that average Arctic temperatures are projected to continue to rise more than those in other regions. The Antarctic is also projected to warm, but there is less certainty about the extent of this warming than there is for other regions. Warming is expected to be higher than the global annual average for all seasons throughout Africa. Furthermore, warming is likely to be significantly above the global average in central Asia, the Tibetan Plateau and northern Asia; above the global average in eastern Asia and South Asia; and similar to the global average in southeast Asia. In Central and South America the annual mean warming is likely to be larger than the global mean except for southern South America, where warming is likely to be similar to the global mean warming. The annual mean warming in North America and in Europe is likely to exceed the global mean warming in most areas, whereas the warming in Australia and New Zealand is likely to be comparable to the global average. The small island developing states (SIDS) will most likely experience less warming than the global annual average (Christensen et al., 2007).

Temperature increases are associated with changes in precipitation, and the seasonal and regional variability is substantially higher for changes in precipitation than it is for changes in temperature (Trenberth et al., 2007). Already, significant increases in precipitation have been observed in northern Europe, northern and central Asia, as well as in the eastern parts of North and South America. By contrast, parts of southern Asia, the Mediterranean, the Sahel and southern Africa have become drier.

In the future, substantial increases in annual mean precipitation are expected in most high latitude regions, as well as in eastern Africa and in central Asia (Emori and Brown, 2005, Christensen et al., 2007). Substantial decreases are, on the other hand, expected in the Mediterranean region (Rowell and Jones, 2006), the Caribbean region (Neelin et al., 2006) and in most of the sub-tropical regions (Christensen et al., 2007). It is not only the changes in annual averages that are important. Seasonal changes, as well as changes in the frequency and intensity of heavy precipitation events, are likely to have significant social and economic impacts on livelihoods, mortality, production and productivity, including management of human and natural systems infrastructure, etc. These aspects are addressed further in the subsections on extreme events and regional and sectoral climate change impacts.

b) Sea level rise and changes in snow, ice and frozen ground

Warming of the climate system has several implications for sea level rise. First, consistent with the findings on increased global average temperatures, there is a consensus in the literature on the subject that ocean temperatures have already increased, contributing to a rise in sea level through thermal expansion (Levitus et al., 2005, Willis et al., 2004). Between 1961 and 2003, the global average sea level rose at a rate of approximately 1.8 millimetres (mm) per year. This rate was significantly faster, i.e. approximately 3.1 mm per year, over the period 1993 to 2003 (IPCC, 2007a, Rahmstorf et al., 2007).

Rising sea levels, combined with human activities such as agricultural practices and urban development, already contribute to losses of coastal wetlands and mangrove swamps, leading to an increase in damage from coastal flooding in many developing countries (IPCC, 2007d)). New evidence further supports the theory that the changes which have been observed in marine and freshwater biological ecosystems are related to changes in the temperatures, salinity, oxygen levels, circulation (i.e. how water circulates around the globe) and ice cover of the earth's oceans, seas, lakes and rivers.[12]

Moreover, the literature points out that decreasing snow cover and melting ice caps and glaciers have direct implications for rising sea levels (Lemke et al., 2007). The effect does not only accrue directly from the melting of the snow and/or ice. Ice and snow have a bright surface that reflects the sunlight; when this cover melts, darker marine or terrestrial layers with less reflective surfaces appear, resulting in a "feedback effect" that accelerates the melting. In other words, the effect of the sun is amplified by the dark surfaces which absorb and re-emit the heat. It is complicated to create accurate computer models of these processes, and the projected rises in sea level have varied in each of the four IPCC Assessment Reports published to date, primarily due to diverging views on sea ice cover, the rate of melting in Greenland and Antarctica, and the rate of glacier melt.

Thus, sea level was projected to rise 0.2 metres by 2030 and 0.65 metres by 2100 in the first IPCC Assessment Report (IPCC, 1990), whereas the Second Assessment Report (IPCC, 1995) projected a rise from 0.15 to 0.95 metres from the present to 2100. In the Third Assessment Report (IPCC, 2001a), sea level projections were 0.09 to 0.88 metres between 1990 and 2100, while the Fourth Assessment Report (IPCC, 2007a) projects a rise in sea level of 0.18 to 0.59 metres for 2090-2099 relative to 1980-1999.

There are two main reasons for the more conservative estimates in the most recent IPCC report. First, a narrower confidence range, i.e. projections with lower degrees of uncertainty, is used in the Fourth Assessment Report compared to the Third Assessment Report. Secondly, uncertainties in the feedbacks of the climate-carbon cycle are not included in the Fourth Assessment Report and the full effect of changes in ice sheet flows is also not included, because at the time of the report it was not possible to draw firm conclusions based on the existing literature on the topic. Although the effect of increased ice flow from Greenland and Antarctica (at the rates observed during the period 1993-2003) was incorporated in the model used to project sea rise levels for the Fourth Assessment Report, it acknowledges that the contributions from Greenland and possibly Antarctica may be larger than projected in the ice sheet models used, and that there is thus a risk of sea level rise above the figures stated in the report.

A number of recent scientific contributions seem to suggest that not only may the climate system be responding more quickly than climate models have indicated, but that climate impacts are, in fact, escalating (Levin and Pershing, 2008). With regard to sea ice, glacier and snow melt, and the associated sea level rise, several new studies shed more light on the extent of the problem and on the dynamic feedback processes outlined above that were not fully incorporated in the ice sheet models used for the projections in the IPCC Fourth Assessment Report.

Based on observations using NASA satellite data, NASA (2007) concludes that the levels of sea ice were at a record low from June to September 2007.[13] The ice melt was found to accelerate during periods with warmer temperatures and few clouds, when more solar radiation reaches the earth's surface. Similar findings on substantial decreases in sea ice are reported for perennial sea ice (i.e. ice which remains year-round, and does not melt and re-form with the changing of the seasons) for the period 1970-2000, with an increase in the rate of loss during 2005-2007 (Ngheim et al., 2007). As outlined above, when ice or snow melts, darker marine or terrestrial surfaces with less reflective surfaces appear, which can produce a warming feedback effect that accelerates further melting, and which may negatively affect the re-formation of ice during the following cold season. This was suggested by Mote (2007) as a potential explanation for the dramatic increase observed in surface-ice melting for Greenland in 2007.

Mote (2007) finds that the observed melting could have arisen from previous melting episodes in 2002-2006, and that the most plausible explanations are a decrease in surface reflectivity, warmer snow due to higher winter temperatures, or changes in the accumulation of winter snow due to precipitation changes.

These findings not only indicate that sea level rise may have been underestimated in the IPCC Fourth Assessment Report, but also that it may only be a question of years or of a few decades before changes in sea ice, particularly in the Arctic, lead to the accessibility of new shipping routes – which would have significant implications for transport, as well as for the exploitation of resources, including fossil fuels. For example, in 2007, the Northwest Passage, which is the shortest shipping route between the Atlantic and the Pacific, was free of ice and navigable for the first time in recorded history (Cressey, 2007). The duration of the navigation season for the Northern Sea Route is likewise expected to increase in the coming decades (ACIA, 2005). The potential for new shipping routes has already led to discussions on sovereignty over these routes, seabed resources and off-shore developments (ACIA, 2005). The decline in Arctic sea ice and the opening of new navigable passages will also have a number of implications on tourism, commercial fishing, and hunting of marine wildlife.

More generally, the observed increase in the size and number of glacial lakes, changes in some ecosystems (particularly in the Arctic), and the increasing ground instability in permafrost regions due to thawing of the frozen surface layer, are clear indicators that natural systems related to snow, ice and frozen ground are affected by climate change (Lemke et al., 2007). This has a number of additional implications for transport, industry and infrastructure. Certain industries, notably oil and gas companies, depend heavily on reliable snow cover and temperatures, as they use ice roads in the Arctic to gain access to oil and gas fields.

In order to protect the tundra ecosystem, before a company builds an ice road, certain criteria on temperature and snow-depth must be met, and these are compromised by climate change (UNEP, 2007a). The Arctic Climate Impact Assessment (ACIA) (2005), for example, reports that, in the Alaskan tundra, the number of travel days on frozen roads of vehicles for oil exploration decreased from 220 to 130 per year over the period 1971-2003. Thawing of permafrost has additional severe impacts for housing and other infrastructure (Lemke et al., 2007).

Another area where recent studies suggest that the climate system may be responding more quickly than climate models predicted is on the capacity of the oceans to absorb carbon dioxide. For instance, although the IPCC (2007c) concludes that the capacity of the oceans and the terrestrial biosphere to absorb the increasing carbon dioxide emissions would decrease over time, Canadell et al. (2007) find that the absorptive capacity of the oceans has been falling more rapidly than the rates predicted by the main models used by the IPCC. This finding is mirrored by Schuster and Watson (2007), whose results suggest that the North Atlantic uptake of CO_2 declined by approximately 50 per cent between the mid-1990s and 2002-2005.

Le Quéré et al. (2007) studied the CO_2 "sink" (i.e. the capacity for carbon dioxide absorption) in the Southern Ocean over the period from 1981 to 2004 and report a similar significant weakening of the carbon sink. Whereas Schuster and Watson (2007) find that sink weakening is attributable to a combination of natural variation and human activities, Le Quéré et al. (2007) suggest that the decrease is a result of changes caused by man (i.e. anthropogenic changes) predominantly in wind temperatures, but also in air temperatures.

Until now, the oceans have been absorbing over 80 per cent of the heat being added to the climate system (IPCC, 2007a), and sequestered 25-30 per cent of the annual global emissions of CO_2 (Le Quéré et al., 2007). However, if the above-mentioned decline in the oceans' capacity to absorb carbon dioxide carries on, and that trend continues on a global scale, a significantly greater proportion of emitted carbon will remain in the atmosphere, and will exacerbate future warming trends (Levin and Pershing, 2008).

c) Climate variability and extremes

It is reasonable to argue that climate change will be experienced most directly through changes in the frequency and intensity of extreme weather events. Such weather events are "hidden" in the changes in climatic averages and have immediate short-term implications for well-being and daily livelihoods (ADB, 2005, and IPCC, 2007a).[14]

Even with small average temperature increases, the frequency and intensity of extreme weather events are predicted to change, and the type of such weather events (such as hurricanes, typhoons, floods, droughts, and heavy precipitation events) that regions are subject to is projected to change (UNFCCC, 2008). A number of changes in climate variability and extremes have already been observed and reported, including increases in the frequency and intensity of heatwaves, increases in intense tropical cyclone activity in various regions, increases in the number of incidences of extreme high sea level, and decreases in the frequency of cold days or nights and the occurrence of frost (Meehl et al., 2007). One of the most pronounced findings relates to changes in the frequency and intensity of heavy precipitation, which have increased in most areas, although there are strong regional variations.

In general, incidences of heavy precipitation have increased in the regions that have experienced an increase in average annual precipitation, i.e. northern Europe, northern and central Asia, as well as in the eastern parts of North and South America (Trenberth et al., 2007). However, increases in the frequency of heavy precipitation have been observed even in many regions where the general trend is a reduction in total precipitation (i.e. most sub-tropical and mid-latitude regions). In addition, longer and more intense droughts have been observed, especially in the tropics and sub-tropics, since the 1970s (Trenberth et al., 2007).

As will be seen below, most of the changes which have been observed are expected to become more widespread and to intensify in the future. However, it should be noted that there are a number of difficulties in assessing long-term changes in extreme events. First, extremes, by definition, refer to events that occur rarely, which means that the number of observations on which to base statistical analyses is limited. The more infrequent an event is, the more difficult it is to identify long-term trends (Frei and Schär, 2001, and Klein Tank and Können, 2003).

Lack of data, statistical limitations and the diversity of climate monitoring practices have, in general, limited the types of extreme events that could be assessed, and the degree of accuracy of conclusions reached in the past (Trenberth et al., 2007). Many of these issues have been addressed over the past five to ten years, and substantial progress has been made in terms of generating improved data in the form of daily regional and continental data sets. In addition, the systematic use and exchange between scientists of standards and common definitions, has allowed the generation of an unprecedented global picture of changes in daily extremes of temperature and precipitation (Alexander et al., 2006, and Trenberth et al., 2007).

The most notable improvements in the reliability of model analyses of extremes relate to the improvement of regional information concerning heatwaves, heavy precipitation and droughts. It should be noted, however, that for some regions, model analyses are still scarce. This is the case for extreme events in the tropics, in particular, where the projections are still surrounded by uncertainty. Information is improving, however. For instance, Allan and Soden (2008) used satellite observations and computer model simulations to examine the response of tropical precipitation to changes due to natural causes in surface temperature and atmospheric moisture content. Their results indicate that there is a distinct link between temperature and extremes in rainfall, with warm periods associated with increases in heavy rain and cold periods associated with decreasing incidences of heavy rain. The observed increase of rainfall extremes was found to be greater than predicted by models, which implies (as they pointed out) that current projections on future changes in rainfall extremes may be under-estimations.

Based on current knowledge, Table 1 provides an overview of the major impacts that changes in climate variability and extremes are projected to have on various sectors.

Table 1 illustrates the considerable range of likely impacts arising from changes in climate variability and extremes. It illustrates that although a few of the impacts are positive – most notably increases in agricultural yields in mid to high latitudes and reductions in mortality from reduced exposure to cold – the impacts of most changes will be adverse.

In addition, the table illustrates that most changes will be associated with a number of direct as well as indirect consequences across various sectors. Thus, the impacts of heavy precipitation may not be limited to direct impacts (such as damage to agricultural crops, buildings, roads, bridges and other infrastructure, or injuries and deaths), but may also have an indirect negative impact on trade (through disruption to infrastructure, or as a result of damage to agricultural outputs), which in turn may also have detrimental effects on nutrition. Vector-borne diseases (i.e. diseases carried by insects or parasites) may also rise if climatic conditions favour increases in insect populations through for example rising mean temperatures and changes in precipitation patterns, and if water supplies are contaminated (which may occur as a result of floodings, etc.) increases in diarrheal diseases and cholera epidemics may follow incidences of heavy precipitation.

Table 1. Potential impacts of climate change due to changes in extreme weather and climate events, based on projections to the mid- to late 21st century.

Phenomenon and direction of trend	Examples of major projected impacts by sector			
	Agriculture, forestry and ecosystems	Water resources	Human health	Industry, settlement and society
Over most land areas, warmer and fewer cold days and nights; warmer and more frequent hot days and nights	Increased yields in colder environments; decreased yields in warmer environments; increased insect outbreaks	Effects on water resources relying on snow melt; effects on some water supplies	Reduced human mortality from decreased cold exposure	Reduced energy demand for heating; increased energy demand for cooling; declining air quality in cities; reduced disruption to transport due to snow, ice; effects on winter tourism
Warm spells/ heatwaves. Frequency increases over most land areas	Reduced yields in warmer regions due to heat stress; increased danger of wildfire	Increased water demand; water quality problems, e.g. algal blooms	Increased risk of heat-related mortality, especially for the elderly, chronically sick, very young and socially isolated	Reduction in quality of life for people in warm areas without appropriate housing; impacts on the elderly, the very young and the poor
Heavy precipitation. Frequency increases over most areas	Damage to crops; soil erosion; inability to cultivate land due to waterlogging of soils	Adverse effects on quality of surface and groundwater; contamination of water supplies; water scarcity may be relieved	Increased risk of deaths, injuries, and infectious respiratory and skin diseases	Disruption of settlements, commerce, transport and societies due to flooding; pressures on urban and rural infrastructures; loss of property
Area affected by droughts	Land degradation; lower yields/crop damage and failure; increased livestock deaths; increased risk of wildfire	More widespread water stress	Increased risk of food and water shortage; increased risk of malnutrition; increased risk of water- and food-borne diseases	Water shortage for settlements, industry and societies; reduced hydropower generation potentials; potential for population migration
Increases in intense tropical cyclone activity	Damage to crops; wind throw (uprooting) of trees; damage to coral reefs	Power outages causing disruption to public water supply	Increased risk of deaths, injuries, water- and food-borne diseases; post-traumatic stress disorders	Disruption by flood and high winds; withdrawal of risk coverage in vulnerable areas by private insurers; potential for population migrations; loss of property
Increased incidence of extreme high sea level (excludes tsunamis)	Salinization of irrigation water, estuaries and fresh-water systems	Decreased fresh-water availability due to saltwater intrusion	Increased risk of deaths and injuries by drowning in floods; migration-related health effects	Costs of coastal protection versus costs of land use relocation; potential for movement of populations and infrastructure; see also tropical cyclones above

Source: Adapted from IPCC 2007a, table SPM 3. Note that changes or developments in the capacity to adapt to climate change are not taken into account in the table.

The examples in Table 1 point to an implicit aspect of climate change impacts: the magnitude of such impacts will be location-specific and will depend on pre-existing underlying stresses, development characteristics and ongoing processes. For example, the consequences of an incidence of extreme rainfall will be less severe for a population in an area where building construction is of a high standard; roads, railways, etc., have sufficient drainage; water supply and quality are assured; and only a small percentage of the population relies directly on the natural resource base for sustaining their livelihoods.

In other words, the magnitude of the consequences of climate change impacts depends on the vulnerability of a given human or natural system. Vulnerability refers to the degree to which a human or natural system is susceptible to, and unable to cope with, the adverse effects of climate change, including climate variability and extremes (IPCC, 2007d). In this way, it is a function not only of the character, variation, magnitude and rate of climate change to which a system is exposed, but also of its sensitivity and its adaptive capacity (IPCC, 2007d). The sensitivity and adaptive capacity of the systems or societies is, in turn, influenced by the development characteristics, including economic development and distribution of resources, pre-existing stresses on humans and ecosystems, and the functioning and characteristics of social and governmental institutions (Adger et al., 2007, Turner et al., 2003, Smit and Wandel, 2006, and Yohe and Tol, 2002). The following subsections will address these and related aspects in more detail.

3. Projected regional and sectoral impacts of climate change

The regional and sectoral impacts of climate change are analysed extensively in the existing literature on this subject (see UNFCCC, 2007a, Nyong, 2008, Boko et al., 2007, Cline, 2007, Cruz et al., 2007, Hennessy et al., 2007, Alcamo et al., 2007, Magrin et al., 2007, Anisimov et al., 2007, Field et al., 2007, Mimura et al., 2007, and IPCC, 2007d). Drawing on these and other sources, the current subsection provides a brief overview of the key projected regional and sectoral impacts of climate change. Rather than attempting to cover all the findings of the literature on climate change impacts at the regional and sectoral level, the emphasis of this subsection is on results that are particularly relevant for trade, productive resources and human livelihoods, and thus not all impacts are covered.[15]

a) General findings on sectoral and regional impacts

Future global, regional and sectoral climate change impacts will depend on the extent of the increase in global average temperatures, as indicated in the section on greenhouse gas emission projections and climate change scenarios. Figure 8, from the IPCC (2007d), further illustrates the relationship between global average annual temperature change and the key impacts on different sectors, and relates these changes to the different SRES emission scenario projections discussed earlier. As the figure shows, the impacts of climate change increase with increasing average temperatures in all cases, and in most situations negative impacts arise even with small increases in global average temperatures. An immediate observation can be made that mitigation is required to avoid the impacts associated with large temperature increases, and adaptation is necessary to address the impacts that are unavoidable.

Figure 8 illustrates that vulnerability is a function of the character, magnitude and rate of climate change. In addition, it gives an initial indication of the areas, sectors and population groups that will be affected the most by climate change. Agriculture is highly vulnerable both directly through temperature increases and, as shown in the previous subsection, through incidences of extreme climate events, and indirectly through the changes to the hydrological cycle (i.e. the cycle of water between the earth and the atmosphere, through evaporation, precipitation, runoff, etc.) which accompany temperature increases, such as changes related to glacial and snow melt and to water supply, including changes in precipitation patterns. Low-lying coastal areas and their populations, economic activities and infrastructure are similarly vulnerable to global warming. Water availability poses another key impact area, with hundreds of millions of people predicted to be exposed to increased water scarcity and declining water quality. Ecosystems and species will be significantly affected depending on the extent of global warming, and additional – potentially severe – risks to health will be imposed by climate change.

Figure 8 gives an indication that low latitudes will be hit the hardest. The picture becomes clearer when a specific regional dimension is added. Table 2 summarizes some of the key projected climate change impacts by region. While the impacts will depend on the rate of temperature change, as indicated in Figure 8, and will vary according to the extent of adaptation, and socio-economic development pathways, several general observations can be made.

First, it can be observed from Table 2 that issues related to the hydrological cycle, such as increased glacial and snow melt, changes in precipitation patterns, erosion from runoff, etc., are pertinent in all regions and that coastal areas and mega-deltas around the world will be negatively affected. Second, the most significant adverse impacts on agricultural production arc projected for Africa, for the mega-deltas in Asia, and for Latin America, although agricultural production is also projected to decrease in parts of Australia and New Zealand and in southern Europe. Furthermore, the climate change impacts within regions vary significantly. And last, the stresses induced by climate change will accentuate existing development challenges for developing regions of the world.

In the next subsection, the most significant projected regional climate impacts are summarized for key sectors and issues.

FIGURE 8. Key climate change impacts as a function of increasing global average temperature change

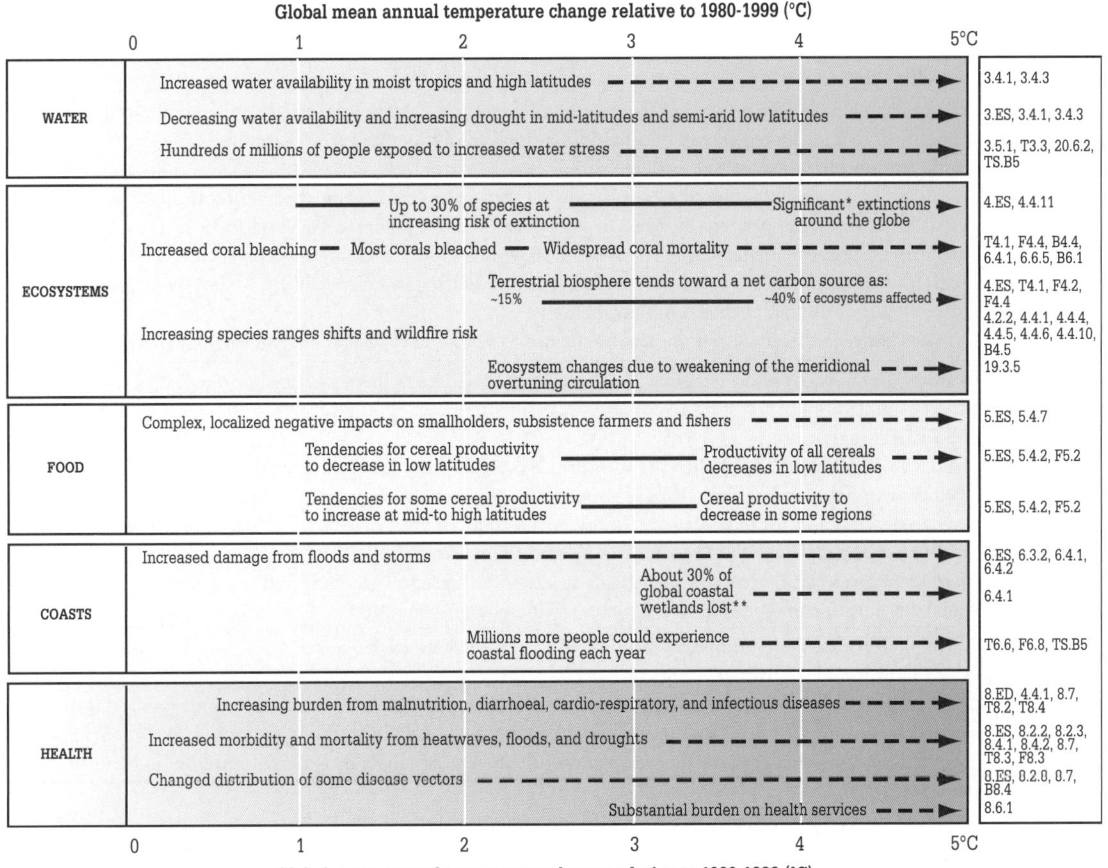

Source: IPCC 2007d, Figure SPM.2.

Table 2. Examples of projected regional impacts of climate change

Africa	By 2020, between 75 and 250 million people are projected to be affected by water shortages due to climate change. By 2020, in some countries, yields from rain-fed agriculture could be reduced by up to 50 per cent. Agricultural production, including access to food, in many African countries is projected to be severely compromised. This would have a further adverse effect on the supply of food and would exacerbate malnutrition. Towards the end of the 21st century, projected sea level rise will affect low-lying coastal areas with large populations. The cost of adaptation could amount to at least 5 to 10 per cent of gross domestic product (GDP). By 2080, an increase of 5 to 8 per cent of arid and semi-arid land in Africa is projected under a range of climate scenarios.
Asia	By the 2050s, freshwater availability, particularly in large river basins, in central, south, east and southeast Asia is projected to decrease. Coastal areas, especially heavily populated mega-delta regions, in south, east and southeast Asia, will be at greatest risk due to increased flooding from the sea and, in some mega-deltas, flooding from the rivers. Climate change is projected to compound existing pressures on natural resources and the environment resulting from rapid urbanization, industrialization and economic development. Endemic morbidity and mortality due to diarrhoeal diseases primarily associated with floods and droughts are expected to rise in east, south and southeast Asia due to projected changes in the hydrological cycle.
Australia and New Zealand	By 2020, significant loss of biodiversity is projected to occur in some ecologically rich sites, including the Great Barrier Reef and the Queensland Wet Tropics. By 2030, water security problems are projected to intensify in southern and eastern Australia and, in New Zealand, in Northland and some eastern regions. By 2030, production from agriculture and forestry is projected to decline over much of southern and eastern Australia, and over parts of eastern New Zealand, due to increased drought and fire. However, in New Zealand, initial benefits are projected in some other regions. By 2050, ongoing coastal development and population growth in some areas of Australia and New Zealand are projected to exacerbate risks from sea level rise and increases in the severity and frequency of storms and coastal flooding.
Europe	Climate change is expected to magnify regional differences in Europe's natural resources and assets. Negative impacts will include increased risk of inland flash floods and more frequent coastal flooding and increased coastal erosion (due to storms and sea level rise). Mountainous areas will face glacier retreat, reduced snow cover and diminished winter tourism, and extensive species losses (up to 60 per cent by 2080 in some areas under high emission scenarios). In southern Europe, climate change is projected to worsen conditions (high temperatures and drought) in a region already vulnerable to climate variability, and to reduce water availability, hydropower potential, summer tourism and, in general, crop productivity. Climate change is also projected to increase the health risks due to heatwaves and the frequency of wildfires.
Latin America	By mid-century, increases in temperature and associated decreases in soil water are projected to lead to gradual replacement of tropical forest by savannah in eastern Amazonia. Semi-arid vegetation will tend to be replaced by arid-land vegetation. There is a risk of significant biodiversity loss through species extinction in many areas of tropical Latin America. Productivity of some important crops is projected to decrease and livestock productivity to decline, with adverse consequences for food security. In temperate zones, soybean yields are projected to increase. Overall, the number of people at risk of hunger is projected to increase. Changes in precipitation patterns and the disappearance of glaciers are projected to significantly affect water availability for human consumption, agriculture and energy generation.
North America	Warming in the western mountains is projected to cause decreased snowpack, more winter flooding and reduced summer flows, exacerbating competition for over-allocated water resources. In the early decades of the century, moderate climate change is projected to increase aggregate yields of rain-fed agriculture by 5 to 20 per cent, but with important variability among regions. Major challenges are projected for crops that are near the warm end of their suitable range, or which depend on highly utilized water resources. Cities that currently experience heatwaves are expected to be further challenged by an increased number, intensity and duration of heatwaves during the course of the century, with potential for adverse health impacts. Coastal communities and habitats will be increasingly stressed by climate change impacts interacting with development and pollution.

Source: IPCCa 2007, Table SPM.2

b) Projected sectoral impacts of climate change at the regional level

i) Agriculture and food security

Agriculture is highlighted as the sector which is most vulnerable to climate change throughout the literature on this issue (see Cline, 2007, Nyong, 2008, or IPCC, 2007d). As indicated in Figure 7, local temperature increases of between 1° C and 3° C and the associated changes in average precipitation levels, are likely to have beneficial impacts on agricultural outputs in mid- to high-latitude regions. These changes would affect the main cereal crops grown in these areas, including rice, wheat and maize (IPCC, 2007d). If warming rises beyond the 1 to 3° C range, however, increasingly negative impacts will be likely, and will affect all regions of the world.

In low-latitude regions, where most developing countries are located, the picture is different, even for small temperature increases. In these regions, moderate local temperature increases of around 1° C are projected to result in a 5 to 10 per cent decline in yields for major cereal crops (World Bank, 2008a, Nyong, 2008). In considerable areas of semi-arid and dry sub-humid zones in Africa, the duration of the growing period is expected to fall by 5 to 20 per cent by 2050 (World Bank, 2008a).

According to Boko et al. (2007), crop yield in some African countries has been projected to drop by up to 50 per cent as early as by 2020, and net crop revenues could fall by as much as 90 per cent by 2100, with small-scale farmers being the worst affected. Fischer et al. (2005) estimate that some countries, including Sudan, Nigeria, Somalia, Ethiopia, Zimbabwe, and Chad, could lose their cereal-production potential by 2080. In South Asia, cereal yields are projected to decrease by up to 30 per cent by 2050 (Cruz et al., 2007), while generalized reductions in rice yields are projected by the 2020s in Latin America (Nyong, 2008).

The fact that temperatures in developing countries are already near or above certain thresholds – beyond which further warming will decrease rather than increase agricultural productivity – provides part of the explanation for such substantial projected impacts in response to even small temperature increases (Cline, 2007). Combined with socio-economic and technological challenges such as low income and educational levels, lack of irrigation infrastructure and lack of access to financing, the projected decreases in precipitation in these already dry areas and the predominance of "rainfed agriculture" (i.e. crops which are not irrigated, but rely on precipitation or on subsurface water) in many developing countries and regions, mean that small increases in temperatures have significant implications for yields.

Rainfed agriculture is highly vulnerable to changes in precipitation patterns, indicating that reduced rainfall or changes in the seasonal timing and intensity of rainfall will have direct implications for farmers' income and livelihoods, and thus for agricultural GDP. Indeed, studies of semi-arid economies, particularly in Africa and south Asia, show that agricultural GDP and farmers' incomes closely mirror rainfall variations (World Bank, 2008a).

As previously noted, in addition to the changes in local average temperatures and precipitation, climate change is likely to include a higher frequency of extreme weather, such as floods and droughts. Such incidences may cause direct damage to crops at specific developmental stages. Moreover, heavy rainfall could increase soil erosion, resulting in loss of agricultural land.

Droughts have also been shown to affect rates of livestock death, particularly in Africa, where several studies have established a direct relationship between drought and animal death (Nyong, 2008). Furthermore, higher temperatures and longer growing seasons have led to increased pest and insect populations in several regions of the world.

The magnitude of the projected impacts reported above depends on the climate change scenario chosen for the modelling exercises. In addition, the scale of the impacts projected depends to a considerable extent on whether the beneficial effects of carbon fertilization on agricultural yields[16] are included in the analyses and on the extent to which they materialize in practice. In an extensive analysis of the impacts of climate change on agriculture at the country level by 2080,

Figure 9. Projected changes in per cent in agricultural productivity by 2080 due to climate change

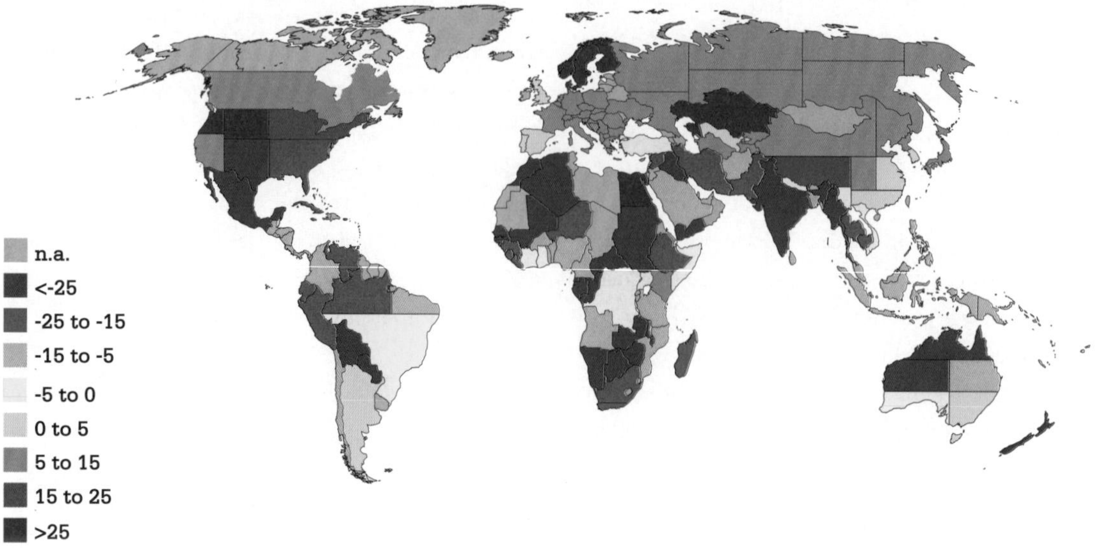

n.a.
<-25
-25 to -15
-15 to -5
-5 to 0
0 to 5
5 to 15
15 to 25
>25

Source: Adapted from Cline, 2007. Note that the effects of carbon fertilization are incorporated.

Cline (2007) provides further evidence on the concentration of agricultural losses in developing countries. Figure 9 provides an overview of his findings on the projected regional changes in agricultural productivity as a result of climate change by 2080. The projections mirror the findings reported above. In addition, beneficial effects of carbon fertilization are included in the projections shown in the figure, and thus the projected impacts are likely to lie in the lower, more conservative range of estimated outcomes.

The projections discussed above indicate that issues of access to and availability of food, as well as food utilization, will be an increasing challenge in the future, particularly for the poorest and most vulnerable population groups within developing countries (Boko et al., 2007). Fischer et al. (2005) estimate that approximately 768 million people will be undernourished by 2080, and that undernourishment will be particularly severe in Sub-Saharan Africa and in southern Asia. Nyong (2008) reports that a projected 2 to 3 per cent reduction in African cereal production by 2030 would be enough to increase the risk of hunger for an additional 10 million people, and that by 2080 the total populations of the 80 countries with insecure food supplies are projected to increase from approximately 4.2 billion to 6.8 billion.

From a trade perspective, changes in productivity and in agricultural outputs may lead to an increase in trade, with most developing countries depending increasingly on food imports (Easterling et al., 2007). However, as pointed out by Cline (2007), among others, the scope for adapting to the impacts of climate change by increasing the levels of trade would be constrained by the limited purchasing power of those developing countries needing to increase their food imports in response to adverse climate impacts. This argument is reinforced by the projections on future purchasing power with respect to food: these projections suggest that, although purchasing power would initially increase in response to declining agricultural "real prices" (i.e. prices that are adjusted to reflect the relative exchange ratio between real goods) as global agricultural output increases in the period up to 2050, it would diminish from 2050 onwards, when global agricultural output is expected to decrease and cause real prices for food to rise (Nyong, 2008).

ii) Hydrology and water resources

Figure 8 and Table 2 above gave a general illustration of the importance of climate change impacts on hydrology[17] and on water resources at both sectoral and regional levels. Many of the climate change impacts related to hydrology and water resources are addressed in the subsections on sectoral climate change impacts at the regional level, and will thus not be repeated here. The following findings are not, however, directly mentioned in other subsections.

Climate change is projected to have an impact on access to water, availability of and demand for water, and on water quality, and in many areas these impacts could be exacerbated by population increase and by weak infrastructure (Kundzewicz et al., 2007, Nyong, 2008). In Africa, for example, between 75 and 250 million people are projected to be exposed to increased water stress due to climate change by 2020; and this figure is expected to rise to between 350 and 600 million people by 2050 (IPCC, 2007a). A rise in temperature of 3° C could lead to an additional 0.4 to 1.8 billion people being exposed to the risk of water stress in Africa. Globally, it is projected that between 120 million and 1.2 billion people will experience increased water stress by the 2020s, rising to 185 to 981 million people by the 2050s (Arnell, 2004).

The loss of glacial meltwater sources for irrigated agriculture and other uses in the Andes, central Asian lowlands, and parts of south Asia, represents a serious long-term climate risk (World Bank, 2008a). These regions, as well as other regions facing projected decreases in average precipitation, will most likely need to reconsider and optimize how their water resources are distributed among different sectors, particularly in the case of agriculture, which accounts for approximately three-quarters of total water use in developing countries. For example, the decline in annual flow of the Red River in Asia by 13 to 19 per cent and that of the Mekong River by 16 to 24 per cent by the end of the 21st century will contribute to increasing water shortages (ADB, 1995).

It is estimated that the ice caps on Mount Kilimanjaro could disappear by 2020 (Thompson et al., 2002) and glacial melting, in general, together with the associated risks of glacial melt outburst floods (GLOF), created when water dammed by a glacier or a moraine is released, are projected to have significant adverse effects in some regions.

In the small island states, the wet and dry cycles associated with El Niño/Southern Oscillation (ENSO)[18] episodes will have serious impacts on water supply (Nyong, 2008). In Asia, ENSO events have also contributed to intensifying water shortages, while a 6 to 10 per cent increase in water demand for agricultural irrigation is expected to occur in response to a 1° C rise in surface air temperature by the 2020s (Cruz et al., 2007), further exacerbating water shortages.

In addition to its effect on water availability and demand, climate change will also affect water quality: over-exploitation of groundwater (the reserves of water below the earth's surface) in many coastal countries has resulted in a drop in its level, leading to "saltwater intrusion" (i.e. seepage of salt water from the oceans into the groundwater, making the sub-surface water saline). As a direct impact of global warming, the coastal regions of Africa, India, China and Bangladesh, as well as small island developing states, are especially susceptible to increasing salinity of both their groundwater and their surface water resources due to increases in sea level. In Latin America, the increase in arid zones resulting from climate change, coupled with inappropriate agricultural practices (such as deforestation, farming methods which lead to soil erosion, and the excessive use of agrochemicals) are projected to diminish the quantity and quality of surface water and groundwater, and will further aggravate the situation in areas which have already deteriorated (UNEP, 2007b).

iii) Coastal areas, settlements and infrastructure

All coastal areas, including those situated in industrialized countries, are vulnerable to future climate change impacts. In North America, for example, climate change impacts, interacting with economic development and pollution, will pose increasing stresses on coastal communities and habitats (Field et al., 2007). In Australia, where more than 80 per cent of the population lives in coastal zones, there are potential risks from large storm surges and long-term sea level rise (Hennessy et al., 2007).

Developing countries, however, are found to be most vulnerable to the impacts of increased frequency and intensity of tropical storms, storm surges and sea level rise (World Bank, 2008a). Large sections of the populations in developing countries are clustered in low-lying areas, and much or most of the physical development and infrastructure in these regions are therefore concentrated close to the coasts (Nyong, 2008).

In general, south, southeast and east Asia, Africa, and the small island developing states are projected to be most vulnerable to coastal climate change impacts (Nicholls et al., 2007), although the coastal areas of Latin America are also expected to experience significant impacts by 2050 to 2080 (Magrin et al., 2007). As noted by the World Bank (World Bank, 2008a), rising sea levels over time present the greatest threat to the world's most vulnerable regions. As Cruz et al. (2007) point out, a 40 cm increase in sea level by the end of the century (which is probably a conservative estimate), is projected to increase the number of coastal inhabitants at risk of annual flooding from 13 million to 94 million.

The expected changes in sea level, weather, and climatic variability and extremes are very likely to result in significant economic losses, as well as other detrimental effects on human well-being (Wilbanks et al., 2007a, and Nyong, 2008). A long list of projected impacts can be compiled, based on a review of the current literature on this topic. Impacts on infrastructure will include damage to buildings, roads, railways, airports, bridges, and to port facilities due to storm surges, flooding and landslides. The potential economic losses directly associated with infrastructure damages are relatively easy to assess; however, the resulting impacts would also have a knock-on effect on other key sectors and services, including health and delivery of health services, tourism, agriculture, access to and availability of safe water, local trade and delivery of supplies, and food security. Moreover, population growth and migration of people to large cities in coastal areas put additional pressure on coastal settlements that would add to the challenges to be faced.

A wide range of other climate change impacts are projected for coastal areas and settlements. For example, projected sea level rise may exacerbate flooding, and increase the salinity of rivers, bays, and aquifers (the water-containing layers under the earth's surface), in addition to eroding beaches and inundating coastal marshes and wetlands. Other impacts reported relate to population displacement; increased erosion and changing coastlines; disruption of access to fishing grounds; negative impacts on biodiversity, including mangrove swamps; over-exploitation of water resources, including groundwater; and pollution and sea-water acidification in marine and coastal environments (Magrin et al., 2007).

iv) Health

Already today, climate change poses a number of threats to health and, as noted in the previous subsections, the majority of the health threats and impacts are concentrated in developing countries, with Africa being disproportionately affected. Figure 10 illustrates this by giving an overview, by region, of the actual (in 2000) mortality rates which are estimated to have resulted from climate change. As seen from the figure, the African continent is deemed to have experienced the largest health-related burden of climate change impacts, followed by the eastern Asia and Pacific region. Latin America and the Caribbean and China are also projected to be exposed to a significant increase in mortality attributable to climate change.

For developed countries, the main health impacts, both present and predicted, resulting from climate change are reductions in the death rate as a result of less exposure to the cold, an increase in the death rate during heatwaves, and other deaths arising from extreme climate events. Furthermore, alterations in the seasonal distribution of some allergenic pollen species have been observed and are expected to have negative impacts on health in the future (Confalonieri et al., 2007). In Australia, projected increased risks of forest and bush fires may cause result in an increased risk of respiratory diseases and breathing problems, as

FIGURE 10. Estimated climate change related deaths in 2000 by sub-region

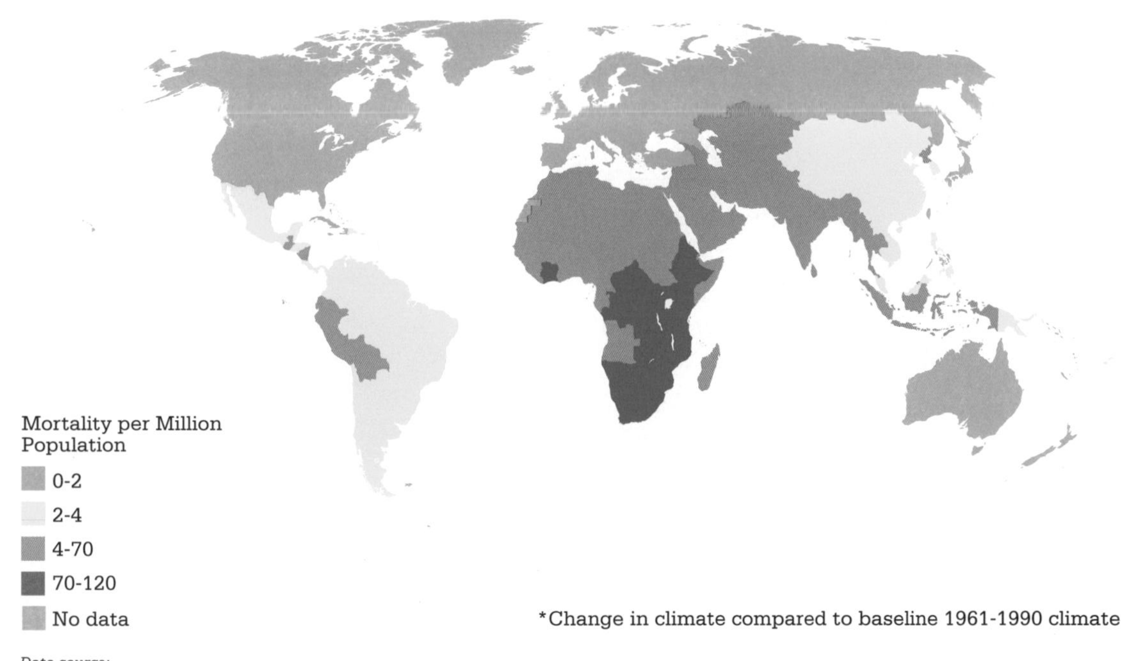

Data source:
McMichael, J.J., Campbell-Lendrum D., Kovats R.S., et al. Global Climate Change. In comparative Quantification of Health Risks: Global and Regional Burden of Disease due to Selected Major Risk factors. M.Ezzati, Lopez, AD. Rogers A., Murray GJL. Geneva, World Health Organisation, 2004

Source: Patz et al., 2005.

well as the danger of burns or of death (World Health Organization, 2000).

For developing countries too, the projected health impacts related to climate change include increases in the number of people dying or suffering from diseases or injuries brought about by extreme climate events, such as heatwaves, floods, storms, fires and droughts. In addition, these countries are likely to witness increased levels of malnutrition arising both directly from climate change impacts, and indirectly from the impacts on agriculture and water resources, as described in previous subsections (Confalonieri et al., 2007). In both cases, existing development challenges exacerbate the negative health impacts resulting from climate change.

Projected trends in climate change-related health impacts in developing countries also include increased instances of malaria, dengue fever, cholera, diarrhoeal diseases and other food- and water-borne diseases that have been shown to be linked to changes in temperatures, precipitation and extreme events (Confalonieri et al., 2007, and Menne and Ebi, 2006).

v) The natural resource base: ecosystems and biodiversity

Biodiversity and ecosystems are important for all people and societies, but particularly so for the large parts of the populations in many developing countries, whose livelihoods depend directly upon the natural resource base and the ecosystems for food, shelter, energy needs, etc. Analyses in Africa, Asia and Latin America carried out under the Assessments of Impacts and Adaptations to Climate Change (AIACC) project (AIACC, 2003-2007), for example, show that marginalized populations which are dependent on natural resources are particularly vulnerable to climate change impacts, especially if their natural resource base is severely degraded by overuse, as is often the case.

A number of potentially significant climate change impacts on both terrestrial and aquatic ecosystems have also been identified in recent assessments. The risk of species extinction due to climate change impacts is projected to be particularly high in Central and Latin America – where seven out of the 25 most critical ecosystems with high concentrations of endemic species (i.e. species which are found only in a specific area) are located – and in Asia, where up to 50 per cent of the region's total plant and animal species is projected to be at risk due to climate change (Thomas et al., 2004, Nyong, 2008, Cruz et al., 2007, and Magrin et al., 2007).

As a result of temperature changes, non-indigenous invasive species including insects, mites, nematodes (i.e. "roundworms"), and various plants are projected to become a problem in the middle and high-latitude and in small island states, and changes in forest structure and composition, are projected in most developing regions of the world, including Africa, Latin America and Asia (UNEP, 2007b, Cruz et al., 2007, and Nyong, 2008). Furthermore, it is expected that the combined effect of climate change impacts and changes in land use in Latin America will result in the loss of forests, and their replacement by savannas (Thomas et al., 2004, and Magrin et al., 2007).

By the end of this century, the natural grassland coverage and the grass yield in Asia are projected to decline by around 10 to 30 per cent as a consequence of climate change, with consequent negative impacts on livestock production in the region (Nyong, 2008). Grasslands in Africa are also projected to be impacted by climate change and this could, among other issues, negatively affect the availability of migration routes for both cattle and wild animals (Thuiller et al., 2006).

Major impacts on coastal ecosystems which have been reported in various regions include coral bleaching and the disappearance of low-lying corals, as well as the possible extinction of endangered species associated with these ecosystems (such as manatees and marine turtles), and losses of migratory birds and of biodiversity in general. As noted by Nyong (2008), all of these impacts will also have negative effects on fisheries and tourism.

B. Responding to climate change: mitigation and adaptation

Mitigation and adaptation are the two major approaches for dealing with climate change and its associated impacts. Mitigation refers to policies and options for reducing greenhouse gas emissions and/or enhancing carbon sinks (such as forests or oceans). Adaptation, on the other hand, refers to responses aimed at attenuating the negative impacts of climate change or exploiting its potential beneficial effects.

In this section, the concepts of mitigation and adaptation and how they are related are examined, and current knowledge on the potentials, practices and technologies available for mitigation and adaptation are reviewed. This section builds on subjects covered in previous sections and focuses, particularly with reference to mitigation, on options related to technology. The final part examines key issues regarding the role of technology and technology transfer, specifically in the context of mitigation and adaptation.

1. Mitigation and adaptation: defining, comparing and relating the concepts

The projections of future climate change and of its impacts, which were discussed in the previous section, amply illustrate the necessity of reducing current and future greenhouse gas (GHG) emissions, and of intensifying strategies for dealing with the impacts of climate change that are unavoidable due to past emissions. There is now general recognition that both adaptation and mitigation are necessary elements of any comprehensive strategy to manage the risks and to respond to the impacts of climate change (see, for example, IPCC, 2007f, McKibben and Wilcoxen, 2004, IPCC, 2001b, and Wilbanks et al., 2003).

Mitigation is defined by the IPCC (2007b) as "technological change and substitution that reduce resource inputs and emissions per unit of output". In the context of climate change, mitigation thus means implementing policies to reduce greenhouse gas emissions and/or enhance carbon sinks. Adaptation, on the other hand, refers to responses to the impacts of climate change, and is defined by the IPCC (2007b) as "adjustment in natural or human systems in response to actual or expected climatic stimuli or their effects, which moderates harm or exploits beneficial opportunities"

In other words, mitigation reduces the rate and magnitude of climate change and its associated impacts, whereas adaptation increases the ability of people or natural systems to cope with the consequences of the impacts of climatic changes, including increased climate variability and the occurrence of extreme weather (Jones and Preston, 2006, and Wilbanks et al., 2007b). Thus, mitigation and adaptation deal with different aspects of the risks imposed by climate change and are, to a large extent, targeted at managing risks at opposite ends of the range of projections on climate change.

Adaptation is, in many ways, best suited to dealing with the impacts of climate variability and change that are already being experienced as a result of historical GHG emissions, or that have a high probability of occurring within a relatively short time-frame. Mitigation is aimed at reducing the volume of accumulated emissions in the future, thereby reducing or avoiding the "worst-case" climate change scenarios, for instance among the SRES scenarios described in previous subsections. By reducing the volume of accumulated emissions, mitigation also increases the chances that the remaining climate risks can be successfully managed through adaptation (McKibben and Wilcoxen, 2004, and Wilbanks et al., 2003).

In addition to managing different parts of the risks imposed by climate change, mitigation and adaptation differ in terms of time and geographical scales. In this way, although the costs of emission reductions are location-specific, the benefits of mitigation are global, since emission reductions contribute equally to decreasing overall atmospheric concentrations of greenhouse gases, regardless of the geographical location of the emission-reduction activities. Moreover, mitigation benefits are long-term because of the long atmospheric lifetimes of most greenhouse gases and the resulting time lapse between the moment of emission and the response by the climate system. Adaptation, by contrast, is characterized by benefits in the short to medium term, and both adaptation costs and benefits are primarily local (IPCC, 2007a, and Jones and Preston, 2006).

Based on the differences outlined above, mitigation and adaptation have followed separate paths in scientific studies, as well as in national and international climate change response efforts, and until recently such efforts have been characterized by a major focus on mitigation (Burton, Diringer and Smith, 2006). The emphasis on mitigation reflects a belief, widely held until the end of the 1990s, that an internationally coordinated effort to reduce greenhouse gas emissions would be sufficient to avoid climate change impacts on a significant scale (Burton, Diringer and Smith, 2006, and Wilbanks et al., 2007b), and a related belief that climate change was an emission problem (i.e. that it was related to the volume of emissions) rather than a concentration problem, resulting from GHG concentrations in the atmosphere.

As discussed earlier, it is now undisputed that climate change is taking place, and that some climate change impacts are unavoidable. This realization, and the gradually increasing evidence on the magnitude of the adaptation effort which will be necessary to manage the impacts of climate change, are reflected in the findings on climate change risks and impacts, and the increasing confidence in the accuracy of these findings throughout the four IPCC Assessment Reports (IPCC, 1990, 1995, 2001 and 2007a).

In many ways, the focus on mitigation resulted in a relative lack of emphasis on the potential synergies between climate change and development. In addition, it focused attention away from development needs and priorities which could provide a less polarized way of addressing climate change challenges in a global context. To give an example, in many developing countries, energy initiatives and other climate favouring activities have emerged as side-benefits of sound development programmes. Price reform, agricultural soil protection, sustainable forestry initiatives, and energy sector restructuring are all examples of policies and initiatives that can have substantial effects on the growth rates of greenhouse gas emissions, although they are often undertaken without any reference to climate change mitigation and adaptation. This observation suggests that in many cases it is possible to build environmental and climate policy upon development priorities that are vitally important to national decision-makers in developing countries. It opens the potential that climate change policies may be seen not as a burden to be avoided but as a side-benefit of sound and internationally supported development. By introducing specific requirements for sustainable development, the Clean Development Mechanism (one of the three flexibility mechanisms introduced under the Kyoto Protocol), can be seen as one of the first steps towards recognizing the need for an integrated approach to development and climate issues.

Following the IPCC Fourth Assessment Report (IPCC, 2007a) and the Stern Review (Stern, 2006), there appears to be an increased focus on building on the potential synergies between adaptation and mitigation efforts, while at the same time making sure that they also contribute to achieving broader development goals. More generally, with the growing body of evidence on the magnitude of the burden that climate change adaptation may impose on the poorest and most vulnerable countries and populations, there has been increasing recognition of the need to take climate change into consideration during development planning and policy-making.

In the subsections below, options for climate change mitigation and adaptation will be addressed. The area of mitigation is generally well defined and there is considerable knowledge on the opportunities, technologies, and costs of achieving a given reduction of greenhouse gas emissions.

Adaptation, vulnerability and adaptive capacity are, on the other hand, more difficult to define and measure. Adaptation is, as previously noted, intrinsically linked to existing development contexts such as income and educational levels, structure of the economy and governance structures. Since the end results of changes in adaptation, vulnerability and adaptive capacity are location, context, and development specific, it is difficult to attribute such outcomes or end results to any single intervention. Furthermore, adaptation – unlike mitigation, where it is possible to assess the outcome in terms of changes in CO_2 equivalent emissions – cannot be evaluated by the use of a single, unambiguous indicator. Finally, there is still limited evidence on the costs of adaptation and on the insurance aspects related to it: for example, how much are we willing to pay for a given reduction in the risk of a given climate change impact or event?

2. Mitigation: potential, practices and technologies

a) Mitigation sectors

In the section on greenhouse gas emission trends and structure, it was noted that, between 1970 and 2004, global greenhouse gas emissions caused by human activity increased by 70 per cent from 28.7 to 49 Giga tonnes of CO_2-equivalent (see note 7 for a definition). It was also noted that carbon dioxide is the principal greenhouse gas and its emission levels are increasing the fastest. There is broad agreement – as reflected by the IPCC (2007a), the Stern Review (Stern, 2006), and the International Energy Agency (IEA, 2006a) – that GHG emissions must be dramatically reduced to limit the severity of climate change impacts on developing and developed countries alike. The data outlined in the previous subsections offer further support to this conclusion. As illustrated in the subsections on observed and projected climate change impacts and on projected regional and sectoral impacts, significant impacts will accompany even small increases in temperature and for larger temperature increases, the impacts are potentially calamitous.

Greenhouse gas emissions arise from almost all economic activities and aspects of society, indicating that the range of practices and technologies potentially available for achieving greenhouse gas emission reductions is broad and diverse. Figure 11 illustrates this by showing the global flow of greenhouse gas emissions by sector and end-use.

By volume, the largest contribution to greenhouse gas emissions is accounted for by power generation (electricity and heat production and transformation), followed by industry and fuel combustion. Land-use change, through deforestation and forest degradation, is estimated to account for more emissions globally than the entire transport sector, and emissions arising from agriculture are roughly the same as emissions from transportation.

Figure 11. Global flow of greenhouse gas emissions by sector and end-use activity

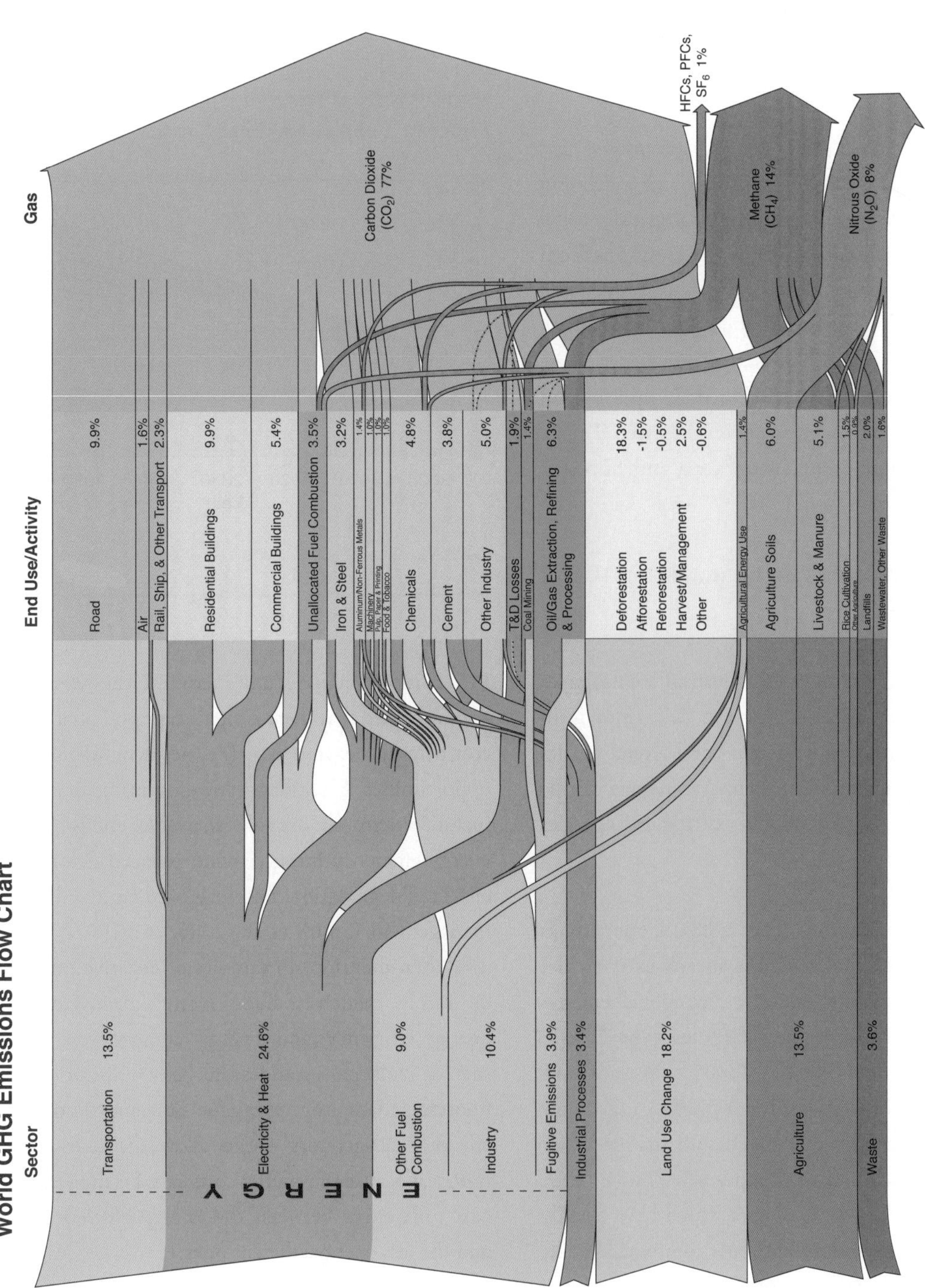

Sources & Notes: All data is for 2000. All calculations are based on CO_2 equivalents, using 100-year global warming potentials from the IPCC (1996), based on a total global estimate of 41,755 $MtCO_2$ equivalent. Land use change includes both emissions and absorptions; see Chapter 16. See Appendix 2 for detailed description of sector and end use/activity definitions, as well as data sources. Dotted lines represent flows of less than 0.1% percent of total GHG emissions.

Source: Baumert et al. (2005).

The figure also indicates that, in order to achieve significant emission reductions, mitigation potentials in all of the sectors above will need to come into play, and this will involve a broad range of technologies. The literature on this topic consequently focuses on the following seven major sectors for mitigation: buildings, transport, industry, energy supply, agriculture, forestry, and waste (IPCC, 2007f).

The information on the flow of greenhouse gas emissions given in Figure 11 also gives a first indication on the key options for climate change mitigation: using energy more efficiently to reduce the emissions from fossil fuel use; switching to zero- or low-carbon energy technologies; reducing deforestation; and introducing better farming practices and waste treatment. There seems to be general agreement on these options and their importance in the literature on the topic (IPCC, 2007e, IEA, 2006c, 2008, and Pacala and Socolow, 2004).

b) Key technologies and practices in the mitigation sectors

A wide variety of options in the form of technologies and practices are available for the achievement of greenhouse gas emission reductions, and several studies conclude that even ambitious emission targets can be achieved through employment of existing technologies and practices (IPCC, 2007e).

For instance, a study from IEA (2008a) demonstrates how employing technologies that already exist or that are under development could reduce global energy-related CO_2 emissions to their 2005 levels by 2050.[19] Similarly, Pacala and Socolow (2004) illustrate how emissions may be stabilized until 2050, and how global reductions after that date could stabilize CO_2 concentrations at levels of around 500 ppm in CO_2 equivalent, based on technologies which have already been deployed in various places on a commercial scale, and without assumptions of further fundamental technological breakthroughs. Their analysis is based on rapid expansion in the deployment of seven so-called "wedges" of alternate technologies, including improved fuel economy in cars, reduced reliance on cars, more energy-efficient buildings, improved power plant efficiency, substituting coal with national gas, and carbon capture and storage in power and hydrogen plants respectively (Pacala and Socolow, 2004). Each of these technology wedges would displace approximately 1 $GtCO_2$-eq per year by 2054.[20] Figure 12 illustrates this approach.

Figure 12. Stabilization through technology wedges

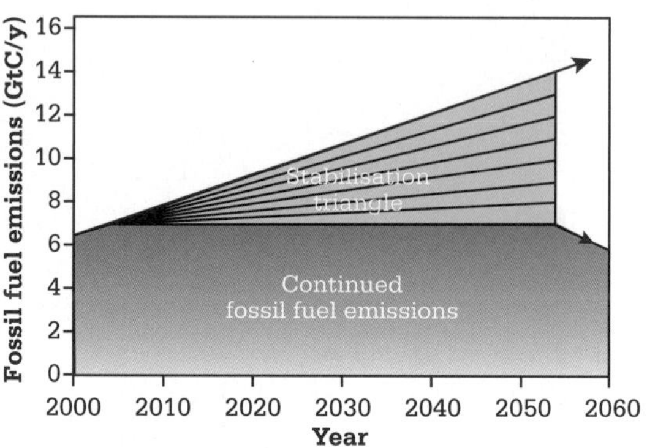

Source: Pacala and Socolow, 2004

In addition, many studies around the world have demonstrated that there is significant potential for low-cost or even negative cost (i.e. net benefit) mitigation opportunities. Examples of low-cost mitigation actions include increased use of renewable energy sources, energy efficiency improvement, reduced deforestation and land degradation, and improved land and forestry management (Smith et al., 2007, and IPCC, 2007e). The often-mentioned examples of negative mitigation options – which include many improvements in energy efficiency and energy conservation actions, such as replacing incandescent light bulbs or compact fluorescent lamps or buying fuel efficient cars or energy efficient refrigerators – can allow the users to save money, because the energy costs saved is more than the cost differences between the energy efficient choices and the less energy efficient ones.

Table 3 provides an overview of the key technologies and practices that are currently commercially available – as well as other technologies which are projected to be commercialized before 2030 – in the seven major "mitigation sectors".[21] These seven mitigation sectors

Table 3. Technologies and practices for the mitigation sectors

Sector	Key mitigation technologies and practices currently commercially available	Key mitigation technologies and practices projected to be commercialized before 2030
Energy supply	Improved supply and distribution efficiency; fuel-switching from coal to gas; nuclear power; renewable heat and power sources (hydropower, solar, wind, geothermal and bioenergy); combined heat and power; early applications of Carbon Capture and Storage (CCS, e.g. storage of CO_2 removed from natural gas).	CCS for gas, biomass and coal-fired electricity generating facilities; advanced nuclear power; advanced renewable energy, including tidal and wave energy, concentrating solar, and solar photovoltaics (PV).
Transport	More fuel-efficient vehicles; hybrid vehicles; cleaner diesel vehicles; biofuels; shifts from road transport to rail and public transport systems; non-motorized transport (cycling, walking); land use and transport planning.	Second-generation biofuels; higher efficiency aircraft; advanced electric and hybrid vehicles with more powerful and reliable batteries.
Buildings	Efficient lighting and day-lighting; more efficient electrical appliances and heating and cooling devices; improved cooking stoves; improved insulation; passive and active solar design for heating and cooling; alternative refrigeration fluids; recovery and recycle of fluorinated gases.	Integrated design of commercial buildings technologies, such as intelligent meters that provide feedback and control; solar PV integrated in buildings.
Industry	More efficient end-use electrical equipment; heat and power recovery; material recycling and substitution; control of non-CO_2 gas emissions; and a wide array of process-specific technologies.	Advanced energy efficiency; CCS for cement, ammonia, and iron manufacture; inert electrodes for aluminium manufacture.
Agriculture	Improved crop and grazing land management to increase soil carbon storage; restoration of cultivated peaty soils and degraded lands; improved rice cultivation techniques and livestock and manure management to reduce CH_4 emissions; improved nitrogen fertilizer application techniques to reduce N_2O emissions; dedicated energy crops to replace fossil fuel use; improved energy efficiency.	Improvements of crop yields.
Forestry/forests	Afforestation; reforestation; forest management; reduced deforestation; harvested wood product management; use of forestry products for bioenergy to replace fossil fuel use.	Tree species improvement to increase biomass productivity and carbon sequestration. Improved remote sensing technologies for analysis of vegetation/soil carbon sequestration potential and mapping land-use change.
Waste management	Landfill methane recovery; waste incineration with energy recovery; composting of organic waste; controlled waste-water treatment; recycling and waste minimization.	Biocovers and biofilters to optimize CH_4 oxidation.

Source: IPCC, 2007f.

and the key technologies and practices that can be expected to deliver GHG emission reductions before 2030 are shown in Table 3.

As mentioned above, there is broad agreement in the related literature on the key categories of technologies that are currently available for application in the various "mitigation sectors" (IPCC, 2007e, IEA, 2006c, 2008, and Pacala and Socolow, 2004). These technologies and practices for the mitigation sectors are described further below.

As Table 3 shows, for the energy sector, these technologies and practices can be classified into three groups: the first group involves technologies for improving the efficiency of energy supply, including "co-generation" (the generation of heat and power at the same time). The second group includes the low- or zero-emission technologies, such as renewable energy, nuclear energy, and replacing coal with natural gas. The third group is focused on using fossil fuels without greenhouse gas emissions, mainly through carbon capture and storage technologies.[22]

A large number of low-carbon energy supply technologies are currently commercially available and are expected to be developed further in the coming decades. The demand for a range of renewable energy technologies, such as wind power, hydropower, solar power, bioenergy and geothermal power, is expected to increase. Within energy supply, this range of renewable energy sources has the largest mitigation potential and its use could almost double from 18 per cent of electricity supply in 2005 to 30-35 per cent by 2030.

The potential increase in nuclear energy is less significant, with a small increase from 16 per cent to 18 per cent projected within the same time-frame. Other technologies and measures also play a role in energy supply-related mitigation, including supply efficiency, combined heat and power, switching boilers from coal to gas, and early applications of carbon capture and storage technologies. Energy investments up to 2030 are expected to total more than US$ 20 trillion, and will accordingly have a major impact on global investment and trade.

The transportation, buildings, and industry sectors are major end-users of energy, and the mitigation technologies in these sectors can be grouped into three categories: end-use energy-efficiency improvement; switching to zero-carbon or less carbon-intensive sources of energy; and reducing the demand for energy needs, for example by eliminating day-lighting, by increasing use of public transport or of bicycles, and by material recycling.

The transport sector also has a potential for mitigation through technologies such as fuel-efficient and hybrid motorized vehicles, rail and public transport systems and biofuels. However, the reduction of greenhouse gas emissions through the use of fuel-efficient vehicles and greater fuel efficiency in aviation may be counteracted by growth in transportation. The potential emission reductions will also depend on the development of second-generation biofuels[23] as well as on the development of electric vehicles. From a trade perspective, trade in alternative fuels will potentially show significant growth, as is the case with vehicle-related technologies.

The residential, commercial and institutional buildings sector is the area with the most important projected potential for greenhouse gas emission reductions (IPCC, 2007e). Since most emissions from this sector are a result of heavy use of energy for heating/cooling, lighting and various electrical appliances, the emission reduction potential can be attained largely through energy-efficiency improvements. Some of the key technologies and products for this purpose are building insulation, efficient lighting options, more efficient heating and cooling systems and efficient electrical appliances (Levine et al., 2007).

Demand-side energy efficiency often proves to be the most cost-effective route to climate change mitigation, and it is expected that, by 2030, close to one-third (30 per cent) of emissions in the buildings sector can be offset with net economic benefits rather than costs (Levine et al., 2007). To some extent these efficiency measures can be integrated in existing residential, commercial and institutional buildings, and for new buildings there is even a higher potential through integrated design and inclusion of solar photovoltaic technology. Building codes and standards are potentially an important means of influencing the adoption of energy-efficiency measures (Levine et al., 2007).

Energy efficiency and energy recovery in the industrial sector can significantly contribute to the reduction of greenhouse gas emissions. This is especially true for the carbon-intensive and energy-intensive industries (such as iron and steel, non-ferrous metals, cement and glass, among others), that accounted for approximately 85 per cent of the industrial sector's energy use in 2004 (Bernstein et al., 2007). There is significant potential for efficient industrial motors, other electrical equipment and process technologies. But there is also a potential for reducing greenhouse gas emissions by using co-generation technologies to recover waste heat and gas for energy production.

Based on the available studies, the largest mitigation potential is found to be in the steel, cement, and pulp and paper industries and in the reduction of non-CO_2 gases. In addition, much of the potential is available at a relatively low cost (i.e. less than US$ 50 per tonne of CO_2-eq). In the medium and longer term, the application of carbon capture and storage (CCS) technologies offers another large potential for reduction of greenhouse gas emissions, although it is associated with higher costs (Bernstein et al., 2007).

In the forestry and agricultural sectors, the mitigation technologies mainly involve increased carbon sinks to remove CO_2 from the atmosphere through enlarging the forest areas and eliminating land degradation; supplying biomass (i.e. organic matter) as a renewable source of energy; and reducing the emissions of methane and nitrous oxide from agricultural activities through improved management practices.

Improvements in techniques and practices, rather than the deployment of actual technologies ("hard" technologies), are expected to play a significant part in emission reductions in agriculture. There is considerable potential for reductions in greenhouse gas emissions through the restoration of degraded lands, soil carbon sequestration and storage, energy efficiency, and combustion of agricultural residues.

As shown in Figure 11, agriculture also has a potential for mitigation of emissions of non-CO_2 gases, such as methane and nitrous oxide through the use of manure management technologies and fertilizer applications. Soil carbon sequestration is estimated to account for 89 per cent of the potential for reducing greenhouse gas emissions through the use of technology in agriculture, whereas mitigation of methane and nitrous oxide emissions from soils account for 9 and 2 per cent of the technical potential, respectively (Smith et al., 2007).

Technology has great scope for reducing greenhouse gas emissions in the agricultural sector, but development and transfer of these technologies is found to be a key requirement for these mitigation potentials to be achieved. For example, while some studies of technology change in Europe show that technological improvement will be a key factor in greenhouse gas mitigation in the future (Smith et al., 2005, and Rounsevell et al., 2006), other studies indicate that, although efficiency improvements (for example, in the use of nitrogen) occur in industrialized countries, this is not the case for many developing countries, because various barriers, such as costs, lack of knowledge and incentives for the farmers, prevent the transfer of these technologies (IFA, 2007).

The mitigation potential in forestry is embodied principally in forestry management practices (such as afforestation and reforestation) to enhance carbon sinks. Also, importantly, the prevention of further deforestation can contribute to emission reductions, and this accounts for about half the forestry mitigation potential.

Finally, the main types of mitigation technologies in the waste sector include reducing the quantities of waste generation, and recycling the usable parts of waste; waste management to avoid methane emissions during the decay of waste; and using waste as a source for energy production. Although waste management is expected to have the smallest potential for greenhouse gas emission reduction of the various mitigation sectors by 2030, it is associated with a number of important technologies: these include the capture of methane gas from landfills for either flaring (i.e. burning without economic purpose) or power generation; burning of waste, such as municipal solid waste, for electricity generation; composting of organic waste; and methane recovery from waste water systems.

c) Mitigation targets, potential and associated cost estimates

i) Stabilization scenarios and targets and associated cost estimates at the macroeconomic level

International negotiations will determine stabilization target(s) at the global level and will thus determine the extent of the greenhouse gas emission reductions which must be achieved. The targets under discussion are, however, influenced by scientific knowledge on the

TABLE 4. Characteristics of stabilization scenarios [a)]

CATEGORY	RADIATIVE FORCING (W/m^2)	CO_2 CONCENTRATION [c)] (ppm)	CO_2-EQ CONCENTRATION [c)] (ppm)	GLOBAL MEAN TEMPERATURE INCREASE ABOVE PRE-INDUSTRIAL AT EQUILIBRIUM, USING "BEST ESTIMATE" CLIMATE SENSITIVITY [b), c)] (°C)	PEAKING YEAR FOR CO_2 EMISSIONS [d)]	CHANGE IN GLOBAL CO_2 EMISSIONS IN 2050 (% OF 2000 EMISSIONS) [d)]	NO. OF ASSESSED SCENARIOS
I	2.5-3.0	350-400	445-490	2.0-2.4	2000-2015	-85 to -50	6
II	3.0-3.5	400-440	490-535	2.4-2.8	2000-2020	-60 to -30	18
III	3.5-4.0	440-485	535-590	2.8-3.2	210-2030	-30 to +5	21
IV	4.0-5.0	485-570	590-710	3.2-4.0	2020-2060	+10 to +60	118
V	5.0-6.0	570-660	710-855	4.0-4.9	2050-2080	+25 to +85	9
VI	6.0-7.5	660-790	855-1130	4.9-6.1	2060-2090	+90 to +140	5
						TOTAL	177

Notes: a) The understanding of the climate system response to radiative forcing as well as feedbacks is assessed in detail in the AR4 WGI Report. Feedbacks between the carbon cycle and climate change affect the required mitigation for a particular stabilization level of atmospheric carbon dioxide concentration. These feedbacks are expected to increase the fraction of anthropogenic emissions that remains in the atmosphere as the climate system warms. Therefore, the emission reductions to meet a particular stabilization level reported in the mitigation studies assessed here might be underestimated.

b) The best estimate of climate sensitivity is 3° C (see IPCC, WG 1 SPM).

c) Note that global mean temperature at equilibrium is different from expected global mean temperature at the time of stabilization of GHG concentrations due to the inertia of the climate system. For the majority of scenarios assessed, stabilisation of GHG concentrations occurs between 2100 and 2150.

d) Ranges correspond to the 15th to 85th percentile of the post-TAR scenario distribution. CO_2 emissions are shown so multi-gas scenarios can be compared with CO_2-only scenarios.

Source: IPCC, 2007f, Table SPM.5.

extent of climate change and the impacts associated with different levels of concentration of greenhouse gases in the atmosphere, and on the costs of achieving stabilization targets which correspond to these levels.

In Table 4, the characteristics of different stabilization scenarios are given. The table provides an overview of the relationship between various targets aimed at stabilizing greenhouse gas concentration levels, their implications in terms of global warming, as well as the reduction in global greenhouse gas emissions that would be needed to achieve the stabilization target.

The two stabilization targets that have been most widely discussed by scientists and policy-makers fall within the concentration ranges of 445-490 parts per million (ppm) and 535-590 ppm CO_2-eq. The first target has been backed primarily by the European Union, which advocates limiting global warming to a 2° C increase in temperature, in order to avoid dangerous anthropogenic interference with the climate system. The second target, more specifically of 550 ppm CO_2-equivalent (CO_2-eq), which would correspond to a temperature increase of around 3° C, has been more extensively studied in science, including by the IPCC.

The main motivation for using 550 ppm as a benchmark for analyses is that it corresponds roughly to a scenario where CO_2 levels in the atmosphere would be stabilized at around twice the pre-industrial level (see Section I.A) – a level which has been suggested by the IPCC as an upper threshold for avoiding dangerous human interference with the climate system. As seen from Table 4, the two targets have quite different implications for the amount of reduction in global greenhouse gas emissions that would be required to achieve them, and in the peaking year of emissions: global CO_2-eq emissions would have to be decreased by 50-85 per cent (relative to emission levels in 2000) by the year 2050 in order to confine global warming to

2.0-2.4° C; whereas confining temperature increases to between 2.8 and 3.2° C by 2050, would only require global emissions to be between 30 per cent lower to 5 per cent higher than emission levels in 2000 (see the 7th column of Table 4).

In addition, the different stabilization targets have very different implications for the estimated macroeconomic costs at a global level, as shown in Table 5. The higher stabilization target of around 550 ppm CO_2-eq is estimated by the IPCC to result in an annual reduction of global gross domestic product (GDP) of 0.2-2.5 per cent, whereas the lower stabilization target would imply an annual reduction in global GDP of more than 3 per cent. For comparison, the Stern Review (Stern, 2006) concludes that the costs of stabilizing emissions at 550 ppm CO_2-eq would be, on average, 1 per cent of global GDP, which would correspond to approximately US$ 134 billion in 2015 or US$ 930 billion in 2050.

The results shown in the table are based on studies using various baselines. These studies also differ in terms of the point in time at which stabilization is expected to be achieved – generally this point is in 2100 or later. Furthermore, it should be noted that for any given stabilization level, GDP reductions would increase over time after 2030 in most models. Thus, the long-term cost ranges (in terms of reduction in GDP) corresponding to the estimates in Table 4 above are respectively –1 to 2 per cent for the 590-710 ppm CO_2-eq stabilization level, from just below zero to around 4 per cent for the 535-590 ppm CO_2-eq stabilization level, and more than 5.5 per cent reduction in GDP for the 445-535 ppm CO_2-eq stabilization level (IPCC, 2007f). Costs in the long term are, however, associated with higher uncertainty.

In order to address stabilization targets and emission reductions from the individual sectoral and technological angles, it is convenient to view the costs from an incentive perspective, i.e. in terms of carbon prices. This implies that, rather than studying the emission reduction requirements for reaching a given stabilization target, the analyses are structured around a "bottom-up" viewpoint: What would be the effects on greenhouse gas emission reductions of introducing a given price on carbon?

In order to be cost-effective, the "marginal cost" of CO_2 emission reductions must be equal for all sources of emissions; otherwise, it would be possible to lower the overall costs by redistributing emission reductions between sources. The most effective tool for achieving this is to put a price on (CO_2-equivalent) greenhouse gas emission reductions (known as "carbon pricing"), measured as the price per tonne of CO_2-equivalent emissions reduced. In addition, "carbon pricing" creates incentives to undertake research and development (R&D) and to innovate energy-saving and climate-friendly technologies (OECD, 2008). The following subsection reviews the potential for emission reductions at the sectoral level, considered in terms of carbon prices.

ii) Potential for emission reductions at the sectoral level as a function of carbon prices

Table 6 shows the global mitigation potential as a function of carbon prices in 2030, based on a review of available studies.[24] It should be noted that since this table does not refer to the same stabilization levels as in Tables 4 and 5, and since, furthermore, Table 4 uses 2050 as the point of reference for changes in emissions, Table 6 cannot be directly compared to those tables. However, a 550 ppm CO_2-eq stabilization level is reported to correspond to an emission reduction of 26 Gt CO_2-eq/year, whereas an emission reduction of 33 Gt CO_2-eq/year would be required to achieve a stabilization level of 490 ppm CO_2-eq, and a reduction in emissions of 18 Gt CO_2-eq/year would lead to a stabilization level of around 700 ppm CO_2-eq (Enkvist, Nauclér and Rosander, 2007).

In addition, since global greenhouse gas emissions in 2000 were 43 Gt CO_2-eq (IPCC, 2007f), the emission reduction potential of 16 to 31 Gt CO_2-eq/year would be equivalent to an emission reduction by 2030 of 36 to 70 per cent relative to 2000 levels of emissions. This indicates that a carbon price of US$ 100 per tonne of CO_2-eq, as suggested in the studies reviewed by the IPCC, could be sufficient for achieving the lower stabilization targets illustrated in Table 4.

Table 6 illustrates a point raised earlier, regarding the existence of mitigation options associated with

TABLE 5. Estimated global macroeconomic costs in 2030[a)] for lowest-cost means of achieving different long-term stabilization [b), c)]

STABILIZATION LEVELS (ppm CO_2-eq)	MEDIAN GDP REDUCTION [d)] (%)	RANGE OF GDP REDUCTIONS [d), e)] (%)	REDUCTION OF AVERAGE ANNUAL GDP GROWTH RATES [d), f)] (percentage points)
590-710	0.2	-0.6-1.2	<0.06
535-590	0.6	0.2-2.5	<0.1
445-535[g)]	not available	<3	<0.12

Notes: a) For a given stabilization level, GDP reduction would increase over time in most models after 2030. Long-term costs also become more uncertain.

b) Results based on studies using various baselines.

c) Studies vary in terms of the point in time stabilization is achieved; generally this is in 2100 or later.

d) This is global GDP based market exchange rates.

e) The median and the 10th and 90th percentile range of the analyzed data are given.

f) The calculation of the reduction of the annual growth rate is based on the average reduction during the period till 2030 that would result in the indicated GDP decrease in 2030.

g) The number of studies that report GDP results is relatively small and they generally use low baselines.

Source: IPCC, 2007f, Table SPM.4.

TABLE 6. Global mitigation potential in 2030 for different carbon prices

CARBON PRICE (US$/t$CO_2$-eq)	ECONOMIC POTENTIAL (GtCO_2-eq/year)	REDUCTION RELATIVE TO SRES A1 B (68 GtCO_2-eq/year) (%)	REDUCTION RELATIVE TO SRES B2 (49 GtCO_2-eq/year) (%)
0	5-7	7-10	10-14
20	9-17	14-25	19-35
50	13-26	20-38	27-52
100	16-31	23-46	32-63

Source: IPCC, 2007f, Table SPM.1.

negative net costs, i.e. where the benefits of the options are larger than the costs. According to the table, such options have the potential to reduce global emissions by around 6 Gt CO_2-eq/year by 2030, equivalent to a reduction by 2030 of around 14 per cent relative to 2000 emissions with associated net benefits.

In Figure 13 and the associated Table 7, the results on mitigation potential as illustrated in Table 6 are broken down by sector and region. The ranges for global economic potentials as assessed in each sector are shown by vertical lines in each of the coloured bands, and Table 7 reports these ranges for the mitigation potential by sector of less than US$ 100/t CO_2-eq.

The figure and table show that, of the seven mitigation sectors, the buildings sector holds the greatest potential for achievement of greenhouse gas emission level reductions in terms of quantity, as was noted earlier, and that a very large share of this potential can be achieved at low carbon prices. Based on a review of more than 80 recent studies from 36 countries worldwide, Levine et al. (2007) estimate that, by 2030, about 30 per cent of the projected greenhouse gas emissions in the buildings sector could be avoided, with net economic benefit, and that the same potential exists in all regions of the world.

The potential reflects the scope for improvements in low-cost energy efficiency options for the buildings

Figure 13. Estimated economic potential for global mitigation by sector for different regions

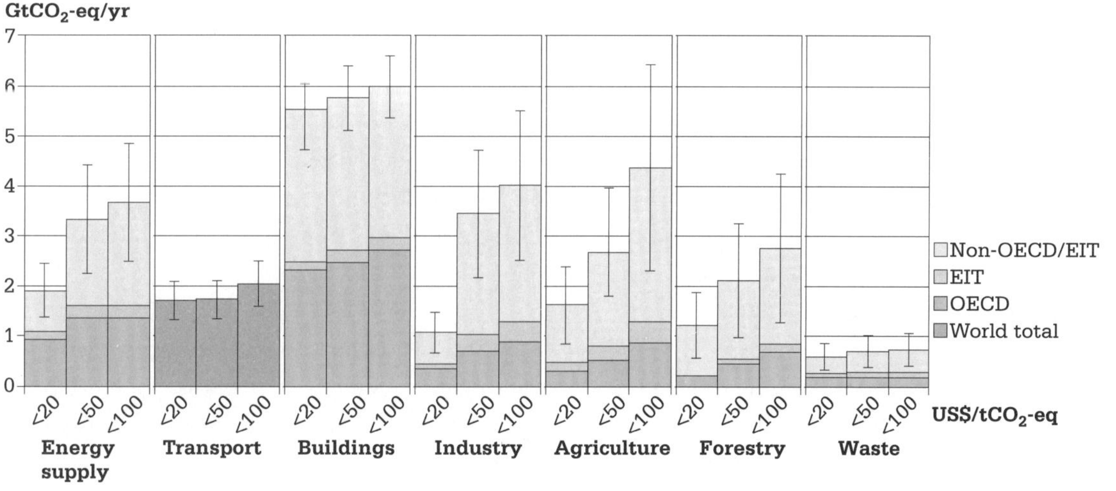

Table 7. Mitigation potential in different sectors at a carbon price of less than US$ 100/tCO_2-eq

Sectors	Energy Supply	Transport	Buildings	Industry	Agriculture	Forestry	Waste	Total	Reduction relative to the baseline of 6 Gt CO_2-eq/year
Mitigation potential (Gt CO_2-eq/year)	2.4-4.7	1.6-2.5	5.3-6.7	2.5-5.5	2.3-6.4	1.3-4.2	0.4-1	15.8-30.1	23%-46%

Source for Figure 13 and Table 7: IPCC, 2007f, Figure and Table SPM.6.

Notes: a) The ranges for global economic potentials as assessed in each sector are shown by vertical lines. The ranges are based on end-use allocations of emissions, meaning that emissions of electricity use are counted towards the end-use sectors and not to the energy supply sector.

b) The estimated potentials have been constrained by the availability of studies particularly at high carbon price levels.

c) Sectors used different baselines. For industry the SRES B2 baseline was taken, for energy supply and transport the WEO 2004 baseline was used; the building sector is based on a baseline in between SRES B2 and A1B; for waste, SRES A1B driving forces were used to construct a waste specific baseline, agriculture and forestry used baselines that mostly used B2 driving forces.

d) Only global totals for transport are shown because international aviation is included [5.4].

e) Categories excluded are: non-CO_2 emissions in buildings and transport, part of material efficiency options, heat production and cogeneration in energy supply, heavy duty vehicles, shipping and high-occupancy passenger transport, most high-cost options for buildings, wastewater treatment, emission reduction from coal mines and gas pipelines, fluorinated gases from energy supply and transport. The underestimation of the total economic potential from these emissions is of the order of 10-15%.

sector. It also reflects the availability of well-developed energy-efficiency technologies that exist already and that have been used with success, such as improved insulation and district heating in the colder climates, and efficiency measures related to space conditioning in the warmer climates, along with cooking stoves in developing countries (Levine et al., 2007). Other measures that rank high in terms of potential energy and emission savings include solar water heating, efficient lighting and appliances, and building energy management systems (Levine et al., 2007).

At carbon prices below US$ 20 per tonne of emission reduction in CO_2-eq, the energy supply sector has the second-largest mitigation potential. This potential increases considerably for carbon prices up to US$ 50 per tonne of CO_2-eq reduced, reflecting the relatively higher costs associated with the implementation of some of the technologies available for emission reductions in the energy sector, as well as the considerable investment requirements. An increase in the carbon price from US$ 50 to US$ 100 per tonne of CO_2-eq does not result in a large increase in the mitigation potential for the energy sector, indicating that the scope for deploying additional technologies is not enhanced substantially by such levels of increase in the price of carbon.

For the industrial sector, the difference in mitigation potential for carbon prices up to US$ 20 and US$ 50 per tonne of CO_2-eq, respectively, is even more significant, with the mitigation potential being approximately three times larger for a carbon price of US$ 50 per tonne of CO_2-eq. An increase in the carbon price up to US$ 100 per tonne of CO_2-eq increases the mitigation potential by around 0.5 $GtCO_2$-eq/year, illustrating the potential for carbon capture and storage technologies in the industry sector (Bernstein et al., 2007).

For the agricultural sector, the increase in mitigation potential is significant over all three levels of carbon prices. The same is the case, although to a lesser extent, for the forestry sector. The mitigation potential in agriculture at carbon prices up to US$ 100 per tonne of CO_2-eq is the second highest of the seven mitigation sectors. Furthermore, in both these sectors the higher carbon prices influence the mitigation potential not only in OECD countries, but also in economies in transition and in developing countries (non-OECD countries/economies in transition).

In the transport and waste sector, increases in carbon prices do not lead to a significant increase of the mitigation potential, although an increase in the carbon price from below US$ 50 per tonne of CO_2-eq to below US$ 100 per tonne of CO_2-eq has some effect.

A further illustration of estimated costs of global mitigation for various technologies is provided in Figure 14. The estimates are from a study on the potentials and costs of measures to reduce global greenhouse gas emissions (McKinsey, 2009), and the figure provides a good overview of the relative costs estimated for various mitigation technologies by sector. Note that the costs are given in euros/tonne of CO_2-eq/yr.

The estimated mitigation potential at negative net costs is comparable in range to the potential mitigation shown in Table 6. The figure supports the findings discussed above, and gives further details on the estimated costs for different technology options.

Based on the cost curve in Figure 14, a carbon price of approximately 40 euros/tonne CO_2-eq/year would be required by 2030 in order to achieve stabilization at 550 ppm CO_2-eq. IPCC (2007e) estimates that carbon prices of US$ 20-80/tonne CO_2-eq would be required by 2030 to aim at achieving stabilization at around 550 ppm CO_2-eq by 2100. These costs are thus comparable in range, and differences mainly reflect variations in the underlying assumptions, such as economic development, costs of technologies and technological progress, energy demand and supply, energy prices, etc., as well as differences in the studies included as a basis for analysis.

It should be noted, however, that estimations of potential greenhouse gas emission reductions at different cost levels are associated with considerable uncertainty, not least because of their differing assumptions regarding technological progress, the rate of deployment of emission reduction technologies,

FIGURE 14. Strategic options for climate change mitigation global cost curve for greenhouse gas abatement measures

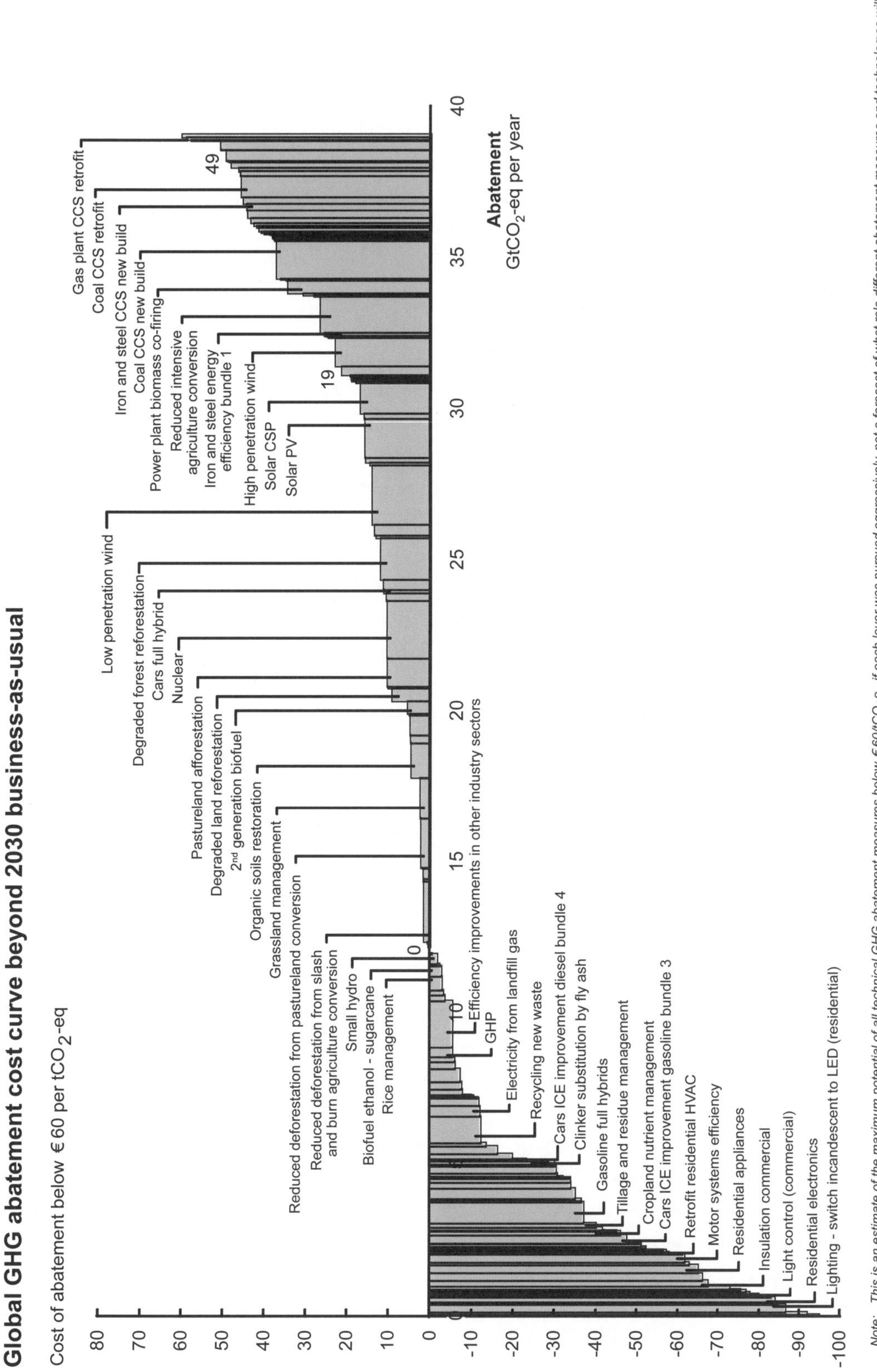

Source: McKinsey, 2009.

and assumptions regarding technology transfer. Some studies estimate that the costs of global mitigation will be or could be significantly higher than the figures reported in this subsection. For example, the IEA (2008b) points out that to reach the target of 50 per cent reduction in global greenhouse gas emissions from the current level by 2050, the marginal cost would have to be at least US$ 200 per tonne of CO_2-eq reduced, and could be as high as US$ 500 per tonne of CO_2-eq if the progress of key technologies does not live up to expectations.

Nonetheless, this subsection has illustrated that there is a substantial potential for global greenhouse emission reductions, and that a considerable portion of this potential, based on estimates in the available literature, is likely to be associated with relatively low costs.

3. Adaptation: potential, practices and technologies

It was noted above that adaptation refers to responses to moderate the negative impacts of climate change or to exploit potential beneficial effects of climate change. The potential for adaptation, in turn, depends on adaptive capacity, i.e. the ability or potential of a system to respond successfully to climate variability and change (Adger et al., 2007). In this subsection, we will focus on how people adapt, leaving out adaptation by ecosystems. As there are significantly fewer concrete results on costs and technologies available in the literature on adaptation than there are on mitigation, this subsection will be briefer than the previous one.

Studies on vulnerability to climate change have, to a large extent, influenced the understanding of adaptive capacity, since the indicators selected in studies of vulnerability often provide insights on the factors, processes and structures that determine adaptive capacity (Eriksen and Kelly, 2007). As noted previously, vulnerability refers to the degree to which a human or natural system is susceptible to, and unable to cope with, the adverse effects of climate change, including climate variability and extremes, and is a function not only of the character, variation, magnitude and rate of climate change to which a system is exposed, but also of its sensitivity and its adaptive capacity (IPCC, 2007d).

Important indicators for determining both vulnerability and adaptive capacity include education, health status, knowledge, technology, institutions and income level. Adaptive capacity is, however, also influenced by the character, variation, magnitude and rate of the climate change impacts that the system is exposed to, as well as by the distribution of resources and by the existence of prior stresses (Turner et al., 2003, Smit and Wandel, 2006, and Yohe and Tol, 2002).

Although adaptive capacity will generally be inversely related to vulnerability (i.e. the greater the adaptive capacity the lower the vulnerability, and vice versa), this may not always be the case. For some types of climate-related impacts, notably those associated with extreme weather and abrupt climate changes, the consequences may be severe even if the adaptive capacity of the system is high (an often-quoted example of this is the impacts of Hurricane Katrina in 2005 on the southern coast of the United States).[25] In addition, and as noted by Adger et al. (2007), high adaptive capacity does not necessarily always translate into actions that reduce vulnerability: taking the example of heat stress, they note that despite high capacity to adapt to extreme temperatures at relatively low cost, residents in European cities, for example, continue to experience high levels of mortality during heatwaves.

Furthermore, contrary to mitigation, which is measured in terms of tonnes of CO_2 reduced, progress or achievement on adaptation cannot be assessed by any one single indicator or measurement standard.

Generally, and as noted in several studies, including Brooks and Adger (2005), the strengthening of adaptive capacity is a necessary condition for the design and implementation of effective adaptation strategies that reduce both the likelihood and the magnitude of negative impacts from climate change.

a) Technologies and practices for adaptation in different sectors

One of the key findings on adaptation is that adaptation actions are rarely based solely on a response to climate change. In most cases, adaptation measures are and will be undertaken as part of larger sectoral and national initiatives related to, for example, planning and policy development, improvements to the water sector, integrated coastal zone management, or as a response to current climate variability and extreme circumstances, including flooding and droughts. In addition, actions that enhance the adaptive capacity (such as education and poverty reduction) may be unrelated to climate issues and considerations.

Table 8 provides examples of adaptation practices and technologies reported in the literature on the subject. It should be noted, however, that categorization by sector only represents one means of differentiating adaptation measures. Since various aspects of adaptation measures will often be interrelated and cross-sectoral, it may be more appropriate in certain contexts to use other types of categorization, such as:

- type of action: physical, technological, regulatory, market-based, or investment oriented
- level: local, regional or national level
- climatic zone: arctic, floodplain, mountains, etc.
- information about those involved: individuals, private sector, local government, international donors, etc.
- development or income level: specific vulnerable groups, least-developed countries, middle-income or industrialized countries, etc.

In addition, it may be appropriate to distinguish and analyze adaptation options based on whether they are for current or future climate changes and their impacts (i.e. a temporal distinction), as is frequently done in adaptation studies. From a temporal perspective, there are three levels of climate risk adaptation, including:

- responses to current variability
- observed medium and long-term trends in climate
- anticipatory planning in response to model-based scenarios of long-term climate change.

As in the case of the types of categorization of adaptation mentioned above, the variations across the three temporal levels are often intertwined, and may even be indistinguishable from each other (i.e. they may form a continuous adaptation measure extending from the present to the future) (Adger et al., 2007).

Table 8 illustrates that a wide range of adaptive responses to climate change are potentially available, covering a range of management, behaviour-related, and policy options, as well as purely technological options.

Furthermore, a large number of the adaptation practices and technologies included in the table are well known, and have been adopted and refined over centuries to cope with climate variability and, more generally, to enhance livelihood resilience to external and prevailing local socio-economic conditions and stresses. Many of these practices represent indigenous expertise, and in addition involve management practices, behaviour-related responses, training, and information and warning systems (Adger et al., 2007). Other types of technology include, for example, infrastructure construction (dykes, sea walls, harbours, railways, etc.) and industrial processes, building codes and design, as well as recent technologies, such as remote sensing, advanced materials science, research, development and deployment of drought resistant crops, etc. (Adger et al., 2007, and UNFCCC, 2006).

As illustrated in the table, financial mechanisms can contribute to climate change adaptation. Property, health and crop insurance are examples of risk spreading, and may reduce risks for individuals, communities, and firms. In addition, capital markets have the potential for addressing financial constraints through the implementation of adaptation. The insurance sector has, in this regard, been the most active to date. This is primarily due to an observed increase in insurance payments related to extreme weather over the past ten years and the expected increase in demand for insurance products, accompanied by a realization that climate change impacts could reduce insurability and threaten insurance schemes (Valverde and Andrews, 2006). The role of the financial sector in adaptation should be assumed to be larger in industrialized countries,

TABLE 8. Examples of adaptation practices and technologies for different sectors

SECTOR	ADAPTATION TECHNOLOGIES AND PRACTICES
AGRICULTURE	Systematic observation and seasonal forecasting; introduction of drought-resistant crops; crop management; land management; improved water use and availability including rainwater harvesting; leakage reduction; hydroponic farming; building of shelter-belts and wind-breaks to improve resilience of rangelands; monitoring of the number of grazing animals and cut trees; national government programmes to recreate employment options after drought; capacity building of local authorities; assistance to small subsistence farmers to increase crop production; adjustment of planting dates and crop variety (e.g. inclusion of drought-resistant plants such as agave and aloe); accumulation of commodity stocks as economic reserve; spatially separated plots for cropping and grazing to diversify exposures; diversification of income by adding livestock operations.
COASTAL ZONE	Dykes, sea-walls, tidal barriers, detached breakwaters; dune or wetland restoration or creation; beach nourishment; indigenous options such as walls of wood, stone or coconut leaf; mangrove afforestation; early warning and evacuation systems; hazard insurance; practices such as using salt-resistant crops; building codes; improved drainage; desalination systems.
INFRASTRUCTURE	Urban planning to improve the efficiency of combined heat and power systems and optimize the use of solar energy; minimize paved surfaces and plant trees to moderate the urban heat island effects and reduce the energy required for air conditioning; limit developments on flood plains or potential mud-slide zones; establish appropriate building codes and standards; provide low-income groups with access to property; use physical barriers to protect industrial installations from flooding; climate proofing investments.
WATER RESOURCES AND HYDROLOGY	Water transfer; water recycling and conservation (soft technologies to support the preparation of on-line, searchable flood risk maps); water harvesting; increase reservoir capacity; desalination; erection of protection dams against avalanches and increased magnitude of potential debris flows stemming from permafrost thawing; changes in livelihood practices (e.g. by the Inuit), including change of hunt locations, diversification of hunted species; use of Global Positioning Systems (GPS) technology; and encouragement of food sharing.
TOURISM	Artificial snow-making; grooming of ski slopes; moving ski areas to higher altitudes and glaciers; use of white plastic sheets as protection against glacier melt; diversification of tourism revenues (e.g. all-year tourism).
FINANCE	Internalize information on climate risks and help transfer adaptation and risk-reduction incentives to communities and individuals; capital markets and transfer mechanisms alleviating financial constraints to the implementation of adaptation measures, including bank loans (e.g. for purchase of rainwater storage tanks, set-up of crop insurance); creation of local financial pools (as alternative to commercial crop insurance), set-up of revolving credit funds; fostering risk prevention through: implementing and strengthening building standards, planning risk prevention measures and developing best practices, and raising awareness of policyholders and public authorities; adopting forward-looking pricing methods in order to maintain insurability (not yet implemented).
BIODIVERSITY	Supporting implementation of adaptation technologies; modelling movements of species due to climate change and the vulnerability of habitat to sea level rise.
HEALTH	Vector control; vaccination; impregnated bed-nets; health education; greater care with water storage; using appropriate clothing; taking siestas in warm climates; using storm shelters; urban planning to reduce heat island effects; air conditioning; health education; early warning systems; implementation of heat health alert plans including measures such as: opening of designated cooling centres at public locations; information to the public through local media; distribution of bottled water to vulnerable people; operation of a heat information line to answer heat-related questions; availability of emergency medical service vehicles with specially trained staff and medical equipment; disease monitoring and prevention/treatment; access to health services and health alert information.

Source: Based on Adger et al. (2007), UNFCCC (2006), ABI (2004) and SBSTA (2007).

at least in the shorter term, due to the fragmented nature of financial markets in many less-developed and developing countries.

b) Key factors influencing adaptation

Common to all of the technologies and practices listed in Table 8 is the impossibility, according to the available literature, of assessing how effective the various options are at reducing the risks of climate change impacts (Adger et al., 2007). This is particularly the case for vulnerable groups and in the presence of higher levels of warming and related climate impacts. The limits to adaptation are, therefore, unclear, since effective options for adaptation depend on specific geographical and climate risk factors as well as on socio-economic, institutional, political and financial constraints (IPCC, 2007d).

Thus the extent to which adaptation options will be implemented and will be effective for reducing climate change risks and vulnerability depends on a large number of factors that are interlocked with development issues. Political stability, governance, market development and public sector service provision, education, income, poverty, and conflicts, are among the key factors. Furthermore, there might be critical thresholds for the resilience of interlinked socio-ecological systems to climate change that may limit the possibilities for adaptation to climate change (IPCC, 2007d, Klein et al., 2007, and Adger et al., 2007).

Technology and technological limits are also highly important. While it is acknowledged that there is a large potential for technologies to adapt to climate change and for the transfer of such technologies, there may be several limitations to the degree to which adaptation can be handled though technological options. First of all, there may be limits to the extent to which technologies can be transferred under specific contexts and to various groups of people. More specifically, adaptation can be location-specific and is not necessarily effective in all settings. Tol et al. (2006) also point out that decision-making in situations of uncertainty may create a barrier both to the development and to the adoption of certain technologies. Furthermore, even when technological options for adaptation are possible, they may not be economically feasible or culturally or socially desirable (Adger et al., 2007).

Finally, there are important financial barriers to the implementation and scale-up of adaptation efforts and options as the following subsection on adaptation costs illustrates.

c) Adaptation costs

There is broad agreement in the literature dealing with this subject that the costs of adaptation will, in almost all cases, be smaller than the benefits, and that climate change impacts and the associated need for adaptation will increase the cost of, and potential for, economic development in developing countries (see e.g. Agrawala and Fankhauser, 2008, and IPCC, 2007d). However, very few adaptation cost and benefit estimates have been carried out to date.

The literature on the costs and benefits of adaptation is, however, growing rapidly. These studies have so far mostly been carried out at the regional or project level for a number of specific adaptation options, including agriculture, energy demand for heating and cooling, sea level rise, water resource management and infrastructure. They indicate that a number of adaptation options are feasible at low cost and/or with high returns. However, comprehensive estimates of adaptation costs and benefits are currently lacking, and a number of studies tend to focus on qualitative rather than quantitative assessments. In addition, due to the fact that adaptation practices and technologies will be location- and context-specific and may involve differing definitions, assumptions and indicators, it is difficult to compare the costs of specific types of adaptation measures in different geographical locations or in other contexts.

The availability of global adaptation cost figures is even more limited, and the assumptions about climate change impacts and adaptation activities and technologies underlying their derivation are much less refined (Adger et al., 2007). The broader macroeconomic and economy-wide implications of adaptation on economic growth and employment remain largely unknown (Aaheim and Schjolden, 2004).

A few global sectoral adaptation cost estimates are available for energy, heating and cooling, and for sea-level rise. Tol (2002) estimates that for a sea-level rise of 1 metre the global costs would be around US$ 1,055 billion. He also estimates that for global warming of 1° C by 2100, the global benefits from reduced heating would be around US$ 120 billion, and global costs resulting from increased cooling would be around US$ 75 billion. For a 2° C increase in temperature by 2100, Mendelsohn et al. (2000) estimate that global energy costs related to heating and cooling would increase by US$ 2 billion to US$ 10 billion (at 1990 values) and by US$ 51 billion to US$ 89 billion (at 1990 values) for a 3.5° C increase.

Currently, no comprehensive multi-sectoral estimates of global adaptation costs and benefits are available, but there are some rough estimates available on the generic global adaptation costs in developing countries. These are provided in Table 9.

While their scientific basis might be questionable, such estimates are useful in underlining the order of magnitude of the international funding required to address adaptation challenges on a sufficient scale in developing countries, especially when considering that currently the annual flow of official development assistance is around US$ 100 billion.

Table 9. Estimates of global annual adaptation costs in developing countries

Assessment	Annual Cost	Year
Stern Review, 2006	$4-37 billion	present
World Bank, 2006	$9-41 billion	present
Oxfam, 2007	$50 billion	present
UNFCCC, 2007a	$28-67 billion	2030
UNDP, 2007	$86 billion	2015

Source: Based on data from Bapna and McGray (forthcoming) and Agrawala and Frankhauser (2008).

4. Technology and technology transfer in the context of climate change mitigation and adaptation

It is generally recognized that technological innovation, together with the transfer and widespread implementation of climate-friendly technologies, will be central to global efforts for handling the many challenges associated with climate change (IPCC, 2000a, and Philibert, 2003). As we have seen, a broad spectrum of technological measures will be required, covering both greenhouse gas emission mitigation technologies and climate change adaptation technologies, and will include "soft"' as well as "hard" technologies.[26]

Adaptation technologies are applied in a variety of projects to assist countries which are adversely affected by climate change to adapt, and to reduce their vulnerability to further changes. Strategic adaptation technologies include improved design and construction for safer and more resistant buildings, innovative agricultural and forestry practices and products, and regulation and protection of water supplies and coastal zones (UNFCCC, 2006).

Furthermore, the transfer and deployment of greenhouse gas mitigation technologies offers an opportunity to achieve significant and cost-effective emission reductions on a global basis (Petersen, 2007, and Wilkins, 2002). In some cases, for example in relation to energy-efficiency measures, the transfer and implementation of technological mitigation solutions may involve very low or even negative reduction costs (IPCC, 2000a).

The principal mitigation technologies encompass energy generation (including renewable energy), energy efficiency, switching to cleaner fuels, and environmentally-friendly waste management, among others. Given the growth in emission levels which is expected to occur both on a global level and in developing countries, technology transfer between industrialized and developing countries will also play a key role in finding a more climate-friendly route to economic development than has been used in the past (Thorne, 2008).

a) Technology and technology transfer pathways

The international transfer of technologies in the context of climate change is an area that has been addressed extensively both in published academic studies and in non-published literature, such as technical reports or working papers (Rip and Kemp, 1998, Worrel et al., 2001, Bennett, 2002, and Thorne, 2008). Scholars and practitioners from a variety of academic backgrounds, such as economics, political science, international law, business and management, engineering, and industrial relations have all addressed the subject, marking it out as an interdisciplinary field of study (Martinot et al., 1997, IPCC, 2000b, and Petersen, 2007).

As a result, a variety of different theoretical and analytical perspectives have been applied to study and understand technology transfer, and together with other factors such as the inherent complexity of the subject, this may have contributed to the absence of any coherent comprehensive theories of technology transfer (Reddy and Zhao, 1990, and Sagafi-Nejad, 1991). The various approaches, for example in relation to evaluation of the effectiveness and success of technology transfer programmes, have each emphasized different aspects concerning the actors involved, the nature of the processes, the effects, indicators, goals, and more (Kumar et al., 1999, and Bennett, 2002). A fundamental issue concerns the various aspects which characterize a technology, since these are reflected in the transfer process.

Technology transfer may broadly be understood as involving two aspects (Bell, 1997, and Andersen et al., 2007). The first aspect is the transfer of technology embodied in tangible physical assets or capital goods, such as industrial plant and equipment, machinery, components, and devices (Rosenberg, 1982, and Ramanathan, 1994).

The second aspect relates to the transfer of the knowledge and information inherent in any given technology or technological system (Edquist and Edquist, 1979, Metcalfe, 1995, and Jacot, 1997). This information includes the accumulated technical, managerial and commercial knowledge; the process know-how; engineering design and plant construction; organization and operating methods; quality control; and market characteristics – and all of this information may be firm-specific: for example, the engineering design may be known only to the firm which invented the technology (Sharif, 1994, Bell, 1997, and Chandra and Zulkieflimansyah, 2003).

Owing to the often tacit and cumulative nature of the knowledge, technology transfer processes imply more than the simple purchase of capital goods, and therefore entail a complex process of learning (Bijker et al., 1989, Kuada, 2003, Bell and Pavitt, 1993, Chen, 1996, and Levin, 1997). In addition, technology may be embodied in manuals, blueprints, technical specifications, handbooks and patents (Archibugi and Coco, 2005, Mytelka, 2007, and Dutrénit, 2004).

As indicated above, it is predominantly private companies which retain ownership of various technologies, and it is therefore relevant to identify the channels or pathways within the private sector that can facilitate technology transfer (Hoekman and Javorcik, 2006). These pathways may involve international trade in equipment and in capital goods used for production under arm's length transactions such as purchase of industrial machinery and plant components, through foreign direct investment (FDI), or through licence or royalty agreements, turnkey projects e.g. complete delivery of landfill gas recovery and utilization systems, joint ventures, technical agreements, or other forms of cooperation arrangements (Bell, 1997, and Kumar et al., 1999). These technology transfer pathways are related to the commercial and trade linkages between companies. It is key to take them into consideration in the broader debate on the role of trade and technology transfer in mitigating climate change.

The pathways play a key role in relation to facilitating access to the different dimensions of technology and thereby the quality and substance of the transfer process (Hagedoorn, 1990, and Bell and Pavitt, 1993). However, much research still needs to be done in the area of climate change related technologies, as studies carried out to date have focused mainly on technologies relevant for productivity and efficiency gains.

Bilateral and multilateral technical assistance programmes can play a key role in the transfer of technology. So far, the most important such programme has been the Global Environment Facility (GEF) under the UNFCCC. Through GEF, low-carbon projects, mainly focused on renewable energy and energy efficiency, have been financed in a number of developing countries. The Kyoto Protocol's Clean Development Mechanism (CDM) is another example of a market-based framework that may result in the transfer of technology to the developing world, although only about one-third of the projects carried out to date claim to involve some aspect of technology transfer (see Section III.A).

b) Intellectual property rights and technology transfer

A continuing debate within political discussions and academic forums has focused on whether the protection of intellectual property rights (IPRs), in particular patents, impedes or facilitates the transfer of technologies to developing countries (Hutchison, 2006, Barton, 2007, and Littleton, 2008).

The Fourth Assessment Report of the IPCC underlined that a wide array of mitigation technologies is currently commercially available or expected to be commercialized soon (IPCC, 2007a, Table 4.2). A recent study found that, for the period 1998-2008, some 215,000 patents were registered worldwide for several low- or zero-emission energy technologies (such as waste and biomass energy; or solar, fuel cell, ocean, geothermal and wind power) (Copenhagen Economics and IPR Company, 2009 and Dechezleprêtre et al., 2008). Moreover, the growth rate in patent registrations for these technologies has been high in recent years, including in several developing countries.

One key rationale for the protection of intellectual property rights, and in particular patents, is to encourage innovation (López, 2009): patent protection could ensure the innovators' ability to reap the benefits (through revenues from commercial exploitation of the invention) and recoup the costs of R&D investments. It has been argued that strong and enforceable intellectual property rights are an essential catalyst for the development of climate-friendly goods and technologies (Harvey, 2008). Studies have shown that stronger protection of patent rights is closely related to increased trade flows (Maskus, 2005).

However, it has also been argued that, in some cases, stronger protection of IPRs might act as an impediment to the acquisition of new technologies and innovations in developing countries. Patents, or other intellectual property rights, give their holders market power by allowing them to limit the availability, use, and development of technologies, and this may result in higher costs for the acquisition of technologies (Hutchison, 2006 and Littleton, 2008). While strong patent laws provide the legal security for technology-related transactions to occur, firms in developing countries may not have the necessary financial means to purchase expensive patented technologies.

More systematic information is needed on the geographic scope of patent protection for key climate change technologies, and several initiatives are in progress.[27] Recent initiatives to create open licensing structures for environmentally friendly patented technology[28] and studies addressing the potential role of the patent system in promoting competition in the development of mitigation technologies have highlighted the need to consider not merely the formal legal scope of patents, but also to review the full range of licensing mechanisms that should be deployed and to consider how patents are deployed in practice in the market place, including to construct collaborative innovation structures and to leverage technology diffusion, in conjunction with measures to encourage competition.[29]

A study on the link between intellectual property protection and access to clean technologies such as photovoltaic, biomass and wind power generation suggests that the most likely patent issues will arise from the latest technologies, where it is not excluded that extensive patent protection might slow down the development of new and more efficient or less expensive technologies. In photovoltaic power generation, for example, it is likely that the newer thin-film technologies will be subject to much more extensive patenting than the older silicon-slice technology. In the field of biomass for fuels, the patents of older technologies have long since expired, while there is enormous patenting activity in the new biomass technologies (Barton, 2007).

Finally, the importance of intellectual property rights needs to be set in a relevant context. When climate-friendly technologies are protected by intellectual property rights, the most relevant of these rights in the context of technology transfer are patents and trade secrets, particularly in the case of mitigation technologies. In the area of adaptation technologies, patents or the protection of plant varieties for climate-resistant crops could play an important part in the transfer of technology.

However, many of the technologies which are relevant to addressing climate change, whether they are "soft" technologies (such as better energy management or agricultural practices) or "hard" technologies (such as building insulation, minor technological components or subsystems) may not, in fact, be protected by patents or other intellectual property rights (Barton, 2007). Moreover, even where technologies and products benefit from intellectual property protection, for instance for mitigation, the likelihood of alternative technologies and substitute products being available is thought to be high (Barton, 2007, Copenhagen Economics and IPR Company, 2009). Further studies in this area would be useful.

Endnotes

1 The IPCC was initially established by UNEP and the WMO to provide decision-makers and other parties interested in climate change with an objective source of information. It should be noted that the IPCC does not conduct any primary research or monitor climate-related data. Rather, its role is to assess the latest scientific, technical and socio-economic literature relevant to climate change, its impacts and options for adaptation and mitigation. See IPCC, "About IPCC", http://195.70.10.65/about/index.htm.

2 Note that this definition differs from the one adopted by the UNFCCC, where the focus is on anthropogenic climate change (i.e. climate change caused by human activities).

3 For a detailed description of the interactions between greenhouse gas emissions and the climate system, see e.g. Le Treut et al. (2007).

4 The enhanced greenhouse effect is defined as "[a]n increase in the natural process of the greenhouse effect, brought about by human activities, whereby greenhouse gases such as carbon dioxide, methane, chlorofluorocarbons and nitrous oxide are being released into the atmosphere at a far greater rate than would occur through natural processes and thus their concentrations are increasing." (NOVA, 2009).

5 Climate models are applied as a research tool to study and simulate the climate system. The climate system can be represented by models of varying complexity, but common to all climate models is the numerical representation of the climate system based on the physical, chemical and biological properties of its components, their interactions and feedback processes, and accounting for all or some of its known properties. General Circulation Models (GCMs) and Coupled Atmosphere-Ocean General Circulation Models (AOGCMs) provide a representation of the climate system that is near the most comprehensive end of the spectrum currently available (IPCC, 2007b).

6 See e.g. Stephens, 2005, or Bony et al., 2006, for a review of the strengths and weaknesses of the methods used to diagnose climate feedbacks in GCMs.

7 CO_2-equivalence refers to equivalent carbon dioxide (CO_2) concentration. It is a unit of measurement used for aggregating and comparing emissions from different greenhouse gases and is defined as the concentration of carbon dioxide that would cause the same amount of radiative forcing as a given mixture of carbon dioxide and other greenhouse gases.

8 The OECD baseline scenario assumes world economic growth averaging just over 3.5 per cent in purchasing-power-parity terms up to 2050, with a gradual catching-up of the living standards of developing countries to those of developed countries. In terms of emissions and resulting concentrations, the baseline is quite close to the average of other recent studies; some are more optimistic, but others less so. The figures reported are based on these assumptions and on data from OECD Environmental Outlook to 2030 (OECD, 2008b) and the OECD ENV-Linkages model (Burniaux and Château, 2008).

9 Note that these data do not take account of emissions resulting from land clearing prior to 1850 in the now-developed countries (World Bank, 2008a).

10 World Resources Institute 2009, Climate Analysis Indicators Tool (CAIT) Version 6.0. Based on total greenhouse gas emissions in 2005, excluding land use change.

11 The four SRES scenario "families" contain a total of 40 individual scenarios.

12 There is also increasing evidence of climate change impacts on coral reefs, but it remains difficult to separate the impacts of climate-related stresses from other stresses, such as over-fishing and pollution.

13 More specifically, 38 per cent below average levels and 24 per cent below the previous record low from 2005.

14 This will be addressed in the section on regional and sectoral climate change impacts, as well as in the section on adaptation, but it should be noted that the impacts will in turn depend on a number of issues, including the vulnerability, resilience and adaptive capacity of the society or natural system in question.

15 For a full and detailed overview of regional and sectoral impacts of climate change, please consult the publications referred to above.

16 Carbon fertilization refers to a positive effect on agricultural yields due to increases in atmospheric concentrations of carbon dioxide (Cline, 2007).

17 Hydrology is defined as: "The scientific study of the waters of the earth, especially with relation to the effects of precipitation and evaporation upon the occurrence and character of water in streams, lakes, and on or below the land surface. In terms of the hydrologic cycle, the scope of hydrology may be defined as that portion of the cycle from precipitation to re-evaporation or return to the water of the seas. Applied hydrology utilizes scientific findings to predict rates and amounts of runoff (river-forecasting), estimate required spillway and reservoir capacities, study soil-water-plant relationships in agriculture, estimate available water supply, and for other applications necessary to the management of water resources." (BioGlossary, 2009).

18 ENSO is a global coupled ocean-atmosphere phenomenon. El Niño is a periodic warming of the tropical eastern Pacific Ocean associated with a fluctuation in the low latitude pressure system known as the Southern Oscillation. This atmosphere-ocean interaction is known as ENSO, and normally occurs on irregular time-scales of between two to seven years. ENSO is associated with floods, droughts, and other disturbances in a range of locations around the world.

19 For instance, the IEA study notes that strong energy efficiency gains in the transport, industry and buildings sectors; "decarburization" of electricity supply through a shift in power-generation mixes towards larger shares in nuclear power, renewable energy sources, natural gas, and coal with CO_2 capture and storage (CCS); and increased use of biofuels for road transport, could together limit CO_2 emissions to their 2005 levels.

20 Please note that Pacala and Socolow (2004) use Giga tonnes of carbon equivalent as the unit of measurement. One tonne of carbon equivalent is equal to 44/12 tonne of CO_2 equivalent, based on the weight of respectively a carbon atom and a CO_2 molecule.

21 Table 3 and the subsequent discussion mainly draws on the findings of IPCC (2000, 2007e).

22 Carbon capture and storage involves the collection of CO_2 emissions from large point sources such as fossil fuel power plants, transportation of the CO_2 and its injection it into various deep geological formations (including saline formations and exhausted gas fields), liquid storage in the ocean, and solid storage by reaction of CO_2 with metal oxides to produce stable carbonates.

23 First generation biofuels are produced by fermenting plant-derived sugars to ethanol, using a similar process to that used in beer and wine-making. The large-scale production of first generation biofuel leads to the problem of competing land use with food production. Second generation biofuel technologies substantially extend the amount of biofuel that can be produced by using biomass consisting of the residual non-food parts of current crops, such as stems, leaves and husks that are left behind once the food crop has been extracted, as well as other crops that are not used for food purposes, such as switch grass, jatropha and cereals that bear little grain, and also industry waste such as wood chips, skins and pulp from fruit pressing, etc.

24 The estimates are taken from bottom-up studies. See IPCC (2007e).

25 This does not suggest that hurricane Katrina was caused by climate change: it is used only as an example of the impacts of an extreme weather event on a society characterized by many indicators as having high adaptive capacity.

26 Hard technologies, sometimes referred to as capital goods, hardware or embodied technologies, include tools, machinery, equipment, and entire production systems. Examples of hard adaptation technologies include seawalls and irrigation technologies. Soft technologies, sometimes referred to as software or disembodied technologies, concerns the knowledge of methods and techniques for the production of goods and services, or for choosing optimal courses of action. Examples of soft technologies include crop rotation, data and information, as well as early warning systems.

27 For instance, UNEP, the European Patent Office and the International Centre for Trade and Sustainable Development are currently undertaking a patent mapping and licensing analysis of energy generation technologies, and there is a proposed review of the International Patent Classification (IPC) under consideration by the IPC Union within WIPO, Project C456, Environmentally sound technology, available at www.wipo.int/ipc-ief.

28 For example, World Business Council for Sustainable Development (WBCSD), The Eco-Patent Commons at www.wbcsd.org.

29 Copenhagen Economics and IPR Company, 2009.

Part II

Trade and Climate Change: Theory and Evidence

This part reviews the available economic literature on trade and climate change. It deals with questions such as: "To what extent do trade activities change greenhouse gas emissions?" or "Will trade opening lead to more emissions?"

It focuses on the mechanisms by which trade and trade opening can affect greenhouse gas emissions. The evidence which has been gathered so far on the links between trade and climate change is then reviewed. This evidence includes econometric studies, as well as environmental assessments of the impact of trade agreements. Since there is a close connection between trade and transport, it also looks at some of the available data regarding the role trade plays in generating transport emissions. Beyond these effects, this part examines the contributions that international trade can make to help societies both mitigate and adapt to climate change and its economic consequences. Finally, it considers how climate change can, in turn, affect the pattern and volume of international trade flows.

This part will concentrate on the link between trade and greenhouse gas emissions rather than examining the broader question about how changes in trade policy can affect economic efficiency and social welfare in cases where pollution extends beyond national borders (transboundary pollution). There are three reasons for narrowing this focus: first, there has been only limited research[1] aimed at analysing the welfare and policy consequences of trade when production (or consumption) in one sector of the economy is the source of pollution in other countries; second, how trade opening affects greenhouse gas emissions has implications for economic welfare; and finally, how trade affects greenhouse gas emissions is, in itself, of interest to policymakers, to the general public and also to economists. This explains the extensive economic literature on the links between trade and the environment, a substantial amount of which looks precisely at this question of how trade affects various indicators of environmental quality, from pollutants to biodiversity.

While the focus of this part is on trade opening, it is necessary to point out that there are other trade-related policy changes – such as reduction of environmentally harmful subsidies – which may help to mitigate climate change but which are not covered in this discussion.

A. Effects of trade and trade opening on greenhouse gas emissions

1. Trends in global trade

The past half a century has been marked by an unprecedented expansion of international trade. In terms of volume, world trade is nearly thirty-two times greater than it was in 1950.[2] By way of comparison, the level of world gross domestic product (GDP) increased by little more than eight times during the same period. As a consequence, the share in world GDP that international trade accounts for has risen from 5.5 per cent in 1950 to 21 per cent in 2007 (see Figure 1).[3] During this sixty-year period, trade expanded at an even faster pace than it did during the first wave of globalization in the late 19th to early 20th centuries.[4] This dramatic expansion may be one reason why trade is increasingly being taken into consideration in climate change discussions.

A number of reasons have been given to explain the enormous expansion in world trade. Foremost among these reasons is technological change, which has dramatically reduced the cost of transportation and communications. In the second half of the 20th century, the introduction of the jet engine and the use of containers in the transportation of goods (allowing rapid and efficient loading, unloading and transfer of shipments) have significantly reduced the cost of air and maritime transportation (Hummels, 2007). This, in turn, expanded the range and volume of goods that could be traded. The information and communication technology (ICT) revolution led to a dramatic reduction in the cost of communications, making it easier, for example, to coordinate the production of a final good whose parts and components may have been produced in several different countries (referred to as "unbundling" production).

A second reason for the expansion in trade is the spread of more open trade and investment policies. Many countries have liberalized their trade regimes through unilateral changes in their national policies, through bilateral or regional trade arrangements, or through multilateral trade negotiations. Measures that

FIGURE 1: **Rising trade share of global output, 1950-2007**

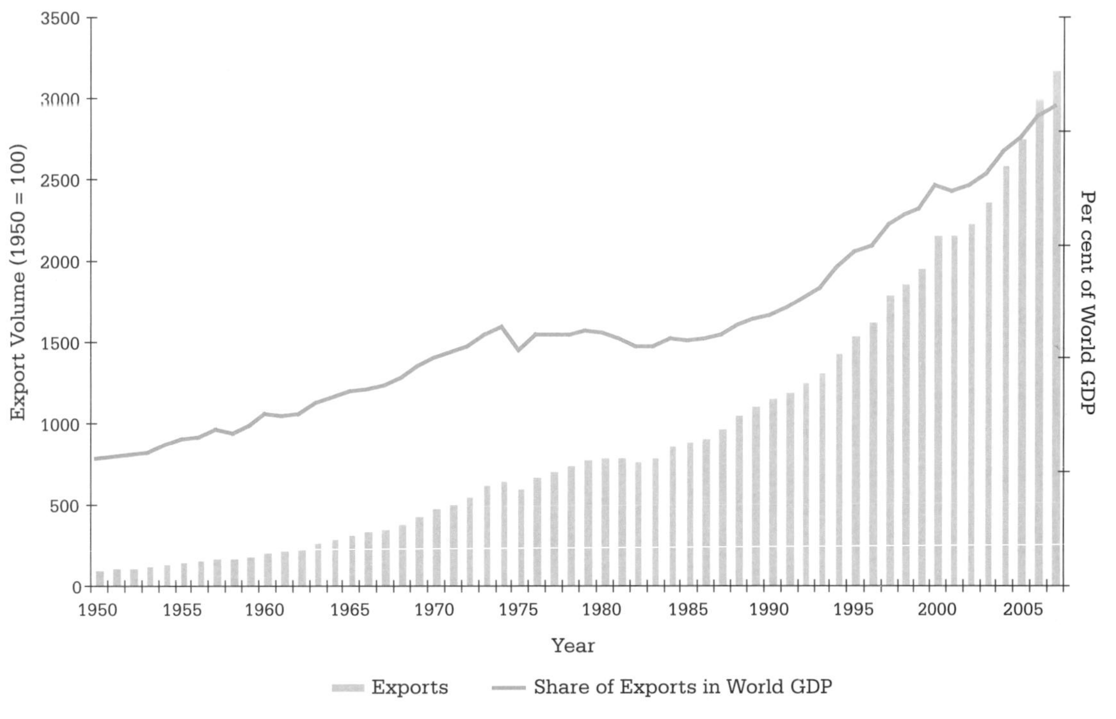

Sources: WTO (2008b) and Maddison (2001).

previously taxed, restricted or prohibited trade have been either eliminated or reduced significantly. These changes in economic policies have increased the number of countries participating in global trade expansion. In 2007, developing countries accounted for 34 per cent of world merchandise trade – approximately double their share of this trade in the early 1960s.[5]

Thus, technological innovations and the opening of trade and investment policies have both increased participation in trade and, at the same time, made it easier to "unbundle" production across a range of countries. The parts and components that make up a final product may be manufactured in different locations around the globe. Many of these manufacturing plants are located in developing countries that, as a result, become increasingly integrated in global supply chains. Compared to the past, more trade can be involved in the manufacture of a final product, and more countries can take part in the process. For example, each of the dozens of electronic components that make up a personal computer may be manufactured in a different country, with each component being produced in the country which has the "comparative advantage" in its production.

2. Scale, composition and technique effects

How does trade opening affect greenhouse gas emissions? Trade economists have developed a conceptual framework to examine how trade opening may affect the environment. This framework, first used to study the environmental impact of the North American Free Trade Agreement (NAFTA), breaks down the impact of trade opening into three "effects": the scale effect (i.e. how greenhouse gas emissions may increase as a result of increased economic activity); the composition effect (i.e. the way trade opening, and consequent changes in relative prices, may affect the relative size of the various sectors that make up a country's production); and the technique effect (i.e. the manner in which technological improvements may be adopted to reduce the emission-intensity of the production of goods and services) (Grossman and Krueger, 1993).

Copeland and Taylor (2003) provide a definition of these effects from a general equilibrium model of trade and the environment. Some international organizations, such as the Organization for Economic Cooperation and Development (OECD) (1994), have adopted or extended this conceptual framework in order to evaluate the environmental impact of trade agreements.[6] This analytic framework can be applied to investigate the link between trade and climate change. While the scale effect may worsen climate change, the technique effect may help to mitigate it. There is some uncertainty, however, about the impact the composition effect would have on climate change.

The "scale effect" refers to the increase in greenhouse gas emissions resulting from an expanded level of economic activity. According to Copeland and Taylor (2004), the scale effect can be defined as the increase in the value of production, measured in world prices as they were prior to trade opening.[7] If there are unemployed resources (labour, capital or land) prior to liberalization, trade opening will allow greater utilization of these resources and will thus lead to an expansion in the level of production.[8] This increased level of economic activity will, in turn, require greater energy use and since most countries rely on fossil fuels as their primary energy source, the scale effect will lead to higher levels of greenhouse gas emissions. Furthermore, increased trade will give rise to a greater use of cross-border transportation services, which will increase greenhouse gas emissions even further.

The scale effect is conceptually different from economic growth, since the latter is a result of capital accumulation, population growth and technological change.[9] Nevertheless, there is a presumption that, in theory, greater trade opening will lead to economic growth through (indirect) mechanisms that affect the rate of capital accumulation and improvements in productivity.[10] Given that economic growth is closely linked with energy use, this will magnify the impact on greenhouse gas emissions.

Despite this, it has not been easy to demonstrate a statistically significant relationship between trade barriers, in the form of tariff and non-tariff measures, and the rate of economic growth (Baldwin, 2000). In the 1990s, a number of studies appeared to show that "open" economies (with liberal trade policies) grew faster than "closed" economies. Dollar (1992), for example, estimated that the growth rate of Latin American and African economies would increase by between 1.5 and 2.1 per cent if they adopted more open trade policies.

A study by Sachs and Warner (1995) finds that developing countries with more open trade policies grew at a rate of 4.5 per cent per year, while closed economies grew by only 0.7 per cent per year. However, these studies have been criticized for the use of measures of openness which are closely linked with other indicators of good economic performance, such as lack of restrictions on foreign exchange markets (Rodriguez and Rodrik, 1999). There is also a problem involving the endogeneity of trade and growth (Edwards, 1998). This refers to the possibility of a two-way rather than a one-way relationship between trade and economic growth. In other words, while more trade may have a positive impact on economic growth, growth may, in turn, lead to an increase in trade. Thus, a positive relationship between trade and growth does not automatically tell us that trade is causing higher growth. Baldwin's (2000) survey is careful to point out, however, that these problems should not be interpreted as indicating that international economic policies in general or international trade have only an insignificant effect on economic growth.

The "composition effect" refers to the way that trade opening changes the share that each sector represents in a country's production in response to changes in relative prices, resulting in the expansion of some sectors and the contraction of others. The consequent increase or decrease of greenhouse gas emissions will depend on whether the emission-intensive sectors are expanding or contracting. Changes in the structure of a liberalizing country's production will depend on where the country's "comparative advantage" (in terms of resources and capacity) lies: if its comparative advantage is in sectors which are less emission-intensive, then trade opening will lead to lower greenhouse gas emissions, but if it is in the more emission-intensive sectors, then liberalization will lead to greater emissions of greenhouse gas.

In addition, the "pollution-haven hypothesis"[11] implies that the composition of production in a liberalizing economy will also respond to differences between countries in environmental regulations. If a country has stringent environmental protection measures in place, the increased competition brought about by trade opening may lead emission-intensive sectors to relocate to countries with weaker regulations. In the context of greenhouse gas emissions, the effect of international differences in climate change policies raises the likelihood of "carbon leakage". This term refers to a situation in which the measures taken by some countries to limit their carbon dioxide (CO_2) emissions at a national level do not ultimately result in a global CO_2 reduction, because industries emitting high levels of CO_2 simply relocate to countries which do not impose such strong penalties on emissions. This topic is reviewed in Part IV.

Changes in the composition of the liberalizing country's production, whether resulting from its "comparative advantage" or from the pollution-haven hypothesis, will have an effect on how the production of its trade partners is changed. If trade opening results in a country producing fewer emission-intensive goods, then they must be procured elsewhere, giving rise to an expansion in the production of those goods in other parts of the world. The pattern of expansion and contraction of certain sectors of industry in the liberalizing country will be mirrored in reverse in the rest of the world. This suggests that trade opening can lead to some countries "specializing" in more emission-intensive industries, while other countries concentrate on "cleaner" industries. The net effect on greenhouse gas emissions at the global level will depend on the relative strengths of these effects.

Finally, the technique effect refers to improvements in the methods by which goods and services are produced, so that the quantity of emissions released during the production process declines. Following Grossman and Krueger (1993), this reduction in greenhouse gas emission may come about in two ways.

First, more open trade will increase the availability and lower the cost of climate-friendly goods and services. This is particularly important for countries which do not have access to climate-friendly goods and services, or whose domestic industries do not produce such goods and services in sufficient amounts or at affordable prices. Access to the technologies used in the production of climate-friendly goods and services should reduce the energy required during production, and thus reduce emissions. For exporters, the prospect of increased market access would provide an incentive to develop new goods and services that help mitigate climate change. Such potential benefits of more open trade highlight the importance of the current negotiations under the Doha Round, which aim to liberalize environmental goods and services (see Section III.B).

Second, the increase in income levels that trade opening brings about can lead the general public to demand lower greenhouse gas emissions (a cleaner environment is a "normal" good).[12] Increased incomes or wealth gives populations the freedom to be concerned about other aspects of their well-being, such as better environmental quality. Grossman and Krueger (1993) conjecture that this public demand is perhaps the most important outcome of the technique effect. For rising income to lead to environmental improvement, however, governments need to respond to the public's demands with the appropriate fiscal and regulatory measures. Only if such measures are put in place will firms adopt cleaner production technologies, so that a given level of output can be produced with lower greenhouse gas emissions than previously.

Torras and Boyce (1998), who examined the available evidence on international variations in seven indicators of air and water quality, find that the degree of inequality in incomes, as well as inequalities in levels of literacy, political rights and civil liberties, had a substantial impact on the quality of environmental protection in low-income countries. Countries which had a more equitable distribution of income and which achieved greater equality in literacy, political rights and civil liberties tended to have better environmental quality. This evidence suggests that increases in income from trade opening may not translate into environmental improvements if the economic benefits are not shared more equitably among the population. While trade openness does not appear to be a major factor in income inequality in developed countries, the evidence is more mixed for developing countries.[13]

Due to the opposing nature of the scale and technique effects, Grossman and Krueger's study suggests that the relationship between per capita income and environmental quality may be non-linear. For countries with low levels of per capita income, increased economic growth may initially lead to deterioration of environmental quality. Only once a certain income threshold has been crossed do further increases in per capita income lead to gains in environmental quality. The "environmental Kuznets curve" (as this inverted U-shaped relationship between environmental quality and income has been called) has generated a great deal of research interest.

Much of the theoretical literature on this topic has attempted to explain the nature and causes of this non-linear relationship between per capita income and environmental quality. The explanations have been varied. Some have alluded to indivisibilities in technologies, which means that below a certain threshold of income only polluting technologies are used, while cleaner technologies are used only when income rises above that threshold (Stokey, 1998).

Some attribute the non-linearity between income and environmental quality to the fact that pollution is generated by consumption while there are increasing "returns to scale" in abatement, which implies that abatement of pollution becomes more efficient as an economy becomes richer (Andreoni and Levinson, 2001). Still other explanations ascribe the environmental Kuznets curve to the presence of pollution stock externalities, which means that if the stock of pollution depreciates quickly the net benefits from pollution control will rise with income (Kelly, 1997). While others, still, have described it as a consequence of developed countries exporting their older, more pollution-intensive technologies to developing countries (Suri and Chapman, 1998). In terms of political economy, the presence of advanced collective decision-making institutions (such as representative democracy) in developed countries and the absence of such institutions in some developing countries may explain this inverted U-shaped relationship (Jones and Manuelli, 1995).

However, the "environmental Kuznets curve" might not be applicable to global pollution. Since greenhouse gas emissions are released into the "global commons" (the atmosphere), and part of their cost is therefore borne by people in other countries, there would not be a strong incentive for nations to take action to reduce such emissions, even if their citizens' incomes were improving.

Since the scale effect and the technique effect tend to work in opposite directions, and the composition effect depends on the countries' "comparative advantage" and on the pollution-haven hypothesis, the overall impact of trade on greenhouse gas emissions cannot be easily determined. The answer will depend on the magnitude or strength of each of the three effects, and determining these will require detailed analysis of empirical evidence. Finally, although the literature on this subject has not touched on the timing of these effects, it is possible to hazard a few remarks on the issue.

First, how quickly these effects occur will depend on how rapidly trade opening measures are implemented and how far-reaching they are. Bilateral agreements or free trade agreements generally involve deeper commitments and more accelerated time-frames than multilateral agreements. Despite this, some studies have found that most bilateral or free trade agreements only manage to liberalize 90 per cent of their tariff lines for goods by the tenth year of implementation (Estevadeordal et al., forthcoming).[14] There may also be politically sensitive sectors where these periods span more than a decade. Second, the reallocation of resources within an economy in response to the removal of trade barriers may be subject to adjustment costs. The extent to which governments reduce these adjustment costs through retraining of workers and provision of job search assistance will determine how smoothly this reallocation of resources takes place. Thus, while it is possible that the scale, composition and technique effects will be discernible in the first year of implementation of a trade agreement, it is more likely that it may be many years later before they become fully apparent.

3. Assessments of the effect of trade opening on emissions

This section focuses on the available evidence about the effects of trade and trade opening on greenhouse gas emissions.

Much of this literature is recent, and the body of work continues to grow. The evidence that is assembled in this section consists of both econometric studies and environmental assessments of trade agreements. Most of the econometric studies suggest that more open trade would be likely to increase CO_2 emissions. It would appear that the scale effect tends to dominate the technique and composition effects. Some studies, however, suggest that there may be differences in impact on emissions between developed and developing countries, with improvement being observed in OECD countries and deterioration in developing countries. Although many developed countries now require environmental assessments of any trade agreements that they enter into, these assessments tend to focus on national rather than cross-border or global pollutants. A few of these assessments have raised concerns about the possible increase in greenhouse gas emissions from increased transport activity, although few have attempted a detailed quantitative analysis of the effects on emission levels of increased transportation.

A separate subsection looks at the empirical evidence on whether an environmental Kuznets curve exists for greenhouse gas emissions. This literature has produced inconsistent results, although recent studies tend to show that no such curve exists for CO_2 emissions. Studies that differentiate between OECD and non-OECD countries tend to find an environmental Kuznets curve for the first group of countries but not for the second.

a) Econometric studies on the scale, composition and technique effects

Since the pioneering study by Grossman and Krueger on the impact of NAFTA on emissions of sulphur dioxide, more and more econometric studies have examined the environmental impact of trade openness.[15] A study by Antweiller, Copeland and Taylor (2001), which estimates the scale, composition and technique effects using a general equilibrium model of trade and environment, also looks at sulphur dioxide emissions.[16] A more recent study by Grether, Mathys and de Melo (2007) analyzes the impact of trade on worldwide sulphur dioxide emissions.[17] For the most part, these studies tend to find that the technique effect played the dominant role: in all three studies, the technique effect was strong enough that trade opening resulted in environmental improvements. None of these studies, however, has examined greenhouse gas emissions, although this situation has started to change with the growing awareness of the problems posed by climate change.

In econometric studies, it is often more convenient to analyze a cross-section of countries than to study the effects over time within a single country, since there are more observations available for analysis. This means, however, that countries may be observed at a point when no trade opening is taking place. One remedy to this problem is to use the degree of trade *openness*, which is usually defined as the proportion represented by trade (exports plus imports) in GDP, as a stand-in for the degree of trade *liberalization*. Of course, there may also be a separate interest in knowing how the trade orientation of a country (how open it is relative to other countries) affects its greenhouse gas emissions.

Following the approach of Antweiller, Copeland and Taylor, a study by Cole and Elliott (2003a) considers the effect of trade openness on four environmental indicators, including carbon dioxide (CO_2) emissions. The data on CO_2 which they used covered 32 developed and developing countries during the period 1975-95. They find that, overall, more trade openness would be likely to increase CO_2 emissions, due to a large scale effect and only a small technique effect (in other words, increased trade openness would lead to increased production and therefore increased emissions, without a large enough increase in the use of emission-reduction technologies to counter such growth). For the median country in their sample, the composition effect was also positive, with a 1 per cent increase in trade intensity increasing per capita CO_2 emissions by 0.04 per cent.

Frankel and Rose (2005) examine evidence from several countries on the relationship between seven indicators of environmental quality (including CO_2 emissions) and trade openness, for a given level of per capita income. In the case of CO_2 emissions, their data allows them to study nearly 150 countries. Their paper also takes account of the possible "endogeneity" of trade and per capita income through the use of instrumental variables techniques.[18] The endogeneity of trade openness and per capita income arises because there may be a two-way rather than a one-way relationship between trade openness and per capita income. In other words, while more openness may increase per capita income, the latter may in turn lead to increased trade. When this endogeneity is not taken into account, the statistical results of their study indicate that trade openness would lead to increased CO_2 emissions. On the other hand, by including the possible endogeneity of trade in their calculations, the detrimental effect of trade openness on CO_2 emissions becomes statistically insignificant.

Nevertheless, Frankel and Rose conclude that the main instance where trade and growth might have a detrimental effect is on the amount of CO_2 emissions. They recognize that this is due to the global nature of the externality (emissions are released into the global commons and the costs of the pollution are partly borne by foreigners) and that, as a result, CO_2 emissions are unlikely to be addressed by national environmental regulations.

McCarney and Adamowicz (2005) use "panel data"[19] for 143 countries, spanning the period 1976 to 2000, to examine the link between trade openness and CO_2 emissions. Their results indicate that more open trade significantly increases emissions of CO_2, although they are not able to give a breakdown of the overall outcome into the individual contributions of the scale, composition and technique effects. The fact that the data covered differences between countries over different periods of time allowed heterogeneity across countries to be taken into account, so that comparisons could be drawn about how different national characteristics influence the environmental impact of more open trade. One such difference among the countries that they examined is the effect of democratic governance, as compared to autocratic governance. Interestingly, they find that greater democracy may be linked to increased levels of CO_2 emissions. In their view, this may be the result of an indirect effect of governance on environmental quality, whereby the lack of good governance reduces prosperity, thus reducing per capita income levels and, in consequence, emissions.

Managi (2005) uses data for 63 developed and developing countries over the period 1960 to 1999 to examine the link between trade openness and levels of CO_2 emissions. As in the case of the study by Frankel and Rose, the possibility of endogeneity between trade openness and income was taken into account in the estimation. The results of the study suggest that further trade opening would result in increased emissions with an estimated elasticity (a measure of the responsiveness of CO_2 emissions to trade openness) of 0.579, with a greater contribution from the scale effect than from the technique effect.

However, a later study by Managi et al. (2008) suggests that the impact of trade openness on CO_2 emissions may differ between developed countries (OECD members) and developing countries. They estimate the overall impact of trade openness on emission levels of carbon dioxide and sulphur dioxide, and on levels of biochemical oxygen demand (BOD) – a measure of the amount of oxygen used by micro-organisms while breaking down organic matter in water, which is used as an indicator of pollution levels. They use panel data on CO_2 and SO_2 emissions of 88 countries from 1973 to 2000 and the BOD levels of 83 countries from 1980 to 2000. The econometric analysis they employed allows them to correct for the endogeneity of income and trade and enabled them to distinguish between the short-term and long-term relationships between trade and CO_2 emissions.[20] They find that trade openness reduces CO_2 emissions in OECD countries because the technique effect dominates the scale and composition effects, but that it has a detrimental effect on carbon dioxide emissions in non-OECD countries, where the scale and composition effects prevail over the technique effect. They also find that the long-term impact of trade on CO_2 emission levels is large, although it is small in the short term.

b) The "environmental Kuznets curve" and greenhouse gas emissions

From the evidence that has been gathered to date, studies on whether or not there is an environmental Kuznets curve for greenhouse gas emissions have produced conflicting results, as Huang et al. (2008) note.

Holtz-Eakin and Selden (1995) examined data on 130 countries for the years 1951 to 1986, with complete sets of data for 108 of these countries. They are able to estimate an environmental Kuznets curve for CO_2 emissions, but find that it differs from the curve for local pollutants (pollutants that are confined within local or national borders) in that the turning point – at which further income growth leads to lower emissions – occurs only at very high income levels.

Roberts and Grimes (1997) looked at a larger sample of countries (147 countries) and a longer time period (1962-91). They find that the relationship between CO_2 emissions per unit of GDP and level of economic development has changed from essentially linear in 1962 (i.e. each change in GDP and in level of economic development gave rise to a constant amount of change in CO_2 emission levels), to strongly curvilinear in 1991 (in other words, the amount of change in emission levels became larger and larger in response to each change in GDP and economic development level). They also find that, during a brief period in the early 1970s, and increasingly since 1982, the environmental Kuznets curve reached statistical significance. They conclude, however, that this is not the result of groups of countries passing through stages of development, but is due to improvements in production efficiency in a small number of developed countries, combined with reduced efficiency in low and middle-income countries.

The study by McCarney and Adamowicz (2005) which was discussed above also estimates an environmental Kuznets curve for CO_2 emissions, with the turning point being found at lower levels of per capita income in autocratic countries as compared to democratic ones. This result suggests that emissions would begin declining at lower levels of income in autocratic countries compared to more democratic countries.

Other empirical studies find no environmental Kuznets curve for greenhouse gas emissions. The World Bank (1992) finds that per capita CO_2 emissions always increase with income. The study by Shafik (1994) shows that although some environmental indicators (such as water and sanitation) improve with rising incomes, others (such as particulates and sulphur oxides) initially deteriorate before eventually improving, while others become steadily worse (carbon dioxide emissions, dissolved oxygen in rivers and municipal solid wastes, for example).

Moomaw and Unruh (1997) identify 16 countries (a subset of OECD members) that demonstrate sustained income growth with stable or decreasing levels of CO_2 emissions per capita. Using these 16 countries, they then compare two models – an environmental Kuznets curve and what they term a structural transition model of per capita CO_2 emissions and per capita GDP – to see which model best matches the experience of these 16 countries. The structural transition model attempts to find a sudden change in the pattern of the data and relate it to some precipitating event. They find that improvements in levels of CO_2 emissions per capita are not correlated with income levels, but are closely linked with historic events related to the oil-price shocks of the 1970s and to the policies that followed. They conclude that an environmental Kuznets curve for CO_2 emissions and income does not provide a reliable indication of future behaviour.

Using more recent data from the period 1990 to 2003, Huang et al. (2008) test for the existence of an environmental Kuznets curve for greenhouse gas emissions in transition economies and (Kyoto Protocol) Annex II countries. They conclude that the evidence for most of these countries does not support the environmental Kuznets curve hypothesis. The Frankel and Rose (2005) study discussed earlier is also unable to find an environmental Kuznets curve for CO_2 emissions.

There is also within-country studies. Aldy (2005) analyzes state-level CO_2 emissions in the United States from 1960 to 1999, and is able to estimate production-based CO_2 environmental Kuznets curves and consumption-based CO_2 environmental Kuznets curves. But in testing the robustness of these relationships, he finds that estimated environmental Kuznets curves appear to vary by state. Furthermore, in some states with non-stationary income and emissions data (data whose statistical properties vary with time), he concludes that the estimated relationship between income and emission levels does not accurately reflect the true situation.

c) Environmental assessments of trade agreements

The environmental assessments of trade agreements that have been undertaken by countries engaged in negotiating multilateral and bilateral free trade agreements are another possible source of information on the expected impact of trade on greenhouse gas emissions. Negotiations under the Doha Round are still ongoing, but a large number of other free trade agreements have been negotiated and come into force over the past two decades. The WTO has been notified of 243 regional trade agreements (RTAs) which are currently in force.[21]

A significant number of the agreements that were concluded during the current decade have been the subject of formal environmental assessments. Among WTO members, Canada,[22] the European Communities[23] and the United States[24] have required environmental assessments of the trade agreements that they have entered into. A WTO report (2007) provides an inventory of the environmental assessments that have been notified to the WTO's Committee on Trade and Environment.

Before examining the results of these assessments, it may be helpful to consider their limitations. First, nearly all of these assessments involve an analysis of the likely economic, environmental, and frequently also social, impacts of the trade agreements. As such, the conclusions reached by the studies, if any, are about the anticipated rather than actual impacts of the trade agreements. Only a few of the environmental assessments analyze climate change impacts; most deal with local or domestic environmental impacts. This may be because a study of climate change impacts was not included in the scope of the assessment, or because the impact the trade agreement would have on greenhouse gas emissions was considered to be negligible. Furthermore, although some of the assessments apply the scale, composition and technique effect framework, few are able to provide quantitative estimates of the impact each of these effects would have as a result of the trade agreement.

Despite their limitations, these studies nonetheless offer some insights into the issues that have been of concern to trade negotiators and civil society groups as they examine specific trade agreements for their likely environmental impacts. Of the environmental assessments, those for the Australia-US Free Trade Agreement, the EU-Chile Free Trade Agreement, the EU-Mercosur Association Agreement, the Euro-Mediterranean Free Trade Area and the North American Free Trade Agreement consider their consequences on climate change.

Both Australia and the United States conducted their own environmental assessments of the Australia-US Free Trade Agreement. While the United States' environmental review did not look at climate change, the Australian study concluded that the free trade agreement would entail a significant increase in domestic and international transportation, which would result in an increase in greenhouse gas emissions, as well as in other pollution (Cebon, 2003).

NAFTA is probably the trade agreement that has received the most intensive scrutiny. The North American Commission on Environmental Cooperation, an institution which was established by NAFTA, has produced or commissioned a large number of environmental studies. Several of these have discussed the effects of NAFTA on greenhouse gas emissions. The North American Symposium on Assessing the Linkages between Trade and Environment is a collection of 13 studies on the environmental effects of NAFTA. One of the papers, "NAFTA Transportation Corridors: Approaches to Assessing Environmental Impacts and Alternatives", has managed to assess, in some detail, the greenhouse gas emissions arising from trucking and rail freight of trade within the NAFTA region (CEC, 2002).

North American goods move by a variety of means – highways, railways, waterways, air and pipeline – but trucking and rail freight were judged to produce the most greenhouse gas emissions and to pose the greatest risk to air quality. Several of the main transport routes (or "transport corridors") for NAFTA trade were selected for the analysis: Vancouver-Seattle, Winnipeg-Fargo, Toronto-Detroit, San Antonio-Monterrey and Tucson-Hermosillo. The study determined the current and anticipated future commodity flows, freight-vehicle traffic volumes, and levels of emissions for each of these transport corridors. A range of air pollution emissions, including greenhouse gas emissions, were also examined.

The study's main conclusion is that trade-related emissions of greenhouse gases are expected to rise substantially by 2020. Using estimated growth by the year 2020 as a basis for comparison, it was calculated that the carbon dioxide emissions from NAFTA trade would increase by 2.4 to 4 times over their current levels in the five corridors. However, the study points to opportunities to achieve lower levels of trade-related emissions through the implementation of mitigation strategies. For example, reducing empty-vehicle mileage (by ensuring that vehicles carrying goods from one point to another made their return journey carrying a different cargo) would lower all pollutant emissions from trade.

Based on the analysis of the Toronto-Detroit corridor, reducing the fraction of empty trucks from 15 per cent to 10 per cent would eliminate over 0.5 metric tonnes of nitrogen oxide and 600 metric tonnes of carbon dioxide per day by 2020 (5 per cent of the trade-related truck total). The study suggests that the main US-Mexico transport corridors have the potential for even larger reductions through the implementation of a similar mitigation strategy.

Several studies completed in 1999 also discuss greenhouse gas emissions from various sectors where NAFTA was expected to have a significant impact (CEC, 1999b, 1999c, 1999d). A study of "feedlot" cattle (i.e. cattle being fattened for consumption) identified methane emissions from cattle as being an environmental concern. It concludes that although methane emissions remain a challenge, increased efficiency in beef-feeding, combined with genetic selection of the beef herd, could reduce total methane emission levels.

A second study focused on the electricity-generation sector in NAFTA countries, but also included the industries further up the supply chain that provide the major fuel sources used for electricity generation (notably coal, natural gas and hydroelectric installations) in its analysis. It concludes that the environmental pressures arising from increased demand for and trade in electricity in Canada, Mexico and the United States will depend on two key factors: the domestic environmental regulations imposed on the operation of existing power plants; and the impact of new electricity-generation technologies on fuel production.

The EU's environmental assessment of the EU-Chile Free Trade Agreement did not address this agreement's overall impact on greenhouse gas emissions. However, it did examine the effect of the agreement on the forestry sector, where commercial operation has been increasingly based on forest plantations. The assessment anticipated that growth in demand for forest products would be met by products obtained from plantations. It concluded that these plantations could slow down climate change by capturing carbon dioxide, thus contributing to the reduction of carbon dioxide concentrations in the atmosphere.

With regard to the Euro-Mediterranean Free Trade Agreement, the EU assessment indicated an overall adverse impact on climate change, due both to the increase in greenhouse gas emissions from increased transport and to changes in consumption patterns in the Mediterranean partner countries. It noted that the scale effect – which arises from increased trade and subsequent increases in production and consumption – can, in principle, be countered by technology or by regulation. However, it did not analyse any measures to strengthen the positive effects so as to counteract the adverse ones. The assessment did, however, indicate that the free trade agreement would give rise to an overall economic gain, a part of which, it suggested, could be directed towards measures to mitigate the expected climate change impacts.

As part of its sustainability impact assessment of trade agreements, the EU examined the likely impact of an EU-Mercosur Association Agreement (University of Manchester, 2007), and concluded that the impacts of the proposed trade agreement on climate change are mixed.[25] There would be a small reduction in greenhouse gas emissions from the reallocation of production between Mercosur and the EU. A free trade agreement could lead to less energy consumption during production because the energy-intensive parts of the manufacturing sector would be largely transferred to Europe where, in general, firms are more energy-efficient than their Mercosur counterparts.

The lower energy consumption and increased use of natural gas would lead to a small downturn in the total carbon dioxide emissions from production in both Mercosur countries and in the EU. However, the study concluded that this would be countered by a larger increase in carbon dioxide emissions arising from the increase in international transport. Overall, the association agreement could lead to an increase in global CO_2 emissions of about 0.15 per cent as a result of the full liberalization of agriculture and of manufactured goods.

d) Other approaches

Instead of calculating the impact of trade opening on greenhouse gas emissions, some studies have tried to account for the contribution of international trade to CO_2 emissions. Peters and Hertwich (2008a, 2008b), for example, have suggested that 21.5 per cent of global CO_2 emissions are a result of international trade. Similar studies have been undertaken by the Stockholm Environment Institute and the University of Sydney to estimate the CO_2 emissions associated with UK trade (Wiedmann et al., 2007).[26] What these studies have in common is that they calculate emissions associated with consumption rather than those resulting from production.

Since consumption, by definition, involves trade (consumption = production + imports – exports), it is necessary to estimate the CO_2 emissions "embodied" in trade.[27] (In practice, the studies use emissions from the production of these traded goods to calculate the emissions "embodied" in trade.) However these estimates do not imply that halting international trade would eliminate 21.5 per cent of greenhouse gas emissions, since domestic products would take the place of imported products. These would in themselves be a source of emissions.

Studies employing the same approach, but applied to specific countries or pairs of trade partners, have also been undertaken by McGregor et al. (2008), who estimate the amount of CO_2 emissions contained in trade between Scotland and the rest of the United Kingdom; by Shui and Harriss (2006), who focus on the CO_2 emissions embodied in US-China trade; and by Sanchez-Choliz and Duarte (2004), who examine the CO_2 emissions embodied in Spain's international trade.

4. Trade and transport

One important issue concerning trade's role in greenhouse gas emissions is its link to transportation services. International trade involves countries specializing in the production and export of goods where they have a comparative advantage and importing other goods from their trade partners where they have no such advantage. This process of international exchange requires that goods be transported from the country of production to the country of consumption, and consequently an expansion in international trade is likely to lead to increased use of transportation services.

Merchandise trade can be transported by air, road, rail and water, or via pipelines in the case of oil. In most instances, international trade in merchandise will involve more than one mode of transport, since even goods that are carried by air or by water must often make an overland journey to the seaport or airport, and are generally transported by land on the final stretch of their journey to the ultimate consumer.

At a global level, maritime transport accounts for the bulk of international trade transport by volume, and for a significant share by value. Excluding intra-EU trade, the United Nations Conference on Trade and Development (UNCTAD) (2007b) reported that, in 2006, seaborne cargo accounted for 89.6 per cent of world trade transport by volume; overland and other modes of transport (including pipelines) accounted for another 10.2 per cent; while airborne cargo accounted for the remaining 0.27 per cent (see Figure 2). By value, seaborne trade made up 70.1 per cent of global trade transport, airborne cargo accounted for 14.1 per cent, and land and other modes of transport for the remaining 15.8 per cent.[28] Since 2000, the share by volume of each of these modes of transport appears to have changed very little, with the share of maritime transport remaining almost invariable at 89 per cent. The share by value, however, has been more subject to change, with maritime transport's share varying between 64 and 70 per cent.

The inclusion of trade within the EU changes the picture somewhat. Lloyd's Maritime Intelligence Unit (MIU) estimated that seaborne trade accounted for 76.5 per cent of international trade transport by volume and air transport for 0.3 per cent, while the share of overland transport was 15.9 per cent and that of pipelines was 7.3 per cent. By value, the share of seaborne cargo represented 58 per cent of the total, air cargo 11 per cent, overland cargo 39 per cent and transport via pipelines accounted for 2 per cent.[29] The apparent reduction in the share of maritime transport can be explained by the fact that only a small proportion – 18.1 per cent (by volume) – of trade within the EU is transported by sea although 71.7 per cent of its trade with the rest of the world is by sea (OECD, 2006a).

Figure 2: Modes of transportation of international trade, 2006

[(a) by volume]

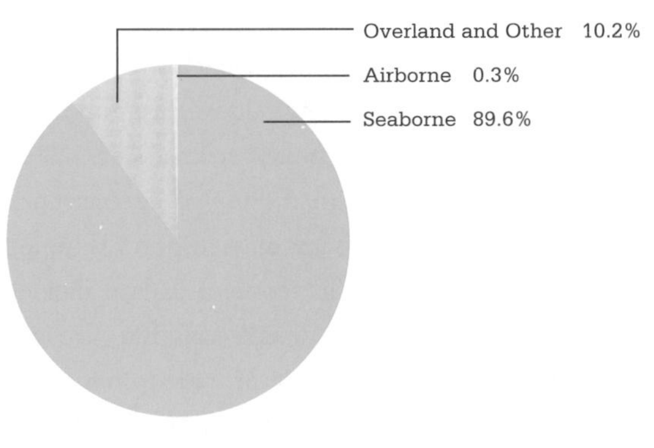

[(b) by value]

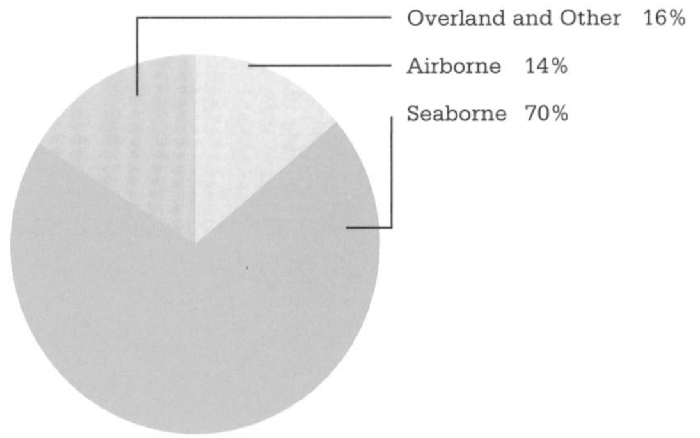

Source: UNCTAD (2007b).
Note: The data used exclude intra-EU trade.

At the regional level, there is of course considerable variation in the importance of the various modes of transport. Countries that share a land border will have a greater share of trade being transported by land. Hummels (2007) estimates that in North America, nearly 25 to 35 per cent of trade by value is transported by land. The OECD (2006a) estimates that, in 2004, 31.1 per cent of trade within the EU was transported by road, another 6.1 per cent by rail and 7.7 per cent by pipeline. The role of international trade in increasing greenhouse gas emissions caused by road transport has been highlighted in a number of environmental assessments of regional trade agreements such as NAFTA (these assessments were reviewed in the previous subsection). By contrast, for countries in Africa, the Middle East and Asia, only between 1 and 5 per cent of trade by value is with neighbouring countries, and thus the bulk of trade is carried by sea or by air.

While the greater part of international trade is transported by sea, the volume of goods shipped by air (tonnes/kilometre) has been growing rapidly: between 1951 and 2004, it grew at 11.7 per cent annually – about twice the rate of other modes of world trade transport.[30] This comparatively faster increase in the use of air transport for the shipment of goods can be explained by technological improvements (e.g. the invention and widespread use of the jet engine) which have resulted in a sharp decline in the cost of air shipping; by a fall in the value-to-weight ratio of manufactured goods; and by the growing importance of speed in international trade (Hummels, 2007).

With the exception of diesel motor vehicles, however, aviation is the most polluting mode of transport for the movement of both passengers and freight (Chapman, 2007), and this may pose an increasingly important challenge, since the use of aviation services to convey internationally traded goods is likely to grow faster than the use of other modes of transport.

Petroleum supplies 95 per cent of the total energy used by world transport, so the transport sector is a significant source of greenhouse gas emissions.[31] There are significant differences, however, in the contribution of the various modes of transport to energy-related greenhouse gas emissions. A recent report by the Intergovernmental Panel on Climate Change (IPCC) (Kahn Ribeiro et al., 2007) estimated that about 74 per cent of the energy-related CO_2 emissions of the transport sector, including the carriage of both goods and people, was produced from road transport, with another 12 per cent from air transport.[32] It should be noted that, since only emissions that arise from international trade are being considered here, these numbers will overestimate the contribution of these two modes of transport, as they include emissions produced during the transport of people.

In the case of maritime transport, the International Maritime Organization (IMO) has recently completed its study of CO_2 emissions of ships (IMO, 2008).[33] The report covers several elements: (i) an inventory of current emissions of CO_2 from international shipping (defined as merchant ships above 100 gross tonnes (GT)[34] in size); (ii) a comparison of the CO_2 emissions from various types of ships with the CO_2 emissions from other sources in the transport sector; and (iii) estimates of future emissions of CO_2 from international shipping. For 2007, the IMO study estimates the CO_2 emissions from international shipping to be about 843 million tonnes of CO_2, which is 2.7 per cent of the total world CO_2 emissions generated by human activity.

The IMO study also compares the "carbon emission efficiency" index (which the IMO defined as CO_2 efficiency = CO_2/tonne-kilometre) of ships with that of other modes of transport. The lower this index, the more carbon-emission efficient a mode of transport is. It found that shipping has the lowest value of the index among the different modes of transport. The study also compares the share of each mode of transport in the sector's total CO_2 emissions and arrives at figures similar to those given by the IPCC report (Kahn Ribeiro et al., 2007): road transport accounted for the biggest share of emissions, with 72.6 per cent, followed by international shipping with 11.8 per cent, then aviation with 11.2 per cent and finally rail transport, which accounted for 2 per cent.[35]

Finally, the study used the scenarios in the IPCC's Special Report on Emission Scenarios (SRES) to estimate future CO_2 emissions from international shipping. The IMO base scenario predicts that emissions from international shipping will increase from current levels by between 125.7 per cent and 218 per cent by the year 2050.[36] The base scenario also predicts that increases over the next decade (to 2020) will range from a low of 9.7 per cent to a high of 25.5 per cent above current emission levels.[37]

The major part of international trade is transported by sea (90 per cent when calculated by weight and 70 per cent when calculated by value). This proportion appears to have remained steady, at least since 2000, despite the rapid growth in the use of air transport. Among the different modes of transport, shipping is also the most efficient in terms of carbon dioxide emissions. It is important to take this into account when assessing the contribution of trade to transport-related emissions. However, it should not be taken as a cause for complacency since there are warning signs that, without significant policy or regulatory changes, CO_2 emissions from international shipping will rise by significant amounts in the next four decades.

B. Contribution of trade and trade opening to mitigation and adaptation efforts

As discussed in the previous section, the technique effect can be a major mechanism through which trade opening can lead to mitigation of climate change. More open trade can increase the availability of goods and services that are more energy efficient. The increased income made possible through trade opening can lead to greater demand for better environmental quality and thus to reduced greenhouse gas emissions. Related to this, trade (or trade opening) encourages the spread from one country to another of technological innovations that are beneficial in mitigating climate change. Furthermore, allowing international markets to remain open could help countries adapt to supply disruptions that may be triggered by climate change, such as a shortage in food supplies.

1. Technological spillovers from trade

International trade can serve as a means for diffusing new technologies and know-how (Grossman and Helpman, 1991). International technology diffusion is important because of the highly skewed distribution of spending on research and development (R&D) around the world. Coe, Helpman and Hoffmaister (1997) estimate that 96 per cent of global expenditure on R&D is undertaken by only a handful of industrialized countries. The distribution of expenditure on R&D is even more skewed than the distribution of world income. Keller (2004) notes that the G-7 countries (the world's leading industrialized countries) accounted for 84 per cent of global spending on R&D in 1995, but represented only 64 per cent of global gross domestic product (GDP). Since Solow (1956), economists have understood the importance of technological change in raising productivity and underpinning economic growth. The greater a country's exposure to the international economy, the more it gains from R&D activities in other countries (Helpman, 1997).

This suggests a similar role for trade in diffusing technologies that mitigate climate change. The available information indicates that 90 per cent of what is termed the environmental goods and services industry is located in member countries of the OECD.[38] Since many OECD countries were among the first to adopt climate change mitigation measures, the already lopsided distribution of technological know-how may become more distorted as the adoption of mitigation measures leads to further innovation in environmental technologies in OECD countries. Porter and van der Linde (1995) have argued that domestic firms' compliance with environmental regulations can trigger technological innovations, since such inventions will lower firms' cost of compliance.[39] The existence of spillovers in climate change technology (i.e. transfers of technological know-how from one country to another) provides one mechanism by which developing countries' own efforts to combat climate change can benefit from innovations in OECD countries. Section III.B provides information on trade opening in goods that may mitigate greenhouse gas emissions.

There are several channels by which technological dissemination through trade can occur (Grossman and Helpman, 1991; Helpman, 1997). As explained in Section I.B.4(a), one channel is through the importation of innovations embodied in both intermediate goods (i.e. manufactured or processed goods which are used in further production processes) and capital goods (e.g. machinery or equipment used in the production of other goods and services) which a country could not have produced on its own. A second channel is through the transfer of knowledge about new production methods and design from developed countries. Third, international trade can increase the available opportunities for adapting foreign technologies to meet local conditions. Lastly, the learning opportunities arising from international economic relations will reduce the cost of future innovation and imitation, making them more accessible to developing countries.

The literature examining evidence of the link between international trade and the dissemination of technology has looked at both trade in intermediate goods (Coe and Helpman, 1995) and trade in capital goods (Xu and Wang, 1999; Eaton and Kortum, 2001). There is also some work based on patent applications that examines how foreign technology is acquired by firms. It shows that contacts with foreigners in the form of trade and foreign direct investment facilitate the transfer of foreign technology (Globerman et al., 2000). A survey by Keller (2004) and Acharya and Keller (2007) of the literature on this subject concludes that imports play a significant role in the international dissemination of technology.

Sijm et al. (2004) surveyed the literature on the ways that technological know-how is transferred from one country to another. They argue that the technological know-how in Kyoto Protocol Annex I countries has a positive impact on non-Annex I countries, given that technology and know-how are transferred through foreign trade and through education. However, the authors also point out that this has not been quantified in a reliable manner. This suggests a fruitful avenue for future research: empirical studies that document the extent of such spillovers and the role that trade plays in the international diffusion of climate change technologies.

2. Trade as a means of economic adaptation to climate change

Climate change threatens to disrupt the conditions under which a wide range of goods and services that are important to economic well-being are produced and consumed. Trade may increase the vulnerability to climate change of some countries because it leads them to specialize in the production of products in which they have a comparative advantage, while relying on imports to meet their requirements for other goods and services. These countries may become vulnerable if climate change leads to an interruption in their supply of imported goods and services. However, trade can also provide a means to bridge the differences in demand and supply conditions, so that if climate change leads to a scarcity of certain goods and services in a country, it will nonetheless be able to obtain what it needs from countries where these goods and services continue to be available. Thus, beyond mitigation, trade can play a valuable role in helping humankind adapt to the consequences of a warmer future.

As discussed in Part I, climate change is likely to significantly affect agricultural production. Without trade, countries facing changed climatic conditions and lower crop yields will confront huge challenges in providing adequate supplies of food and agricultural raw materials to their populations. International trade allows the world to cushion the severity of climate change impacts on global agriculture by making it possible for a country to draw upon its trade partners' supplies to meet part of the demand for food and agricultural raw materials. But the extent to which international trade can play this buffering role depends on how economic scarcity or abundance are transmitted in terms of changes in prices across markets (i.e. agricultural prices rising in response to scarcity or falling in situations of abundance).

Where prices are distorted by the use of certain trade measures, the contribution that trade can make in helping countries to adapt to climate change may be significantly reduced. If, as mentioned earlier, a country becomes vulnerable to climate change impacts because it has specialized in certain sectors of production (in the case, for example, of a country which specializes in mining, or in the manufacture of automobile parts, but which has a very small agricultural sector), matters will only deteriorate if its partners restrict trade to safeguard their own supplies.

A number of economic studies have simulated how trade might help reduce the cost of adapting to climate change in the agricultural or food sectors.

Reilly and Hohmann (1993) used the SWOPSIM (Static World Policy Simulation Model) of world food markets to simulate the effect of a range of climate change scenarios while allowing countries to partly adjust to these impacts through trade. Their scenarios assumed reductions in yield of between 10 and 50 per cent in the US, Canada and the European Communities, and assumed either increases or no change in yield in high-latitude regions (former Soviet Union, Northern Europe, China, Japan, Australia, Argentina, Brazil) and the rest of the world. They find that, even under the assumption of large reductions in food yields, the losses in economic welfare are small relative to GDP (a few hundredths to a few tenths of a per cent) for all the countries identified in the study. The study also finds that Australia and China would experience large net gains (between 2 and 6 per cent of their GDP). Their results illustrate the importance of international trade in promoting interregional adjustments in production and consumption and hence in lowering the costs from climate change.

The study by Rosenzweig et al. (1993) considers the effect that further liberalization in agricultural trade would have on the world's ability to adapt to climate change. The potential variations due to climate change in the yield of some major crops (wheat, rice, maize, and soybeans) were estimated. A number of climate change scenarios were considered in estimating these changes in yields, based on the assumption of a doubling in CO_2 levels (to 555 parts per million) by 2060. Three general circulation models (GCMs) – sophisticated computer models incorporating detailed observations of various weather phenomena and other factors, which are used to study past, present and future climate patterns – were employed to obtain a range of these climate change scenarios. The GCMs employed were from the Goddard Institute for Space Studies, the Geophysical Fluid Dynamics Laboratory and the United Kingdom Meteorological Office. These projected changes in yields were then fed into a world food trade computer model – the Basic Linked System (BLS) – and projections of the world food market up to 2060 were generated. The study finds that, with trade opening, global impacts due to climate change would be slightly reduced. Price increases would be slightly less than those that would occur without full trade opening, and the number of people at risk from hunger would be reduced by about 100 million (from the reference case of about 640 million in 2060).

The study by Hertel and Randhir (2000) continues this focus on trade policies in the agricultural sector and how they may affect adaptation to climate change. The study underscores the importance of reducing or eliminating trade-distorting measures, such as subsidies, so as to make international trade a more effective tool for adapting to climate change. Scenarios where international trade helps a country to adapt to climate change all result in net increases in economic welfare at the global level. But international trade contributes more efficiently as a tool for economic adaptation when agricultural subsidies are eliminated. The global economic welfare gains are nearly six times greater when subsidies are completely eliminated, because large subsidies to agriculture exacerbate inefficiencies in the global agricultural system.[40]

However, other studies demonstrating that agricultural trade opening can increase greenhouse gas emissions should not be discounted. A recent paper by Verburg et al. (2008), for example, employs the Global Trade Analysis Project (GTAP) computable general equilibrium model, together with the Integrated Model to Assess the Global Environment (IMAGE), to simulate the long-term consequences on global emission levels of removing all trade barriers in agriculture, particularly in the milk-livestock sector.

The study first establishes a baseline: the "business as usual" scenario. According to this baseline, by 2050, carbon dioxide (CO_2), methane and nitrous oxide (N_2O) emissions will be 63 per cent, 33 per cent and 20 per cent higher, respectively, than their levels in 2000. The authors simulate various trade opening scenarios. Full agricultural trade opening would add an extra 50 per cent of CO_2 emissions to the baseline scenario by 2015. This initial increase in emissions would, however, decrease over time, so that CO_2 emissions in 2050 would be 30 per cent lower compared to the baseline. Full liberalization would lead to an additional 1.7 per cent of N_2O emissions by 2015, but this would later fall, so that by 2050 N_2O emissions would be equal to the baseline. Methane is the only emission which would have increased, by an extra 5 per cent over the baseline level, in 2050. Despite these complicated evolutions over time, the authors suggest that the full liberalization scenario would lead to a small overall increase in greenhouse gases by 2050.[41]

Given the uncertainties about the impact of climate change on yields across regions and the long time-scales involved in these simulations, the results of these studies should not by any means be seen as forecasts or predictions. Nevertheless, they serve to underline the means by which international trade can assist economies to adjust to changes which may occur in the inter-regional location of agricultural production as a result of climate change.

C. Possible impact of climate change on trade

So far, the discussion has been about how trade can affect greenhouse gas emissions, help mitigate climate change, or assist countries in adapting to future warming. But the link between trade and climate change is not only in one direction, since the physical processes associated with climate change can also affect the pattern and volume of international trade flows. This discussion will be short, given that few studies have considered this specific linkage to trade and more detailed information on the effects of climate change is contained in Section I.A.

There appear to be two likely effects of climate change on international trade. First, climate change may alter countries' comparative advantages and lead to shifts in the pattern of international trade. This effect will be stronger on those countries whose comparative advantage stems from climatic or geophysical reasons. Countries or regions that are more reliant on agriculture may experience a reduction in exports if future warming and more frequent extreme weather events result in a reduction in crop yields.

Warming need not always produce negative impacts on exports, since it may succeed in increasing agricultural yields in other regions. These climate change effects will not necessarily be confined to trade in merchandise goods but might extend to trade in services as well. Many tourist destinations rely on natural assets – beaches, clear seas, tropical climate, or abundant snowfall, for example – to attract holiday-makers. A rise in sea levels or changes in weather patterns might deprive countries of these natural assets. It could be argued, of course, that comparative advantage is never permanent. Technological breakthroughs, shifts in consumer preferences and changes in economic policies constantly buffet economies and alter the relative economic strengths of nations and overall competitiveness. Nevertheless, to the extent that climate change impacts may occur abruptly or that countries may be inadequately prepared, these adjustments can prove costly. In this context, international trade may become an important means of adapation.

Second, climate change may increase the vulnerability of the supply, transport and distribution chains upon which international trade depends. The Fourth Assessment Report of the IPCC refers to some of these vulnerabilities (Wilbanks et al., 2007a). Extreme weather events (such as hurricanes) may temporarily close ports or transport routes and damage infrastructure critical to trade. Transportation routes in permafrost zones may be negatively affected by higher temperatures, which would shorten the length of time that roads would be passable during winters. Coastal infrastructure and distribution facilities are vulnerable to flood damage. Transportation of bulk freight by inland waterways, such as the Rhine, could be disrupted during droughts. Disruptions to the supply, transport and distribution chains would raise the costs of undertaking international trade. While an increase in trade costs would be bad for trade in general, many developing countries whose integration into the global economy has depended on their participation in international production chains may be more vulnerable than developed countries.

Endnotes

1 See, for instance, Markusen (1975a and 1975b), Bui (1993 and 1998), Barrett (1997) and Nordhaus (1997).

2 See Table A1 of WTO (2008b).

3 Based on calculations using Table A1 of WTO (2008b) and Table F-5 in Maddison (2001).

4 WTO (2008c), p. 15.

5 WTO Press/520/Rev.1.

6 There are other assessment approaches or methodologies that have been employed to study the environmental impact of trade agreements. See, for example, UNEP (2001), the Commission on Environmental Cooperation (CEC, 1999a, 1999e), and the European Communities' sustainability impact assessment (Kirkpatrick et al, 2002). Some of the results of these methodologies will be discussed in the section on environmental assessment of trade agreements.

7 The economy's scale (S^A) prior to liberalization can be defined as: $S^A = \Sigma_i^N p_i^A x_i^A$ where p_i^A is the world price and x_i^A is the volume of production of product *i* before liberalization. The summation is to be taken over all *N* goods produced in the economy. The economy's scale after liberalization is $S^F = \Sigma_i^N p_i^A x_i^F$ where x_i^F is the volume of production of product *i* after liberalization. The scale effect is represented by the percentage change in *S* following liberalization with the pre-liberalization world prices p_i^A being used to value the new level of domestic production. Thus, the scale effect is equal to $100^*[(S^F / S^A) - 1] = 100^*\{[\Sigma_i^N (p_i^A x_i^F) / \Sigma_i^N (p_i^A x_i^A)]-1\}$.

8 In the standard textbook treatment of trade liberalization, it is often assumed that all factors of production are fully employed. In this case, the scale effect will reflect changes to the composition of output in response to trade opening.

9 This insight follows from both the traditional growth theory (Solow, 1956) and the new growth theory (Romer, 1986; 1990). While the traditional growth theory does not explain how technological progress comes about, the new theory makes the acquisition of technological know-how, through R&D for example, an integral part of the growth model.

10 This literature includes, among others, Rivera-Batiz and Romer (1991), Grossman and Helpman (1991), Peretto (2003) and Aghion et al. (2005).

11 Copeland and Taylor (2004) distinguish between the pollution-haven *effect* and the pollution-haven *hypothesis*. The pollution-haven effect states that differences in environmental regulations among countries affect trade flows and production-plant location decisions. The pollution-haven hypothesis predicts that countries with weaker environmental regulations will specialize in the polluting industries. Thus, the pollution-haven hypothesis is a stronger form of the pollution-haven effect, since the latter allows for specialization to continue to be determined by comparative advantage.

12 In economics, normal goods are any goods for which demand increases when income increases.

13 Although there is evidence of rising income inequality in industrial countries, this does not appear to be linked to greater trade openness (Borjas et al., 1997; Feenstra and Hanson, 1999; Acemoglu, 2002): a far bigger role is played by skill-biased technological change (Bound and Johnson, 1992; Juhn, Murphy and Pierce, 1993; Haskel and Slaughter, 2002; Autor, Katz and Kearney, 2008). Skill-biased technological change refers to technological change that increases the demand for skilled workers relative to unskilled workers. In developing countries, the evidence of trade leading to greater income inequality is less clear. In some regions (east Asia), trade openness appeared to have resulted in significant income gains and reductions in inequality (Wood, 1999). In other regions (Latin America), evidence suggests that trade liberalization has coincided with an increase in both income inequality and wage inequality between high- and low-skilled workers (Harrison and Hanson, 1999; Goldberg and Pavcnik, 2007).

14 Trade-weighted measures of the depth of liberalization yield similar results.

15 The Grossman and Krueger study concludes that NAFTA was not likely to worsen air pollution in Mexico. Mexico had already reached the income threshold of the environmental Kuznets curve, which they calculate at US$ 5,000; thus, the technique effect suggested that demand for better environmental quality would increase. They used a computable general equilibrium (CGE) model to simulate the composition and scale effects of NAFTA for Mexico. Although NAFTA was expected to increase Mexico's welfare in the order of between 0.9 and 1.6 per cent of gross domestic product (GDP), the composition effect would result in the expansion of Mexico's labour-intensive industries (which were less polluting) relative to its capital-intensive sectors. Overall, it was predicted that the composition and technique effects would offset the scale effect.

16 The Antweiller, Copeland and Taylor study of sulphur dioxide emissions uses a far larger sample of 40 developed and developing countries. They estimate an elasticity of between 0.25 and 0.5 for the scale effect and an elasticity of between -1.25 and -1.5 for the technique effect (in other words, a 1 per cent increase in GDP would increase emissions by between 0.25 to 0.5 per cent for an average country in their sample, but the accompanying 1 per cent increase in income would reduce emissions by between 1.25 and 1.5 per cent. As expected, the composition effect varies from country to country, according to each country's relative income and resources. For an average country in their sample, however, the composition effect is negative.

17 This study breaks down world-wide sulphur dioxide emissions for the period 1990-2000 into the scale, composition and technique effects. It finds that the scale effects are dominated by technique effects (in other words, a large enough increase in the use of emission-reduction technologies counters increased emissions from expanded production) which helps explain the global fall in sulphur dioxide emissions.

18 Ordinary least squares (OLS) estimation assumes that the explanatory variables in a regression are uncorrelated (not statistically related) to the error term. However, this would not be the case if trade openness is determined simultaneously with income and environmental outcomes. In this case, OLS estimates will yield-biased and inconsistent estimates of the coefficient on the explanatory variable, e.g. the wrong conclusion may be drawn about the relationship between openness and CO_2 emissions. The instrumental variable (IV) technique introduces another variable (the instrument), which is directly related to the explanatory variable (openness) but not to the error term. The use of this technique will produce unbiased and consistent estimates of the coefficient on openness, thus enabling the correct interpretation to be made about the relationship between trade and CO_2 emissions.

19 Panel data refer to data which varies across several dimensions – in this case over time and across countries. McCarney and Adamowicz also test the relationship between trade liberalization and biochemical oxygen demand (BOD) but, since this is not a greenhouse gas, their results for this environmental indicator are not discussed.

20 Managi et al use a dynamic Generalized Method of Moment (GMM) approach for their study. The GMM estimator is often used in lieu of Instrumental Variables if the error terms are heteroskedastic (the variance of the error term is not constant). For a description of GMM estimators, see for instance Hayashi (2000), pp. 186-322.

21 This total is as of February 2009. It is broken down as follows: a) 178 RTAs in force have been notified to the WTO under either Article XXIV of the General Agreement on Tariffs and Trade (GATT) 1994 or the Enabling Clause of 1979 and b) 65 RTAs in force have been notified under Article V of the General Agreement on Trade in Services (GATS).

22 In 1999, the Canadian government issued a Cabinet Directive on the Environmental Assessment of Policy, Plan and Program Proposals. The directive requires a strategic environmental assessment to be carried out whenever a policy, plan or programme proposal is submitted to an individual minister or the cabinet for approval, and where implementation of the proposal may result in important environmental effects, either positive or negative. Canada's environmental assessment framework for trade negotiations was finalized in February 2001 (Canada, 2001).

23 In anticipation of the Third WTO Ministerial Conference in 1999, the European Commission prepared a strategy paper outlining its approach for the negotiations. That paper, which was presented to both the European Council and the European Parliament, contained a number of ideas which deserve attention because they explain the European Commission's approach to sustainability impact assessments. Environmental considerations were to be integrated into the European Union's approach and addressed throughout the negotiations, so as to achieve an outcome where environmentally friendly consequences could be identified in the final package. In 1999, the European Commission contracted the University of Manchester's Institute for Development Policy and Management, in collaboration with a number of other institutions, to carry out a sustainability impact assessment (SIA) of WTO trade negotiations. The SIA methodology was finalized by the contractors in April 2002 (Kirkpatrick, Lee, Curran, Franklin, George and Nomura, 2002). While most approaches set out to investigate the environmental impacts of trade agreements, the European Commission framework is more ambitious, since it also examines the sustainability impact of trade and includes not only EU members, but other countries as well.

24 In November 1999, President Clinton signed Executive Order 13141, which committed the US to ongoing assessment and evaluation of the environmental impacts of certain trade agreements. The agreements to be covered by a review include multilateral trade rounds, bilateral or plurilateral free trade agreements and trade liberalization agreements in natural resource sectors. While the focus of the environmental review is the impact on the US, the reviews may also examine global and transboundary effects if that is deemed to be appropriate and prudent.

The guidelines for the implementation of Executive Order 13141 were finalized in December 2000 (US Trade Representative, 2000).

25 These studies were conducted for the European Union by the University of Manchester research consortium.

26 The study was commissioned by the United Kingdom's Department for Environment, Food and Rural Affairs (DEFRA). It estimated that, in 2004, emissions embodied in UK imports were 374 million tonnes of CO_2, while emissions embodied in UK exports amounted to 242.2 million tonnes of CO_2. UK consumer emissions amounted to 762.4 million tonnes of CO_2, and were greater than producer emissions which accounted for 630.6 million tonnes of CO_2. These figures imply that imports accounted for between 49 per cent and 59 per cent of UK emissions of CO_2 for consumption and production, respectively.

27 However, in the case of developing countries, such as China, the interest is not in the carbon emissions embodied in their imports but in those embodied in their exports. See Weber et al (2008), who examine the contribution of Chinese exports to climate change.

28 See UNCTAD (2007b).

29 See Lloyd's Maritime Intelligence Unit (MIU) (2007) at www.lloydsmiu.com.

30 This is based on data from IATA (2007). However, if one were to measure this expansion solely by tonnage so as to make it comparable with seaborne transport, air cargo volume only rose by 7.5 per cent between 1972 and 2004.

31 The International Energy Agency estimated that, in 2004, transport was responsible for 23 per cent of world energy-related greenhouse gas emissions. See IEA (2006c).

32 See Kahn Ribeiro et al. (2007) for the share of road transport. Information on the share of air transport comes from the International Air Transport Association (IATA) at www.iata.org.

33 A second phase covering other greenhouse gases is scheduled to be completed in April 2009.

34 Gross tonnes (GT) is a measure of the overall size of a ship. Tonnage measurements are governed by the IMO's *International Convention on Tonnage Measurement of Ships* (1969), which entered into force on 18 July 1982. The gross tonnage is a function of the moulded volume of all enclosed spaces of the ship.

35 See Table 55 of IMO (2008).

36 See Table 48 of IMO (2008).

37 See Table 47 of IMO (2008).

38 See OECD (2005), page 27.

39 Goulder and Schneider (1999) appear to be making a similar point when they argue that climate policies will bias technical change towards emission saving technologies.

40 The scenario which involves the absence of agricultural border distortions (e.g. tariffs) and domestic subsidies results in welfare gains of US$ 6.9 billion (in 1992 dollars). A similar scenario, which however includes domestic subsidies, generates net economic welfare gains of only US$ 1.2 billion (in 1992 dollars).

41 The authors provide the following explanation for the complicated evolution over time of greenhouse gas emissions. The greenhouse gases produced by agriculture have three components: CO_2, methane and N_2O, each with its own cause and emitter. CO_2 is caused by vegetation clearance (burning of natural vegetation) during the expansion of agricultural areas. This occurs mainly in South America and Asia. Full liberalization would cause current agricultural production taking place in North America and Europe (mainly beef and dairy farming) to move to new production areas in South America and Asia. As a result, these former agricultural areas would be abandoned and re-growth of natural vegetation (mainly forests) would occur. This would lead to a global decrease in CO_2 emissions later during the simulation, because these new forest areas would absorb carbon dioxide. Methane is mostly emitted by ruminants (dairy and beef cows). One of the first impacts of liberalization would be the relocation of this production to South America and Asia. However, the agricultural system in these regions is mostly "extensive" or pastoral (i.e. large areas and minimal capital and labour input, producing low yields). Because of these low yields, more cows need to be fed in these extensive systems to meet a given demand for meat. Subsequently, these systems become more intensive and fewer cows would be needed. In the case of N_2O, manure of all animal types plays an important part. Unlike cattle farming, pigs and poultry (which constitute the largest part of livestock) are always managed in intensive agricultural systems. The relocation of production due to liberalization would not significantly affect the number of animals, since the world demand is assumed to remain constant, and this would cause only a small change in global N_2O emissions between the baseline and projected scenarios.

Part III

Multilateral Work Related to Climate Change

A. Multilateral action to reduce greenhouse gas emissions

An international response to climate change is essential, given its global nature.[1] As early as 1972, in the Stockholm Declaration of the United Nations Conference on the Human Environment, the importance of international cooperation "to effectively control, prevent, reduce and eliminate adverse environmental effects" was recognized.[2] This call for international cooperation to address environmental challenges was reiterated during the 1992 United Nations Conference on Environment and Development (commonly referred to as the "Earth Summit").[3]

The Earth Summit proved to be groundbreaking on many fronts: it was one of the first global dialogues on sustainable development, and led to the signing of the Rio Declaration on Environment and Development. Among other things, the Rio Declaration identified a clear link between sustainable development, economic growth and environmental protection, and called on countries to "cooperate to promote a supportive and open international economic system that would lead to economic growth and sustainable development in all countries, to better address the problems of environmental degradation".[4]

The Earth Summit was also crucial from a climate change perspective, as it led to the adoption of the United Nations Framework Convention on Climate Change (UNFCCC) – the first global effort to address climate change. Although the UNFCCC, which entered into force in March 1994, represented a groundbreaking response to climate change by creating a general framework for action, it did not create legally binding commitments for reducing greenhouse gas emissions.

In view of this, and as scientific consensus and alarm regarding climate change grew during the years following the Earth Summit, there were increased calls for a supplementary agreement with legally binding commitments for reducing greenhouse gas emissions.[5] This increased political momentum ultimately led to the signing of the Kyoto Protocol in 1997.

The Kyoto Protocol requires industrialized countries to meet agreed levels of emission reductions over an initial commitment period that runs from 2008 to 2012. The exact amount of emission reduction commitments varies for each country, but the total collective commitment represents the reduction of greenhouse gas emissions to at least 5 per cent less than their 1990 levels in these industrialized countries.[6]

The challenge now facing climate change negotiators is to agree on a multilateral response to climate change once the Kyoto Protocol's first commitment period has expired (i.e. in the "post-2012" period). Given this, current negotiations are broadly focused on issues such as the extent to which industrialized countries should reduce their emissions in the post-2012 period, and the level of technological and financial support that developed countries should provide to developing economies in order to help them participate in mitigating, and adapting to, global climate change.

1. Framework Convention on Climate Change

Although scientific discussions about human-induced climate change date back more than a century, it was not until the 1980s that the international community started to actively focus on the issue.[7] In 1988, the Intergovernmental Panel on Climate Change (IPCC) was launched by the World Meteorological Organization (WMO) and the United Nations Environment Programme (UNEP) to undertake the first authoritative assessment of climate science. When the IPCC's first report came out in 1990, it confirmed the serious threat that climate change represents, and called for a global treaty to address the challenge.[8]

The IPCC report catalysed governmental support for international negotiations on climate change, which began in February 1991 with the first meeting of the Intergovernmental Negotiating Committee for a Framework Convention on Climate Change, and concluded in 1992 with the adoption of the UNFCCC at the Earth Summit.[9] The Convention entered into force on 21 March 1994,[10] and has been ratified by 192 countries.[11]

a) Principles

The "ultimate objective" of the UNFCCC is the "stabilization of greenhouse gas concentrations in the atmosphere at a level that would prevent dangerous anthropogenic interference (i.e. resulting from human activity) with the climate system."[12] The Convention elaborates a number of principles to guide parties in reaching this objective: for instance, the Convention calls on parties to employ a "precautionary approach" to climate change:

"Parties should take precautionary measures to anticipate, prevent or minimize the causes of climate change and mitigate its adverse effects. Where there are threats of serious or irreversible damage, lack of full scientific certainty shall not be used as a reason for postponing such measures...".[13]

The UNFCCC also reflects the principle of "common but differentiated responsibilities," which recognizes that even though all countries have a responsibility to address climate change, they have not all contributed to the same extent to causing the problem, nor are they all equally equipped to address it.[14] Accordingly, the Convention places the initial burden of greenhouse gas emission reductions on the most industrialized countries, given their disproportionate contribution to climate change since the beginning of the industrial revolution.

Moreover, the Convention explicitly states that "[t]he specific needs and special circumstances of developing country Parties", especially those that would bear a "disproportionate or abnormal burden under the Convention, should be given full consideration".[15] This concept is further reflected in several UNFCCC provisions that require developed countries to provide assistance, particularly additional financing, to enable mitigation measures to be taken by developing countries.

There is also an implicit recognition that responding to climate change may entail substantial costs. In order to minimize the economic costs of mitigating climate change, the Convention calls for all policies and measures that deal with climate change to "be cost-effective so as to ensure global benefits at the lowest possible cost".[16] Closely linked to this "cost-effectiveness" principle, the UNFCCC also reflects an "open economy" principle, which calls for parties to "promote a supportive and open international economic system" that will lead to

Table 1. Country groups and obligation differentiations under the UNFCCC

Country Group	Annex I	Annex II	Non-Annex I
Members	• Industrialized countries (all 24 members of the Organization for Economic Cooperation and Development in 1992, 14 economies in transition (EITs), Monaco, Liechtenstein)[22] and the European Union[23]	• Industrialized countries (only 23 of the OECD members in 1992)[24] and the European Union	• Developing countries[25]
Mitigation	• Adopt policies and measures with the aim of reducing their 2000 greenhouse gas emissions to 1990 levels • EITs have "flexibility" in implementing commitments	• Provide financial resources to enable developing countries to mitigate climate change • Promote and facilitate technology transfer to EITs and non-Annex I parties	• The Conference of the Parties (COP) identifies activities to address non-Annex I needs and concerns • No quantitative obligations • Least-developed countries given special consideration
Adaptation	• Plan, implement, and publish strategies of integrating adaptation to climate change in development	• Assist developing countries to adapt to climate change	• Plan, implement, and publish strategies of integrating adaptation to climate change in development

sustainable economic development.[17] The principle also suggests that measures focused on climate change "should not constitute a means of arbitrary or unjustifiable discrimination or a disguised restriction on international trade",[18] thus reflecting a main principle contained in WTO agreements.[19]

Finally, the Convention supports the principle of "promoting sustainable development", which is based on the idea that each party to the Convention should be free to tailor its response to climate change and to adopt measures which are appropriate for continuing economic development under its own national development strategy.[20]

b) Obligations

The principles discussed above are reflected in the specific commitments made by UNFCCC parties to stabilize their greenhouse gas concentrations. For instance, in keeping with the above-mentioned principle of common but differentiated responsibilities, the Convention divides countries into Annex I countries (industrialized nations, Russia and a number of eastern European countries), Annex II countries (only the most industrialized countries) and non-Annex I countries (developing countries).[21] Each group of countries is assigned a particular set of commitments with regard to mitigation of greenhouse gas emissions and adaptation to the impacts of climate change. These commitments are summarized in Table 1.

The Convention commits Annex I parties to adopt national policies and take measures to mitigate climate change, with the aim of returning to their 1990 emission levels.[26] The Kyoto Protocol (described in greater detail below) builds on this goal of returning to 1990 emission levels, and imposes legally binding commitments on Annex I Parties.

Under the UNFCCC, parties also agree to sustainably manage the carbon sinks (such as forests and oceans) which absorb greenhouse gases[27] and to cooperate in preparing for the effects of climate change, with particular emphasis on preparing coastal zones and on management of water resources.[28] Parties agree to participate and cooperate in research on and assessment of climate change risks,[29] and to exchange "scientific, technological, technical, socio-economic and legal information".[30] Moreover, parties to the UNFCCC agree to take account of climate change concerns when formulating national "social, economic and environmental policies and actions".[31]

In order to ensure that the commitments are being met, all parties have an obligation to "[d]evelop, periodically update, publish and make available to the Conference of the Parties ... national inventories of anthropogenic emissions by sources and removals by sinks of all greenhouse gases not controlled by the Montreal Protocol".[32] This requirement to report such information is the primary means of monitoring compliance with the Convention. Parties must also "[f]ormulate, implement, publish and regularly update national and, where appropriate, regional programmes containing measures to mitigate climate change ... and measures to facilitate adequate adaptation to climate change".[33]

There are a number of provisions requiring developed countries to assist developing countries in meeting their obligations.[34] In fact, the participation of developing country parties in greenhouse gas emission reductions is explicitly linked to financial support and technology transfer from developed country parties.[35] For instance, developed country parties are required to provide financial assistance to help developing country parties fulfil the obligation to update and report their national greenhouse gas emission inventories.[36] Moreover, developed country parties are required to assist those developing country parties that are especially vulnerable to climate change with the costs of adaptation,[37] and must "take all practicable steps" to assist in the transfer of any technology and knowledge which would facilitate compliance with the Convention.[38]

As developing countries become the source of an increasingly larger percentage of the total greenhouse gas emissions, the question of how to engage them in mitigation efforts and how to ensure sufficiently measurable, reportable and verifiable financial support and technology transfer from developed countries has become a central issue in the negotiations for a new post-2012 climate regime.

2. The Kyoto Protocol

As noted above, the UNFCCC establishes the overall framework for international efforts to tackle the challenges posed by climate change, and includes mainly voluntary provisions encouraging national actions and increased international cooperation to stabilize greenhouse gas emissions. Although the UNFCCC contains commitments to report on national emissions and to offer financial assistance, it does not specify binding quantified emission limits or reduction commitments.

Drawing on the positive experience of the negotiations for the Montreal Protocol (1988),[39] which provides legally binding commitments regarding ozone-depleting substances, UNFCCC parties began exploring the development of a legal instrument that would include legally binding greenhouse gas emission reduction targets for Annex I parties. At the 1995 meeting of the UNFCCC Conference of the Parties (COP) in Berlin, Germany, parties formally agreed to negotiate such a commitment in the form of a protocol or other legal instrument.[40] The result of this initiative was the Kyoto Protocol, which was signed in late 1997 at the UNFCCC COP meeting in Kyoto, Japan.[41]

Although the Protocol was signed in 1997, in order to enter into force it had to be ratified by at least 55 parties to the Convention, whose total emissions would account for at least 55 per cent of the global carbon dioxide emissions of Annex I parties in 1990, the agreed base year.[42] Negotiations on the specific rules and procedures for implementing the Protocol continued for another four years after its signature. These negotiations finally culminated in 2001 at the 7th Meeting of the UNFCCC COP in Marrakesh, Morocco, where parties agreed on a comprehensive rulebook for implementing the Kyoto Protocol.[43]

The "Marrakesh Accords" provided the impetus for widespread ratification of the Protocol, which eventually entered into force in February 2005. Currently, a total of 183 individual countries and one regional economic integration organization (the European Community) have deposited instruments of ratification, acceptance, approval or accession to the Kyoto Protocol. The Annex I parties that have ratified, or otherwise acceded to the Protocol, currently represent 63.7 per cent of the total carbon dioxide emissions for Annex I parties in 1990.[44]

a) Obligations

The Kyoto Protocol requires Annex I countries to collectively reduce their emissions of the six main greenhouse gases (i.e. carbon dioxide, methane, nitrous oxide, hydrofluorocarbons, perfluorocarbons, and sulphur hexafluoride) to at least 5 per cent less than 1990 emission levels.[45] This target must be achieved over the five-year period from 2008 to 2012.[46] However, not all Annex I parties are required to reduce their emissions by the same amount. Rather, this overall target is reflected as specific emission reduction targets that vary for each of the Annex I parties.[47] In addition to these binding commitments on emission reductions, the Kyoto Protocol also includes detailed requirements on reporting for Annex I parties,[48] and contains provisions on developed-country financial and technological assistance that are similar to the obligations under the UNFCCC.

i) Binding emission targets

Emission targets for Annex I countries vary considerably (See Table 2). These targets are expressed as percentage reductions, or as caps on increases, based on each party's greenhouse gas emission levels in 1990, which must be met over the 2008-2012 commitment period.[49]

The Protocol allows two or more countries to jointly fulfil their commitments provided that their overall combined emissions are not greater than their total reduction commitments.[52] This is commonly referred to as an emission reduction "bubble". The group of 15 countries which formed the EU member states in 1990 represents the only group of countries to date to participate in this scheme by subdividing its overall target of –8% into different targets for each participating member state (See Figure 1).[53]

Table 2. Emission reduction targets in the Kyoto Protocol for Annex I countries – arranged by percentage of reduction

Countries	Target (1990-2008/2012)
EU-15,[50] Bulgaria, Czech Republic, Estonia, Latvia, Liechtenstein, Lithuania, Monaco, Romania, Slovak Republic, Slovenia, Switzerland	–8%
United States [51]	–7%
Canada, Hungary, Japan, Poland	–6%
Croatia	–5%
New Zealand, Russia, Ukraine	0
Norway	+1%
Australia	+8%
Iceland	+10%

Source: Annex B to the Kyoto Protocol

ii) Reporting requirements and other obligations

Like the UNFCCC, the Kyoto Protocol includes detailed reporting requirements for Annex I parties as a tool for assessing compliance.[54] For instance, the Protocol requires Annex I parties to "have in place, no later than one year prior to the start of the first commitment period, a national system for the estimation" of greenhouse gas emissions and carbon sinks.[55] A national system is defined by the Marrakesh Accords as "all institutional, legal and procedural arrangements ... for estimating anthropogenic emissions by sources and removal by sinks ... and for reporting and archiving inventory information".[56]

Other important obligations set out in the Protocol include:

- an obligation to formulate, to the extent possible, national and regional programmes containing measures to mitigate climate change and facilitate adaptation to climate change;[57]
- requirements for developed countries to provide financial and technological support to developing countries in order to help them implement their reporting and other obligations under the UNFCCC and Kyoto Protocol;[58] and
- a commitment from developed countries to implement policies and measures that, among other things, enhance energy efficiency in relevant sectors, protect and enhance carbon sinks, promote sustainable forms of agriculture, develop and promote renewable forms of energy, and reduce and phase-out market imperfections (i.e. taxes and subsidies) in greenhouse gas emitting sectors.[59]

Figure 1. Burden sharing among EU-15 countries of the Kyoto reduction commitment

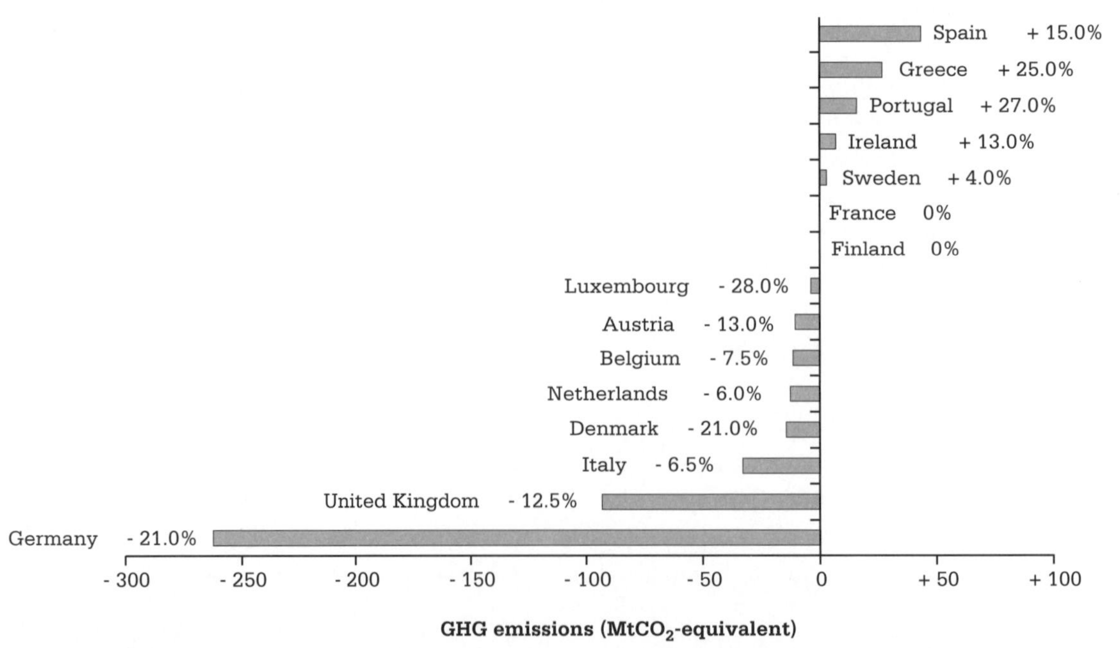

Source: European Environment Agency, 2005.

b) Key provisions

The Kyoto Protocol includes a number of provisions which are intended to help parties meet their obligations and to ensure compliance. In particular, the three "flexibility mechanisms" (Emission Trading, Joint Implementation, and the Clean Development Mechanism) are generally acknowledged to be a unique feature of the Protocol, as they provide parties with the possibility of meeting their obligations in the most cost-effective manner.[60] Moreover, the Protocol's compliance mechanism is considered to be among the most comprehensive and rigorous of the existing multilateral environmental agreements.[61]

i) Flexibility mechanisms

The Kyoto Protocol includes three "flexibility mechanisms" that give Annex I parties freedom to find the most inexpensive method for reducing their emissions.[62] By providing three alternative methods to meet targets, the Protocol relieves the burden of meeting targets only by means of national greenhouse gas emission reductions, and instead allows parties to seek the lowest-cost ways of achieving reductions consistent with the UNFCCC principle of cost effectiveness.

To participate in these flexibility mechanisms, parties must fulfil strict eligibility requirements and obligations, including ratification of the Protocol, establishment of the level of emission reductions to be achieved, maintenance of a national inventory system and national registries, and submission of annual inventories.[63] A more detailed discussion of each of the three flexibility mechanisms follows.

Emission Trading

Emission trading, as set out in the Kyoto Protocol, allows countries that have emission units "to spare" – i.e. countries whose emission levels are lower than their permitted limit – to sell this excess to countries that are over their targets.[64]

Emission trading is a classic example of a cap-and-trade scheme designed to ensure that the overall target, or cap, is maintained, while allowing for internal flexibility. This system has led to the creation of an "international carbon market" – so named because carbon dioxide represents the principal greenhouse gas. It is estimated that the global carbon market in 2009 will grow by 20 per cent in terms of volume to 5.9 $GtCO_2$-eq as compared to 4.9 $GtCO_2$-eq in 2008.[65] The Protocol's emission trading scheme is not limited to the allowable emissions within the overall cap for Annex I Parties. It also includes trade in emission credits from activities such as reforestation, generated from developing countries under the Clean Development Mechanism, which is discussed below.

Joint Implementation

The Joint Implementation flexibility mechanism allows a Kyoto Protocol Annex I country to invest in emission reduction or emission removal projects in another Annex I country, and thus to earn emission reduction units (ERUs), which can be counted towards meeting its emission target.[66] Joint Implementation is seen as mutually beneficial for the participants, as it allows the investing country to ensure a cost-efficient means of fulfilling part of its Kyoto commitments, while the host party benefits from foreign investment, from the potential for technology transfer and from selling a share of the agreed national emission allowance.

The approval process for Joint Implementation projects may follow one of two different "tracks" depending on how the emission reductions are verified. Under the Joint Implementation "Track 1" process, the host party itself (i.e. the country where the emission reduction project is situated) may verify the emission reductions and issue the appropriate quantity of emission reduction units, provided it meets certain eligibility requirements, such as having in place a national system for estimating greenhouse gas emissions and removals by carbon sinks.[67]

Parties which are unable to meet all the eligibility requirements, however, must use a "Track 2" process, and seek external verification from the Kyoto Protocol's Joint Implementation Supervisory Committee (JISC) or from an accredited and independent third party verifier.[68] Thus far, however, only one company has been accredited as a third party verifier of Joint Implementation Track 2 projects.[69]

As of 18 February 2009, there had been 30 Track 1 and 170 Track 2 projects submitted for public comment, which is the first step in the approval and verification process.[70] It has been estimated that the 170 Track 2 projects alone could yield around 300 million tonnes of emission reductions by 2012.[71] However, there is only one project to date – a Track 2 project – that has received final approval and verification.[72] The project involves a cement plant in Ukraine which is expected to produce more than 3 million tonnes of carbon credits from 2009 to 2012. These credits will be purchased by an Irish company.[73]

Clean Development Mechanism

Similar to Joint Implementation, the Clean Development Mechanism (CDM) allows a country with greenhouse gas emission reduction commitments to meet its obligations by implementing emission reduction projects in another country.[74] Unlike Joint Implementation projects, however, CDM involves projects between a developed and a developing country, rather than between two Annex I countries.

Another major difference between these two types of flexibility mechanism is that developing countries do not have emission reduction targets, and thus the emission reductions obtained through CDM projects (known as certified emission reductions ("CERs")) are not deducted from an emission allowance in the country where the project is located.

The CDM therefore requires that emission reductions be "additional" in the sense that they would not have occurred if the CDM project had not existed. This requirement for additional emission reductions is critical to the environmental integrity of the CDM. Typically, project sponsors are required to demonstrate that their project will lower emissions below a baseline estimate of emission levels in the absence of the CDM project.[75] The Kyoto Protocol also requires that the projects qualify through a validation, registration, and issuance process overseen by the CDM Executive Board.[76]

Use of the CDM has been steadily growing over the past few years. From October 2007 to September 2008, the CDM Executive Board received approximately 160 requests per month to validate project activities, representing a 10 per cent increase over the previous year. These validation requests reflect a wide range of focus (about 60 per cent are renewable energy or energy-efficiency projects) and sizes (about 60 per cent are small-scale projects).[77] As of end of May, the CDM has registered over 1,600 projects that are estimated to result in certified emission reductions totalling over 1.5 $GtCO_2$-eq by the end of the first commitment period.[78]

Despite these achievements, concerns remain about the CDM, including whether many of the projects are indeed "additional"; and how the current situation – where the vast majority of projects have focused on only a few of the major developing countries – may be remedied.[79] Concerns also remain about whether the CDM has enabled transfer of skills, know-how, information, capital and goods related to climate technologies.

Although the CDM does not have an explicit technology transfer mandate, it may contribute to technology transfer by supporting projects that use technologies currently unavailable in the host countries.[80] Since technology transfer is not compulsory for qualification as a CDM project no easy way exists to measure the extent of technology transferred under the CDM.[81] However, a UNFCCC study analyzing claims of technology transfer made on CDM project design documents found that 33 per cent of the projects claim to involve technology transfer.[82] Given that there is no common definition of technology transfer used by the project participants, the study was not able to ascertain whether the transfer involved equipment, knowledge, or a combination of both.[83]

ii) Compliance mechanism

The Kyoto Protocol's ultimate effectiveness depends on whether parties comply with their obligations. The Protocol's mechanism to ensure compliance consists of an independent Compliance Committee made up of a facilitative branch and an enforcement branch whose objective is to "facilitate, promote and enforce compliance with the commitments under the Protocol".[84] The compliance mechanism also includes mechanisms to generate information about performance, to facilitate compliance, and to deter non-compliance through penalties.[85]

For instance, an Annex I party that fails to fulfil its emission reduction target during the first commitment period will have its amount of permitted carbon emissions reduced during the second commitment period by the amount of emissions necessary to bring it back into compliance, plus a penalty of a further reduction, equal to 30 per cent of the amount by which it exceeded its emission target.[86]

In addition, a failure to meet eligibility requirements for the three flexibility mechanisms, including the various reporting requirements, can result in a suspension of the right to participate in these mechanisms.[87] For example, in a recent case Greece's eligibility to participate in flexibility mechanisms was suspended because the country was found to be in violation of national reporting requirements.[88] After Greece submitted a compliance plan and an annual report, the suspension on eligibility was lifted.[89]

c) Achievements

The Kyoto Protocol represents a significant step forward in the multilateral response to global climate change by creating specific and legally binding emission reduction commitments for industrialized countries. As the first commitment period of the Kyoto Protocol has just begun, it is too early to determine the ultimate effectiveness of its provisions. Nevertheless, it is possible to consider its short-term impact on greenhouse gas emissions.

Figure 2 shows the relative changes in regulated greenhouse gas emissions (in per cent) from 1990 to 2006 for three different groups of Kyoto Annex I parties: all 40 Annex I parties; the 14 EIT parties in Annex I; and the 26 non-EIT parties of Annex I.[90] While the figure shows that emissions of all Annex I parties were 5.5 per cent lower in 2006 than in 1990 when including emissions/removals from land use change and forestry (LULUCF), this result requires further elaboration.

As shown in Figure 2, emissions from non-EIT parties have increased by 9.1 per cent over 1990 levels. The EIT parties reached a total reduction in emissions of 35 per cent, which was more a result of their economic transition towards market economies in the early 1990s when many of their heavy industries failed, rather than the result of activities to reduce emissions in accordance

FIGURE 2. Greenhouse gas emissions by Annex I parties, 1990-2006

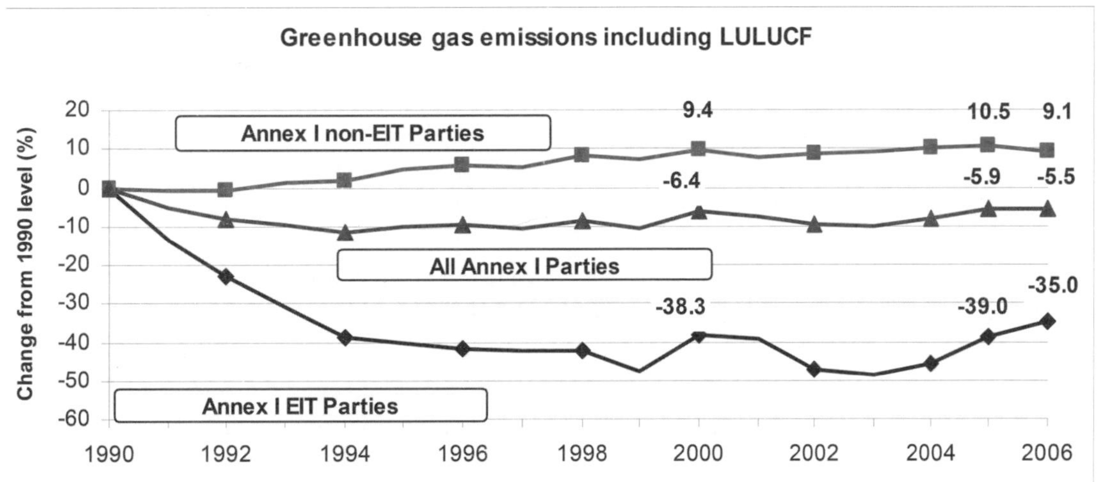

Source: UNFCCC, FCCC/SBI/2008/12 (17 November 2008).

with the Kyoto Protocol.[91] Moreover, greenhouse gas emissions worldwide increased by around 24 per cent between 1990 and 2004, despite action taken under the UNFCCC and the Kyoto Protocol.[92]

Many critics cite the net emission increases during this period as evidence of the failure of the Kyoto Protocol to achieve its goals.[93] The Kyoto Protocol, however, was never intended to address global emissions, as it focuses on achieving emission reductions in the industrialized countries as a first step.

Velders et al. (2007b) calculate that the emission reduction target set by the Kyoto Protocol corresponds to 5.8 per cent of the 1990 baseline of 18.4 $GtCO_2$-eq, in other words a decrease of 0.97 $GtCO_2$-eq per year over the 2008-2012 period. If the emissions avoided since 1990 are added to those from the 2008-2012 period, they estimate that the Kyoto Protocol will actually result in a reduction of about 2 $GtCO_2$-eq per year over the 2008-2012 period, or about 10 $GtCO_2$-eq in total.[94]

3. Post-2012 UNFCCC and Kyoto Protocol negotiations

In 2007, at the 13th UNFCCC Conference of Parties meeting in Bali, Indonesia, parties decided to launch the Bali Action Plan to "enable the full, effective and sustained implementation of the Convention through long-term cooperative action, now, up to and beyond 2012".[95] It was also decided that the Kyoto negotiating process, which began before the Bali meeting, and which focuses on further commitments of Annex I countries after the Kyoto Protocol's first commitment period expires, would continue as a separate and parallel negotiating process.[96]

As a result, climate negotiations for the post-2012 period currently follow two tracks: the Kyoto Protocol negotiations focused on commitments by Annex I parties, and the UNFCCC negotiations under the Bali Action Plan. Each track is represented by an ad hoc working group that oversees the ongoing negotiating process: the Ad Hoc Working Group on further commitments for Annex I parties under the Kyoto Protocol (AWG-KP) conducts the work for the Kyoto Protocol negotiations; and the Ad Hoc Working Group on Long-term Cooperative Action (AWG-LCA) oversees the UNFCCC negotiations. These two negotiating groups are working to achieve agreement at the 15th UNFCCC Conference of the Parties meeting in December 2009, in Copenhagen, Denmark.

While the two working groups are not formally linked, the negotiations around them are closely intertwined. The following section briefly assesses the progress under these two negotiation tracks, and discusses some of the key building blocks for a future agreement, while noting that this process is constantly evolving.

a) Kyoto Protocol negotiations

As noted above, the AWG-KP negotiations focus on achieving further emission reduction commitments for Annex I Kyoto Protocol parties. Early in the deliberations, there was broad agreement among parties that the cap and trade approach embodied in the Kyoto Protocol should be retained, but that the specific mechanisms would require further refinement based on the lessons learned during the Protocol's implementation, and also that any trading should be done as a supplement to domestic emission-reduction measures taken in Annex I countries.[97] By the end of 2008, the negotiations were still focused largely on the negotiating process itself, and no conclusions had been reached on the range of emission reductions to be undertaken by developed countries after 2012.

Table 3 provides a summary of emission reductions required for Annex I and non-Annex I parties to the Kyoto Protocol under different atmospheric carbon concentration scenarios. This illustrates the estimated levels of cuts necessary to stabilize carbon concentrations in the atmosphere.

The scenario of 450 parts per million (ppm) CO_2-eq has been mentioned by several parties as a possible starting point for considering new Annex I party emission reduction commitments.[98] According to Table 3, this would require a reduction of approximately 25-40 per cent from 1990 levels. There is currently, however, no consensus on this point.[99]

Trade issues have also been raised in the context of the AWG-KP negotiations. In particular, the importance of considering the environmental, social and economic consequences, or spillover effects of tools, policies, measures and methodologies available to Annex I parties to achieve their commitments has been raised. The potential impact of tariffs and other measures affecting trade, such as taxes and trade-distorting subsidies, has been highlighted in this context.[100]

b) UNFCCC negotiations

The UNFCCC negotiations, which, as noted above, are taking place within the AWG-LCA, are focused on key issues elaborated in the Bali Action Plan, including enhanced action on mitigation, adaptation, technology transfer, and the provision of financial support.

In terms of mitigation, the Bali Action Plan calls for measurable, reportable, and verifiable emission reduction commitments on the part of developed countries.[101] It also calls for consideration of reducing emissions from deforestation and forest degradation (REDD), and sectoral approaches and sector-specific actions as potential mitigation measures.[102]

Significantly, the Bali Action Plan also considers, for the first time, the involvement of developing countries in mitigation efforts through "[n]ationally appropriate mitigation actions", which are carried out in a sustainable development context and must be enabled by technology, financing and capacity-building support that is measurable, reportable and verifiable.[103]

In terms of adaptation, the Bali Action Plan suggests that measures for adapting to climate change should include international cooperation, especially in conducting assessments of vulnerability and financial need, prioritizing actions, and implementing capacity building and response strategies.[104] The needs of particularly vulnerable developing countries – such as small island nations and African nations susceptible to desertification, drought, or flooding – must also be taken into account.[105] Moreover, the Bali Action Plan calls for risk management and risk-reduction strategies,[106] disaster-reduction strategies,[107] and economic diversification to increase resilience.[108]

In order to assist in the implementation of both adaptation and mitigation strategies, the Bali Action Plan calls on parties to cooperate in technological development and transfer, and to find ways to increase the amount of technology transferred to developing countries.[109] In conjunction with technology transfer, developed countries are called on to provide financial assistance for the adoption of mitigation and adaptation strategies. Such assistance includes improving access to "adequate, predictable and sustainable financial resources and financial and technical support, and the provision of new and additional resources, including official and concessional funding for developing country Parties".[110] Finally, parties are encouraged to

Table 3. Ranges of emission reductions required for various stabilization levels

Scenario category	Region	2020	2050
A-450 ppm CO_2-eq	Annex I	-25% to -40% from 1990 levels	-80% to -95% from 1990 levels
	Non-Annex	Substantial deviation from the baseline in Latin America, the Middle East, east Asia and Central Asia	Substantial deviation from baseline in all regions
B-550 ppm CO_2-eq	Annex I	-10% to -30% from 1990 levels	-40% to -90% from 1990 levels
	Non-Annex	Deviation from baseline in Latin America, the Middle East, and east Asia	Deviation from baseline in most regions, especially in Latin America and the Middle East
C-650 ppm CO_2-eq	Annex I	0% to -25% from 1990 levels	-30% to -80% from 1990 levels
	Non-Annex	Baseline	Deviation from baseline in Latin America, the Middle East, and east Asia

Source: IPCC 2007, Mitigation, pp. 776 and 227.

consider innovative financial mechanisms, such as encouraging climate-friendly public and private sector investment.[111]

These elements of the Bali Action Plan are meant to come together in a shared vision on long-term cooperative action, which includes a "long-term global goal for emission reductions, to achieve the ultimate objective of the Convention, in accordance with the provisions and principles of the Convention".[112] In 2008, a number of proposals regarding the elements discussed above were put forward by various parties. The negotiations are now focused on developing a draft text with the aim of reaching a final agreement at the 15th UNFCCC Conference of Parties meeting in December 2009.[113]

4. Montreal Protocol

While the UNFCCC and its Kyoto Protocol represent the principal agreements addressing climate change, the Montreal Protocol on Substances that Deplete the Ozone Layer[114] has emerged as a significant mechanism for the international regulation and phase-out of certain greenhouse gases with a high global warming potential (GWP). These ozone-depleting industrial gases were intentionally not controlled under the UNFCCC or the Kyoto Protocol, although they are very potent greenhouse gases, and are produced on a large scale worldwide.

The Montreal Protocol was established in 1987 in response to the discovery of an ozone "hole" over Antarctica, and the scientific evidence that ozone in the stratosphere was being destroyed by chlorofluorocarbons (CFCs) and other ozone-depleting chemicals. The Protocol's primary objective is to phase-out the consumption and production of nearly 100 chemicals known as "ozone depleting substances" (ODS). Under the Protocol, both developed and developing countries have binding, time-targeted and measurable commitments, but developing countries are given longer time periods and financial assistance in meeting their targets.

By 2007, the Protocol had led to the phase-out of about 97 per cent of the consumption and production of ozone-depleting potential-weighted ODS worldwide.[115] In fact, the phase-out has been faster, the costs have been lower, and the alternatives and substitutes have been more environmentally acceptable than the parties to the Montreal Protocol anticipated during the initial negotiations.[116] Given all of these factors, the Protocol has often been widely praised as one of the most successful multilateral environmental agreements.[117]

Since many of the ODS and the fluorocarbon gases used as substitutes for ODS are significant greenhouse gases in terms of their global warming potential,[118] the Montreal Protocol plays an important role in mitigating climate change.[119] In fact, the annual contribution of ODS to global warming peaked in 1988, at a value slightly less than half that of global CO_2 emissions.[120] Moreover, it has been estimated that, in the absence of the Montreal Protocol, ODS emissions would have reached 14-18 $GtCO_2$-eq/year by 2010. However, as a result of the Montreal Protocol, it is predicted that ODS emissions will only reach 1.4 $GtCO_2$-eq/year in 2010, thereby resulting in an overall decrease in ODS emissions of 135 $GtCO_2$-eq over the 1990-2010 period.[121] Given this, some experts have argued that, since it was brought into effect in 1987, the Montreal Protocol has achieved significantly greater climate protection (i.e. four to five times) than that foreseen during the first commitment period under the Kyoto Protocol.[122]

The Montreal Protocol recently had another breakthrough that will further contribute to reducing greenhouse gas emissions. In 2007, the parties decided to accelerate the phase-out of hydrochlorofluorocarbons (HCFCs), which are gases with low ozone depletion potential that were developed for use as transitional replacements while CFCs were quickly phased out.[124]

Developing countries must now freeze their HCFC production and consumption at their 2009-2010 level by 2013, and phase-out 10 per cent of production and consumption by 2015, 35 per cent by 2020, 67.5 per cent by 2025, and 100 per cent by 2030, with 2.5 per cent allowed, if necessary, for servicing existing equipment until 2040. Developed countries have also advanced their phase-out schedule by 10 years to completely eliminate HCFC production and consumption by 2020, with 0.5 per cent allowed, if necessary, for servicing existing equipment until 2030.[125]

FIGURE 3. Actual world ODS emissions and estimated world emissions in the absence of the 1987 Montreal Protocol (in $GtCO_2$-eq/year)

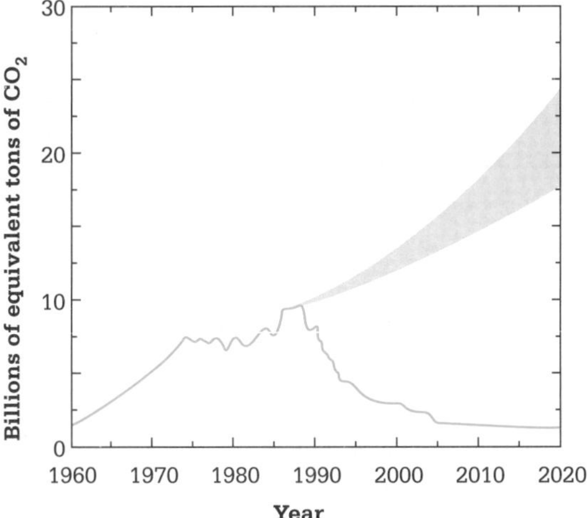

Source: Kintisch Eli, Tougher Ozone Accord Also Addresses Global Warming, Science, Vol. 317, 28 September 2008, p. 1843[123].

The accelerated phase-out of HCFCs presents developing countries with an unprecedented opportunity to adopt ozone- and climate-friendly technologies and policies. This transition to ozone- and climate-friendly options is being financially and technically supported by the Montreal Protocol's Multilateral Fund, through the preparation and implementation of national HCFC Phase-out Management Plans for developing countries. The parties to the Montreal Protocol directed the Multilateral Fund, when providing this assistance, to also focus on substitutes and alternatives that minimize other impacts on the environment, including on climate, taking into account global warming potential, energy use and other relevant factors.[126]

According to various estimates, phasing out HCFCs and their by-products could result in significant climate benefits by 2050. Depending on the implementation and data sets used for calculation, estimated reductions in emission levels range from 17.5 to 25.5 $GtCO_2$-eq overall between 2010 and 2050.

The IPCC and the Montreal Protocol's Technology and Economic Assessment Panel (TEAP) estimated in a joint study that the climate benefits of phasing out HCFCs would be a total reduction in emissions of about 18 $GtCO_2$-eq over the 2015-2050 period.[127] Velders et al. (2007a)[128] and the United States Environment Protection Agency[129] calculate a potential reduction of 17.5 $GtCO_2$-eq between 2010 and 2050, and 17.68 $GtCO_2$-eq between 2010 and 2030 respectively. The Brazilian Government has offered the most positive estimates, with potential reductions of 25.5 $GtCO_2$-eq between 2010 and 2040.[130] Achieving these potential reductions and their associated climate benefits depends on the replacement technologies adopted, and can only be attained if low or zero global warming potential alternatives are adopted as replacements to HCFCs.

B. Trade negotiations

In the Marrakesh Agreement establishing the WTO, members established a clear link between sustainable development and trade opening in order to ensure that market opening goes hand in hand with environmental and social objectives. In the ongoing Doha Round of negotiations, WTO members went further in their pledge to pursue a sustainable development path by launching the first multilateral trade and environment negotiations. The issue of climate change, in itself, is not part of the WTO's ongoing work programme and negotiation agenda. However, the WTO's rules and institutions are relevant because climate change measures and policies intersect with international trade in a number of different ways.

In the context of the Doha Round, ministers have called for the liberalization of environmental goods and services. The mandate of negotiations stipulates "the reduction, or as appropriate, elimination of tariff and non-tariff barriers to environmental goods and services".[131] These negotiations could result in fewer and lower barriers to trade in environmental goods and services, and therefore improve global market access to more efficient, diverse, and less expensive goods and services, including goods that can contribute to climate change mitigation and adaptation.

Another question addressed in the Doha Round is the relationship between the WTO and multilateral environmental agreements (MEAs), such as the UNFCCC. In this area of the negotiations, WTO members have focused on the means for further strengthening cooperation between the WTO and MEA secretariats, as well as promoting coherence and mutual supportiveness between the trade and climate regimes.

With regard to the liberalization of environmental goods and services, as well as to the WTO-MEA relationship, the Doha mandate provides an unprecedented opportunity for the multilateral trading system to contribute to furthering mutual supportiveness of trade and environment.[132] Significant work has been carried out in the Special Session of the Committee on Trade and Environment (CTE in Special Session), which is the negotiating group responsible for overseeing discussions relating to the trade and environment mandate.[133] However, many issues have yet to find a resolution and the outcome of the negotiations remains elusive.

This section provides an overview of key areas identified in the negotiations under Paragraph 31 of the Doha Ministerial Declaration that may be relevant to the goals of climate change mitigation and adaptation.

1. Improving access to climate-friendly goods and services

Climate-friendly technologies include a variety of technologies that can be employed to mitigate and adapt to climate change in diverse sectors. It has been pointed out that no single technology or sub-set of technologies is able to meet the challenge of climate change. Rather, numerous technological options must be pursued simultaneously.[134]

The IPCC has identified a range of mitigation and adaptation technologies that can assist in overcoming the challenges posed by climate change.[135] Many of these technologies involve products which are currently being discussed in the Doha negotiations, such as wind and hydropower turbines, solar water heaters, photovoltaic cells, tanks for the production of biogas, landfill liners for methane collection, as well as the equipment necessary for the operation of renewable energy plants and technologies (e.g. thermostats, AC generators, clutches, gears, etc.).[136] In this context, the WTO environmental goods and services negotiations have a role to play in improving access to climate-friendly goods and technologies.

In the CTE in Special Session[137] a number of countries have identified a broad range of goods serving various environmental purposes, including mitigation of climate change.[138] For instance, the following categories of goods have been discussed:[139] water and waste-water management; air pollution control; management of solid and hazardous waste; renewable energy production; heat and energy management; cleaner or more resource-efficient technologies and products; and environmental monitoring, analysis and assessment. Climate-friendly goods and technologies are contained in several of these categories, particularly in the category of renewable energy.

Environmental services are covered as part of the services negotiations under Article XIX of the General Agreement on Trade in Services (GATS), which form an integral part of the negotiating framework under the Doha Development Agenda. In the negotiations on environmental services, WTO members are seeking specific commitments on activities which may be directly relevant to policies aimed at mitigating climate change.

There is a twofold rationale for reducing tariffs and other trade barriers regarding climate-friendly goods and technologies. First, reducing or eliminating import tariffs and non-tariff barriers for these types of products should reduce their price and therefore facilitate their deployment at the lowest possible cost.[140] Access to lower-cost and more energy-efficient technologies may be particularly important for industries which must comply with climate change mitigation policies that place the burden of emission reductions on the emitters (see Part IV).[141]

A number of studies have shown that tariff reductions can ease the economic barriers to the use of climate-friendly goods and services, particularly in the renewable energy sector, since cost is the principal obstacle to the deployment of renewable energy-based electricity generation.[142] A number of climate-friendly products have high tariffs in some countries. The reduction or removal of these tariffs could therefore contribute significantly to improving access to these goods.

In the category of renewable energy, as it is currently discussed in the Doha negotiations,[143] applied tariff rates in developing countries range from 0 to 60 per cent (with the average tariff being about 6 per cent). In least-developed countries, they range from 0 to 35 per cent (with an average of about 10 per cent) and in developed countries they vary from 0 to 10 per cent (with an average tariff of about 2 per cent).

For instance, a number of countries apply a tariff on the product line which covers solar water heaters (categorized in the Harmonized System[144] under HS 841919) of over 20 per cent (in more than 30 countries), or a tariff of over 15 per cent on hydraulic turbines, parts for hydraulic turbines, and wind-powered generating equipment.[145] Reducing tariffs in these goods could substantially improve the diffusion of these technologies worldwide. It has also been observed, for instance, that lowering tariffs on the components of goods necessary for the exploitation of geothermal energy could help a number of countries to develop this source of energy domestically.[146]

A study of selected climate change mitigation technologies in the electricity-generation and heavy-industry sectors has identified various types of non-tariff measures that may potentially hinder trade in these technologies. These include measures such as burdensome pre-shipment inspection and customs procedures; quantitative import restrictions (for example, through import licensing, import quotas, or prohibitions), import surcharges or border taxes, technical requirements and voluntary standards, burdensome conformity assessment procedures, costly certification and testing procedures, and discriminatory taxes.[147]

The second reason for reducing tariffs and other trade barriers is the fact that trade liberalization of climate-friendly goods would provide incentives to producers and provide them with domestic expertise to expand the production and export of these goods. It is argued that trade liberalization of such goods would allow developing countries, in particular, to promote the industrial diversification of their economies and realize economies of scale.[148]

Indeed, increased trade allows larger markets for climate-friendly goods, leading to profits from economies of scale and giving producers the opportunity to learn and benefit from technological advances.[149] For instance, it has been noted that the reduction of certain import tariffs has encouraged the adoption of energy-efficient lighting in Ghana.[150] Moreover, trade liberalization of climate-friendly goods, in particular in developing countries, could help increase local capabilities for innovation and adaptation of domestic technology rather than foster dependence on transfer of foreign technology. Trade opening could then facilitate the integration of small and medium-sized enterprises into related global supply chains, thereby increasing employment and reducing poverty.[151]

A review of several developing-country case studies has noted a significant shift in the structure of these countries' environmental goods and services industries, from traditional "end-of-pipe" activities to the use of cleaner technologies that reduce pollutants at source.[152] Several other studies have further noted that many developing countries, such as China, Republic of Korea, Malaysia, India and Indonesia, have emerged as leading producers in clean energy sectors, such as wind and solar energy or efficient lighting.[153]

A number of developing countries have a significant export interest in certain product lines which are included in the category of renewable energy. For example, in 2007 the following developing economies were among the top five exporters for at least one HS 6-digit subheading in the category of renewable energy products:[154] Brazil; China; Hong Kong, China; India; Republic of Korea; Malaysia; Mexico; Turkey; Singapore; South Africa; and Thailand.[155] In addition, the following countries were among the top ten exporters: Argentina, Jordan, the Philippines, Saudi Arabia, and the United Republic of Tanzania. Five developing economies are among the top ten exporters of the entire renewable energy category of goods: China; Hong Kong, China; Mexico; Singapore; and Thailand.

Moreover, several developing countries are the top exporter of one or more product lines in the renewable energy category. For instance, Mexico is the top exporter of the product line which covers solar water heaters (HS 841919), while China is the top exporter of lines which include wind turbine towers (HS 730820), static converters that change solar energy into electricity (HS 850440), solar batteries for energy storage in off-grid photovoltaic systems (HS 850720), and concentrator systems used to intensify solar power in solar energy systems (HS 900290).

For certain countries, exports in the renewable energy category represent a substantial part of their overall exports. For instance, in 2007, about 2 per cent of China's exported goods figured in renewable energy product lines, while both Mexico and Thailand's exports of these goods amounted to 2.2 per cent. It should also be noted that in 2007, world exports of goods contained in the 30 product lines (HS 6) of the renewable energy category amounted to US$ 189 billion (i.e. they accounted for 1.5 per cent of world exports).[156] Developing countries' exports in the same category amounted to US$ 59 billion and their imports amounted to US$ 69 billion.

Finally, the trade of climate-friendly goods has seen a considerable increase in the past few years. For instance, between 1997 and 2007 exports of goods contained in the product lines listed in the renewable energy category grew by 598 per cent in developing countries and by 179 per cent in developed countries, representing 62 per cent and 29 per cent of annual average growth respectively.

It should of course be noted that the price of climate-friendly goods is not the only factor that affects the diffusion of these technologies. A number of authors have pointed to other important factors, such as a country's gross domestic product, its level of foreign direct investment and the regulatory framework for climate change action.[157] This last aspect is the focus of Part IV on national efforts to mitigate and adapt to climate change.

2. Mutual supportiveness between trade and environment

The Doha negotiations on trade and environment also provide WTO members with an opportunity to consider the mutual supportiveness between the trade and environment rules, and how institutional cooperation can help foster mutual supportiveness. The objective of Paragraph 31(i) and (ii) of the Doha Ministerial Declaration is to ensure coherence by fostering a positive synergy between the trade and environment regimes.

Paragraph 31(i) calls for negotiations on the relationship between existing WTO rules and the specific trade obligations set out in multilateral environmental agreements (MEAs). In this context, WTO members are discussing ways to ensure a harmonious coexistence between WTO rules and specific trade obligations in the different agreements that have been negotiated multilaterally to protect the environment. The importance of these negotiations cannot be over-emphasized, given the present consensus in the international community on the value of multilateralism and concerted actions to combat climate change.

While, until now, there has been no legal dispute between the trade and environmental regimes, a successful outcome to these negotiations will nevertheless reinforce the relationship between them. The negotiators have drawn on experiences in the negotiation and implementation of multilateral environmental agreements at the national level, and are seeking ways to improve national coordination and cooperation between trade and environment policies.

At the inter-institutional level, Paragraph 31(ii) of the Doha Ministerial Declaration focuses on the exchange of information between the WTO and MEA secretariats, as well as on the criteria for granting observer status in WTO bodies. Certain procedures are being discussed to improve or complement existing practices and cooperation mechanisms. This exchange of information extends to the participation of each body in the meetings of the other, and also to the organization of information exchange sessions and joint technical assistance and capacity-building activities.

Cooperation is already taking place between the WTO and climate change bodies: the UNFCCC participates in meetings of the regular WTO Committee on Trade and Environment and is an ad hoc observer to the CTE in Special Session, while the WTO secretariat attends UNFCCC Conference of Parties meetings.

As negotiations progress for a post-2012 international climate change regime, issues relating to coherence between the trade and climate change regimes, and to the institutional cooperation required to foster such coherence will become increasingly important. A positive outcome to the Doha negotiations on these questions can contribute to further strengthening collaboration, while the trade and climate change regimes continue to evolve in a mutually supportive manner, within their respective spheres of competence.

Endnotes

1 See e.g. Burleson, E. (2007), "Multilateral Climate Change Mitigation", *University of San Francisco Law Review* 41, pp. 373-407; Pfeiffer, T. and Nowak, M.A. (2006), "Climate Change: All in the Game", *Nature* 441:7093, pp. 583-584; Stern (2006), pp. 37-38. See also Choucri, N. (1995), *Global Accord: Environmental Challenges and International Responses*, MIT Press.

2 Stockholm Declaration of the United Nations Conference on the Human Environment (1972), Principle 24; see Hunter, Salzman and Zaelke (2002), pp. 176-177.

3 See Rio Declaration on Environment and Development (1992), Principle 7 (stating that "[s]tates shall cooperate in a spirit of global partnership to conserve, protect, and restore the health and integrity of the Earth's ecosystem").

4 Rio Declaration on Environment and Development (1992), Principle 12.

5 See Hunter, Salzman and Zaelke (2002), p. 589.

6 See Kyoto Protocol, Article 3.

7 Scientific discussion about possible anthropogenic climate change dates back more than a century. See Handel and Risbey (1992), "Reflections on more than a Century of Climate Change Research", *Climate Change* 21: 2.

8 IPCC (1990); see UNFCCC Fact Sheet at http://unfccc.int/resource/ccsites/senegal/fact/fs221.htm.

9 See *Report of the Intergovernmental Negotiating Committee for a Framework Convention on Climate Change on the Work of Its First Session*, A/AC.237/6 (8 March 1991), at paras. 42, 61.

10 See UNFCCC (2002), *A Guide to the Climate Change Convention Process*, available at http://unfccc.int.

11 See *United Nations Framework Convention on Climate Change Status of Ratification*, 22 August 2007, at http://unfccc.int.

12 UNFCCC, Article 2.

13 UNFCCC, Article 3.3. The principle of the "precautionary approach" has been affirmed in a number of international agreements and declarations, including the 1992 Rio Declaration on Environment and Development ("In order to protect the environment, the precautionary approach shall be widely applied by States according to their capabilities. Where there are threats of serious or irreversible damage, lack of scientific certainty shall not be used as a reason for postponing cost-effective measures to prevent environmental degradation."). See Rio Declaration on Environment and Development (1992), Principle 15.

14 UNFCCC, Articles 3.1, 3.2. For an additional elaboration of this principle, see Rio Declaration on Environment and Development (1992), Principle 7.

15 UNFCCC, Article 3.2.

16 UNFCCC, Article 3.3. Unlike cost-benefit analysis, which weighs the cost of a particular action against its potential benefits, cost-effectiveness analysis follows the acceptance of a predetermined goal (such as the mitigation of climate change) and requires that the goal be accomplished as inexpensively as possible. The integration of the cost-effectiveness principle still allows for consideration of costs in regard to specific technologies or methodologies applied, but without the possibility of the claim that taking any action is too expensive. See American College of Physicians, *Primer on Cost-Effectiveness Analysis*, September/October 2000.

17 UNFCCC, Article 3.5.

18 UNFCCC, Article 3.5.

19 See, e.g. GATT, Article XX.

20 UNFCCC, Article 3.4. Although the UNFCCC does not strictly define sustainable development, most definitions focus on recognition of the importance of development occurring in a manner which will meet the needs of today's population while preserving the ability to meet the needs of later generations. Furthermore, sustainable development requires giving priority to the poorest members of society and integrating social, economic and environmental policies. See e.g. United Nations World Commission on Environment and Development (1987), *Our Common Future*.

21 UNFCCC, Article 4.

22 Liechtenstein and Monaco were added as Annex II countries in an amendment to the UNFCCC in 1998, which also makes them Annex I countries.

23 For a complete list of current Annex I Parties see http://unfccc.int.

24 Turkey was an OECD country in 1992, but was deleted from the list of Annex II countries by an amendment to the UNFCCC which entered into force in June 2002.

25 For a complete list of current non-Annex I Parties http://unfccc.int.

26 UNFCCC, Articles 4.2(a)-4.2(b).

27 UNFCCC, Articles 4.1(d), 4.2(a).

28 UNFCCC, Article 4.1(e).

29 UNFCCC, Article 4.1(g).

30 UNFCCC, Article 4.1(h).

31 UNFCCC, Article 4.1(f).

32 UNFCCC, Article 4.1(a). The link between the Montreal Protocol and greenhouse gases is discussed in greater detail below.

33 UNFCCC, Article 4.1(b).

34 UNFCCC, Articles 4.3-4.7. For instance, Article 4.3 requires that developed country parties provide financial assistance to developing country parties in order to assist them in reporting obligations.

35 UNFCCC, Article 4.7.

36 UNFCCC, Article 4.3.

37 UNFCCC, Article 4.4.

38 UNFCCC, Article 4.5.

39 The Vienna Convention for the Protection of the Ozone Layer of 1985 created a broad framework convention, and the Montreal Protocol later created binding commitments which are, arguably, the most successful within international environmental law. See http://ozone.unep.org for more information.

40 This was called the "Berlin Mandate". See UNFCCC (1995), *Report of the Conference of the Parties on its First Session*, FCCC/CP/1995/7/Add.1, available at http://unfccc.int.

41 For a full text of the Kyoto Protocol and additional information, see http://unfccc.int; see also UNFCCC (2007), *Uniting on Climate: A Guide to the Climate Change Convention and the Kyoto Protocol.*

42 Kyoto Protocol, Article 25.

43 For the full text of the Marrakesh Accords and the Marrakesh Declaration, see http://unfccc.int.

44 See UNFCCC, *Status of Ratification of the Kyoto Protocol*, at http://unfccc.int.

45 Kyoto Protocol, Article 3.1.

46 Kyoto Protocol, Article 3.1.

47 These specific targets for each country are enumerated in Annex B of the Kyoto Protocol.

48 See, e.g. UNFCCC, Article 4.1(a) and Kyoto Protocol, Article 7.

49 Kyoto Protocol, Article 3.1, see *Kyoto Protocol Reference Manual on Accounting Emissions and Assigned Amounts* (2007), p. 13.

50 The EU-15, as noted in Table 2, which consists of members of the European Union in 1990 (base year), opted to combine and redistribute their targets. This was then distributed internally according to economic development priorities and agreements, with the result that some countries took on reduction commitments of over 20 per cent, while others were permitted to increase emissions by more than 25 per cent (See *infra* Figure 1). *Kyoto Protocol Reference Manual on Accounting of Emissions and Assigned Amounts* (2007), p. 13; Kyoto Protocol, Article 3.1.

51 While the United States agreed to a target of 7% relative to the 1990 base year in the negotiations, it never ratified the Protocol and still remains outside the Kyoto Protocol process. See Kyoto Protocol, *Targets*, at http://unfccc.int.

52 Kyoto Protocol, Article 4.

53 Kyoto Protocol, Annex B. See also Kyoto Protocol, *Targets*, at http://unfccc.int.

54 See e.g. Kyoto Protocl, Articles 5 and 7; Yamin and Depledge (2004), *The International Climate Regime*, Cambridge University Press, p. 327.

55 Kyoto Protocol, Article 5.

56 See UNFCCC (2005), *Report of the Conference of the Parties serving as the meeting of the Parties to the Kyoto Protocol on its first session*, FCCC/KP/CMP/2005/8/Add.3, Decision 19/CMP.1, Annex, para. 2.

57 Kyoto Protocol, Article 10.

58 Kyoto Protocol, Article 11.

59 Kyoto Protocol, Article 2.1.

60 See Wara, M. (2008), "Measuring the Clean Development Mechanism's Performance and Potential. Symposium on Changing Climates: Adapting Law and Policy to Transforming World", *UCLA Law Review* 55:1759.

61 See Wiser, G. (2002), "Analysis and Perspective: Kyoto Protocol Packs Powerful Compliance Punch", *International Environment Reporter* 25:2, p. 86. The Convention on International Trade of Endangered Species (CITES) is another example of a strong compliance system. The CITES Standing Committee has the authority to impose trade sanctions in certain circumstances, including non-compliance with national legislation requirements, non-compliance with annual reporting requirements and general enforcement matters. See *Countries*

currently subject to a recommendation to suspend trade, CITES website at www.cites.org.

62 Kyoto Protocol, Articles 6, 12, 17.

63 See UNFCCC (2005), *Procedures and Mechanisms Relating to Compliance Under the Kyoto Protocol*, FCCC/KP/CMP/2005/8/Add.3, Decision 27/CMP.1, Article XV.4; see also Yamin and Depledge (2004), *The International Climate Regime*, Cambridge University Press, p. 148.

64 Kyoto Protocol, Article 17; see also the UNFCCC website on emissions trading at http://unfccc.int.

65 See Point Carbon, *5.9 Gt CO_2e to trade globally in 2009 – up 20% in volume – estimates Point Carbon*, 24 February 2009. The emissions of non-CO_2 greenhouse gases are often converted into the common unit of tonne of CO_2 equivalent – $GtCO_2$-eq refers to this measurement in Gigatonnes – by multiplying the mass of the greenhouse gas by a factor of its global warming potential (GWP). The GWP of a particular greenhouse gas is its estimated contribution to global warming, and depends on, among other things, its projected life in the atmosphere and absorption of infrared radiation.

66 Kyoto Protocol, Article 6; see also Kyoto Protocol, *Joint Implementation*, at http://unfccc.int.

67 See UNFCCC (2006), *Report of the Conference of the Parties serving as the meeting of the Parties to the Kyoto Protocol on its first session*, FCCC/KP/CMP/2005/8/Add.2, Decision 9/CMP.1, paras. 21 and 23, see also Kyoto Protocol, *Joint Implementation*, at http://unfccc.int.

68 See UNFCCC (2006), *Report of the Conference of the Parties serving as the meeting of the Parties to the Kyoto Protocol on its first session*, FCCC/KP/CMP/2005/8/Add.2, Decision 9/CMP.1, para. 24; Kyoto Protocol, *Joint Implementation*, at http://unfccc.int.

69 The German company TÜV SÜD Industrie Service GmbH is the first Track 2 third party verifier. See UNFCCC (2009), *Kyoto Protocol's joint implementation mechanism passes milestone with accreditation of first project verifier*, Press Release, 18 February 2009, available at http://unfccc.int.

70 See UNFCCC, *Project Overview*, available at http://ji.unfccc.int.

71 See UNFCCC (2009), *Kyoto Protocol's joint implementation mechanism passes milestone with accreditation of first project verifier*, Press Release, 18 February 2009, available at http://unfccc.int.

72 Russian Regional Environmental Centre, *The First Joint Implementation Project has been Approved*, www.rusrec.ru.

73 Russian Regional Environmental Centre, *The First Joint Implementation Project has been Approved*, www.rusrec.ru . See also Global Carbon website at www.global-carbon.com.

74 Kyoto Protocol, Article 12; see also Kyoto Protocol, *Clean Development Mechanism*, at http://unfccc.int.

75 See UNFCCC (2006), *Report of the Conference of the Parties serving as the meeting of the Parties to the Kyoto Protocol on its first session*, FCCC/KP/CMP/2005/8/Add.1, Decision 3/CMP.1, paras. 43-48.

76 See UNFCCC (2006), *Report of the Conference of the Parties serving as the meeting of the Parties to the Kyoto Protocol on its first session*, FCCC/KP/CMP/2005/8/Add.1, Decision 3/CMP.1, paras. 35-66.

77 See UNFCCC (2008), *Annual report of the Executive Board of the Clean Development Mechanism to the Conference of the Parties serving as the meeting of the Parties to the Kyoto Protocol*, FCCC/KP/CMP/2008/4, p. 6.

78 For the most recent figures see UNFCCC, CDM-Home, http://cdm.unfccc.int.

79 See generally United States Government Accountability Office (2008), *International Climate Change Programs: Lessons Learned from the European Union's Emissions Trading Scheme and the Kyoto Protocol's Clean Development Mechanism*, United States Government Accountability Office.

80 See UNFCCC (2008), *Analysis of Technology Transfer in CDM Projects*, p. 4, at http://cdm.unfccc.int.

81 See generally United States Government Accountability Office (2008), *International Climate Change Programs: Lessons Learned from the European Union's Emissions Trading Scheme and the Kyoto Protocol's Clean Development Mechanism*, United States Government Accountability Office.

82 See UNFCCC (2008), *Analysis of Technology Transfer in CDM Projects*, p. 7, at http://cdm.unfccc.int.

83 See UNFCCC (2008), *Analysis of Technology Transfer in CDM Projects*, p. 5, at http://cdm.unfccc.int.

84 Kyoto Protocol, *Compliance*, at http://unfccc.int; see UNFCCC (2002), *Report of the Conference of the Parties on its Seventh Session*, FCCC/CP/2001/13/Add.3, Decision 24/CP.7, Article II.

85 Danish (2007), pp. 50-51.

86 See UNFCCC (2002), *Report of the Conference of the Parties on its Seventh Session*, FCCC/CP/2001/13/Add.3, Decision 24/CP.7, Article XV; see also Danish (2007), pp. 50-51.

87 UNFCCC (2006), *Report of the Conference of the Parties serving as the meeting of the Parties to the Kyoto Protocol on its first session*, FCCC/KP/CMP/2005/8/Add.3, Decision 27/CMP.1, Article XV.4.

88 Compliance Committee, *Informational Note*, at http://unfccc.int.

89 Compliance Committee, *Informational Note*, at http://unfccc.int.

90 See Table 2 *infra*.

91 Zugravu, Millock and Duchene, *The Factors Behind CO_2 Emissions Reduction in Transition Economies*, Fondazione Eni Enrico Mattei, available at www.feem.it.

92 IPCC (2007a), p. 36.

93 See e.g. Sweet, W. (2008), "Greenhouse Gas Trends", *IEEE Spectrum* 45:1, p. 88; The Economist (2005), *Climate change and politics - Hotting up*, 374:8412, 3 February 2005, pp. 73-74.

94 Velders et al. (2007), "The Importance of the Montreal Protocol in Protecting Climate", *Proceedings of the National Academy of Sciences of the USA* 104:12, p. 4818.

95 UNFCCC, *Bali Action Plan*, Decision 1/CP.13 at 1.

96 See UNFCCC (2006), *Report of the Conference of the Parties serving as the meeting of the Parties to the Kyoto Protocol on its first session*, FCCC/KP/CMP/2005/8/Add.1, Decision 1/CMP.1, paras. 1-3.

97 UNFCCC (2008), *Means, methodological issues, mitigation potential and ranges of emission reduction objectives, and consideration of further commitments*, FCCC/KP/AWG/2008/L.18.

98 See European Council (2005), *European Council Brussels 22 and 23 March 2005: Presidency Conclusions*, Council of the European Union, Brussels.

99 See International Institute for Sustainable Development (IISD) (2008), "Summary of the Fourteenth Conferences of Parties to the UN Framework Convention on Climate Change and Fourth Meeting of Parties to the Kyoto Protocol: 1-12 December 2008", *Earth Negotiations Bulletin* 12:395.

100 See, e.g., UNFCCC (2008), *Ad Hoc Working Group on Further Commitments for Annex I Parties under the Kyoto Protocol, Agenda item 5 Consideration of information on potential environmental, economic and social consequences, including spillover effects, of tools, policies, measures and methodologies available to Annex I Parties*, FCCC/KP/AWG/2008/L.17, Draft Conclusions Proposed by the Chair, p. 2.

101 UNFCCC, *Bali Action Plan*, Decision 1/CP.13 at 1(b)(i).

102 UNFCCC, *Bali Action Plan*, Decision 1/CP.13 at 1(b)(iii), (iv).

103 UNFCCC, *Bali Action Plan*, Decision 1/CP.13 at 1(b)(ii).

104 UNFCCC, *Bali Action Plan*, Decision 1/CP.13 at 1(c)(i).

105 UNFCCC, *Bali Action Plan*, Decision 1/CP.13 at 1(c)(i).

106 UNFCCC, *Bali Action Plan*, Decision 1/CP.13 at 1(c)(ii).

107 UNFCCC, *Bali Action Plan*, Decision 1/CP.13 at 1(c)(iii).

108 UNFCCC, *Bali Action Plan*, Decision 1/CP.13 at 1(c)(iv).

109 UNFCCC, *Bali Action Plan*, Decision 1/CP.13 at 1(d)(i).

110 UNFCCC, *Bali Action Plan*, Decision 1/CP.13 at p. 5, para. 1(e)(i).

111 UNFCCC, *Bali Action Plan*, Decision 1/CP.13 at 1(e)(iii), (v).

112 UNFCCC, *Bali Action Plan*, Decision 1/CP.13 at 1(a).

113 UNFCCC, *Bali Action Plan*, Decision 1/CP.13 at 2.

114 UNEP Ozone Secretariat (2006), *Handbook for the Montreal Protocol on Substances that Deplete the Ozone Layer*, 7th Edition, Nairobi.

115 Ozone Secretariat, ODS data reported by the Parties under Article 7 of the Montreal Protocol as of 8 April 2009. Ozone-depleting potential (ODP) refers to the amount of ozone depletion caused by a substance, and is the ratio of the impact on ozone of a chemical compared to the impact of a similar mass of CFC-11. Thus, the ODP of CFC-11 is defined to be 1.0. See US Environmental Protection Agency (EPA), Ozone Depletion Glossary, available at www.epa.gov.

116 Andersen, S.O. and Sarma, K.M. (2002), *Protecting the Ozone Layer: The United Nations History*, Earthscan, London, pp. 187-233; UNEP Ozone Secretariat, *Economic Options Committee of the Montreal Protocol Technical Economics Assessment Panel* (1991, 1994, and 1998), Reports of the Economic Options Committee.

117 See United Nations Department of Economic and Social Affairs (2007), *The Millennium Development Goals Report 2007*, pp. 24-25; and United Nations Department of Public Information (2000), *We The Peoples - The Role of the United Nations in the 21st Century*, p. 56.

118 The global warming potentials of ODS range from 4,000 to 11,000 for CFCs, to 700 to 2,300 for hydrochlorofluorocarbons. For comparison, the global warming potential of HFCs controlled under the Kyoto Protocol range from 90 to 12,200 (N.B. ODS values and global

warming potential values can be calculated in different ways and therefore values can differ).

119 IPCC (2007c), p. 100.

120 See Velders et al. (2007b).

121 Kaniaru, D., Shende, R. and Zaelke, D. (2008), "Landmark Agreement to Strengthen Montreal Protocol Provides Powerful Climate Mitigation", *Sustainable Development Law & Policy* VIII:II, pp. 46-50 and 87-89.

122 Velders et al. (2007); see generally Kaniaru (2007).

123 Original version from Velders et al. (2007b).

124 The Montreal Protocol on Substances that Deplete the Ozone Layer (Montreal Protocol) (as amended), Article 2.9.

125 UNEP (2007), *Adjustments to the Montreal Protocol with regard to Annex C, Group I, substances (hydrochlorofluorocarbon) of the Report of the Nineteenth Meeting of the Parties*, UNEP/OzL.Pro.19/7, Decision XIX/6, paras. 3, 4 and 13.

126 UNEP (2007), *Adjustments to the Montreal Protocol with regard to Annex C, Group I, substances (hydrochlorofluorocarbon) of the Report of the Nineteenth Meeting of the Parties*, UNEP/OzL.Pro.19/7, Decision XIX/6, para. 11(b).

127 UNEP/TEAP (2007), *Response to Decision XVIII/12: Report of the Task Force on HCFC Issues and Emissions Reduction Benefits Arising from Earlier HCFC Phase-out and other Practical Measures.*

128 Velders (2007a) .

129 US Environmental Protection Agency (2007), *Changes in HCFC Consumption and Emissions from the U.S. Proposed Adjustments for Accelerating the HCFC Phase Out.*

130 Brazilian Ministry of Environment, Powerpoint (2007), *Benefits for the Protection of Ozone Layer and Climate of the Brazilian-Argentinean Proposal*, Fourth Meeting of the Stockholm Group.

131 Doha Ministerial Declaration, Paragraph 31 (iii), WT/MIN(01)/DEC/1.

132 In the context of the negotiations, some WTO members have highlighted the potential contribution of the mandate towards the objectives of MEAs, such as the Montreal Protocol and Kyoto Protocol to UNFCCC; UN Millennium Development Goals; and the Plan of Implementation of the World Summit on Sustainable Development, which advocates support for "voluntary, WTO-compatible market-based initiatives for the creation and expansion of domestic and international markets for environmentally friendly goods and services." See United Nations (2002), *Report on the World Summit on Sustainable Development*, para. 99.

133 It should be noted that the Doha mandate also calls for negotiations to clarify disciplines relating to fisheries subsidies. These negotiations are conducted in the Negotiating Group on Rules.

134 IPCC (2007e), p. 621. Steenblik and Matsuoka (2008), at p. 9.

135 IPCC (2007a), Table 4.2, p. 60. See also Part I.

136 Canada, the European Communities, Japan, Korea, New Zealand, Norway, Chinese Taipei, Switzerland, and the United States (2007), *Continued Work under Paragraph 31 (iii) of the Doha Ministerial Declaration*, Non-Paper, WTO Committee on Trade and Environment Special Session, JOB(07)/54, 27 April 2007, 22 p. European Communities and the United States (2007), *Proposal for a Result under Paragraph 31 (iii) of the Doha Ministerial Declaration*, Non Paper, WTO Committee on Trade and Environment Special Session, JOB(07)/193/Rev.1, 6 December 2007, 5 p.

137 Some ideas have also been put forward with respect to which approach should be taken to eliminate or reduce tariffs and non-tariff barriers (modalities) (e.g. special and differential treatment to be given to developing and least developed countries, for instance in the form of longer implementation periods or exemptions from commitments to reduce and eliminate tariffs and not tariffs barriers).

138 Canada, the European Communities, Japan, Korea, New Zealand, Norway, Chinese Taipei, Switzerland, and the United States (2007), *Continued Work under Paragraph 31 (iii) of the Doha Ministerial Declaration*, Non-Paper, WTO Committee on Trade and Environment Special Session, JOB(07)/54, 27 April 2007, 22 p.

139 It should be noted that there is no universally accepted definition of "environmental goods". Indeed, the notion of a good being "environmental" may vary depending on the environmental challenges faced and the priorities identified to address them, as well as on the country's level of development. The rapidly evolving nature of the technology to address environmental challenges is also another challenge with respect to product coverage. Furthermore, environmental goods cut through a wide range of chapters in the Harmonized System (HS). As goods are not classified under the HS on the basis of their end-use, products included under the HS 6-digit categories identified as environmental goods are often multiple-use goods, i.e. they may be used for environmental purposes, but may also have a range of other applications that are not environmental in themselves.

140 OECD (2001b), p. 49.

141 Howse and Bork (2006), p. 5.

142 Steenblik and Matsuoka (2008), p. 11.

143 The trade and tariff data is presented in order to illustrate the potential importance of the negotiations in this sector, in particular for developing countries. However, the following caveat should be provided. The data presented in this section is based on the category of renewable energy contained in a list of goods developed by a group of nine WTO members for the CTE in Special Session. Also, the data is provided on the basis of all 30 HS 6-digit subheadings included in the category of renewable energy. The data therefore reflects information on more products than just climate-friendly commodities. Canada, the European Communities, Japan, Korea, New Zealand, Norway, Chinese Taipei, Switzerland, and the United States (2007), *Continued Work under Paragraph 31 (iii) of the Doha Ministerial Declaration*, Non-Paper, WTO Committee on Trade and Environment Special Session, JOB(07)/54, 27 April 2007, 22 p.

144 The Harmonized Commodity Description and Coding Systems generally referred to as "Harmonized System" or simply "HS" is a multipurpose international product nomenclature developed by the World Customs Organization (WCO). It comprises about 5,000 commodity groups; each identified by a six digit code. See for more information the website of the WCO at www.wcoomd.org.

145 Philibert (2006a), p. 18. Steenblik (2005), p. 10. Alavi (2007), p. 17.

146 Steenblik (2006), pp. 4, 17-18. Steenblik and Matsuoka (2008), pp. 39-40.

147 Steenblik and Matsuoka (2008), pp. 21-22, 31-33, 40-43, 51-52, 57-58, 67-68, and 72-74.

148 Claro and Lucas (2007), pp. 32-60, at p. 32. OECD (2001b), p. 49.

149 Stern (2006), Chapter 23.7, p. 21.

150 Stern (2006), Chapter 23.7, pp. 10, 21.

151 Claro and Lucas (2007), pp. 32-60, at p. 32. OECD (2001b), p. 49. Philibert (2006a), p. 24. Steenblik (2005), p. 5.

152 Kennett (2005), p. 19.

153 ICTSD (2008b), p. 4. World Bank (2008b), p. 68. Jha (2008a).

154 See endnote 144 above.

155 Comtrade database, 2007 (EU 27, no intra trade).

156 Comtrade database, 2007 (EU 27, no intra trade).

157 OECD (2001b), pp. 49-50. Jha (2008b). ICTSD (2008b), p. 6.

Part IV

National Policies to Mitigate, and Adapt to, Climate Change, and their Trade Implications

Climate change mitigation and adaptation measures and policies intersect with international trade in a number of ways. This part reviews the range of policies to mitigate, and adapt to the effects of, climate change. It provides examples of national efforts on climate change mitigation and adaptation, whether voluntary or mandatory, public or private. It is based mainly on national experiences and key literature on the topic. In broad terms, it provides an overview of the rationale behind these mitigation and adaptation policies and their potential implications for the environment and trade. The key aspects in the design of climate change related measures are presented in order to draw a clearer picture of their overall potential and effects on environmental protection, development and trade.

A number of policy measures have been used or are available at the national level to mitigate, and adapt to, climate change. They are typically distinguished as either regulatory measures (i.e. regulations and standards) or economic incentives (e.g. taxes, tradable permits, and subsidies). Climate change resulting from emissions of greenhouse gases is, in economic terms, a negative externality.[1] In order to correct such negative externalities and to "internalize" environmental costs, setting a price on carbon dioxide (CO_2) emissions is a key policy response. However, the existence of a number of market imperfections[2] means that carbon pricing alone may not be sufficient or may be difficult to implement. Therefore, apart from national efforts to internalize the environmental costs of greenhouse gas emissions (see Section IV.A below), other policies are being considered and implemented by governments, including financial measures to promote development and deployment of climate-friendly goods and technologies (see Section IV.B below), and technical requirements to promote the use of such goods and technologies (see Section IV.C below). These distinctions also provide a useful framework for considering the potential relevance of trade rules, and this is how this report is structured below.

In addition, it should be noted that a number of adaptation and mitigation measures in the area of agriculture with related impacts on forestry and biodiversity are being explored at the national level. As noted in Parts I and II of this Report, a changing climate will likely have a profound impact on current agricultural production systems and may require farmers to adapt. For some this may present new opportunities, but for others, particularly farmers in developing countries, this could present significant challenges. Adaptation in the agricultural sector has taken place throughout history and often without specific policy interventions. As farmers recognise the impact of a changing climate on agricultural yields, they alter their practices, such as the timing of operations, the choice of crops or livestock breed or the mix of their production, to account for the new situation.

However, the risk of a rapidly changing climate caused by greenhouse gas emissions may require policy interventions to ensure that farmers can respond in a timely manner and that support is available as farmers consider their options. Support for research will also become increasingly important to ensure the knowledge base required to deal with new pests and diseases and the changing climate is available. In this context, the WTO Agreement on Agriculture and the Agreement on Sanitary and Phytosanitary Measures (SPS) may play an important role. For example, the Agreement on Agriculture, in particular through its "Green Box" provisions for permissible subsidies, provides exemptions for research and development. Similarly, the SPS Agreement would help countries align their response to new types of pest and disease outbreaks as a result of climate change.

There are also opportunities within national agriculture policy to focus on mitigation. Notwithstanding the difficulties of calculating agricultural emissions, there is an expectation that emissions from agriculture should be reduced. At a practical level, a reduction in emissions can be achieved through a wide range of activities, including adopting energy saving practices, changing livestock feeding methods, reducing the application of pesticides, and improving manure and slurry storage. Moreover, enhancing carbon storage in soils and biomass by removing land from production (thereby avoiding soil disturbance) or by creating new woodlands are seen by many as providing a useful mitigation opportunity. From a trade policy perspective, the removal of trade barriers that currently encourage carbon-intensive agricultural practices may be an option. For instance, several commentators have called for the reduction and removal of the most harmful kinds of trade-distorting agricultural subsidies; a step that is currently being addressed in the Doha Round.

Although national policies related to agriculture may offer important adaptation and mitigation opportunities, an in-depth analysis of these policy areas is beyond the scope of this Report. Additional studies are clearly required to address these and other types of national adaptation and mitigation measures currently under consideration. Rather, as previously stated, the analysis below focuses on price and market-based mechanisms to internalize the environmental costs of greenhouse gas emissions, and on financial and technical measures to encourage the development, deployment and use of climate-friendly technologies.

In this Part, the universe of relevant WTO rules is addressed in connection with the presentation of the different types of domestic policies and not in relation to specific measures. Broadly speaking, WTO rules and case law that relate generally to environmental issues are relevant to the examination of climate change measures. The general approach under WTO rules has been to acknowledge that trade measures may be used to achieve certain policy objectives as long as a number of carefully crafted conditions are respected. Moreover, WTO rules, as a whole, offer a framework for ensuring predictability, transparency and the fair implementation of such measures.

A number of WTO rules may be relevant to the examination of mitigation and adaptation measures and most of them are explained in this Part in detail. First, several provisions of the General Agreement on Tariffs and Trade (GATT) should be mentioned, including: the disciplines on tariffs, essentially prohibiting members from collecting tariffs at levels higher than that provided for in their WTO scheduled consolidation; a general prohibition against quantitative restrictions; a general non-discrimination principle, consisting of the most-favoured-nation and national treatment principles; and the general exceptions of the GATT that allows WTO members to adopt policy measures to protect the environment. Moreover, specific rules on technical regulations and standards as contained in the Agreement on Technical Barriers to Trade (TBT) may be relevant, and for instance the rules that such measures may not be more restrictive than necessary to fulfil a legitimate objective, must respect the principle of non-discrimination and be based on international standards, where they exist.

Also, rules of the Agreement on Subsidies and Countervailing Measures (SCM) may be relevant as they define the concept of "subsidy", establishe the conditions under which WTO members may or may not employ subsidies, and regulate the remedies that may be taken against subsidized imports. The disciplines of the General Agreement on Trade in Services (GATS) should also be mentioned: it imposes general obligations such as most-favoured-nation treatment, as well as further obligations in sectors where individual members have undertaken specific commitments such as environmental and energy services. The provisions of the Agreement on Trade-Related aspects of Intellectual Property Rights (TRIPS Agreement) may also be relevant, for instance in relation to the development and diffusion of climate-friendly technologies. Finally, other disciplines may be applicable, for instance those on import licensing and rules of origin and those related to the plurilateral Government Procurement Agreement.

A. Price and market mechanisms to internalize environmental costs of GHG emissions

This section discusses domestic efforts to internalize the environmental costs of greenhouse gas emissions and therefore to set a price on such emissions. The section starts by presenting two types of internalization mechanisms: internal taxes on greenhouse gas emissions, and emission trading schemes (see subsection IV.A.1 below). Generally, such domestic climate change policies alter the relative prices of traded goods covered by such schemes and taxes and may affect conditions for international trade. Therefore, a discussion of the disparities in domestic levels of carbon pricing among countries, and the risk of "carbon leakage"[3] will follow (see subsection IV.A.2 below). In this context, the options discussed in the literature on this subject and suggested by some policy makers to counterbalance these disparities (e.g. border measures) will also be addressed. Finally, the section will present WTO rules that may be relevant to domestic efforts to internalize environmental costs of greenhouse gas emissions, including related border measures (see subsection IV.A.3 below).

1. Domestic measures

a) Taxes on greenhouse gas emissions, and in particular "carbon taxes"

Of the range of measures available to reduce greenhouse gas emissions, one possibility, which is widely discussed in the relevant literature and has already been implemented by several countries, is the use of taxation to put a price on the release of CO_2 into the atmosphere. The main tax base of a "carbon tax"[4] is the combustion-related CO_2 emissions of fossil fuels (which are the key source of CO_2 emissions). Such a tax is usually calculated by measuring the carbon content of fossil fuels,[5] which is directly proportional to the amount of CO_2 that is produced during their combustion.[6] The tax base typically varies for each of the fossil fuels to reflect their varying carbon content, i.e. higher carbon-content fuels, such as coal and oil, are often taxed more, and relatively lower carbon-content fuels, such as natural gas, taxed less.[7] The CO_2 tax may also be based on measured emissions.[8] However, a review of the relevant literature and existing legislation did not identify any example of taxes on the emissions of CO_2 during production of goods (e.g. in the cement and steel sectors).

Broadly speaking, a carbon tax may be levied on two main points of taxation or application: consumers and producers. Although the revenue implications of one collection point over another are considered to be relatively minimal, whether the consumer or the producer is taxed may have an effect on the incentives for switching fuel and thus on the overall environmental impact of the tax, as well as on the costs of collection and enforcement.[9] Most countries implementing a "carbon tax" levy it directly on consumers through a tax on fuel consumption "at the pump".[10]

National carbon taxes are already in use in some countries, including Finland,[11] which was the first country to enact a carbon tax in 1990, and was later followed by seven other European countries.[12] Several other non-European countries have also envisaged the introduction of a carbon tax, but ultimately decided not to proceed with it.[13] Carbon taxes have also been discussed or introduced at the city or state level. For instance in Canada, the province of Quebec introduced a carbon tax in October 2007[14] and in July 2008 the province of British Columbia began phasing in a carbon tax on all fossil fuels;[15] and in the United States, the San Francisco Bay Area (California) adopted a greenhouse gas fee in May 2008.[16]

Often, governments use a combination of a tax on CO_2 emissions and a tax on energy use.[17] A "carbon tax" and an "energy tax" have different tax bases: an energy tax is based on the energy content of energy sources, while a carbon tax is based on their carbon content. Therefore, energy taxes can be imposed on both fossil fuels and on carbon-free energy sources.[18] Since energy taxes apply to fossil fuels, they have a *de facto* effect on CO_2 emissions and can be considered as "implicit carbon taxes".[19] An energy tax falls more heavily on oil and gas than a carbon tax, because oil and gas have a greater energy content than coal. A carbon tax, on the other hand, places a greater burden on coal than on gas and oil, because coal releases more CO_2 during combustion than gas or oil do.[20]

For example, Finland[21] and Sweden combined a tax on CO_2 emissions and a tax on energy use.[22] Other countries have not adopted explicit carbon taxes but have introduced general energy taxes aimed at promoting energy efficiency and energy savings, thereby reducing greenhouse gas emissions. This is the case, for example,[23] in the United Kingdom with the Climate Change Levy[24] as well as in Germany,[25] in the context of a general environmental tax reform aimed at promoting energy saving and efficiency.[26]

Other greenhouse gases are also subject to taxation. For example, France introduced a tax on nitrous oxide (N_2O) emissions in its general tax on polluting activities.[27] In Norway, taxes on the import and production of hydrofluorocarbons (HFCs) and perfluorocarbons (PFCs) were introduced in 2003.[28] In Denmark, imports of industrial gases, HFCs, PFCs, and sulphur hexafluoride (SF_6) have been subject to taxation since 2001.[29] In 2003, the government of New Zealand proposed a methane (CH_4) tax on sheep and cattle, which has, however, never been adopted.[30]

b) Emission trading schemes

Another way of setting a price on activities that have a negative impact on the environment is to: (i) fix a cap on total emissions, (ii) translate this cap into "allowed emissions" or allowances to cover emissions, and (iii) create a market in which these allowances can be auctioned and/or traded, at a price set by the market (i.e. a tradable allowance system).[31] In theory, the market price of these allowances should reflect the marginal cost[32] of emission reductions and thus encourage emitters to reach a specified emission reduction target. The price paid for the allowance is in effect, the carbon price.[33]

The first such emission trading scheme (ETS) was introduced in the United States following the Clean Air Act Amendments of 1977 in order to reduce emissions of air pollutants in certain regions.[34] In the following years, several other emission trading programmes were implemented in the United States,[35] including provisions for trading sulphur dioxide (SO_2) allowances among electric utilities in order to reduce the emissions that contributed to acid rain, in line with the 1990 Amendments to the Clean Air Act.[36]

A provision for international emission trading for greenhouse gases was subsequently included in Article 17 of the 1997 Kyoto Protocol to the UNFCCC, as explained in Section III.A.[37] It was intended to enable parties to Annex I of the Kyoto Protocol to reduce emissions through international emission trading. Annex I parties can acquire units from other parties and use them towards meeting their emission targets under the Kyoto Protocol. Since the conclusion of the Kyoto Protocol, the use of emission trading at the domestic level has received increased attention as an efficient and effective tool in complying with greenhouse gas emission targets under the Kyoto Protocol.

There are a limited number of mandatory emission trading schemes implemented at the national level. The European Union introduced, in January 2005, the world's largest greenhouse gases emission trading scheme (the EU-ETS), which currently covers more than 10,000 installations in the energy and industrial sectors that are collectively responsible for about half of the EU's emissions of CO_2.[38] Denmark implemented, in 2001-2004, an emission trading scheme to control CO_2 emissions from producers in the electricity sector (in 2005, the EU-ETS superseded this scheme).[39] In 2005-2007, Norway implemented an emission trading scheme on CO_2 emissions, which covered 10 per cent of the country's total greenhouse gas emissions. The scheme has now merged with the EU-ETS, although installations that were already subject to Norwegian CO_2 taxes are not included in the EU scheme.[40] In Switzerland, since 2008, companies wishing to be exempted from the CO_2 tax must undertake a legally binding commitment to reduce their energy-related CO_2 emissions and, in return, receive emission allowances that can be traded directly on the domestic and international markets.[41] New Zealand also adopted legislation on an emission trading scheme in 2008.[42]

Other proposals have been discussed, or announced for the near future. In Australia, a mandatory national emission trading scheme is planned.[43] Since 2007, Canada has also been developing a greenhouse gas emission reduction plan, which includes the creation of a carbon emission trading market by 2010.[44] In the United States, since 2007, several climate change and energy bills are being discussed, including the possibility of introducing a mandatory cap-and-trade scheme.[45]

Voluntary national emission trading schemes have also been put in place. For instance, in 2002-2006, the United Kingdom implemented an ETS based on voluntary participation that is open to both the public and private sectors.[46] In 2005, Japan launched a voluntary ETS covering CO_2 emissions from companies that agreed to commit to reaching emission reduction targets.[47] Another example of a voluntary emission trading system is the Chicago Climate Exchange, launched in 2003 in North America.[48] Its members are business firms and governmental and non-governmental organizations that choose to make voluntary commitments to reduce emissions of all six major greenhouse gases.[49] Once these voluntary commitments are made, they become legally binding.

At the sub-national level, the state of New South Wales in Australia introduced, in 2003, the Greenhouse Gas Abatement Scheme, which is the second-largest mandatory scheme, after the EU-ETS.[50] In the United States, the Air Resources Board of the state of California recently approved a framework for implementing a cap-and-trade programme for the electricity generation sector, which will be implemented in 2012.[51] Seven western states of the United States and four Canadian provinces[52] also committed, in 2007, to the Western Climate Initiative, under which a regional cap-and-trade programme will be implemented in 2012.[53] In 2009, ten northeast states[54] of the United States, as part of the Regional Greenhouse Gas Initiative, launched the first cap-and-trade scheme for greenhouse gas emissions within the United States.[55]

Emission trading schemes share a number of design characteristics that are briefly discussed below: the scope; the allocation of emission allowances; the linkages with other existing schemes; and some other features.[56] These design characteristics are important, as they determine the cost burden for participants, and influence the overall trade implications of the schemes.

i) Scope

First, domestic trading schemes can be linked to two types of emission targets:[57] (i) an overall emission level (the cap-and-trade system); or (ii) an emission standard for each source (the rate-base system). In a cap-and-trade system, the government defines an overall maximum amount of greenhouse gases, usually set in physical units (e.g. tonnes), that regulated sources can emit over a specified time-frame.[58] To achieve the goal of decreased emissions, this maximum quantity of allowable emissions is often capped at a lower level than the amount of past emissions, and this cap typically decreases over time. The government then creates a number of "allowances" to cover emissions equal to the size of the cap.

In contrast, under a rate-based system (also called relative cap, "baseline and credit"[59] or carbon intensity-based), the government determines a standard of emissions for each source, usually expressed in either emissions allowed per unit of production, or emission-intensity.[60] For instance, the Greenhouse Gas Abatement Scheme in New South Wales (Australia) and the emission trading market currently under discussion in Canada use rate-based cap-setting.[61] In Canada, the baseline of each firm is planned to be its emission-intensity target.[62]

There are two key differences between cap-and-trade and rate-based systems.[63] A rate-based model does not set a general cap on emissions and therefore gives rise to uncertainty about the overall emission level that may be achieved. Moreover, the administrative burden involved is higher with a rate-based system than with cap-and-trade: as with an environmental tax, the regulating authorities would need to periodically recalculate and adjust rate standards to achieve a certain emission target and correct for additional emissions that may result from increased production.[64]

Second, the number of participants in an emission trading scheme is also an important element in determining the potential impact on emission reduction of any given scheme.[65] However, the extent to which small and large emitters contribute to reaching the overall emission target is uneven, and the cost-effectiveness of including small installations in emission trading schemes has been questioned.[66] In fact, existing and proposed schemes usually provide for minimum thresholds of CO_2 emissions so as to exclude small installations. For instance, in the third phase of the EU-ETS, installations emitting under 25,000 tonnes of CO_2 per year will be allowed to opt out of the ETS, provided that alternative reduction measures are put in place.[67] The proposed Canadian,[68] Australian[69] and Californian[70] emission trading schemes also include minimum thresholds.

Third, sectoral coverage varies. Some schemes cover a wide range of sectors or allow for the gradual inclusion of more sectors. For instance, in the post-2012 period, the scope of the EU-ETS – which currently covers power generation, iron and steel, glass, cement, pottery and bricks, among others – will be extended to include new sectors, including petrochemicals, ammonia and the aluminium sector.[71] The proposed Canadian scheme is also intended to cover a wide array of sectors: electricity generation produced by combustion; oil and gas; forest products; smelting and refining; iron and steel; some mining; and cement, lime and chemicals.[72]

Finally, concerning the type of gases covered, most regimes cover only CO_2, as is the case for the EU-ETS, the United States' Regional Greenhouse Gas Initiative and Switzerland's trading scheme. In contrast, New South Wales (Australia) and the proposed Canadian scheme also cover other greenhouse gases.[73] The EU-ETS post-2012 phase foresees the inclusion of two new greenhouse gases: nitrous oxide (N_2O) and perfluorocarbons (PFCs).[74]

ii) Allocation of emission allowances

In an emission trading system, allowances are the common currency. Usually, one allowance gives the holder the right to emit one tonne of CO_2, as in the case of the EU-ETS, or the right to emit one tonne of CO_2-equivalent (CO_2-eq), as, for example, in the New South Wales scheme.[75] Companies that keep their emissions below the level of their allowances can sell their excess allowances. On the other hand, companies that emit more than the level of their allowances usually have two possibilities, which may also be combined: take measures to reduce their emissions (such as investing in more climate-friendly technologies), or buy the extra allowances they need on the market.

The method of allocating allowances may have important implications on the distribution of costs among covered companies as well as how costs are passed on to consumers, and therefore may influence the potential loss or gain in competitiveness for certain industries.[76] In this regard, both the point of application (or regulation) of the scheme and how allowances are distributed are important considerations.

Broadly speaking, there are two points of application, which may also be combined.[77] In an "upstream" design, the overall limit on emissions applies to producers and importers of fossil fuels and to producers of other energy sources. The emission costs are typically passed on to consumers in the form of higher prices. It is argued that one key advantage of an upstream system is that it involves relatively low administrative costs because it regulates the emissions of a limited number of entities. However, since there are no real options for suppliers of fossil fuels to reduce the carbon content of these fuels, it is argued that an emission cap amounts to a simple fuel cap, with the related negative impact on the profits of fossil fuel producers and importers. Moreover, an upstream design may be insufficient to encourage end-user energy efficiency and emission reductions.

In a "downstream" design, the emission limit applies to sources of emissions, e.g. to end-users of fossil fuels, who are the actual emitters of CO_2.[78] The downstream system offers the advantage of a potentially wide and efficient market for emission trading. Its main drawback lies in higher administrative costs, as it may apply to potentially large numbers of participants.[79]

Most existing schemes are designed in a downstream fashion, as for example the EU-ETS, which applies to single installations in the targeted sectors.[80] The appropriate point of application may differ from sector to sector. For instance, where emissions linked to the transport sector are concerned, it is considered that a downstream point of application would be difficult to implement, as it would have to include all owners and operators of vehicles,[81] and therefore an upstream point of regulation is usually favoured, at the level of refiners and importers of fuels.

Currently, there are two key methods used by the regulator to distribute allowances to existing installations:[82] allocation free of charge and/or auctioning. Free allowances can be based on historical emission levels ("grandfathering"), or on projected sectoral emissions, or they can be distributed by another method, for example on the basis of emissions per unit of output ("benchmarking").[83] The advantages of the free distribution of allowances are that it reduces the risk of losing competitiveness in energy-intensive and trade-exposed sectors; and it may also be a first step in the progressive phase-in of an emission trading scheme.

With auctioning, companies are required to bid for the number of allowances they need to purchase in order to cover their emissions, as opposed to receiving an initial amount free of charge.[84] Reasons in favour of auctioning include the following: it is likely to provide an immediate price signal in the allowances market, which should increase the scheme's overall effectiveness, as the consumers of CO_2-intensive products will adjust demand accordingly; it provides higher incentives to take early action to reduce emissions; and it may attenuate the windfall benefit problem[85] and therefore be more in keeping with the "polluter pays" principle.[86]

In practice, allowances have often been distributed for free, mainly to address the competitiveness concerns of energy-intensive industries.[87] For instance, Switzerland has distributed 100 per cent of its allowances for free.[88] In the third phase of the EU-ETS, there will be a substantial increase in the amount of auctioning (from less than 4 per cent in Phase II to more than 50 per cent in Phase III).[89] Also, under Australia's emission trading scheme a high proportion of free allowances will be allocated to emission-intensive and trade-exposed industries.[90] On the other hand, under the Regional Greenhouse Gas Initiative, several participating northeast states of the United States have decided to auction 100 per cent of their annual allowances.[91]

iii) Linkages with existing schemes, including offsets

A number of emission trading schemes have already been established or are planned for the near future. Although it may be very challenging to link several schemes, as they often vary in some of their key characteristics (such as size, environmental stringency, reporting and monitoring mechanisms, or CO_2 price), there are some clear advantages in doing so. For example, linking emission trading systems could lead to the creation of a larger market, which may in turn bring down the overall cost of reducing greenhouse gas emissions, increase liquidity[92] and reduce volatility of allowance prices.[93]

Two types of links may be distinguished. First, direct links can be set up, whereby emission allowances are traded across several different emission trading schemes.[94] For instance, in the third phase of the EU-ETS, linking and mutual recognition of allowances will be allowed between the EU-ETS and the cap-and-trade systems of any country at the national or sub-national levels, as long as the design of the other emission trading schemes do not undermine the "environmental integrity" of the EU-ETS.[95]

Second, indirect links (which are quite common)[96] may also be established, whereby emission trading schemes are linked to project-based offsets.[97] "Carbon offsetting" (or "offsets") refers to the act of reducing or avoiding greenhouse gas emissions in one place in order to "offset" greenhouse gas emissions occurring somewhere else.[98] Offsets are credits typically generated from emission-reducing projects, such as tree planting, or investments in renewable energy, energy conservation or methane capture.

Credits from project-based offsets can be generated from abroad, for example through the Clean Development Mechanism (CDM).[99] For instance, under the EU-ETS, operators are allowed, within a certain limit, to cover their emission allowances by buying credits generated by emission-saving projects undertaken in other countries.[100] These projects must be officially recognized under the Kyoto Protocol's Joint Implementation mechanism or the CDM. CDM projects are also accepted as offsets in Norway, Japan, the Chicago Climate Exchange, Switzerland[101] and in the proposed Australian emission trading scheme.[102]

Some ETSs also provide for the possibility to use domestic offsets from domestic projects that are not part of the emission trading scheme.[103] For instance, in the Regional Greenhouse Gas Initiative (United States) and the New South Wales (Australia) schemes, other types of offsets from United States[104] and New South Wales-based projects,[105] respectively, can be used. In the third phase of the EU-ETS, it will also be possible to use domestic offset credits from domestic projects that reduce greenhouse gas emissions but that are not covered by the ETS.[106]

iv) Other features

Most emission trading schemes provide for a banking mechanism in order to help stabilize the fluctuations of allowance prices and limit the risk of non-compliance.[107] Banking enables allowances to be carried over from one phase to the other, i.e. allowances not used during the trading period for which they were issued can be banked for use at a later trading period.[108] Banking typically achieves early results in emission reduction, as most firms reduce their emission levels further than required, or buy more allowances than they need, in order to be sure of avoiding non-compliance penalties.[109] The banking of allowances can help firms meet emission targets while providing flexibility to undertake large investments that are necessary to reduce emissions. Provisions allowing the banking of allowances are, for instance, incorporated in the EU-ETS (from the second period onwards),[110] in the emission trading schemes of New South Wales in Australia, in the Chicago Climate Exchange, in the United States' Regional Greenhouse Gas Initiative, in Switzerland, in the national scheme proposed in Australia, and in California's proposed scheme.[111]

Borrowing is another flexibility mechanism that allows a greenhouse gas-emitting entity to use allowances from a future time-period to cover current emissions: the entity borrows from potential reductions that have not been realized yet, but are anticipated to occur in the future, presumably at lower cost than current reductions.[112] Borrowing can constitute an insurance mechanism against price spikes in the event of sustained demand for allowances. For instance, Australia's scheme will allow a limited degree of borrowing, using allowances from the following year, in order to increase flexibility.[113] However, there are some limitations to the use of borrowing, such as the fact that the environmental objective of reduced emissions could be undermined if companies launch into borrowing against future rights and thus delay their emission reductions for several years.[114]

Emission trading schemes may also include some enforcement mechanisms, including possible sanctions.[115] The effectiveness of such mechanisms will depend on the regulator's technical ability to monitor and detect violations, and legal ability to deal with violations once detected.[116] For instance, under the EU-ETS, if an installation does not possess sufficient allowances to cover its annual emissions, it will be financially penalized, and the amount of the deficit in allowances will be carried over to the following period. The fine for non-compliance in the first phase of the EU-ETS was 40 euros/tonne CO_2, and is 100 euros/tonne CO_2 for the second phase.[117] From 1 January 2013 onwards, the fine for non-compliance will increase in accordance with the European Index of Consumer Prices.[118]

c) Environmental effectiveness

Carbon taxes and emission trading schemes may have two key environmental effects:[119] (i) a "direct effect", i.e. a reduction of greenhouse gas emissions, a stimulation of energy-efficient measures, the switching to low-carbon fuels and products, and changes in the economy's production and consumption structures; and (ii) an "indirect effect", through the "recycling" of the fiscal or auctioning revenues to fund, for instance, investment in more climate-friendly technologies, or to enhance emission-reducing changes in investment and consumption patterns.

The "direct effect" stems from the fact that a carbon tax or an emission trading scheme internalizes the environmental cost of carbon by setting a price on the carbon content of energy and on the CO_2 emissions generated in production and/or consumption. In theory, an appropriate price signal on carbon should have the following consequences: ensure that emitting entities pay the full environmental cost of their actions; encourage individuals and businesses to move away from the use of high-carbon goods and services, and to invest in low-carbon alternatives; and, in the long run, promote innovation in new production methods and products that meet consumer demand while reducing pollution.[120]

In order to be fully efficient, a carbon tax should be set at a level that internalizes the costs of environmental damage, so that prices reflect the real environmental costs (the so-called "Pigouvian tax").[121] Most of the integrated assessment models that have been employed to determine the optimal trajectory of a carbon tax show it rising over time. For example, Nordhaus's (2008) study based on his DICE (Dynamic Integrated Model of Climate and the Economy) model shows that the optimal carbon tax begins at $34 (in 2005 prices) per metric ton carbon in 2010, then rises to $42 per ton in 2015, $90 per ton in 2050, and $220 per ton carbon in 2100. The explanation for this is that the carbon tax should be set to equal the marginal damage caused by the emissions.[122] Over time, this marginal damage will increase as the stock of carbon in the atmosphere accumulates so that to fully internalize these rising costs, the carbon tax must increase accordingly. However, the literature and regulations reviewed in this section show that such optimal carbon taxes have rarely been used by policy makers, given, *inter alia*, the difficulty in estimating environmental damage cost and the fluctuations of energy prices.

It seems, however, that countries have rather followed the more pragmatic "Baumol-Oates" approach, pursuant to which the tax rate is set so as to simply influence taxpayers' behaviours to achieve a given environmental objective.[123] This more pragmatic concept is easier to implement in a context where the cost of environmental damage is difficult to evaluate.[124] In practice, the carbon tax rate used varies from country to country: for instance, in Nordic countries, the average CO_2 tax revenue ranges from 7.8 euros/tonne CO_2 in Finland to 23 euros/tonne CO_2 in Sweden.[125]

The "indirect effect" of a carbon tax or an emission trading scheme (under auctioning) may vary depending on how the public revenue which has been raised is used. The revenue can either be included in the government's general budget, or can be redistributed in order to: finance specific programmes, in particular environmental ones (this is known as "earmarking"); compensate industries that are most affected by the tax or the emission trading scheme (and hence alleviate competitiveness concerns); or reduce the burden imposed by some other taxes (such as labour and value-added taxes).[126] Moreover, it has been argued that some additional benefits may be generated by the manner in which the revenues collected with carbon taxes or pursuant to auctioning under an emission trading scheme are "recycled", i.e. reinvested in the economy (this is known as a "double dividend").[127] In addition to an "environmental double dividend" (i.e. reducing CO_2 emissions may be accompanied by a decrease in local pollution), there may also be an "economic double dividend", i.e. recycling the revenues from carbon tax or from auctioning by reducing some other taxes may have a beneficial impact on economic growth, employment or technological development.[128]

Even though recycling the collected revenue, in particular with certain earmarked programmes, might result in environmental advantages, such "fiscal cushioning" may undermine the environmental effectiveness of climate policies and therefore circumvent the intended effect of a carbon tax or emission trading scheme. A number of problems related to this practice have been underlined, among them: firms may delay giving up polluting modes of production; revenue recycling might not motivate companies to fully face up to the environmental cost of their emissions; and earmarking may create obstacles to necessary tax re-evaluations, based on economic and environmental rationales, because the use of the revenue is fixed in advance by the regulator.[129]

In practice, countries often use a mix of possibilities for redistributing the revenues generated from emission trading schemes or carbon taxes. For instance, Finland uses carbon tax revenues both to promote renewable forms of energy and energy efficiency (earmarking), and to reinvest in the general national budget.[130] In Denmark, fiscal revenues are recycled to industry through investment grants for energy-efficient production measures, through reductions of employers' contributions to labour funds, as well as through a special fund for small and medium-sized enterprises.[131] In Sweden, tax-relief rules have been introduced for sectors "subject to competition" and a strategy was adopted in 2000 for a "green tax shift", under which increased carbon taxes are offset by reduced taxes on labour.[132] Norway uses part of the revenues from the carbon tax to reduce income tax.[133] Finally, in the third phase of the EU-ETS, a substantial portion of the revenues which will be generated by the auctioning of allowances as from 2013 will be used to reduce greenhouse gas emissions and adapt to the impacts of climate change, through contributions to certain funds for third countries, investment in renewable energies, and afforestation and reforestation measures in developing countries, among others.[134]

How successful have carbon taxes and emission trading schemes been in practice? Overall, most studies on the results of carbon taxes show relatively small but positive effects on CO_2 emissions. For instance, a 2004 survey of evaluations of CO_2-based taxes concluded that all these taxes, either on their own or as part of a wider package, had generally contributed to the reduction of emissions.[135] Also, a 2000 assessment showed that Finland's CO_2 emissions would have been 7 per cent higher in 1998 had the energy taxes been kept at the 1990 level.[136] The relatively low levels of environmental effectiveness are usually explained by the extensive tax exemptions and the relatively inelastic demand in the sectors that were taxed.[137] When looking at specific sectors, however, emission reductions seem larger. For instance, in Sweden, emissions from district heating, and from the industrial and housing sectors decreased by 19 per cent from 1987 to 1994 and 60 per cent of this reduction could be attributed to the CO_2 taxation.[138] A 1996 study in Norway also found a decrease of 21 per cent in emissions from stationary combustion plants from 1991 to 1995, due to the introduction of the carbon tax.[139]

In theory, a well-functioning emission trading scheme should limit emissions to the specified caps, and should therefore achieve a high level of environmental effectiveness.[140] However, due to the political, practical and economic reasons analysed in the previous section, most emission trading schemes until now have had limited scope and thus a limited ability to curb emissions. Moreover, assessments of the results are still at an early stage, since existing emission trading schemes have not been in operation for long.[141] For instance, the performance of the EU-ETS to date cannot be evaluated without recognizing that the first three years (2005-2007) constituted a "trial" period aimed at developing the cap-and-trade infrastructure needed to reduce greenhouse gas emissions.[142]

Both carbon taxes and emission trading schemes are mechanisms that set a price on greenhouse gas emissions and therefore aim at internalizing the environmental cost of such emissions, with a view to reducing the quantity of emissions to environmentally optimal levels, at the minimum cost.[143] In the case of a carbon tax, the price is determined directly by the regulators through the tax rate (i.e. exogenously), while the quantity of emissions that will be reduced is a result of measures adopted by the industry to reduce emissions (i.e. endogenously). On the other hand, in the case of an emission trading scheme, the quantity of emissions that will be reduced is determined by the regulators (i.e. exogenously) while the price is determined by the market (i.e. endogenously) according to the supply of and demand for emissions, and the price adjusts itself to the marginal abatement costs (i.e. the cost of reducing one additional unit of emissions).[144]

The regulator's choice of instrument is arguably dependent on the relative value assigned to price versus the need to ensure the certainty of an environmental outcome. A carbon tax may be more appropriate when the costs of achieving a desired level of emissions are uncertain. An emission trading scheme may be preferable in situations where greater environmental certainty is needed. For instance, a typical case where greater environmentai certainty is relatively more important than price certainty is where there is a risk of reaching a threshold of damage. This is the case when the environmental damage is relatively limited below a certain threshold, and potentially catastrophic above the threshold. In this situation, if a safe emission threshold can be identified, a cap is the preferable option in order to avoid severe environmental consequences.[145]

On the other hand, when there is no threshold of damage, and the marginal abatement costs are relatively sensitive to the level of pollution identified as being acceptable, a tax may be preferable. For instance, in the case of stock pollutants (defined as pollutants that accumulate over time), it is generally argued that every unit of pollution has roughly the same effect on the environment. In this situation, greater price certainty is relatively more important than environmental certainty, and therefore a tax would be preferable to an emission cap.[146]

In the case of climate change, the harmful environmental effects derive from the accumulation over time of stock pollutants such as greenhouse gases. This would make a case for the adoption of a tax. On the other hand, in the long term, the continued concentrations of greenhouse gases in the atmosphere may eventually reach a certain threshold that could give rise to catastrophic environmental consequences, as discussed in Part I of this publication. In such cases, stabilizing emissions below a threshold level would be very important, providing a rationale for setting an emission cap.[147]

2. Border measures

In the absence of an internationally agreed price on carbon[148] and since emission reduction policies, such as taxes and/or trading schemes, are not applied universally, the implementation of emission reduction policies has given rise to concerns about competitiveness as well as about environmental efficiency, i.e. "carbon leakage". Concerns about competitiveness and carbon leakage, particularly in relation to energy-intensive industries, have recently come to the forefront of climate change discussions, triggered by the consideration and implementation of emission trading schemes in several developed countries.

To reduce the cost of compliance for potentially affected industries, mechanisms such as free allowances or exemptions are used.[149] Another mechanism is to use trade measures at the border to impose a similar cost on importers. This type of trade policy is also argued to be an incentive for other countries to reduce their greenhouse gas emissions, so that the environmental objectives of domestic legislation are achieved and at the same time the global nature of climate change is taken into account.

The following sections first clarify the concepts of "competitiveness" and "carbon leakage", and then present the various types of border mechanisms that are being suggested to remedy them: border tax adjustments to carbon or energy taxes; border measures in relation to an emission trading scheme; and some other types of border measures.

a) Rationale: competitiveness effects and carbon leakage

Both unilateral carbon taxes and emission trading schemes affect relative costs of goods and hence, to a certain extent, also affect the competitiveness of firms and sectors.[150] The competitiveness of a sector may be defined as its ability to maintain profits and market shares.[151] Effects on competitiveness arise in particular if environmental policies in different countries impose different levels of costs on competing firms, thus creating a price advantage for firms located in countries with less stringent environmental policies.[152]

The effects of climate change measures on the competitiveness of sectors will depend on a number of factors that relate to: (i) the specific characteristics of the sector (e.g. its trade exposure; how energy-intensive or CO_2 emission intensive it is; its direct and indirect carbon costs;[153] its production costs; the ability to pass on cost increases through prices; the market structure; transportation costs; its capacity to reduce emissions and/or energy consumption; the possibility to evolve towards cleaner production technologies and processes); (ii) the design of the regulation (e.g. the amount of the carbon charge; the stringency of the regulation; the availability of alleviations and exemptions; and in the case of an emission trading scheme the allocation method for allowances); and (iii) other policy considerations (e.g. energy and climate policies adopted by other countries).[154] The influence of each of these factors may be industry-specific and quite complex to determine. Two of these factors have been at the centre of discussions on the effects on competitiveness of recent emission trading schemes and of those under consideration: the "cost pass-through capability" of companies, and their trade exposure.

The "cost pass-through capability" of a company is its capacity to transfer to consumers any increases in the cost of its production processes by increasing its product prices, without losing profitability (in other words the cost recovery potential). The price increase needed to recover costs incurred due to emission reduction schemes may be determined by adding the direct costs of meeting the emission cap to the indirect carbon costs. Direct carbon costs depend on the carbon intensity and energy intensity of the production process and the availability of emission abatement techniques. In addition to direct costs, industries may also face indirect carbon costs related to increases in the cost of energy inputs in reaction to an increased "carbon constraint" (such as an increase in electricity price).[155]

The ability to "pass through" costs depends on a number of elements, including: the elasticity of demand, i.e. the price responsiveness of demand for a product; the market structure; and the trade exposure.[156] For example, electricity companies can more easily pass on their costs to consumers because electricity demand is relatively price-inelastic (i.e. demand remains nearly constant, whether prices increase or fall), the market structure is usually highly regulated, and there is very limited international competition from countries with no carbon emission reduction policies.[157] Moreover, it is argued that producers of internationally traded commodities will have far less scope to offset their carbon costs through price increase, as they fear loss of market share.[158] Exposure to international trade is seen as the main constraint to companies' ability to pass through costs to consumers.[159]

Studies done to date have generally found that the effects on competitiveness of environmental regulations, including climate change policies, are relatively small, or are likely for only a small number of sectors, because the costs of compliance with a regulation are a relatively minor component of a firm's overall costs, which also include, for example, exchange rate fluctuations, transportation costs, energy prices and differences across countries in the costs of labour.[160] For instance, a study examining the literature on competitiveness effects of a carbon price concluded that it would negatively impact the competitiveness of only a few energy-intensive manufacturing industries and would be likely to have a limited impact on output and employment levels.[161] It should be noted, however, that the carbon constraint in some emission trading schemes (e.g. in Phase III of the EU-ETS) is expected to be increasingly stringent, with fewer free allowances, which will therefore increase the potential impact on the competitiveness of a number of sectors.[162]

Related to the potential impact of climate change mitigation policies on competitiveness, the issue of "carbon leakage", or the risk of energy-intensive industries relocating to countries with weaker environmental policies, has recently received a great deal of attention. It is clear that the price of carbon will be different between countries that have implemented carbon constraining regulations such as a carbon tax or an emission trading scheme and countries that have not. Moreover, among countries that use such a pricing instrument or which have enacted different regulatory measures to mitigate climate change, the price of carbon may also vary considerably.[163]

The concerns related to carbon leakage are usually linked to two risks: a risk of creating "carbon havens", i.e. countries with less stringent carbon policies which attract carbon-intensive industries, thereby endangering the global effectiveness of carbon-constraining environmental policies, and a risk of job relocation resulting from the relocation of industries to countries where climate change mitigation policies are less costly.[164]

Some countries have proposed – or have already introduced in their legislation on emission trading schemes – criteria to identify sectors or sub-sectors that would be at risk of carbon leakage. These criteria include the following: increases in production costs induced by the introduction of the new regulation; trade exposure; emission intensity; the extent to which it is possible to reduce emissions or electricity consumption; and the extent to which other countries are taking comparable action to reduce emissions and improve carbon efficiency.[165] Identification of the sectors that may be at risk of carbon leakage may prove to be a challenging task in practice, mainly because of the difficulties involved in collecting the data for the above-mentioned indicators.

In the context of emission trading, free allocation of emission allowances to energy-intensive industries or output-based rebates have been considered to be a means to prevent carbon leakage. For instance, in the third phase of the EU-ETS certain sectors could continue to receive all their allowances for free for the period 2013-2020 if the European Commission determines that they are "at significant risk of carbon leakage".[166]

But alleviations and exceptions may not be sufficient to prevent carbon leakage, and the question that then arises is whether the concerns over carbon leakage and competitiveness impact warrant government intervention in the form of border adjustments.[167]

b) Key characteristics

In complement to the domestic implementation of carbon taxation or of an emission trading scheme, the introduction of border measures aimed at offsetting possible asymmetries in competitiveness and preventing carbon leakage has been widely discussed in the literature on the subject, and in some countries. The following sections address border tax adjustments to carbon taxes or energy taxes, border measures in relation to emission trading schemes, and other types of border measures.

i) Border tax adjustments to carbon taxes or energy taxes

As shown in Subsection IV.A.1(a), the term "carbon tax" has been used by countries and in the related literature to refer to two broad types of climate change related taxation: (i) taxes on the consumption of fossil fuels in relation to their carbon content; and (ii) taxes on the emissions of CO_2 during the production process (e.g. in the cement and steel sectors) – although the general review of countries' taxation in the previous subsection did not identify any examples of this type. In addition, countries usually impose a number of taxes on the consumption of energy in general (i.e. taxes that are not linked to the carbon content of fossil fuels, but are aimed at reducing the consumption of all energy sources).

The 1970 report of the *GATT Working Party on Border Tax Adjustments*[168] referred to a definition of border tax adjustment used in the OECD.[169] Under this definition, a border tax adjustment (BTA) consists of two situations: (i) the imposition of a tax on imported products, corresponding to a tax borne by similar domestic products (i.e. BTA on imports); and/or (ii) the refund of domestic taxes when the products are exported (i.e. BTA on exports).

Border tax adjustments are commonly used with respect to domestic taxes on the sale or consumption of goods.[170] BTAs are considered by tax experts to be a means to implement in a government's fiscal policy the "destination principle", according to which goods are taxed in the country of consumption.[171] The overall economic objective of a BTA is to level the playing field between taxed domestic industries and untaxed foreign competitors by ensuring that internal taxes on products are "trade-neutral".[172] For example, many tax schemes adjust for taxes on products such as cigarettes or alcohol.[173] Countries also commonly adjust domestic taxes on fossil fuels when importing such fuels.[174]

However, not all internal taxes may be suitable for adjustment. The question whether domestic carbon/energy taxes are eligible for border tax adjustment pursuant to GATT and WTO rules is discussed below in Section IV.A.3(a).

ii) Border adjustments in relation to an emission trading scheme

Border adjustments in relation to an emission trading scheme (for instance in the form of an obligation on importers to hold emission allowances) have not yet been put in place. However, as part of the discussion on domestic emission trading schemes, a debate is currently taking place in certain countries on possible means to impose border adjustments.[175]

For instance, it has been envisaged to link an emission trading scheme to certain requirements on imports from countries that do not impose similar emission reduction obligations on their industries. In such cases, importers would have to submit emission allowances or certified emission credits to cover the emissions created during the manufacturing process of the imported good; or they would be allowed to purchase allowances in the domestic emission trading markets on equal terms with domestic industries.[176]

iii) Other border measures

A number of other types of border measures have been envisaged by governments and in literature on the subject, in particular with a view to encouraging certain countries to agree to emission reduction commitments.[177] Such measures would be imposed on imported products, especially energy-intensive ones, originating from certain countries, and include for instance: an import charge or a higher tariff.[178]

Academics have also discussed the possibility of raising a countervailing duty (against "*de facto* subsidies") or an anti-dumping duty (against "environmental dumping") on imported goods produced in countries that do not impose climate change related regulations, in order to offset the emission-reduction costs those imports have avoided paying, or the *de facto*, or "hidden" subsidy that those goods are receiving.[179] It has been argued that inaction involves a benefit, and therefore the avoided cost of fighting climate change could be considered to be a hidden subsidy on emissions which could be countervailed.[180] A number of other authors, however, are of the view that it would be difficult to qualify a country's failure to adopt climate legislation as a "subsidy" or environmental "dumping" in terms of WTO law.[181]

Another type of measure that has been discussed is the possibility of imposing a tax on certain means of international transport – for example on trucks driving through a country's territory – based on their evaluated emissions of CO_2.[182] Such a measure mainly aims at internalizing the costs of means of transport to better reflect their true impact on society and the environment, and also aims at promoting a more equitable taxation for the use of road infrastructure based on principles such as "user-pays" and "polluter-pays".[183]

c) Practical challenges

There are, however, a number of practical difficulties involved in the implementation of a border tax adjustment in relation to a carbon or energy tax, and further difficulties in designing a mechanism to adjust the cost of emission allowances and calculate the proper level of border adjustment. The main challenges relate to (i) the difficulty in assessing product-specific emissions, and (ii) the fluctuations of the carbon price (or allowance price) in the context of an emission trading scheme. An additional difficulty may arise in cases where imported products are subject, in the country of origin, to other climate change regulations, such as technical regulations, rather than price mechanisms such as taxes.[184] Compliance with certain regulations, such as a fuel efficiency standard, may also involve a cost (e.g. investment in more energy-efficient technologies) that may be complex to evaluate and transform into an adjustable price or a "comparable action".

The main difficulty in assessing products' emissions comes from the fact that greenhouse gas emissions involved in the production process may vary depending on the product, the company and the country.[185] The CO_2 intensity of a product (i.e. embedded CO_2 divided by its value) depends on the quantity of fuels used, the production process of a particular good, the energy efficiency of the production process, the type of fuels or energy used, the source of the energy (i.e. the particular energy mix used in the country of production).[186] If the input is not recognizable in the final product, then it will not be possible to calculate the tax or charge from merely inspecting the product at the border, and alternative methods of assessment of the amount of border adjustment to be imposed on imported products will therefore be necessary.[187] Several methods are usually discussed. First, the country of import could require that imported products be accompanied by some sort of certification or labelling as to the relevant aspects of the production process used.[188] The second potential method would be for the importing country to assume that the imported product has been made according to the "predominant method of production" used in the country of import or the "best available technology" currently available and to tax the product accordingly.[189]

It is generally considered that the first approach requiring that the imported products be accompanied by certification or other information documents may raise a number of practical issues, such as: (i) the difficulty of precisely assessing the actual quantity of CO_2 emitted during the production of a specific item; and (ii) the fact that producers may not be willing to share confidential information on the composition of their products.[190] Such an approach had been envisaged by the United States in relation to chemical products. In the GATT *Superfund* case, the panel found that a United States tax on certain chemicals that was imposed directly on products was eligible for border tax adjustment and consistent with GATT Article III.2.[191] Importers were required to provide sufficient information regarding the chemical inputs of taxable substances to enable the tax authorities to determine the amount of BTA to be imposed.[192]

A case that arose under European Union law is also often referred to concerning the practical difficulties involved in the estimation of the amount of border adjustment to a carbon/energy tax: the 1998 *Outokumpu Oy* case.[193] The Finnish government had imposed a tax on electricity using different rates depending on how it was generated. Finland taxed imports at a flat rate set to approximate an average of the domestic rates, because it argued that it was impossible to determine how imported electricity was produced once it had entered the distribution network. Outokumpu Oy, an electricity importer, complained that this flat rate was a violation of the European Communities Treaty, which forbids direct and indirect discrimination against imported products. The European Court of Justice agreed and explained that Finland's law did not give the importer the opportunity to demonstrate that its electricity was produced by a particular method in order to qualify for the rate applicable to domestic electricity produced by the same method.[194] However, the Court also held that, provided that a tax differential was based on objective criteria and applied to domestic and foreign products alike, it was lawful for member states to tax the same or similar products differentially.[195]

In cases where industries are not in a position to disclose any such information, the second option that has been suggested is for the country imposing the adjustment to assume that the imported products have been produced using the "best available technology" versus the average technology.[196] It has been argued that the "best available technology" chosen could be one that has a certain world market share for the production of the products concerned. The level of the tax would then correspond to the quantity of greenhouse gases that would have been emitted if all components had been manufactured with the "best available technology". It has also been suggested, for credibility reasons, that elaboration of the best available technology standards should be entrusted to an independent body that would receive all required information from the industry.[197]

Some authors argue[198] that a similar approach has been implicitly accepted by the GATT Panel in the *Superfund* case. Under the Superfund Act, if the importer failed to provide information regarding the chemical inputs of taxable substances, the United States could impose instead a rate equal to the amount that would be imposed if the substance were produced "using the predominant method of production".[199] The panel did not find that this method would constitute an infringement of the national treatment principle, as contained in Article III.2, first sentence.[200]

The fluctuations of the carbon price in an emission trading scheme is in fact one of the major differences with an adjustment on a carbon/energy tax (which establishes a fixed carbon price).[201] The actual cost of allowances varies from firm to firm due, for example, to grandfathering, different experiences in emission allowance markets, or worldwide differences in emission profiles within a given industry.[202] In fact, a single firm might also hold different types of allowances: some received free of charge, some purchased from the government in an auction, and others purchased on the open market. Therefore, it may be difficult to base a border adjustment on the current market price of allowances, especially when some free allocations have been distributed.[203]

3. Relevant WTO rules

Several WTO disciplines may come into play if a carbon/energy tax or an emission trading scheme and/or their adjustments affect international trade.[204] The literature has been very prolific on the extent to which GATT and WTO rules would apply to border measures based on the carbon content of products or based on the adoption of "comparable" climate change mitigation measures.[205]

The discussion has been triggered by a number of factors, including: (i) the recent design by governments of new policy mechanisms to mitigate climate change; (ii) the concerns over competitiveness and carbon leakage and the related risk of protectionism; (iii) the absence of universal commitment to reduce greenhouse gas emissions and the related temptation to use trade measures to encourage reduction in emissions; and (iv) some perceived legal uncertainties in GATT and WTO provisions about measures on production processes (in particular "non-product related PPMs"), as they have not yet been clarified in the dispute settlement system of the WTO.

The following subsections first focus on GATT and WTO disciplines that deal specifically with border tax adjustments and then address more general rules that may be relevant to different types of border measures and to domestic regulations that have an effect on trade.

a) Rules specific to border tax adjustments

Generally speaking, two types of internal taxes may be distinguished: taxes on products (called indirect taxes) and taxes on producers (i.e. direct taxes).[206] In its examination of BTAs, the 1970 GATT Working Party indicated that taxes directly levied on products (i.e. so-called indirect taxes, such as excise duties, sales taxes and the tax on value added) were eligible for adjustment, while certain taxes that were not directly levied on products (i.e. direct taxes such as taxes on property or income) were normally not eligible for adjustment.[207]

In 1976, a GATT panel, in the *United States Tax Legislation (DISC)* case,[208] confirmed, for the export side and in relation to GATT rules,[209] the distinction between direct and indirect taxes and the ineligibility of direct taxes (on producers) for adjustment.[210] The question of whether domestic carbon/energy taxes are eligible for border tax adjustment pursuant to GATT and WTO rules and, if so, under which conditions, is addressed in this subsection.

i) Border tax adjustments on imported products

Pursuant to GATT Article II on tariff concessions and customs duties, for a BTA on imports to be characterized as a tax adjustment and not a customs duty,[211] the charge imposed on the imported product needs to be equivalent to the tax imposed on the "like" domestic product. In other words, there is a difference between a "border tax" and a "border tax adjustment". A "border tax" is a tax (or customs duty) imposed on imported goods, while a "border tax adjustment", is an adjustment of the taxes imposed domestically on products when the goods are imported. Therefore, GATT Article II.2(a) allows WTO members, at any time, to impose on the importation of any product a charge equivalent to an internal tax (e.g. a border tax adjustment).[212]

There is an extensive legal debate over the eligibility, for border adjustment, of domestic carbon/energy taxes. Some authors have also discussed whether the price paid by an industry to participate in an emission trading scheme (in the form of an obligation to hold emission allowances) could be qualified as an "internal tax or other internal charge of any kind" under GATT Article III.2,[213] and would therefore be comparable to a carbon/energy tax for the purpose of introducing border adjustments. According to these authors, GATT and WTO rules on border tax adjustment could then become relevant.

Two GATT provisions are at the centre of the discussion on border tax adjustments in relation to carbon/energy taxes: (i) Article II.2(a) and its phrase "articles from which the imported product has been manufactured or produced in whole or in part"; and (ii) Article III.2, first sentence and the terms "applied, directly or indirectly, to like domestic products".

Article II.2(a) allows two types of import charges (i.e. border tax adjustments): (i) charges imposed on imported *products* that are like domestic products; and (ii) charges imposed on *articles* from which the imported product has been manufactured or produced in whole or in part. The first type could refer, for instance, to charges imposed on domestic fuels and imported "like" fuels.[214]

Concerning the second type of charges, however, extensive discussion has taken place on the extent to which the energy inputs and fossil fuels used in the production of a particular product could be considered to be "articles from which the imported product has been manufactured or produced in whole or in part".[215] It has been suggested by some that the wording of Article II.2(a) may restrict the application of Article II to inputs physically incorporated into, or part of, the final product, which would therefore exclude the possibility to adjust taxes on the energy or fossil fuels used during the production of goods (other than taxes on fuels themselves).[216]

Article II.2(a) also states that internal taxes and equivalent charges on imported products need to be imposed consistently with GATT Article III.2 and the preamble to Ad Note Article III.[217] Under Article III.2, border adjustments on imported products is only allowed in respect of taxes "applied, directly or indirectly, to like domestic products" (i.e. indirect taxes).[218] The meaning of the words "directly or indirectly" has been extensively debated in the literature related to adjustments of taxes on CO_2 emissions. In particular, the focus of the debate has been the question whether, pursuant to both Articles II.2(a) and III.2, only the environmental taxes on inputs which are physically incorporated into the final product may be eligible for adjustments when the final product is imported.[219]

It has been argued by some that the word "indirectly" contained in Article III.2 may be interpreted as allowing the use of border tax adjustments on taxes that are charged on inputs used during the production process of a particular product, i.e. applied indirectly to products.[220] According to this argument, a tax on the energy or fuels used in the production process or the CO_2 emitted during production (neither of which are physically incorporated in the final product) could therefore be considered to be applied indirectly to products.[221]

The GATT *Superfund* case[222] has been mentioned in this context. In this case, the dispute panel found that a US tax on certain substances (used as inputs in the production process of certain chemicals)[223] which was imposed directly on products was eligible for border tax adjustment.[224] It has been argued that this case confirms that the GATT allows border tax adjustments on imported products in relation to an internal tax on certain inputs used in the production process.[225]

ii) Border tax adjustments on exported products

GATT and WTO rules permit, under certain conditions, the use of border tax adjustments on exported products. Export BTAs cannot be subject to anti-dumping duties imposed on goods that are deemed to be "dumped" (i.e. exported at less than the cost price in the domestic market) nor can they be subject to countervailing duties that an importing country introduces to offset certain subsidies provided in the exporting country.[226] Export BTAs do not constitute subsidies.[227] Export BTAs are therefore neither prohibited nor "actionable" under the WTO Agreement on Subsidies and Countervailing Measures (SCM) and GATT rules. Footnote 1 of the SCM Agreement reads:

"In accordance with the provisions of Article XVI of GATT 1994 (Note to Article XVI) and the provisions of Annexes I through III of this Agreement, the exemption of an exported product from duties or taxes *borne by* the like product when destined for domestic consumption, or the remission of such duties or taxes in amounts not in excess of those which have accrued, shall not be deemed to be a subsidy." [emphasis added]

GATT Article VI:4, the Ad Note to Article XVI and footnote 1 of the SCM Agreement refer to taxes "borne by" products and not "applied to" or "subject to" as contained in GATT Article III:3. In 1970, i.e. before the SCM Agreement came into effect, the GATT Working Party on Border Tax Adjustments took note of these differences in wording in the GATT and concluded that they had not led to any differences in interpretation of the provisions.[228] It also noted that GATT provisions on tax adjustment applied the "principle of destination" identically to imports and exports.[229]

Furthermore, Items (e) and (g) of the Illustrative List of Export Subsidies contained in Annex I of the SCM Agreement endorse the distinction between direct and indirect taxes.[230] Border tax adjustments on exports with respect to direct taxes are considered to be export subsidies (Item (e)) and are therefore prohibited under Article 3 of the SCM Agreement.[231] On the other hand, border tax adjustments on exports with respect to indirect taxes are considered an export subsidy only when the BTAs are "in excess" of taxes "levied in respect of the production and distribution of like products when sold for domestic consumption" (Item (g)). Item (g) provides that the following is an export subsidy:

"The exemption or remission, in respect of the production and distribution of exported products, of indirect taxes [footnote omitted] in excess of those levied in respect of the production and distribution of like products when sold for domestic consumption."

Item (g) therefore allows, for instance, a tax on domestically produced fossil fuels to be rebated when a product is exported, provided that the rebate is not larger than the actual tax levied on "like" products "when sold for domestic consumption".[232] Moreover, Item (g) allows border tax adjustment (if not "in excess" of taxes that are charged on like products) in relation to indirect taxes levied "in respect of the production and distribution" of like domestic products. This has been interpreted by some authors as including taxes on energy or fuel consumption, since those taxes are levied in respect of the production of the goods.[233]

It has also been argued that carbon and energy taxes are a particular type of indirect tax and would fall under the category of "taxes occultes" (literally, "hidden taxes").[234] The 1970 GATT Working Party on Border Tax Adjustments included, under this category, taxes on "advertising, *energy*, machinery and transport" (emphasis added).[235] In fact, the Working Party noted a divergence of views among delegations regarding the eligibility for adjustment of "taxes occultes" and even indicated that adjustment was not normally made for "taxes occultes" except in countries having a cascade tax.[236] However, it has been argued by some authors that certain of the "taxes occultes" that were mentioned by the GATT Working Party are now explicitly allowed by the SCM Agreement: the Working Group listed taxes on "machinery and transport" as examples of "taxes occultes", whereas the SCM Agreement allows border tax adjustments on taxes not in excess of domestic indirect taxes in respect of the "production and distribution" of like products, which potentially could include transport taxes.[237]

Finally, there has been extensive discussion on the extent to which Item (h)[238] on "prior stage cumulative indirect taxes" (PSCI taxes)[239] of the Illustrative List of Export Subsidies read together with footnote 61[240] to Annex II on "Guidelines on consumption of inputs in the production process" could be interpreted as implying that carbon and energy taxes are eligible for border tax adjustment on both the product and the related production process of the product.[241]

b) General disciplines

The following subsections will focus on one of the key disciplines of the GATT and WTO agreements: the non-discrimination principle (i.e. national treatment principle and the most-favoured nation clause). Moreover, if a trade-related climate change measure is found to be inconsistent with one of the core provisions of the GATT (e.g. Articles I, III or XI), justification could still be sought under Article XX. This will be the focus of the last subsection.

Other disciplines and WTO agreements may be also relevant to climate change related measures such as the prohibition of quantitative restrictions[242] and disciplines on technical barriers to trade.[243] Also, the provisions of the Agreement on Subsidies and Countervailing Measures (SCM) may be relevant to emission trading schemes, for instance if allowances are allocated free of charge. Some authors[244] are of the view that free allowances could constitute actionable subsidies covered by the SCM Agreement.[245] It should be noted however that if free allowances are found to be actionable subsidies covered by the SCM Agreement, "adverse effects" would have to be demonstrated for action to be taken by another WTO member.[246]

i) Non-discrimination principle

National treatment

The national treatment principle may be particularly relevant in cases where a climate change related regulation is applied differently to domestic and foreign producers. The national treatment principle is a key discipline of the WTO and GATT. In accordance with GATT Article III, a member shall not discriminate between its own and like foreign products (giving them "national treatment").

Article III.2 deals specifically with internal taxes or other internal charges. For a tax or charge on imports to fall under this provision, it needs to apply "directly or indirectly, to like domestic products". As already briefly discussed in previous subsections, the key question is whether a potential tax on CO_2 emissions released during the production process will be considered to be a tax applied indirectly to products. For taxes or charges on imports to be consistent with Article III.2, they should not be applied "in excess" to taxes levied on like domestic products. Moreover, in accordance with GATT Article III.2, second sentence, and the Ad Note, "directly competitive or substitutable" imported and domestic products shall incur similar taxes, and these shall not be applied so as to afford protection to domestic production.

GATT Article III.4 addresses "all laws, regulations and requirements affecting the internal sale, offering for sale, purchase, transportation, distribution or use" of products. As indicated by the Appellate Body in the *US – FSC (Article 21.5, EC)* case, the word "affecting" in Article III.4 can be interpreted as having a "broad scope of application".[247] Article III.4 provides that, in respect of all such regulations and requirements, imported products shall not be accorded treatment less favourable than that accorded to like domestic products. In the *Korea – Various Measures on Beef* case, the Appellate Body found that imported products are treated less favourably than like products if a measure modifies the conditions of competition in the relevant market to the detriment of imported products.[248]

The national treatment principle is also found in several other WTO agreements, such as the Technical Barriers to Trade (TBT) Agreement (Articles 2, 5, Annex 3.D) and the Sanitary and Phytosanitary Measures Agreement (Article 2). On the other hand, it should be noted that in the GATS, Article XVII allows a WTO member to maintain discriminatory conditions on its national treatment obligations unless it commits otherwise.

Most-favoured nation clause

According to the most-favoured nation clause, a WTO member shall not discriminate between "like" products from different trading partners (giving them equally "most favoured-nation" status). GATT Article I.1 provides that "any advantage, favour, privilege or immunity" granted by any member to any product originating in or destined for any other member shall be accorded immediately and unconditionally to the like product originating in or destined for the territories of all other members. As explicitly provided in Article I.1, the scope of application of this provision also extends to all matters referred to in paragraphs 2 and 4 of Article III (see above). The most-favoured nation clause is also found in other WTO agreements, including Article II of the GATS and Article 2 of the TBT Agreement.

Definition of like products

One of the key questions discussed in relation to the application of the non-discrimination principle as contained in GATT Articles I and III relates to the "likeness" of domestic and imported products. This is an important question: when a domestic product and an imported product are found to be "like", their treatment must be consistent with the national treatment principle and the most-favoured nation clause.

The question of the definition of "likeness" has been addressed by a number of dispute settlement cases. As rephrased[249] by the Appellate Body in the *EC – Asbestos* case, the analysis of the likeness of products is based on four categories of "characteristics" that the products involved might share:[250] "(i) the physical properties of the products; (ii) the extent to which the products are capable of serving the same or similar end-uses; (iii) the extent to which consumers perceive and treat the products as alternative means of performing particular functions in order to satisfy a particular want or demand; and (iv) the international classification of the products for tariff purposes".[251]

The Appellate Body has made it clear that the concept of likeness is one that needs to be addressed on a case-by-case basis:[252] the four criteria are simply tools to assist in the task of sorting and examining the relevant evidence and not a closed list of criteria that determine the legal characterization of products.[253] An important question in relation to the application of the four above-mentioned criteria to climate change measures is whether products may be considered "unlike" because of differences in the way in which they have been produced (referred to as non-product-related processes and production methods (PPMs)), even though the production method used does not leave a trace in the final product, i.e. even if the physical characteristics of the final product remain identical.

ii) GATT exceptions

A number of authors have underlined the importance of the case law related to GATT Article XX on General Exceptions in the context of climate change related measures.[254] If a particular measure is inconsistent with one of the core provisions of the GATT (e.g. Articles I, III or XI), it could still be justified under Article XX. Article XX lays out a number of specific instances in which WTO members may be exempted from GATT rules.[255] Two exceptions are of particular relevance to the protection of the environment: paragraphs (b) and (g) of Article XX. According to these two paragraphs, WTO members may adopt policy measures that are inconsistent with GATT disciplines, but necessary to protect human, animal or plant life or health (paragraph (b)), or relating to the conservation of exhaustible natural resources (paragraph (g)).

GATT Article XX on General Exceptions consists of two cumulative requirements. For a GATT-inconsistent environmental measure to be justified under Article XX, a member must perform a two-tier analysis proving: first, that its measure falls under at least one of the exceptions (e.g. paragraphs (b) and/or (g), two of the ten exceptions under Article XX); and, second, that the measure satisfies the requirements of the introductory paragraph (the "chapeau" of Article XX), i.e. that it is not applied in a manner which would constitute "a means of arbitrary or unjustifiable discrimination between countries where the same conditions prevail", and is not "a disguised restriction on international trade".[256]

Environmental policies covered by Article XX

WTO members' autonomy to determine their own environmental objectives has been reaffirmed on a number of occasions (e.g. in *US – Gasoline*, *Brazil – Retreaded Tyres*). The Appellate Body also noted, in the *US – Shrimp* case, that conditioning market access on whether exporting members comply with a policy unilaterally prescribed by the importing member was a common aspect of measures falling within the scope of one the exceptions of Article XX.[257] In past cases, a number of policies have been found to fall within the realm of paragraphs (b) and (g) of Article XX: (i) policies aimed at reducing the consumption of cigarettes,[258] protecting dolphins,[259] reducing risks to human health posed by asbestos,[260] reducing risks to human, animal and plant life and health arising from the accumulation of waste tyres[261] (under Article XX(b)); and (ii) policies aimed at the conservation of tuna,[262] salmon and herring,[263] dolphins,[264] turtles,[265] petroleum,[266] and clean air[267] (under Article XX(g)).

Although policies aimed at climate change mitigation have not been discussed in the dispute settlement system of the WTO, the example of the *US – Gasoline* case may be relevant. In this case, the panel had agreed that a policy to reduce air pollution resulting from the consumption of gasoline was a policy concerning the protection of human, animal and plant life or health as mentioned in Article XX(b).[268] Moreover, the panel found that a policy to reduce the depletion of clean air was a policy to conserve a natural resource within the meaning of Article XX(g).[269] Against this background, some authors have argued that policies aimed at reducing CO_2 emissions could fall under Article XX(b), as they intend to protect human beings from the negative consequences of climate change (such as flooding or sea-level rise), or under Article XX(g), as they intend to conserve not only the planet's climate but also certain plant and animal species that may disappear because of global warming.[270]

Also in the *US – Shrimp* case, the Appellate Body accepted as a policy covered by Article XX(g) one that applied not only to turtles within the United States' waters but also to those living beyond its national boundaries. The Appellate Body found that there was a sufficient nexus, or connection, between the migratory and endangered marine populations involved and the United States for purposes of Article XX(g).[271] This point is particularly important in the context of climate change mitigation policies. Some authors have indeed argued that this finding could be relevant to establishing a sufficient nexus between a member's domestic mitigation policy or a border measure and the intended objective of this policy, the protection of a global common asset, the atmosphere.[272]

Degree of connection between the means and the environmental policy objective

In order for a trade-related climate change measure to be eligible for an exception under Article XX, paragraphs (b) and (g), a connection needs to be established between its stated climate change policy goal and the measure at issue. The measure needs to be either: *necessary* for the protection of human, animal or plant life or health (paragraph (b)) or *relating to* the conservation of exhaustible natural resources (paragraph (g)).

To determine whether a measure is "necessary" to protect human, animal or plant life or health under Article XX(b), a process of weighing and balancing a series of factors has been used by the Appellate Body, including the contribution made by the environmental measure to the policy objective, the importance of the common interests or values protected by the measure and the impact of the measure on international trade. If this analysis yields a preliminary conclusion that the measure is necessary, this result must be confirmed by comparing the measure with its possible alternatives, which may be less trade-restrictive while providing an equivalent contribution to the achievement of the objective pursued.[273]

For instance, in the *Brazil – Retreaded Tyres* case, the Appellate Body found that the import ban on retreaded tyres was "apt to produce a material contribution to the achievement of its objective", i.e. the reduction in waste tyre volumes.[274] The Appellate Body also found that the proposed alternatives, which were mostly remedial in nature (i.e. waste management and disposal), were not real alternatives to the import ban, which could prevent the accumulation of tyres.[275]

In *EC – Asbestos*, the Appellate Body also found, as a result of a process of weighing and balancing a series of factors, that there was no reasonably available alternative to a trade prohibition. This was clearly designed to achieve the level of health protection chosen by France and the value pursued by the measure was found to be "both vital and important in the highest degree".[276] The Appellate Body made the point that the more vital or important the common interests or values pursued, the easier it was to accept as necessary measures designed to achieve those ends.[277]

For a measure to be "relating to" the conservation of natural resources in line with Article XX(g), a substantial relationship between the measure and the conservation of exhaustible natural resources needs to be established. In the words of the Appellate Body, a member has to establish that the means (i.e. the chosen measure) are "reasonably related" to the ends (i.e. the stated policy goal of conservation of exhaustible natural resources).[278] Moreover, in order to be justified under Article XX(g), a measure affecting imports must be applied "in conjunction with restrictions on domestic production or consumption" (the even-handedness requirement).[279]

For instance, in the context of the *US – Gasoline* case, the United States had adopted a measure regulating the composition and emission effects of gasoline in order to reduce air pollution in the United States. The Appellate Body found that the chosen measure was "primarily aimed at" the policy goal of conservation of clean air in the United States and thus fell within the scope of paragraph (g) of Article XX.[280] As far as the second requirement of paragraph (g) is concerned, the Appellate Body ruled that the measure met the "even-handedness" requirement, as it affected both imported and domestic products.[281]

In the *US – Shrimp* case, the Appellate Body considered that the general structure and design of the measure in question were "fairly narrowly focused" and that it was not a blanket prohibition of the importation of shrimp imposed without regard to the consequences to sea turtles;[282] thus, the Appellate Body concluded that the regulation in question was a measure "relating to" the conservation of an exhaustible natural resource within the meaning of Article XX(g).[283] The Appellate Body also found that the measure in question had been made effective in conjunction with the restrictions on domestic harvesting of shrimp, as required by Article XX(g).[284]

In the context of climate change, according both to Article XX(b) and to Article XX(g), a substantial link will need to be established between the trade measure and the environmental objective. It should be noted that in *Brazil – Retreaded Tyres*, the Appellate Body recognized that certain complex environmental problems may be tackled only with a comprehensive policy comprising a multiplicity of interacting measures. The Appellate Body pointed out that the results obtained from certain actions – for instance, measures adopted in order to address global warming and climate change – can only be evaluated with the benefit of time.[285]

The importance of the manner in which trade-related environmental measures are applied

The introductory clause of Article XX (its "chapeau") emphasizes the manner in which the measure in question is applied. Specifically, the application of the measure must not constitute a "means of arbitrary or unjustifiable discrimination" or a "disguised restriction on international trade".

The chapeau requires that the measure does not constitute an abuse or misuse of the provisional justification made available under one of the paragraphs of Article XX, that is to say, is applied in good faith.[286] In *Brazil – Retreaded Tyres*, the Appellate Body recalled that the chapeau serves to ensure that WTO members' right to avail themselves of exceptions is exercised in good faith in order to protect legitimate interests, not as a means to circumvent one member's obligations towards other WTO members.[287] In other words, Article XX embodies the recognition by WTO members of the need to maintain a balance between the right of a member to invoke an exception, and the rights of the other members under the GATT.

WTO jurisprudence has highlighted some of the circumstances which may help to demonstrate that a measure is applied in accordance with the chapeau. These include relevant coordination and cooperation activities undertaken by the defendant at the international level in the trade and environment area, the design of the measure, its flexibility to take into account different situations in different countries, as well as an analysis of the rationale put forward to explain the existence of a discrimination (the rationale for the discrimination needs to have some connection to the stated objective of the measure at issue).

For instance, in the *US – Gasoline* decision, the Appellate Body considered that the United States had not sufficiently explored the possibility of entering into cooperative arrangements with affected countries in order to mitigate the administrative problems raised by the United States in their justification of the discriminatory treatment.[288] Moreover, in the *US – Shrimp* case, the fact that the United States had "treated WTO Members differently" by adopting a cooperative approach regarding the protection of sea turtles with some members but not with others also showed that the measure was applied in a manner that discriminated among WTO members in an unjustifiable manner.[289]

At the compliance stage, in *US – Shrimp (Article 21.5)*, the Appellate Body found that, in view of the serious, good faith efforts made by the United States to negotiate an international agreement on the protection of sea turtles, including with the complainant, the measure was now applied in a manner that no longer constituted a means of unjustifiable or arbitrary discrimination.[290] The Appellate Body also acknowledged that, "'as far as possible', a multilateral approach is strongly preferred" over a unilateral approach.[291] But, it added that, although the conclusion of multilateral agreements was preferable, it was not a prerequisite to benefit from the justifications in Article XX to enforce a national environmental measure.[292]

Moreover, in the *US – Shrimp* case, the Appellate Body was of the view that rigidity and inflexibility in the application of the measure (e.g. by overlooking the conditions in other countries) constituted unjustifiable discrimination.[293] It was deemed not acceptable that a WTO member would require another member to adopt essentially the same regulatory programme, without taking into consideration that conditions in other members' territories might be different, and that the policy solutions might be ill-adapted to their particular conditions.[294]

In order to implement the panel and Appellate Body recommendations, the United States revised its measure and conditioned market access on the adoption of a programme comparable in effectiveness (and not essentially the same) to that of the United States. For the Appellate Body, in *US – Shrimp (Article 21.5)*, this allowed for sufficient flexibility in the application of the measure so as to avoid arbitrary or unjustifiable discrimination.[295] The Appellate Body pointed out, however, that Article XX does not require a WTO member to anticipate and provide explicitly for the specific conditions prevailing in every individual member.[296]

Finally, an environmental measure may not constitute a "disguised restriction on international trade", i.e. may not result in protectionism. In past cases, it was found that the protective application of a measure could most often be discerned from its "design, architecture and revealing structure". For instance, in *US – Shrimp (Article 21.5)*, the fact that the revised measure allowed exporting countries to apply programmes not based on the mandatory use of turtle excluder devices (TEDs), and offered technical assistance to develop the use of TEDs in third countries, showed that the measure was not applied so as to constitute a disguised restriction on international trade.[297]

B. Financial mechanisms to promote the development and deployment of climate-friendly goods and technologies

The previous section discussed efforts to internalize the environmental costs of greenhouse gas emissions. Through such efforts, a price signal on emissions is set and individuals and businesses are encouraged to switch away from high-carbon goods and services and to invest in low-carbon alternatives. Government funding to enhance the deployment and utilization of new climate-friendly technologies and renewable energy is another type of economic incentive commonly used in climate change mitigation policies. This section introduces and gives examples of the wide range of governmental policies that are in place, or being discussed, to facilitate the innovation process or address the additional costs related to the use of climate-friendly goods and technologies so as to encourage their development and deployment.

1. Rationale

The Fourth Assessment Report of the Intergovernmental Panel on Climate Change (IPCC) underlined that many mitigation technologies are currently commercially available, and more are expected to be commercialized soon.[298] However, the development and deployment of new technologies, including technologies for the use of renewable and/or cleaner energy sources, may be occurring at a slower pace than is desirable from an environmental point of view, and may therefore need to be reinforced by national policies.

Although the private sector plays the major role in the development and diffusion of new technologies, it is generally considered that a closer collaboration between government and industry would stimulate the development of a broad range of low-carbon technologies at more affordable prices.[299]

A number of factors may hamper the development of new climate-friendly goods and technologies, and may inhibit innovation in the climate change technology sector.[300] First, there is the problem of "environmental externality": because carbon emissions do not have a cost, firms and consumers have no direct incentive to find ways to reduce them. Second, companies' incentive to invent and develop new technologies may be reduced due to the "knowledge effect": in other words, individual companies may not always be able to profit fully from their investment in innovation because "knowledge" about such technologies (and therefore the opportunity to make a profit from them) may spread to other companies, and to other countries. Third, companies may not always be able to convince private investors of the relevance and interest of a research project in the climate change area, because they may not be in a position to demonstrate the environmental effectiveness of their product until it has been brought into use on a wide scale.

Furthermore, a number of factors may affect the cost of deployment of climate-friendly and renewable energy technologies.[301] First, the cost of energy from renewable sources – except large hydropower installations, combustible biomass (for heat) or large geothermal projects – is generally not competitive with wholesale electricity and fossil fuel prices. One of the biggest challenges facing renewable energy technologies is therefore the development of options that can generate energy at costs that are competitive with conventional energy sources. Public funding policies may be able to make the price of energy from renewable sources competitive with that of fossil fuels.

Second, it has been observed that the removal of subsidies on fossil fuels, by changing patterns of energy use and encouraging the development and widespread application of more energy-efficient technologies could be an important mechanism for reducing greenhouse gas emissions.[302] A number of studies have analysed the economic and environmental impact of removing or significantly reducing fossil fuel public subsidies.[303] Such studies usually demonstrate that there would be a substantial reduction in CO_2 emissions. The Agreement on Subsidies and Countervailing Measures (SCM) may be relevant in this regard. Also, some experts have attempted to draw a link between the current Doha Round negotiations on disciplining fisheries subsidies and future multilateral action to address fossil fuel subsidies. It should be noted that a number of countries have engaged in a policy of reduction in subsidies for fossil fuels and coal, both on the production and on the consumption side. In China, for instance, fuel prices rose substantially (over 40 per cent) between 2004 and 2006, as the country removed fuel subsidies.[304] Pre-existing fuel subsidies have also been reduced in other countries, such as Pakistan[305] and Nigeria.[306]

Third, low-emission energy technologies in sectors other than electricity generation (such as transport and industry) are also generally more expensive than conventional technologies. Here, too, governmental funding for industries and individuals using less energy-intensive or emission-intensive technologies – such as purchasing more energy-efficient products or installing meters to measure electricity use – may also help to offset the additional cost involved in the use of these cleaner technologies.

Finally, putting new renewable energy or climate-friendly technologies on the market is also associated with a "learning cost", i.e. the additional cost involved in adapting to the new technology.[307] If the learning rate is low, and/or the time before the technology becomes competitive spans decades, the learning cost will be high, and private sector firms may be unwilling to risk deploying the new technology. In fact, new technologies may not become cost-effective until significant investment has been made and experience has been accrued, and such "learning cost" may reduce the incentive to deploy climate-friendly goods and technologies.

In response to all these factors affecting the cost of climate-friendly and renewable energy goods and technologies, governmental funding may contribute to their faster deployment and increased use, and may also help reduce the gap between their cost and that of conventional technologies and sources of energy.[308] The following subsections introduce the wide range of existing or proposed governmental policies to facilitate the innovation process or to reduce the additional costs related to the use of climate-friendly goods and technologies, and thus encourage their development and deployment.

2. Scope

Policies to promote the development and deployment of goods and technologies aimed at mitigating or adapting to the effects of climate change have been established by certain national and/or sub-national bodies. A number of countries[309] have set up funding programmes at the national level to support climate change policies, such as Denmark's Energy Technology Development and Demonstration Programme[310] or Finland's BioRefine Programme on biomass.[311]

Programmes based on financial incentives (rather than direct payments) usually occur at the national level. For instance, Germany[312] and Spain[313] have both established renewable energy feed-in tariffs (i.e. this refers to a regulated minimum guaranteed price per kilowatt-hour that an electricity company must pay for renewable energy fed into the national electricity grid by a private independent producer. At the sub-national level, some bodies also provide funding.[314] For instance, some provinces in Germany, such as North Rhine-Westphalia,[315] have set up energy research programmes. Another example is Kristianstad, a Swedish municipality, which in 1999 declared its intention of becoming a "Fossil Fuel Free Municipality".[316] This programme, funded by a combination of municipal and state grants, includes promotion of the use of biomass and biogas, energy efficiency and sustainable community planning.

Depending on the type of projects being financed by national and sub-national policies, the population targeted by the policy may vary. A distinction may be made between measures targeted at consumers ("demand-pull") and measures targeted at producers ("supply-push").[317] "Demand-pull" policies are designed to increase the demand for mitigation technologies by reducing their cost for end-users, and are mainly used in the energy, transport and building sectors. "Supply-push" policies aim at providing entrepreneurs with the right incentive to invent, adopt and deploy mitigation technologies. Such production support programmes are mainly used in the energy sector (especially in renewable energy production) and in the transport sector.

Furthermore, certain industries may be specifically targeted by funding programmes, such as the "Wave and Tidal Stream Energy Demonstration scheme" in the United Kingdom, which gives support to businesses using the newly developed technologies for wave and tidal stream power generation.[318] "Energy aid" in Finland is another such programme available to enterprises: it is state aid intended to promote the development of less CO_2-intensive energy production and consumption.[319]

In Germany, since 1990, a public bank has provided private companies with low-interest loans for specified renewable energy projects.[320] Some programmes may also be addressed to a wider public, as is the case of the "Sustainable Development Technology Canada" foundation,[321] whose "SD Tech Fund" aims at stimulating research, development and demonstration of technologies related, among other things, to climate change and air quality. Eligible beneficiaries include the private sector, academic bodies and non-governmental organizations.

3. Type of support

Usually, incentive policies related to climate change may focus on three areas: (i) increased use of renewable and/or cleaner energy sources; (ii) development and deployment of energy-efficient and/or low carbon-content goods and technologies; and (iii) development and deployment of carbon sequestration technologies.[322]

It should be noted that, in recent years, a large number of incentive policies, in particular fiscal measures, have focused on the development and deployment of liquid biofuels (fuel ethanol and biodiesel). There is an extensive body of literature, which is not reviewed here, on the contribution of different types of biofuel support measures to achieving their intended objectives, including greenhouse gas emission reduction, minimizing environmental implications, assuring food security, or contributing to the improvement of rural areas for developing countries.[323]

There are numerous stages in the technology innovation process. Subsection IV.B(a), below, presents governmental efforts to foster research and development of climate-friendly goods and technologies. Subsection IV.B(b) focuses on policies aimed at increasing the deployment of such goods and technologies (including their commercialization and diffusion).[324]

a) Incentives to promote invention of new climate-friendly technologies and goods

Because of the deterrents to investment outlined above – including the "knowledge" and "learning" effects – basic research must often be stimulated through grants and awards to encourage innovators to invent new technologies and processes.[325] A number of governmental grants are intended to facilitate the development of greenhouse gas emission-reducing technologies or renewable energy technologies by financing the cost of research.[326] For example, in New South Wales (Australia), the Climate Change Fund provides, *inter alia*, grants aimed at supporting the demonstration and early commercialization of new renewable energy technologies.[327]

Another example is New Zealand's Plan of Action for Sustainable Land Management and Climate Change, which provides, *inter alia*, research grants for the agriculture and forestry sectors aimed at increasing their resilience and their adaptability to a changing climate.[328] In Korea, too, the Automobile Low Emission Technology Development Support funded research institutions developing, *inter alia*, hybrid vehicles for use as public shuttle buses.[329]

There is also growing interest in other means of encouraging innovation, such as awards for the development of new technologies.[330] Such awards may be provided *ex post* by recompensing existing innovations, i.e. by making a return on investments which have already been made in R&D. Grants may also be awarded *exante* to encourage new research and development projects, in which case the technological improvement to be achieved is generally specified prior to the research process. This type of award is more likely to be used when specific innovations are needed.

For instance, the Bright Tomorrow Lighting Prizes (L Prize), sponsored by the US Department of Energy under the Energy Independence and Security Act of 2007, will be awarded to participants that develop technologies for a new "21st Century Lamp" to replace 60 watt incandescent light bulbs and PAR 38 halogen lamps.[331] The competition will award significant cash prizes and offer other benefits for the winning designers (including opportunities for federal purchasing).

A number of governmental support measures for innovation are implemented on fulfilment of certain conditions, such as reaching performance targets. Performance conditions relate mainly to the achievement of a particular emission target. For instance, in Australia, to be eligible for the Low Emissions Technology Demonstration Fund, technologies had to demonstrate a potential to be commercially available by 2020 to 2030 and able to reduce the energy sector's greenhouse gas emissions by at least 2 per cent per annum from 2030.[332] Australia has also set up the Greenhouse Gas Abatement Program, which provides capital grants to projects that are expected to result in quantifiable emission abatement.[333]

b) Incentives to encourage the deployment of climate-friendly goods and technologies and the increased use of renewable sources of energy

Deployment incentives mainly take the form of financial assistance or support that concerns the cost of production or of use of climate-friendly goods and services. Governmental support measures to encourage the deployment of climate-friendly goods and technologies and the increased use of renewable sources of energy may be implemented upon the fulfilment of certain conditions and criteria.

First, governmental support may be linked to output.[334] Such output-linked support is usually provided through a feed-in tariff (i.e. a minimum guaranteed price per kilowatt-hour) or through direct payments and tax credits provided in proportion to the volume of production. Second, governmental support for climate-friendly production may target intermediate inputs in the production process, such as the energy sources that are used for heat and electricity. Finally, production support may also focus on value-adding factors such as capital and labour. In the United Kingdom, for instance, the Offshore Wind Capital Grants Scheme provided support covering up to 40 per cent of eligible costs, for the deployment of offshore wind electricity-generating facilities with certain minimum generation levels.[335]

There may also be some conditions related to the origin of production. For instance, in some US states, tax credits are only awarded if the raw materials used during production have been produced in the same state in which the production plant is situated. This is the case in Montana, for example, where ethanol producers receive a tax credit only if their ethanol is produced from Montana agricultural products, or is produced from non-Montana agricultural products only when Montana products were unavailable.[336]

The following sections outline three types of financial incentives which are used or are being considered for use by governments to encourage the deployment of climate-friendly goods and technologies: fiscal measures, price support measures and investment support.

i) Fiscal measures

Typically, two types of fiscal measure are used to encourage participation in climate change mitigation efforts: tax reductions (i.e. tax exemptions, tax deduction and tax rebates) and tax credits (i.e. income tax credits, personal tax credits, corporate tax credits, production tax credits and investment tax credits). Such fiscal measures may be either targeted at consumption (i.e. they may reward the purchase and installation of certain technologies) or at facilitating investment in the production of climate-friendly goods and renewable energy.[337]

Fiscal measures aimed at consumption, for instance, can be illustrated by the reduction in value-added tax (VAT) for small hydroelectric, wind and biogas power generation plants in China, while measures targeting investment decisions can be seen in the Chinese government's reduction of income taxes for producers of wind and biogas power projects.[338]

Another fiscal measure, which is used mainly to encourage the use of renewable energy sources, is "accelerated depreciation", which allows investors in renewable energy technologies to depreciate the value of their plant and equipment at a faster rate than is typically allowed, thereby reducing their stated income for the purposes of income taxation.[339] Examples[340] of countries which use such policies include Mexico,[341] the Netherlands,[342] India[343] and the United States.[344]

ii) Price support measures

In the past, feed-in tariffs have been a primary price-support mechanism, used both in Europe and in the United States to encourage the generation of electricity by means of renewable energy sources. A "feed-in tariff" usually refers to a regulated minimum guaranteed price per kilowatt-hour that an electricity company must pay for renewable energy fed into the national electricity grid by a private independent producer.[345]

This type of programme was first implemented in the United States in 1978, with the Public Utilities Regulatory Policies Act (PURPA).[346] PURPA required public utilities to purchase power from renewable energy producers and to pay the utility's avoided cost. Another example is Germany's feed-in tariff, introduced in the 1991 Electricity Feed Act, and its successor, the 2000 Renewable Energy Sources Act.[347] Other countries followed these early examples, including Spain,[348] Italy,[349] France,[350] and the state of South Australia (for solar photovoltaic installations only).[351] Feed-in tariffs have also been introduced in a number of developing countries,[352] including Algeria[353] and Thailand.[354] In China, the Renewable Energy Law (2006) established feed-in tariffs for biomass and wind power.[355]

Feed-in tariffs have proved successful for a number of reasons.[356] First, feed-in tariffs for renewable energy sources usually have a long time-frame and therefore offer long-term price guarantees, providing a high level of security for investors. Moreover, feed-in tariffs are flexible in design and can be adjusted to account for advances in technology and changing market conditions, making them more effective and efficient.

It has also been argued that feed-in tariffs encourage the development of local production of renewable energy, thereby increasing price competition, and also contribute to increasing companies' profit margins, thus encouraging innovation. The literature on this topic shows that feed-in tariffs have been particularly successful when they form part of a broad package of support measures, including tax deductions, "soft" loans (i.e. at subsidized rates) as well as investment incentives (such as subsidies or partial debt relief) for selected technologies.[357]

"Net metering" is another common measure aimed at reducing costs for owners of small-scale on-site renewable energy power generation equipment.[358] If the amount of power that a consumer's renewable energy equipment (such as solar panels or wind turbines) supplies to the national electricity grid is greater than the amount the consumer takes from the grid during a certain billing period, the consumer receives a credit for that amount on future energy bills. In the United States, net metering is available in most states,[359] while in Canada it is offered in the provinces of Ontario and British Columbia.[360] Net metering has also been adopted in Thailand[361] and Mexico.[362]

iii) Investment support

Investment support policies are used to reduce the capital cost of installing and deploying renewable energy technologies:[363] a specified percentage of the costs of constructing or installing climate-friendly technologies is returned to the investor in the form of a capital grant, resulting in significant reductions in the overall cost of such technologies.[364] For instance, between 1994 and 2002, in order to stimulate the development and use of photovoltaic (i.e. solar) power systems, Japan set up a capital grant programme[365] which is considered to have been the driving force behind the rapid deployment of photovoltaic power systems in that country.

In 2006, the state of California approved the California Solar Initiative, which provides rebates to homeowners, businesses and farmers for the installation of rooftop solar systems.[366] Grants to encourage energy-efficient modernization or renovation programmes are offered in many countries, as for instance in Canada, where property owners can apply for EcoENERGY Retrofit grants for improving the energy efficiency of their home.[367]

Investment support policies may also take the form of favourable lending conditions, or low-cost financing with subsidized interest rates for investors in climate-friendly technologies or goods.[368] For instance, in Germany the "100,000 Roofs Programme", launched in 1999, offered "soft loans" (i.e. at subsidized rates) to encourage the installation of photovoltaic systems.[369] Another example is the Indian Solar Loan Programme, which provides low-cost financing for solar energy systems.[370]

In Bangladesh, the micro-financing institutions Proshika and Grameen have started to offer assistance aimed at increasing adaptability and reducing vulnerability to the effects of climate change, through the use of loans for construction of safer housing, for helping people to diversify from agriculture and for undertaking more disaster-proof activities, and through the provision of rapid credit facilities to promote fast recovery in the immediate aftermath of a disaster.[371]

4. Relevant WTO rules

Governmental funding policies to increase the development and deployment of renewable energy sources and of low-carbon goods and technologies may have an impact on the price and production of such goods. From an international trade perspective, such policies lower the costs for producers, leading to lower product prices. In turn, lower prices may reduce exporting countries' access to the market of the subsidizing country or may increase the exports of the subsidizing country.[372]

Moreover, some countries may provide domestic energy-consuming industries with subsidies to offset the cost of installing emission-reducing technologies, thus enabling them to maintain international competitiveness.[373] Since the renewable energy and low-carbon technology sectors are open to international trade, WTO disciplines on subsidies (as contained in the Agreement on Subsidies and Countervailing Measures (SCM)) may become relevant to certain support policies. Moreover, the WTO Agreement on Agriculture may be relevant: it contains a category of permissible green subsidies, known as Green Box, which could allow countries to pursue climate adaptation and mitigation measures in the area of agriculture.

The SCM Agreement aims at striking a balance between the concern that domestic industries should not be put at an unfair disadvantage by competition from goods that benefit from government subsidies, and the concern that countervailing measures to offset those subsidies should not themselves be obstacles to fair trade.[374] The rules of the SCM Agreement define the concept of "subsidy", establish the conditions under which WTO members may or may not employ subsidies, and regulate the remedies (countervailing duties) that may be taken against subsidized imports.[375]

The SCM Agreement also contains surveillance provisions: Article 25 requires each member to notify the WTO of all the specific subsidies it provides, and Article 26 calls for the Committee on Subsidies and Countervailing Measures to review these notifications.[376]

Article 1 of the SCM Agreement defines a subsidy as having three necessary elements: (a) a financial contribution has been provided; (b) the contribution was made by a government or a public body within the territory of a WTO member; and (c) the contribution confers a benefit.[377]

A "financial contribution" is defined by an exhaustive list of measures, which include direct transfers of funds (for example grants or loans), potential direct transfers of funds (such as loan guarantees), government revenue forgone (e.g. fiscal incentives through tax credits), the provision by government of goods and services other than general infrastructure, and government purchase of goods.[378] The range of governmental measures which may be described as subsidies is broadened further by Article 1.1(a)(2), which includes any form of income or price support.[379]

The SCM Agreement does not provide guidance on how to evaluate whether or not a "financial contribution" confers a "benefit". However, the Appellate Body ruled in the *Canada – Aircraft* case that the existence of a benefit is to be determined by comparison with the market-place (i.e. on the basis of what the recipient of the benefit would have received in the market).[380] Moreover, the SCM Agreement's operative provisions only apply to subsidies that are "specific"[381] to a certain enterprise or industry or to a group of enterprises or industries, because it is assumed that non-specific subsidies will not distort the allocation of resources within the economy.[382]

The Agreement makes a distinction between two categories of subsidies:[383] (i) prohibited subsidies (i.e. subsidies contingent upon the export or use of domestic rather than imported products);[384] and (ii) actionable subsidies (i.e. subsidies that cause adverse effects to the interests of other WTO members).[385] Subsidies in the second category are open to challenge by other members only if they are believed to cause adverse effects. In either case, the complaining member may challenge the subsidizing member's subsidies in WTO dispute settlement.

Three types of adverse effect are identified in the Agreement:[386] "injury" to the domestic industry of another WTO member; nullification or impairment of benefits accruing under GATT 1994; and "serious prejudice" to the interests of another member, as defined in the SCM Agreement.[387] These adverse effects generally occur when a subsidy has a negative impact on the access to the subsidizing member's market or to a third country's market, or affects domestic producers in the home market of the complaining member.[388]

In addition to challenging subsidies through WTO dispute settlement, a member may impose countervailing measures on imported products in order to offset the benefits of specific subsidies that have been granted uponthe manufacture, production or export of those goods.[389] However, a WTO member may not impose a countervailing measure unless three specific conditions are met: (i) it must determine that there are subsidized imports; (ii) it must establish that there is injury to the domestic industry; and (iii) it must show that there is a causal link between the subsidized imports and the injury.[390] The SCM Agreement also includes rules on procedures for initiating and conducting investigations, and rules on the implementation and duration (normally five years) of countervailing measures.[391]

Finally, the Agreement on Trade-Related Aspects of Intellectual Property Rights (TRIPS Agreement) may be relevant to the development and diffusion of climate-friendly technologies.[392] The essential objective of the grant and enforcement of intellectual property rights, as set out in the TRIPS Agreement, is to both promote necessary innovation and facilitate the diffusion of technology, balancing legitimate interests in a socially beneficial manner. Intellectual property protection should "contribute to the promotion of technological innovation and to the transfer and dissemination of technology, to the mutual advantage of producers and users of technological knowledge and in a manner conducive to social and economic welfare, and to a balance of rights and obligations".[393]

While the TRIPS Agreement sets out general standards for the protection of intellectual property under national laws, achieving this "balance" in practice is a matter for domestic policymakers and legislators to establish, through an appropriate mix of law, regulation and administrative measures within the policy space defined by the TRIPS Agreement, including through the use of flexibilities in the application of TRIPS standards. Specifically concerning the promotion of climate-friendly innovation and the diffusion of climate friendly technology, patent-related measures that have been raised in policy discussions include promoting technology sharing and patent pooling,[394] technology brokering and clearing house initiatives, more effective use of patent information tools to locate useful technologies, and the facilitation of patent examination of green technologies,[395] as well as limitations or exceptions to patent rights such as research exceptions and specific regulatory interventions such as non-voluntary licensing,[396] government use authorizations and disciplines or guidelines on patent licensing to promote competition.[397] Beyond patent law, other areas of TRIPS standards are relevant to the protection of marks certifying environmentally friendly products and suppressing acts of unfair competition such as making misleading representations about the positive environmental qualities of products (so-called "greenwashing").[398]

C. Technical requirements to promote the use of climate-friendly goods and technologies

In addition to economic incentives such as carbon pricing and financial measures, another approach commonly taken in environment and climate strategies is to develop technical requirements – e.g. in the form of mandatory technical regulations or voluntary standards – for products and production methods, so as to bring about emission reductions and gains in energy efficiency.

In relation to climate change, such regulations and standards intend generally to: (i) improve the energy efficiency of products and processes; and (ii) reduce their energy consumption and/or the quantity of greenhouse gases emitted during the production of a product, or emitted while it is being used. Moreover, some regulations and standards are being developed to facilitate the adaptation to the consequences of climate change. However, as indicated in Part I, adaptation measures are usually undertaken in the context of larger national initiatives related mainly to urban planning, the water sector and coastal management, and few such measures have been put in place so far; this section, therefore, does not review specific examples of such policies.

Since the 1980s, countries have made increasing use of mandatory regulations and voluntary standards to promote the use of more energy-efficient equipment and electric appliances[399] thereby reducing the levels of greenhouse gas emissions associated with their usage. It is estimated that energy-efficiency improvements have resulted in savings of more than 50 per cent in energy consumption over the last 30 years.[400] Furthermore, according to the Stern Review, there is a considerable potential for increased energy efficiency in the buildings, transport, industry, agriculture and power sectors in particular.[401]

This section examines the range of technical requirements aimed at reducing greenhouse gas emission levels and promoting energy efficiency, and discusses related implementation and enforcement instruments, such as information tools, procedures for assessing conformity to regulations, and restrictions and prohibitions. The various aspects of the design of such instruments will determine their potential for climate change mitigation. Furthermore, since the fulfilment of certain regulatory requirements may have an impact on conditions of competition, there can be implications for international trade, and thus the relevant WTO rules and work are also reviewed.

1. Key characteristics

a) Scope

Technical requirements to promote energy efficiency and reduce emissions levels are mainly developed and implemented at the national level. Standards and technical regulations, targeting energy efficiency in particular, have been adopted by most developed countries and by a growing number of developing countries.[402] Such national measures can be public (such as the minimum energy-efficiency performance standards for major domestic appliances, set by the federal government in Canada)[403] or private (such as the Leadership in Energy and Environmental Design (LEED), which is a set of standards in the building sector developed by the US Green Building Council).[404]

In addition, national measures can be either mandatory or voluntary. For instance, in Australia the Minimum Energy Performance Standards (MEPS) for appliances are mandatory regulations;[405] while in the United States, ENERGY STAR is a voluntary labelling endorsement programme.[406] Moreover, technical requirements may also be instituted at the sub-national level, as is the case in the United States, with California's appliance efficiency regulations[407] or in Italy, with Umbria's energy-efficiency building standards.[408]

Standards that aim at enhancing energy efficiency and that set targets for emission reductions are also developed internationally. Such international standards are often used as a basis for regulations at the national level.[409] Currently, examples of areas where international standards may offer practical tools for the application of climate-related regulations include: (i) measurement and methodological standards to measure energy efficiency and greenhouse gas emissions; and (ii) standards related to the use and development of new energy-efficient technologies and renewable energy sources.

Examples of the first category include standards prepared by the International Organization for Standardization (ISO) that can be used to calculate the thermal properties of a building or of individual construction materials.[410] Similarly, the International Electrotechnical Commission (IEC) has developed standards for measuring the efficiency of power conditioners because of their widespread use in solar power generation systems.[411]

Examples of international standards related to the use and development of new energy-efficient technologies and renewable energy sources include the ISO standards on solar energy, hydrogen and wind technologies, and solid and liquid biofuels.[412] In the sector of biofuels in particular, endeavours to promote collaboration are being made in order to reduce the significant differences in the specifications of biofuels between the major producers and users of biofuels (in particular with respect to biodiesel).[413] Such efforts include the Tripartite Task Force, whose members are Brazil, the European Union and the United States;[414] the Energy Working Group in the context of Asia-Pacific Economic Cooperation (APEC);[415] the International Biofuels Forum[416] (which includes Brazil, China, the European Union, India, South Africa and the United States); international efforts within the ISO;[417] as well as private sector collaboration efforts, such as the Roundtable on Sustainable Biofuels.[418]

b) Key specifications

Regulators may establish measures that specify requirements on products and/or processes and production methods in order to achieve reductions in emission levels or other energy-efficiency objectives.

Product-related requirements may achieve indirect results, depending on consumers' purchasing choices and after-sale consumption behaviour. In the context of climate change, such product-related requirements mainly address the energy efficiency and the greenhouse gas emissions related to the use of the product. On the other hand, requirements targeting production methods may result in direct environmental outcomes during production processes, as they improve energy efficiency or limit greenhouse gas emissions to a certain level.

Moreover, standards and regulations, whether related to products or to processes, can be based either on design or descriptive characteristics, or in terms of performance.[419] These different characteristics are outlined in the following subsections.

i) Design-based requirements

Technical requirements for energy efficiency or emission reduction that are based on design or descriptive characteristics specify the particular features a product must have, or the specific actions to be undertaken during production, and determine which goods to use, or which technologies to install. For instance, several governments have developed technical measures with respect to the quality and specifications of biofuels[420] (e.g. Brazil,[421] India,[422] the European Union,[423] and the United States).[424] Japan's standards for business owners concerning the rational use of energy in factories are an example of descriptive requirements for a production process, as they specify, *inter alia*, that combustion facilities must use a certain type of energy-efficient equipment.[425]

Regulations such as design standards (also called technology standards) that are based on descriptive characteristics are best used when there are few options to the polluter for controlling emissions; in this case, the regulator is able to specify the technological steps that a firm should take to control pollution.[426] Moreover, when emissions cannot be measured, or when concerns exist about the feasibility of other policy options, design standards related to existing technologies may provide a practical way to reduce pollution by helping eliminate the least efficient technologies from the market and promoting the use of more efficient ones.[427]

ii) Performance-based requirements

Performance-based requirements for emission reduction or energy efficiency (also known as performance standards) dictate the standards of performance to be achieved for products or processes, or mandate specific environmental outcomes per unit of production (e.g. they may limit emissions to a certain number of grams of CO_2 per kilowatt-hour of electricity generated). In other words, they stipulate environmental outcomes to be delivered by products or production methods, without pronouncing how the outcomes should be achieved. Such requirements are especially prevalent in efforts to improve energy efficiency in such areas as appliances, buildings and transport.

Often, performance requirements are established to encourage the removal of cost-ineffective, energy-inefficient products from the marketplace, and to stimulate the development of more efficient alternatives and processes. Performance-based requirements generally provide more flexibility than design-based requirements, and costs may be lower because firms can choose how they will meet the stipulated environmental target. Indeed, performance standards increase the number of ways that compliance can be achieved, by offering more than a single mandated technology. These compliance options may include finding solutions through changes in the production process, reduction in output, switching to different fuels or other inputs, and alternative technologies.[428] Costs can be further reduced in performance standard implementation by the introduction of additional flexibility, for example through the use of averages.

The performance of a product or process may be set in various ways. Standards may be established, for instance, in terms of maximum CO_2 emissions levels, maximum energy consumption levels, minimum energy performance levels, or minimum fuel economy. For instance, in the European Union, a directive provides that the electricity consumption of domestic refrigeration appliances must be lower than or equal to a specific maximum allowable value;[429] in Australia, all inefficient incandescent light bulbs are to be phased out through the introduction of minimum energy performance standards for lighting products;[430] and in the United States, the US Corporate Average Fuel Economy (CAFE) Standard sets a target in terms of minimum fuel efficiency.[431]

The calculation of the level of performance to be achieved by a standard may be based on different factors. It may be based, for example, on the most efficient product in its category, or on the average energy consumption or emissions of all products in a particular category.[432] Japan's Top Runner Program is an example of the first type of performance calculation: the most efficient model on the market is identified, and the energy performance of this "top runner" is used to set a target for all manufacturers.[433] An example of the second approach may be found in the new US CAFE standard, which is based on the combined average fuel economy of all passenger cars and light trucks sold in a given year in the United States.[434]

Measures may also set out performance standards which apply uniformly across an entire product line (e.g. all light vehicles must achieve the same minimum fuel economy level), or may provide for variation depending on categories within the product line (e.g. based on aspects such as vehicle weight or engine size). For instance, an EU regulation on emission performance standards for new passenger cars defines a "limit value curve" of permitted emissions of CO_2 for new vehicles, depending on the mass of the vehicle: producers will therefore be required to ensure that the average emissions of all new cars which they manufacture are below the average of the permitted emissions for cars of that mass, as given by the curve.[435]

2. Key compliance tools

a) Information tools

Labelling schemes are intended to provide information to consumers, allowing them to make rational decisions which take into account the environmental consequences of specific products, and thus to stimulate manufacturers to design products that achieve higher ratings than the minimum standard.[436] In other words, labelling schemes also aim to stimulate market innovation in energy-efficient products.

Labels, displayed on products at the time of purchase, encourage responsible action with regard to energy use by providing consumers with information on the environmental consequences of the use of specific products and/or the environmental impact of their production process. Labels are often based on, and/or are used in conjunction with, standards. For example, the Seasonal Energy Efficiency Ratio label in the United States, which displays the efficiency of central air-conditioning units, is used in conjunction with a minimum energy performance standard.[437]

One of the main objectives of energy labelling is to encourage manufacturers to develop and market the most efficient products, by ensuring that the benefits of such products can be recognized by the customer. By increasing the visibility of energy costs and providing an energy benchmark (i.e. a reference point to compare the energy performance of one product against that of another), labelling schemes also aim to stimulate market innovation in energy-efficient products, transforming the suppliers of such energy-efficient products from "niche markets" to market leaders.[438]

i) Scope

Labelling schemes have been adopted in many countries across different sectors.[439] While most OECD countries have used energy-efficiency labelling for a number of years, a growing number of non-OECD countries are now also using such measures.[440] For instance, South Africa,[441] Argentina,[442] Ghana,[443] Sri Lanka[444] and Tunisia[445] have adopted energy-efficiency labelling schemes.[446] However, a study done by the World Energy Council (WEC) (2008) finds that labels, despite their recent proliferation, are not as widespread in Africa, the Middle East, or non-OECD Asia: for example, less than 20 per cent of the countries in these regions have refrigerator labels (a common energy-efficiency label in other regions).[447]

In addition, labelling schemes can be either mandatory or voluntary. Examples of mandatory labels include the energy rating labelling programmes for household appliances in Australia;[448] the CO_2 emission labels for new cars in Switzerland;[449] or the fuel consumption labels of new cars in Canada.[450] There are examples of voluntary comparative labelling programmes in several countries,[451] including several developing economies, such as Thailand,[452] India,[453] Brazil[454] and Hong Kong, China.[455]

ii) Type of information covered

Most labelling schemes provide information on the energy efficiency of products or production processes. Energy-efficiency labels are informative labels that are affixed to a product and that describe its energy performance (such as its energy use, efficiency or energy cost), thereby providing consumers with the data necessary for making informed decisions.[456] Many countries have introduced energy-efficiency labels for electrical appliances.[457] Energy-efficiency labels are also present in the building sector. For instance, Denmark requires large and small buildings to display labels that evaluate the building's consumption of heat, electricity, and water.[458] Also, general ecolabels such as the Nordic Swan, and the German Blue Angel, use energy efficiency as one of the many criteria used to award the label to a product.[459]

Moreover, several countries have implemented labels showing the levels of CO_2 emitted by new products. For instance, at the point of sale, new vehicles in Australia must carry a label on the windscreen giving information on the vehicle's fuel consumption and CO_2 emissions.[460] In the European Union, new cars are also required to display labels showing levels of CO_2 emissions in units of grams per kilometre.[461]

In the same way as standards and regulations, on which they are very often based, labelling schemes can be directed at products' characteristics and/or production processes. However, most environmental labels use a criterion that focuses on a product's performance while in operation, such as its energy-efficiency or CO_2 emissions. Such labels mainly concern household appliances and cars. For example, Australia,[463] the European Union,[462] Canada[464] and the United States[465] all require energy-efficiency labels for several household appliances.

Labels may, however, also use broader criteria, such as a product's entire life-cycle, including its production, use and disposal. Such labels focus on ways of reducing the overall environmental impact of a product, including improved energy efficiency. Examples of eco-labels, which include energy-efficiency criteria and life-cycle analysis, are the Nordic Swan,[466] the German Blue Angel[467] and the EU's eco-label Flower.[468] The Carbon Reduction Label in the United Kingdom is another example of a label that focuses on the whole life-cycle of the products it labels.[469] Some companies have also introduced their own labels to indicate the energy used in the production process of their products.[470]

Labelling schemes have also been used by companies to show the origin of products, how far they have travelled in order to reach the consumer, and the emissions generated during their transport.[471] In particular, the term "food mile" is used to refer to the distance food travels from the location where it is grown to where it is consumed. There is some debate, however, over the validity of food miles as an accurate indication of the energy use and greenhouse gas emissions associated with agricultural products. More specifically, it has not only been argued that high food mile ratings do not necessarily mean that more greenhouse gas emissions were produced during the life cycle of a product, but it has also been suggested that airfreight is not a useful indicator of environmental damage.[472]

Instead of simply focusing on airfreight of food products, a number of authors argue that emissions from the entire transport chain need to be considered.[473] Others call for the total energy used from "production to plate" to be examined.[474]

iii) Type of instrument

It is possible to distinguish between two main types of energy-efficiency labels: comparative labels and endorsement labels. Comparative labels provide consumers with information enabling them to compare performance among similar models using categories of performance (such as a rating of 1 to 5 stars) or a continuous scale (showing where the product stands in energy consumption in relation to the amount used by the most and least energy-efficient models in that category).[475]

Comparative labels do not explicitly rank different products or brands; they simply provide the information necessary for consumers to make the comparison. Most comparative labels are of a mandatory nature to ensure that the least-performing products will also be labelled.[476] Comparative energy labels for household appliances are in place, for instance, in Australia,[477] the European Union,[478] Canada[479] and the United States.[480] Comparative labels have also been introduced in some developing countries, for instance in Brazil,[481] Tunisia,[482] China,[483] Iran,[484] Thailand[485] and Korea,[486] and are often modelled on successful developed country labels.[487]

Finally, endorsement labels are also used in some cases: these are essentially seals of approval given by an independant party, assuring consumers that a product meets certain criteria. Endorsement labelling programmes are usually voluntary.[488] An example of an endorsement label is the voluntary Energy Star label in the United States, which is now used for over 60 product categories.[489] The Energy Star label has also been adopted by a number of other countries over the years, in an effort to provide a single set of energy-efficiency qualifications.[490]

A number of developing countries have implemented their own voluntary endorsement labelling programmes, similar to the Energy Star: for instance Brazil,[491] Thailand,[492] and China, whose "China Certificate for Energy Conservation Product" labelling scheme has been run by the China Standards Certification Center (CSC) since 1998.[493] Endorsement labels can also been used in conjunction with comparative labels, as, for example, in the United States, where the Energy Star and EnergyGuide labels may be used together.[494] Finally, there are examples of labels which are used to endorse production methods, as is the case of the Carbon Reduction Label in the United Kingdom.[495]

b) Conformity assessment tools

A conformity assessment procedure is used to determine whether the mandatory and/or voluntary requirements have been fulfilled. Conformity assessments give consumers confidence in the integrity of products, and add value to manufacturers' marketing claims. This section presents the key conformity assessment procedures (testing, inspection, certification, accreditation and metrology) and provides examples in relation to climate change mitigation efforts.

The first of these procedures involves testing a product against specific standards, and is the most common form of conformity assessment, providing the basis for other types of procedures, such as inspection and certification. A test is a technical operation carried out according to a specified procedure, in order to verify one or more characteristics of the product undergoing conformity assessment.[496]

Products can be tested at different stages of their life. For example, the Electricity Generating Authority of Thailand (EGAT) conducts "*ex post* testing" on labelled appliances to ensure their compliance with efficiency standards. Failure to meet the previously awarded efficiency rating results in a downgrading on the efficiency rating scale or complete removal of the label.[497] Similarly, in Hong Kong, China, the authorities monitor the accuracy of energy-efficiency claims on energy labels through sampling and *ex post* testing.[498]

A second procedure – inspection – is the examination of a product design, a product, or a process or installation, and determination of its conformity with specific requirements or, on the basis of professional judgement, with general requirements.[499]

Examples of inspection in relation to climate change related requirements are mainly found in the building sector. For instance, the Leadership in Energy and Environmental Design (LEED) standards, administered by the US Green Building Council, are voluntary environmental standards for commercial buildings. Conformity with these standards is assessed through on-site inspection of five key criteria: sustainable site development, water savings, energy efficiency, selection of materials and indoor environmental quality.[500] Similarly, in order for homes in the United States to qualify for the Energy Star label, they must be inspected by an Independent Home Energy Rater.[501] Another example, in the European Union, is the requirement for regular inspection of boilers and air conditioning systems in buildings in order to ensure compliance with minimum energy performance requirements.[502]

A third type of conformity assessment tool, certification, involves written assurance (the certificate) issued by an independent external body, stating that a product, building or company conforms to specific energy-efficiency or emission standards.[503] Carried out by an independent certification body, certification programmes help create transparency in markets, where energy costs are not always visible. Certification gives confidence to consumers and helps suppliers build their reputation, expand their market and promote new products.[504] Testing and inspection are often integral steps in certification being awarded. For example, all regulated energy-using products (such as domestic electrical appliances) sold in Canada must carry a mark indicating that the energy performance of the product has been verified. The mark must be that of an accredited independent certification body or a provincial authority.[505]

Accreditation is another conformity assessment tool, and is the procedure by which an authority gives formal recognition that a particular person or organization is competent to carry out specific conformity assessment tasks.[506] This can apply to testing laboratories, inspection bodies or certification bodies. Accreditation bodies do not deal directly with the verification of product specifications themselves; instead they assess the bodies carrying out such functions.[507] For example, under the Hong Kong Mandatory Energy Efficiency Scheme, energy test reports must be issued by a laboratory that has been assessed and evaluated by a recognized independent certification body, or that has been accredited by the competent bodies of Hong Kong, China, or their counterparts in other countries, according to mutual recognition agreements.[508] Also, in the United States, the Department of Energy requires accreditation of the laboratories that perform energy-efficiency testing on lighting and electric motors.[509]

A final example of a conformity assessment tool is metrology, which involves ensuring that the measuring equipment used in conformity assessments complies with the requirements for such use.[510] For example, in order to facilitate its compliance assessments on minimum-efficiency standards developed by the US Department of Energy, the National Institute of Standards and Technology developed a specialized power-loss measurement system for testing the power transformers used in the transmission and distribution of electrical power.[511]

c) Restrictions and prohibitions

Measures have been taken by governments to restrict the sale or prohibit the import of certain energy-inefficient products or to ban the use of certain greenhouse gases in the composition of products. It is common for governments to restrict the use of certain substances for environmental reasons.[512] However, since bans and prohibitions have a direct impact on trade (by removing or reducing trade opportunities), governments commonly try to take account of factors such as availability of viable alternatives, technical feasibility and cost-effectiveness, when applying such measures.

Such quantitative restrictions include, for example, bans to prevent and minimize emissions of fluorinated greenhouse gases (such as hydrofluorocarbons (HFCs), perfluorocarbons (PFCs) and sulphur hexafluoride (SF_6)). A number of governments have set up regulatory measures to phase out the use of such gases, in particular pursuant to the Montreal Protocol.[513] For instance, national legislation is in place in Austria,[514] Denmark,[515] Switzerland[516] and the European Union[517] to limit and control the use of HFCs, for example in refrigeration equipment, foams and solvents.

In addition, some other regulations and standards may also effectively ban certain less energy-efficient products from the market. For example, several countries are beginning, or planning, to prohibit the sale of inefficient lighting products, such as incandescent light bulbs, as, for instance, in Australia,[518] the European Union,[519] Canada,[520] Chinese Taipei[521] and Argentina.[522]

3. Environmental effectiveness

The extent to which energy-efficiency and emission-reduction regulations and standards actually contribute to achieving their environmental objectives can be estimated by comparing measurements of the average annual energy efficiency and energy consumption achieved for a given product when regulations are in place with a baseline scenario that assumes no regulations were implemented.[523] In addition, some other means of measurement may be used, in particular to evaluate the environmental effectiveness of a labelling scheme: such measurements may include consumer awareness and acceptance of labels (credibility and understanding) and changes in consumer and manufacturer behaviour.[524]

A number of studies have shown the potential of regulations and standards for increasing the energy efficiency of specific products, particularly electrical equipment.[525] For instance, it has been shown that, in California, the energy-efficiency standards implemented and regularly updated since the late 1970s have significantly contributed to the reduction of energy consumption of major household appliances, such as refrigerators: the energy use of refrigerators in 2000 was more than two-thirds lower than it had been in 1974.[526] Some other studies have calculated the amount of emission reductions resulting from energy-efficiency policies. For instance, in the United States, it was calculated that, if the energy-efficiency standards for household appliances had not been put in place, the total projected CO_2 emissions from the residential sector would have been 8 per cent higher by 2020.[527]

The environmental effectiveness of labelling schemes aimed at promoting energy efficiency and reducing emission levels can be evaluated through examination of the behavioural changes of consumers and manufacturers.[528] Studies show that consumer awareness of environmental labels varies from country to country.[529] For instance, mandatory energy-efficiency rating labels in Australia are recognized by more than 95 per cent of consumers.[530] In Nordic countries, the Nordic Swan label, which covers a wide range of environmental criteria, including energy efficiency, is recognized by 90 per cent of consumers.[531] In the United States, several surveys have been conducted to assess consumer awareness and understanding of the mandatory Energy Guide label. Although recognition of the label was found to be quite good, understanding was limited, with respondents unable to accurately describe the information provided on the label or to determine which appliance was more energy-efficient, based on the labels.[532]

A number of factors may affect the recognition and understanding of labels, which, in turn, influence the market penetration of labelled products and the overall environmental effectiveness of the scheme. These factors include: (i) the size and diversity of the market (i.e. where there is a wide array of brands, models, sizes, designs and features, the purchasing decisions of consumers may be more complex); (ii) the credibility of the labelling programme sponsor (i.e. some studies show that government-run labels tend to be more credible, better recognized and more financially stable); (iii) their clarity and consumer friendliness; and (iv) the link to a certification programme.[533]

Finally, the environmental effectiveness of energy-efficiency conformity assessment may depend on a number of other factors, including: (i) the accuracy of testing results; (ii) the competence of testing laboratories; (iii) the capacity of testing laboratories to keep up to date with changes in technology in order to be more effective; and (iv) the existence of compliance monitoring.[534]

Certain conformity assessment procedures, such as certification and testing, may have a positive environmental effect by ensuring the introduction of more efficient technologies. For instance, in the US automobile sector, *ex post* testing and potential recalls of vehicles have been an effective way of influencing manufacturer behaviour: the expense and consumer dissatisfaction related to "emission recalls", when vehicles fail to meet emission limits, has encouraged many manufacturers to implement standards that are stricter than the existing legal standards, and to design more effective and durable emission-control systems.[535]

4. Relevant WTO rules and work

As outlined in the previous sections, countries have developed a number of climate change related standards and regulations, including procedures to assess conformity. The key WTO instrument governing these measures is the Agreement on Technical Barriers to Trade (TBT). In addition, certain rules of the General Agreement on Tariffs and Trade (GATT) may be relevant, such as GATT Article I (the "Most-Favoured

Nation" clause), Article III (National Treatment principle) and more specifically, Article III:4.[536]

Other provisions of the GATT 1994 may also be relevant. For instance, Article XI requires the general elimination of quantitative restrictions on the importation or exportation of products. Article XI 2(b) introduces an exception to the general rule contained in Article XI and allows import and export prohibitions or restrictions "necessary to the application of standards or regulations for the classification, grading or marketing of commodities in international trade". Furthermore, Article XX establishes exceptions to GATT obligations which may be applicable to certain technical measures.[537]

a) Coverage of the TBT Agreement

The TBT Agreement covers three sets of activities: (i) the preparation, adoption and application of technical regulations by governments;[538] (ii) the preparation, adoption and application of standards[539] by standardizing bodies; and (iii) the conformity assessment procedures used to determine whether the relevant requirements in technical regulations or standards are fulfilled.[540]

The scope of the TBT Agreement extends to all technical regulations, standards and conformity assessment procedures that apply to trade in goods, i.e. to all agricultural and industrial products.[541] However, two areas of trade in goods are excluded from the TBT Agreement:[542] sanitary and phytosanitary measures, which instead are subject to the provisions of the Agreement on the Application of Sanitary and Phytosanitary Measures (SPS); and government procurement specifications, which are addressed in the plurilateral Agreement on Government Procurement (GPA). Technical measures which relate to services are dealt with under Article VI.4 of the General Agreement on Trade in Services (GATS).

i) Mandatory regulations, voluntary standards and conformity assessment procedures

The TBT Agreement makes a distinction between technical regulations (with which compliance is mandatory), and standards (which are voluntary). A fair number of climate-related requirements are voluntary standards and labelling schemes, including some adopted by private entities.[543]

Although the key legal principles are broadly similar for regulations, standards and conformity assessment procedures, there are some differences among each set of provisions, as well as important differences in the level of obligation of members with regard to mandatory regulations and voluntary standards. Indeed, as regards mandatory regulations, members have an obligation to ensure that these regulations are consistent the provisions of the TBT Agreement. On the other hand, with regard to voluntary standards, members are only required to take "reasonable measures" to ensure, for example, that standardization bodies within their territories respect certain disciplines of the TBT Agreement.[544]

An annex to the TBT Agreement contains the Code of Good Practice for the Preparation, Adoption and Application of Standards. This Code of Good Practice includes all the key legal principles of the TBT Agreement (e.g. non discrimination, avoidance of unnecessary obstacles to trade and harmonization). The Code can be accepted, and its provisions followed, by any standardizing body within a WTO member's territory; by any governmental regional standardizing body of which one or more members are also WTO members; and by any non-governmental regional standardizing body which has one or more members situated within the territory of a WTO member.[545] Given the recent proliferation of private carbon labelling (in particular, "food miles" schemes), some authors have also discussed the potential relevance of the TBT Agreement to requirements of this type, which are developed and adopted by private entities (e.g. food supply chains).[546]

Finally, given the number of energy-efficiency and emission-reduction standards that are based on performance requirements, TBT Article 2.8 is an important element. This provision states a preference for regulations based on performance – which may also be seen as less trade-restrictive measures to regulate – rather than for regulations based on design. Indeed, the idea of this provision is to allow producers to find the most cost-effective way of fulfilling the requirements of a technical regulation. What counts is the result, i.e. the performance of a product, rather than the way in which this outcome is achieved.

ii) Products, processes and production methods

A technical regulation is defined under the TBT Agreement as a document which lays down product characteristics or their related processes and production methods, including the applicable administrative provisions, with which compliance is mandatory.[547]

The Appellate Body, in the *EC – Asbestos* and the *EC – Sardines* cases, has set forth three criteria in order to identify a technical regulation: (i) the document must apply to an identifiable product or group of products. A product does not necessarily have to be mentioned explicitly in a document for that product to be an identifiable product, as "identifiable" does not mean "expressly identified";[548] (ii) the document must lay down one or more characteristics of the product. This has been interpreted as meaning that the term "product characteristics" includes not only features and qualities intrinsic to the product itself, but also related "characteristics", such as the means of identification, the presentation and the appearance of a product;[549] and (iii) compliance with the product characteristics must be mandatory.

As outlined in the definitions of technical regulations and standards contained in the TBT Agreement,[550] such requirements include documents which specify requirements relative to "processes and production methods" (PPMs) that are *related* to the product characteristics. However, the second sentence of the definition of technical regulations and standards states that they "may also include or deal exclusively with terminology, symbols, packaging, marking or labelling requirements as they apply to a product, process or production method".[551]

The fact that the second sentence of both definitions leaves out the term "related" when "labelling" (among others) is mentioned, has been interpreted by some as providing some scope for the labelling of a non-product related process or production method (i.e. that does not leave a trace in the final product, so-called "unincorporated PPMs") to be covered by the TBT Agreement.[552] As has been seen in the previous Subsection IV.C.1, a number of energy-efficiency and emission-reduction standards and labelling schemes are based on non-product related PPMs (i.e. the emissions involved in the production of a product do not leave a trace in the characteristics of the final product).

b) Non-discrimination and the avoidance of unnecessary barriers to trade

The TBT Agreement applies the core GATT principle of non-discrimination to each set of activities described above. Technical regulations, standards and conformity assessment procedures are to be applied to products imported from other WTO members in a manner no less favourable than that accorded to "like" (i.e. similar) products of national origin (national treatment principle) and to like products originating in any other WTO member (most-favoured nation treatment).[553] A key question in this context is whether goods produced with a different emission intensity or energy intensity may be considered "unlike" pursuant to the TBT Agreement.[554]

Moreover, technical regulations, standards and conformity procedures must also not be prepared, adopted or applied with the intention or effect of creating unnecessary obstacles to trade.[555] It is important to note, however, that the TBT Agreement recognizes the right of members to take regulatory measures to achieve their legitimate objectives, including: national security; the prevention of deceptive practices; protection of human health or safety, animal or plant life or health, or the environment.[556] Thus, the protection of human, animal or plant life or health and of the environment could be relevant to an energy-efficiency or emission-reduction regulation.

The TBT Agreement also provides a number of guidelines and tests to avoid unnecessary obstacles to trade. For instance, a technical regulation would be considered an "unnecessary" obstacle to trade if it was found to be more trade-restrictive than necessary to fulfil a legitimate objective.[557] Similarly, conformity assessment procedures should not be stricter than is necessary to give confidence that products conform with technical regulations and standards.[558] Although the provisions of the TBT Agreement mentioned in this subsection have never been tested in the Dispute Settlement Body, it may be relevant to refer to the panels' and the Appellate Body's interpretation of the word "necessary" in the context of GATT Article XX.[559]

The non-discrimination principle has also not been tested in the context of the TBT Agreement. However, it may be interesting to note an unadopted GATT panel report; the *United States – Automobiles* case. In this case, the panel examined three US measures on automobiles: the luxury tax on automobiles, the "gas guzzler" tax on automobiles, and the Corporate Average Fuel Economy regulation (CAFE). The luxury tax of 10 per cent was imposed on the first retail sale of vehicles over US$ 30,000 (a tax paid by customers).[560] The gas guzzler tax was an excise tax on the sale of automobiles within "model types" whose fuel economy failed to meet certain fuel-economy requirements (a tax imposed on manufacturers).[561] The CAFE regulation required a minimum average fuel economy for passenger automobiles (or light trucks) manufactured in the United States, or sold by any importer.[562] For companies that were both importers and domestic manufacturers, the average fuel economy was calculated separately for imported passenger automobiles and for those manufactured domestically.

The GATT panel found that both the luxury tax and the gas guzzler tax were consistent with the national treatment principle.[563] However, it found the CAFE regulation to be inconsistent with this principle,[564] because the separate calculations of fuel economy for the foreign vehicles discriminated against foreign cars, and because the fleet averaging requirement differentiated between imported and domestic cars on the basis of factors relating to control or ownership of producers or importers (i.e. based on origin), rather than on the basis of factors directly related to the products themselves.[565]

c) Harmonization

Energy-efficiency standards and regulations and their related conformity assessment procedures may act as a barrier to trade, in particular when they differ from country to country.[566] Differing requirements raise the cost of information, and make exporting to other markets more difficult. A solution to this obstacle is the harmonization of norms, which may be described as the adoption by several countries of common norms on the same subject, where previously each might have had its own set of requirements.[567] Harmonization is a core principle of the TBT Agreement, and the importance of international standards is enshrined in its Preamble. The TBT Agreement strongly encourages efforts by WTO members to harmonize technical regulations, standards and conformity assessment procedures.

The TBT Agreement provides for three approaches to harmonization. First, WTO members are to give positive consideration to accepting the technical regulations of other members as being equivalent to their own.[568] The TBT Agreement urges countries to recognize the equivalence of the norms set by their trading partners, even when they differ from their own, provided they achieve the same final objective. Second, the Agreement encourages mutual recognition of conformity assessment results.[569] Countries are encouraged to recognize the procedures that their trading partners use to assess compliance with regulations if they are convinced of the reliability and competence of their conformity assessment institutions.

Third, and most importantly, WTO members are urged to use international standards as a basis for their own technical regulations, standards and conformity assessment procedures,[570] except when such international standards would be an ineffective or inappropriate means for the fulfilment of the legitimate objectives pursued.[571] Moreover, in order to encourage members to base their regulations on international standards, the Agreement contains a "rebuttable presumption" that any technical regulation which is prepared in accordance with (and not only "based on") relevant international standards will not be considered an unnecessary obstacle to trade.[572] In this context, the TBT Agreement also provides that members, within the limits of their resources, must play a full part in the preparation of international standards, with a view to harmonizing technical regulations.[573]

Although a list of international standardizing bodies for the purposes of the TBT Agreement does not exist, guidance on the identification of these bodies may be found in a decision adopted in 2000 at the Second Triennial Review by the TBT Committee on principles for the development of international standards, guides and recommendations.[574]

d) The TBT Committee and transparency requirements

Transparency is a core principle of the WTO and features in many WTO agreements, including the TBT Agreement. It is an important tool to ensure that trade flows as smoothly, predictably and openly as possible. In the TBT Agreement, WTO members are required to share information on any draft technical regulations and conformity assessment procedures that may have an impact on trade: such measures must be notified to other members.[575] Notifications can make an important contribution towards avoiding unnecessary obstacles to trade and can provide members with the opportunity to influence proposed regulations of other members.[576]

Moreover, a Committee on Technical Barriers to Trade,[577] composed of representatives from each WTO member, meets three to four times a year. An official record of the discussions held during formal meetings is prepared, and is made available to the public. About half of each meeting of the TBT Committee is dedicated to the discussion of specific trade concerns that members may have in relation to technical regulations or conformity assessment procedures which have been proposed or adopted by other members. The Committee therefore provides an important forum to discuss technical requirements to mitigate climate change. Such concerns are often based on a notification of a technical regulation or conformity assessment. Usually, before raising a specific trade concern in the TBT Committee, members go through several stages of information exchange and consultation.

Most trade concerns are in relation to the implementation of transparency procedures and claims that certain measures adopted by WTO members are more trade-restrictive than necessary. In recent years, a number of measures related to the reduction of emissions of certain equipment or the improvement of energy efficiency of electrical appliances have been discussed in the TBT Committee and/or notified to other members.

For instance, in 2007 Brazil notified a draft technical regulation which sets down minimum energy performance standards for non-electric water heaters;[578] in 2008, the European Communities notified a draft regulation that established CO_2 emission performance standards for new passenger cars;[579] Singapore notified a regulation that stipulates that motor vehicles must be registered and labelled to provide information on their levels of fuel consumption and CO_2 emissions;[580] and China notified several technical regulations related to the energy efficiency and energy conservation of electrical storage water heaters, copy machines and computer monitors.[581]

e) Technical assistance provisions

The TBT Agreement contains detailed provisions on technical assistance to developing countries and least-developed countries.[582] These provisions are mandatory but most of them are accompanied by one or more qualifications, such as "take such reasonable measures as may be available to them" or "on mutually agreed terms and conditions". These provisions combine two sorts of obligations: obligations to advise other members, especially developing-country members, on certain issues, and obligations to provide them with technical assistance.

Members have an obligation, if so requested, to advise developing-country members and provide them with technical assistance, on mutually agreed terms and conditions, regarding the establishment of national standardizing bodies, and participation in international standardizing bodies; the establishment of conformity assessment bodies; the steps that should be taken by developing countries' producers if they wish to have access to systems for conformity assessment operated by governmental or non-governmental bodies within the territory of a developed-country member; and the establishment of the institutions and legal framework which would enable developing-country members to fulfil the obligations of membership or participation in international or regional systems for conformity assessment.[583] Some members regularly inform the Committee of their technical assistance programmes in the TBT field.[584]

Moreover, WTO members have, in relation to the activities of bodies within their territories, the obligation to encourage their national standardizing bodies to advise developing-country members and provide them with technical assistance regarding the establishment of national standardizing bodies, and participation in international standardizing bodies. WTO members are also obliged to arrange for the regulatory bodies within their territories to advise developing-country members and to grant them technical assistance regarding the establishment of regulatory bodies, or conformity assessment bodies, and regarding the methods by which their technical regulations can best be met. Another obligation of WTO members is to encourage bodies within their territories which are members or participants of international or regional systems for conformity assessment to advise developing-country members, and to consider requests for technical assistance from them regarding the establishment of the institutions which would enable the relevant bodies within their territories to fulfil the obligations of membership or participation.

Endnotes

1 Charles D. Kolstad defines an externality as follows: "An *externality* exists when the consumption or production choices of one person or firm enters the utility or production function of another entity without that entity's permission or compensation". Kolstad (2000), p. 91. In other words, negative externalities arise when an action by an individual or group produces harmful effects on others.

2 According to Alan V. Deardorff, a market imperfection is "[a] ny departure from the ideal benchmark of perfect competition, due to externalities, taxes, market power, etc." Deardorff (2006), p. 172.

3 See Section IV.A.2.

4 Carbon tax is shorthand for carbon dioxide tax or CO_2 tax.

5 See United Nations (1997); Zhang and Baranzini (2004), p. 508.

6 Fossil fuels contain carbon atoms, which are converted to CO_2 when they are burned. Burning 1 tonne of carbon creates 3.67 tonnes of CO_2.

7 The United States Environmental Protection Agency (EPA) reports the following carbon content coefficients (in Tera Grams Carbon/ Quadrillion British thermal units) for 2005: coal (26), natural gas (14), crude oil (20). For more details see US Environmental Protection Agency (2007), Table A-23.

8 See for instance, Estonia's CO_2 levy. European Environment Agency (2005), p. 54 and Estonia (2005), *Fourth National Communication under the UNFCCC*, 156 p., at pp. 86-87.

9 Baron (1997), p. 28; OECD (2001c), p. 25.

10 OECD (2001c), p. 72.

11 In Finland, the carbon tax is levied on the carbon content of fuels used for heating and transportation. See the website of Finland's Ministry of the Environment on *Environmentally related energy taxation in Finland* available at www.ymparisto.fi/default.asp?node=11865&lan=en.

12 Since 1991, in Sweden, the CO_2 tax is levied on petrol, oil, liquefied petroleum gas, natural gas, coal and coke, and in fossil carbon in household refuse; see Swedish Tax Agency (2007), *Facts about Swedish Excise duties*, 7 p. Since 1991 in Norway, the CO_2 tax is levied on mineral oil, petrol and production of oil and natural gas on the continental shelf; see website of Norway's Ministry of Finance on *Existing green taxes*, at www.regjeringen.no. Since 1992, in Denmark, the CO_2 tax is levied on coal, oil, natural gas and electricity. See Skatteministeriet (2007), *Tax in Denmark 2007*. Slovenia has had a carbon tax since 1997. See Slovenia (2006), *Fourth National Communication under UNFCCC*, 149 p., at p. 73. Since 1999, in Italy, the CO_2 tax is imposed on coal, petroleum coke and "Orimulsion" used in combustion plants, as well as on coal and mineral oils used for electricity production. See Newman (2005), p. 13. See Article 8.7 of the Italian regulation of 23 December 1998. Since 2000 in Estonia, the CO_2 levy is imposed only on the emissions of large combustion plants (thermal input exceeding 50 MW) and is based on measured emissions. See European Environment Agency (2005), p. 54 and Estonia (2005), *Fourth National Communication under the UNFCCC*, 156 p., pp. 86-87. Since 2008, Switzerland has had a tax on CO_2 emissions from imported heating fossil fuels (e.g. heating oil, natural gas, coal, petroleum coke). See Swiss Federal Customs Administration (2007), *Taxe sur le CO_2 sur les combustibles. Que faut-il savoir à ce sujet?*

13 For instance, in New Zealand an extensive discussion of the potential contribution of a carbon tax to climate change mitigation took place in 2002-2005. See e.g. "New Zealand Announces Trading Scheme For Carbon Emissions; Abandons Carbon Tax" (2007), *International Environment Reporter, BNA* 30:20, p. 769. A proposal for a carbon tax has also been discussed in Japan since 2003 but has not yet been adopted. See e.g. "Japan's Ruling Party to Discuss Carbon Tax" (2006), *International Environment Reporter, BNA* 29:7, p. 247.

14 "Climate Change: Canada's Quebec Province Plans Carbon Tax" (2007), *International Environment Reporter, BNA* 30:12, p. 470.

15 Ministry of Small Business and Revenue (2008), *British Columbia Carbon Tax Update, Carbon Tax Act*, Notice 2008-023, 11 p.

16 See Engineering Division Bay Area Air Quality Management District (2008), *Proposed Amendments to BAAQMD Regulation 3: Fees*, Staff Report. Bay Area Air Quality Management District (2008), "Air District Implements Greenhouse Gas Fee", *News*.

17 Bundesamt für Energie Schweiz (2007), pp. 39-41.

18 Usually, renewable sources of energy are exempted. See Zhang and Baranzini (2004), p. 508.

19 OECD (2001c), pp. 116-117.

20 Zhang and Baranzini (2004), p. 508.

21 See the website of Finland's Ministry of the Environment on *Environmentally related energy taxation in Finland* at www.ymparisto.fi.

22 Swedish Tax Agency (2007), *Facts about Swedish Excise duties*, 7 p.

23 See also The Netherlands' Regulatory Energy Tax that applies on fossil energy (gas, electricity and certain mineral oils) and was introduced in 1996 for households and medium-small enterprises. This is a tax on energy, not based on carbon content, but renewable energy is exempted. See IEA Climate Change database (2008, last update).

24 Department for Environment, Food and Rural Affairs (DEFRA) (2001), *United Kingdom's Third National Communication under the UNFCCC*, 121 p., at pp. 29-30, and DEFRA website at www.defra.gov.uk.

25 On the website of the German Finance Ministry on *Oekologische Steuerreform* at www.bundesfinanzministerium.de. See also Bundesamt für Energie Schweiz (2007), pp. 39, 65-66, 94.

26 Bundesministerium für Umwelt, Naturschutz und Reaktorsicherheit (2004), *The ecological tax reform: introduction, continuation and development into an ecological fiscal reform*, 20 p., at pp. 1, 3.

27 Ministère français de l'écologie et du développement durable (2006), *Quatrième communication nationale à la Convention cadre des Nations unies sur les changements climatiques*, 71 p., at p. 14.

28 Norwegian Ministry of the Environment (2005), *Norway's fourth national communication under the Framework Convention on Climate Change*, 92 p., at p. 33.

29 Danish Ministry of the Environment (2005), *Denmark's Fourth National Communication on Climate Change under the United Nations Framework Convention on Climate Change*, 404 p., at p. 108.

30 "New Zealand to Tax Livestock Farmers To Fund Greenhouse Gas Emissions Research" (2003), *International Environment Reporter, BNA* 26, p. 699.

31 See e.g. IEA (2001), p. 25; OECD-IEA (1997), p. 3; UNEP-UNCTAD (2002), p. 5; and IMF (2008), p. 11.

32 The marginal cost can be defined as the "increase in cost that accompanies a unit increase in output". See Deardorff (2006), p. 169.

33 This alternative to the tax approach finds its origins in the Coase Theorem suggested in 1960 by Ronald Coase, and has been applied specifically to pollution control in 1968 by John Dales in the context of waste disposal. The scheme suggested by Dales was based on the sale of property rights: the government would decide what level of pollution society was prepared to tolerate and would then offer for sale "rights to pollute". See Coase (1960), p. 42; Tietenberg (2006), p. 3; Dales (1968); and Sewell (1969), p. 386.

34 See e.g. Meidinger (1985), pp. 457-489; Tietenberg (1998), pp. 2-4; Tietenberg (2006), p. 7; UNEP-UNCTAD (2002), p. 4.

35 Emission trading schemes have also been applied to control lead in gasoline and ozone-depleting chemicals, in accordance with the Montreal Protocol. See Tietenberg (1998), pp. 15-20. Tietenberg (2002), p. 275.

36 Fossil fuel-burning utilities are endowed with a certain number of allowances each giving the right to emit 1 tonne of SO_2. In Phase I (1995-1999) of the programme, the 261 most polluting electric power-generating units were covered by this system. In Phase II (starting in 2000) most fossil fuel-fired electric generating units with a minimum capacity were covered by the system. See e.g. Tietenberg (1998) pp. 7-8; See also *Acid Rain program SO_2 allowances fact sheet* on the website of the Environmental Protection Agency at www.epa.gov; Arimura (2002), p. 271.

37 See UNFCCC website at http://unfccc.int.

38 European Commission (2008), Question 1.

39 See Sigurd Lauge Pedersen (2006), *Danish Domestic CO_2 Cap & Trade Scheme*, 7 p., at pp. 1 and 7.

40 For the period 2008-2012, the scope of the scheme has been widened in order to adapt it to the EU-ETS. See e.g. Norwegian Ministry of the Environment (2008), *Norwegian National Allocation Plan for the Emissions Trading System in 2008-2012*, 34 p.

41 See the website of Switzerland's emission trading at www.bafu.admin.ch.

42 New Zealand's scheme is currently under parliamentary review. See Goldb, E. (2009), "New Zealand: Government to Review Emissions Trading, Streamline Law on Resource Management", *International Environmental Reporter* 32:45.

43 See website of the Australian Department of Climate Change at www.climatechange.gov.au. See also Griffin, M. (2009), "Climate Change: Australian Lower House Passes Legislation For Cap-and-Trade; Senate Showdown Looms", *International Environmental Reporter* 32:516.

44 Canada (2008), 8 p. However, since the plan was announced, some Canadian provinces have introduced their own carbon taxes or have joined United States emission trading schemes (British Columbia, Ontario, Manitoba and Quebec have joined the Western Climate Initiative). See Szabo, M. (2008), "Problems plague Canada's emissions trading plans", *Reuters*, 8 May 2008.

45 See US Committee on Energy and Commerce (2007). See also Office of Management and Budget (2009), *A New Era of Responsibility. Renewing America's Promise*, 134 p., at p. 100, available at www.whitehouse.gov.

46 Eligible installations joined the EU-ETS in 2007. ENVIROS Consulting Limited (2006), *Appraisal of Years 1-4 of UK Emissions Trading Scheme*, Department for Environment, Food and Rural Affairs, p. 4.

47 See "Subsidies-Driven Voluntary Emissions Trading Scheme, Japan" in IEA Climate Change database (2008, last update). See also Reinaud and Philibert (2007), p. 11.

48 See the website of the Chicago Climate Exchange at www.chicagoclimatex.com. See also Capoor and Ambrosi (2007), pp. 18-19.

49 See www.chicagoclimatex.com.

50 At the end of 2005, the scheme was extended to 2020 and beyond. See the website of the Greenhouse Gas Abatement Scheme at www.greenhousegas.nsw.gov.au.

51 Young, S. (2008), "ARB says yes to climate action plan. Plan will slash greenhouse gases, fight global warming and provide economic stimulus for jobs and clean energy future", *News Release*, 08-102, 11 December 2008.

52 The seven states of the United States are the following: Arizona, California, Montana, New Mexico, Oregon, Utah and Washington. The four Canadian provinces are British Columbia, Manitoba, Ontario and Quebec.

53 See the website of the Western Climate Initiative at www.westernclimateinitiative.org.

54 Connecticut, Delaware, Maine, Massachusetts, New Hampshire, New Jersey, Rhode Island, Vermont, Maryland and Pennsylvania.

55 This is a mandatory programme that covers CO_2 emissions from fossil fuel-fired electricity generating units. See the website of the Regional Greenhouse Gas Initiative at www.rggi.org.

56 See in particular Reinaud and Philibert (2007). See also Kollmuss, Zink and Polycarp (2008); Boom and Nentjes (2003), pp. 45-67.

57 Reinaud and Philibert (2007), p. 21.

58 Aulisi et al. (2005), p. 4.

59 European Environment Agency (2005), pp. 16-17.

60 US Environmental Protection Agency (2003), p. 2.9.

61 See the website of the New South Wales Greenhouse Gas Abatement Scheme at www.greenhousegas.nsw.gov.au.

62 Canada (2007), p. 14.

63 Convery (2003), p. 7; US Environmental Protection Agency (2003), p. 2.9. European Environment Agency (2005), p. 19.

64 Fischer (2003), p. 2.

65 See e.g. European Environment Agency (2005), p. 20. Baron and Bygrave (2002), p. 21.

66 European Commission (2008), Question 19. US Committee on Energy and Commerce (2007), at p. 9.

67 European Parliament (2008a), Paragraph 27 concerning Articles 27 and 28. European Commission (2008), Question 7.

68 Canada (2008), p. 8.

69 Australia (2008), Vol. I, p. 6.8.

70 See California Energy Commission & California Public Utilities Commission (2008), *Final Opinion and Recommendations on Greenhouse Gas Regulatory Strategies*, 297 p., pp. 225-226.

71 European Commission (2008), Question 18. Road transport and shipping remain excluded, although the latter is likely to be included at a later stage. Agriculture and forestry are also left out due to the difficulties related to measuring emissions from these sectors with accuracy. European Parliament (2008a), Recital 3.

72 Canada (2007), p. iv.

73 For a list of the six main greenhouse gases, see Part I.

74 European Parliament (2008a), Annex 1.

75 A certificate represents one tonne of carbon dioxide equivalent (tCO_2-eq) of greenhouse gas emissions. See GGAS (2007), *Scheme Glossary*, 5 p., at p. 1. In the Chicago Climate Exchange, each Carbon Financial Instrument contract represents 100 metric tonnes of CO_2 equivalent. See website of the Chicago Climate Exchange at www.chicagoclimateexchange.com.

76 Reinaud and Philibert (2007), pp. 21-27. Boom and Nentjes (2003), pp. 45-67.

77 See Peterson (2003), p. 9; Reinaud and Philibert (2007); Pizer (2007), p. 73; and Boom and Nentjes (2003), p. 48.

78 Reinaud and Philibert (2007), p. 22.

79 Boom and Nentjes (2003), pp. 50-55.

80 Reinaud and Philibert (2007).

81 US Committee on Energy and Commerce (2007), p. 13.

82 New entrants and closure provisions are also important elements of the distribution of allowances. See Reinaud and Philibert (2007), p. 27.

83 European Environment Agency (2005), pp. 21-22. Reinaud and Philibert (2007), pp. 24-25. Hourcade et al. (2007), p. 15.

84 United States Environmental Protection Agency (2003), p. 3.16.

85 I.e. unexpected gain for high emitters, see Section IV.A.1.b) (iii).

86 United States Environmental Protection Agency (2003), p. 3.17. European Environment Agency (2005), p. 21. See also European Commission (2008), p. 4.

87 For more information on competitiveness concerns, see Section IV.A.2.a).

88 See the website of the Swiss Federal Office of the Environment at http://www.bafu.admin.ch/.

89 European Parliament (2008a), Paragraph 10 concerning Article 10. European Commission (2008), Question 5.

90 Australia (2008), Vol. II, pp. 12.44.

91 Holt et al. (2007), p. 5.

92 Liquidity may be defined as "[t]he capacity to turn assets into cash, or the amount of assets in a portfolio that have that capacity". Deardorff (2006), p. 164.

93 See e.g. Stern (2006), p. 480. European Commission (2008), Question 24. Volatility may be defined as "[t]he extent to which an economic variable, such as a price or an exchange rate, moves up and down over time". Deardorff (2006), p. 289.

94 Ellis and Tirpak (2006), p. 8.

95 See European Parliament (2008a), Paragraph 26 concerning Article 25.

96 Reinaud and Philibert (2007), p. 29.

97 Ellis and Tirpak (2006), p. 8.

98 Clean Air-Cool Planet (2006), *A Consumers' Guide to Retail Carbon Offset Providers*, 26 p., at p. VII. See also UNEP (2002), p. 10.

99 For a detailed explanation of Kyoto's flexibility mechanisms, see Section III.1.

100 European Commission (2008), Question 20.

101 See the website of Switzerland's emission trading at www.bafu.admin.ch.

102 See Australia (2008), Vol. I, pp. 11.10-11.15.

103 Reinaud and Philibert (2007), p. 29.

104 Regional Greenhouse Gas Initiative (2007), *Overview of RGGI CO_2 Budget Trading Program*, 12 p., at p. 9.

105 See Greenhouse Gas Reduction Scheme (2008), *Introduction to the Greenhouse Gas Reduction Scheme*, 20 p., at p. 7.

106 European Commission (2008), Question 22.

107 Reinaud and Philibert (2007), p. 31. Philibert and Reinaud (2004), p. 34.

108 Philibert and Reinaud (2004), p. 26. European Environment Agency (2005), p. 20.

109 Convery (2003), p. 8.

110 European Commission (2008), Question 23.

111 Ellis and Tirpak (2006), pp. 11-13, Tables 1 and 2.

112 Baron and Bygrave (2002), p. 29. Philibert and Reinaud (2004), p. 26. European Environment Agency (2005), p. 20.

113 Australia (2008), Vol. I, pp. 8.16-8.17.

114 Philibert and Reinaud (2004), p. 26.

115 See e.g. Peterson (2003), p. 10.

116 Boemare and Quirion (2002), p. 13.

117 See *Directive 2003/87/EC of the European Parliament and of the Council of 13 October 2003, establishing a scheme for greenhouse gas emission allowance trading within the Community and amending Council Directive 96/61/EC*, Article 16 on Penalties.

118 See European Parliament (2008a), Paragraph 19 concerning Article 16, paragraph 4.

119 Baranzini, Goldemberg and Speck (2000), p. 396. See also Rich (2004), p. 3; and Stern (2006), pp. 318-319.

120 Zhang and Baranzini (2004), p. 508. OECD (2001c), p. 25. Stern (2006), p. 308. OECD (2008b), p. 434.

121 European Environment Agency (2005), p. 45 and OECD (2001c), p. 22.

122 The marginal damage cost is the amount of harm done by adding one more unit of emissions to the current stock of greenhouse gases in the atmosphere (see Nordhaus (1993)).

123 European Environment Agency (2005), p. 46.

124 See Baumol (1972), pp. 307-322; and Baumol and Oates (1971), pp. 42-54.

125 Eurostat (2003), p. 24.

126 On recycling of carbon tax revenues, see Baranzini, Goldemberg and Speck (2000), pp. 399-400, 404 and OECD (2001c), pp. 25-27. On recycling of auctioning revenues, see European Environment Agency (2005), p. 21; Dinan (2007), p. 4; and Bohm (2003), p. 3.

127 Baranzini, Goldemberg and Speck (2000), at p. 400. Stern (2006), p. 319. IPCC (2007e), p. 756. For empirical evidence on the double dividend, see for example OECD (2001c), pp. 37-39.

128 See Stern (2006), p. 319.

129 Aldy, Baron and Tubiana (2003), p. 100. OECD (2001c), p. 26; Stern (2006), p. 319.

130 Bundesamt für Energie Schweiz (2007), pp. 39-40. Baranzini, Goldemberg and Speck (2000), p. 399. Alakangas, E. (2002), *Renewable Energy Source in Finland*, OPET Report 9.

131 Baranzini, Goldemberg and Speck (2000), p. 399. World Bank (2008b), Annex 2 at p. 110.

132 Ministry of Sustainable Development (2005), *Sweden's Fourth National Communication under the UNFCCC*, 149 p., at p. 39.

133 Bundesamt für Energie Schweiz (2007), pp. 39-40.

134 European Parliament (2008a), Article 10, p. 95.

135 Agnolucci (2004), p. 50.

136 Marjukka Hiltunen (2004), *Economic environmental policy instruments in Finland*, Helsinki, Finnish environment institute, 35 p., at p. 24. See also OECD (2001c), p. 105.

137 See e.g. OECD (2001c), p. 105.

138 Naturvårdsverket (1995), Utvärdering av koldioxidskatten – har utsläppen av koldioxid minskat? Papport number 4512, Stockholm, in Swedish, quoted in OECD (2001c), p. 105.

139 Larsen and Nesbakken (1997), *Environmental and Resource Economics*, Vol. 9(3), pp. 275-290, quoted in OECD (2001c), p. 105.

140 United States Environmental Protection Agency (2003), p. 1.2.

141 Betz and Stato (2006), p. 354. See also, Ellerman and Joskow (2008); Åhman (2007); Stefano (2008).

142 Ellerman and Joskow (2008), pp. iii, 35.

143 See for example Missfeldt and Hauff (2004), pp. 115-146.

144 United States Environmental Protection Agency (2003), p. 2.5.

145 Pizer (1999), p. 6. United States Environmental Protection Agency (2003), pp. 2.5-2.6.

146 Pizer (1999), p. 6. Philibert (2006b), pp. 8, 16. Kolstad (2000), p. 164.

147 See Philibert (2006b), pp. 21-22.

148 Stern (2006), pp. 470-471.

149 Houser et al. (2008), p. 29.

150 It is more meaningful to use a definition of competitiveness that applies to firms or sectors rather than countries. See *inter alia* Cosbey and Tarasosfky (2007), pp. 3-4; Krugman (1994); Sinner (2002), pp. 3-8; Baron and ECON-Energy (1997), p. 15; and Reinaud (2008b), p. 17.

151 Klepper and Peterson (2003), p. 3. Reinaud (2008b), p. 17.

152 Ekins and Barker (2002), p. 99. Hourcade et al. (2007), p. 13.

153 The direct carbon costs of an emissions trading scheme may be defined as the sum of abatement costs and CO_2 allowance costs. Indirect carbon costs include: increase in the price of other products covered by the carbon constraint; additional costs following higher risks perceived by investors; increase in the value of low-carbon energy sources. See Reinaud (2008b), pp. 19-21.

154 See e.g. OECD (2006b), p. 69. Baron, with Reinaud, Genasci and Philibert (2007), p. 17. Reinaud (2008a), p. 9. Reinaud (2005), p. 81. Sinner (2002), p. 10. Zhang and Baranzini (2004), p. 513. Morgenstern et al. (2007), p. 97. Parker (2008), pp. 5-16. Carbon Trust (2004), p. 6. Demailly and Quirion (2006), p. 111. Hourcade et al. (2007), p. 16.

155 Reinaud (2008b), pp. 19-21, 43-54.

156 Parker (2008), p. 10. Carbon Trust (2004), p. 6.

157 Parker (2008), p. 10.

158 Carbon Trust (2004), p. 6. Reinaud (2008b), p. 46.

159 Reinaud (2008b), p. 46.

160 See for example: Jaffe et al. (1995), p. 158; Harris, Kónya and Mátyás (2002); Xu (2000); Cole and Elliott (2003b), pp. 1167-1168; Hoerner and Müller (1996), p. 14; and OECD (2006b), pp. 10-11. Reinaud (2008b), pp. 6, 29, 56. Reinaud (2005). Some other studies have found however significant effects of environmental regulation on trade flows. See for instance Ederington and Minier (2003).

161 Reinaud (2008b), p. 39. See also Reinaud (2005).

162 Reinaud (2008b), p. 67. European Commission (2008).

163 Carbon leakage is calculated by dividing the increase in CO_2 emissions outside the region affected by the climate protection policy by the reduction in emissions inside that region. See IPCC (2007e), p. 665.

164 Reinaud (2008b), p. 27.

165 European Parliament (2008a), Article 10, pp. 100-101. Australia (2008),Vol. II, p. 12-2.

166 European Parliament (2008a), Paragraph 11 concerning Articles 10a, 10b and 10c.

167 Sinner (2002), pp. 9, 15.

168 The Working Party was established by the Council on 28 March 1968 to examine the provisions of the GATT relevant to border tax adjustments, the practices of contracting parties in relation to such adjustments and the possible effects of such adjustments on international trade. In light of this examination, the Working Party had to consider any proposals and suggestions that had been put forward and report its findings and conclusions on these matters to the Council or to the CONTRACTING PARTIES. See GATT Working Party (1970), para. 1.

169 It reads as follows: "Any fiscal measures which put into effect, in whole or in part, the destination principle (i.e. which enable exported products to be relieved of some or all of the tax charged in the exporting country in respect of similar domestic products sold to consumers on the home market and which enable imports sold to consumers to be charged with some or all of the tax charged in the importing country in respect of similar domestic products)". GATT Working Party (1970), para. 4.

170 Demaret and Stewardson date the use of BTAs back to the 18th century. Demaret and Stewardson (1994), p. 7. Hoerner and Müller (1996), p. 20. Goh (2004), p. 399.

171 See Demaret and Stewardson (1994), p. 6. The destination principle, according to which goods are taxed in the country of consumption, is to be distinguished from the origin principle, whereby the products are taxed in the country of production. Under the origin principle, there would be no need for border tax adjustment, since all products would be taxed at their point of origin. WTO (1997), para. 28.

172 Kraemer, Hinterberger and Tarasofsky (2007), p. 42. Bierman et al. (2003), pp. 30-31. Dröge et al. (2004), p. 175. Zhang and Baranzini (2004), p. 514. Goh (2004), p. 398.

173 Biermann and Brohm (2005b), p. 292.

174 Baron (1997), p. 83. OECD (2006b), p. 92.

175 For instance, in the context of the discussion of future climate change legislation in the United States, a White Paper prepared by the Committee on Energy and Commerce has mentioned such possible approaches. US Committee on Energy and Commerce (2008).

176 US Committee on Energy and Commerce (2008), p. 9. Janzen (2008), p. 23. Genasci (2008), p. 41. Saddler, Muller and Cuevas (2006), p. 46. Pauwelyn (2007), p. 22.

177 Charnovitz (2003), p. 157.

178 See for instance, Bhagwati and Mavroidis (2007), p. 301. Stiglitz (2007); Stiglitz (2006), p. 2.

179 Stiglitz (2006), p. 2. Zhang (1998), pp. 233-234. Doelle (2004), p. 101. Pauwelyn (2007), pp. 13-16.

180 Stiglitz (2007), pp. 177, 185.

181 Pauwelyn (2007), pp. 13-16; Bhagwati and Mavroidis (2007), p. 302.

182 Reuters (2007), *France's Sarkozy seeks EU carbon tax, truck tax*, 25 October 2007. Sarkozy, N. (2007), *Presentation of the Grenelle Environment Forum conclusions speech by M. Nicolas Sarkozy, President of the Republic*, 2 November 2007.

183 *Le Grenelle de l'Environnement. Promouvoir des modes de développement écologiques favorables à la compétitivité. Synthèse Rapport Groupe 6*, 2007, 43 p., at p. 8.

184 Demaret and Stewardson (1994), p. 63. Cosbey (2007), p. 16.

185 Demaret and Stewardson (1994), p. 32. Zhang (1998), pp. 231-232. Houser et al. (2008), p. 32.

186 Demaret and Stewardson (1994), p. 32. Voigt (2008), pp. 57-58. Reinaud (2008b), p. 92. Houser et. al. (2008), pp. 33-34.

187 Demaret and Stewardson (1994), pp. 32-33. Genasci (2008), p. 35.

188 Demaret and Stewardson (1994), p. 33. Zhang and Assunção (2004), p. 380. Ismer and Neuhoff (2007), p. 14.

189 Demaret and Stewardson (1994), p. 33. Zhang (1998), p. 232. See also *Superfund* case, paras. 2.4-2.6. 5.2.9. Ismer and Neuhoff (2007).

190 Ismer and Neuhoff (2007), p. 14.

191 *Superfund* case, paras. 5.2.4, 5.2.7 and 5.2.10.

192 *Superfund* case, paras. 2.6 and 5.2.9. See also Cendra (2006), p. 143.

193 *Excise duty on electricity - Rates of duty varying according to the method of producing electricity of domestic origin - Flat rate for imported electricity*, Judgment of the Court of 2 April 1998, Case C-213/96.

194 Krämer (2002), pp. 146-147. Snape and de Souza (2006), p. 297.

195 Snape and de Souza (2006), p. 297.

196 Ismer and Neuhoff (2007), pp. 4 and 16. Cendra (2006), p. 143.

197 Ismer and Neuhoff (2007), pp. 10, 16.

198 Demaret and Stewardson (1994), p. 33; Biermann and Brohm (2005a), p. 255.

199 *Superfund* case, para. 2.6.

200 *Superfund* case, paras. 5.2.9-10.

201 Saddler, Muller and Cuevas (2006), p. 45.

202 Genasci (2008), pp. 33, 39.

203 Pauwelyn (2007), p. 22; Muller and Hoerner (1997), pp. 5-6.

204 Charnovitz (2003), p. 152. Werksman (1999), p. 257.

205 See e.g. Cosbey (2008); Genasci (2008); Goh (2004); Ismer and Neuhoff (2007); Meyer-Ohlendorf and Gerstetter (2009); Pauwelyn (2007); Sindico (2008); Werksman (1999).

206 Footnote 58 to Annex I, "Illustrative List of Export Subsidies" to the SCM Agreement provides useful definitions that apply in the context of this agreement: "direct taxes" are "taxes on wages, profits, interests, rents, royalties, and all other forms of income, and taxes on the ownership of real property"; and "indirect taxes" are "sales, excise, turnover, value added, franchise, stamp, transfer, inventory and equipment taxes, border taxes and all taxes other than direct taxes and import charges".

207 "[T]here was convergence of views to the effect that taxes directly levied on products [i.e. indirect taxes] were eligible for tax adjustment. Examples of such taxes comprised specific excise duties, sales taxes and cascade taxes and the tax on value added. It was agreed that the TVA, regardless of its technical construction (fractioned collection), was equivalent in this respect to a tax levied directly – a retail or sales tax. Furthermore, the Working Party concluded that there was convergence of views to the effect that certain taxes that were not directly levied on products [i.e. direct taxes] were not eligible for tax adjustment. Examples of such taxes comprised social security charges whether on employers or employees and payroll taxes." GATT Working Party (1970), para. 14. See also WTO (1997), paras. 31 and 33.

208 The United States Domestic International Sales Corporation (DISC) legislation allowed certain types of corporations to be partially exempt from federal income tax on their export earnings. The panel considered that the DISC legislation should be regarded as an export subsidy and therefore not as a BTA on exports. The GATT Panel thereby confirmed that direct taxes such as income tax could not be adjusted. GATT Panel, *US – DISC*, paras. 12, 69.

209 In relation to GATT Article XVI:4 and the Declaration of 19 November 1960 giving effect to the provisions of that paragraph.

210 See e.g. Demaret and Stewardson (1994), p. 12; WTO (1997), para. 35; Cendra (2006), p. 138; Biermann and Brohm (2005b), p. 293.

211 On the difference between a customs duty (pursuant to Article II.1.b) and an internal charge (pursuant to Article III.2) see *China – Measures affecting imports of automobile parts*. The Panel, upheld by the Appellate Body, found that "if the obligation to pay a charge does not accrue based on the product at the moment of its importation, it cannot be an "ordinary customs duty" within the meaning of Article II:1(b), first sentence of the GATT 1994: it is, instead, an "internal charge" under Article III:2 of the GATT 1994, which obligation to pay accrues based on internal factors". Appellate Body, *China – Auto Parts*, para. 131.

212 Article II.2(a) should be read together with the preamble to Ad Note Article III, which reads as follows: "Any internal tax (...) which applies to an imported product and to the like domestic product and is collected or enforced in the case of the imported product at the time or point of importation, is nevertheless to be regarded as an internal tax (...) and is accordingly subject to the provisions of Article III".

213 Pauwelyn (2007), p. 21. Cendra (2006), pp. 135-136.

214 For a discussion on "likeness", see Subsection IV.A.3(a).

215 See WTO (1997). Pitschas (1995), p. 493. Dröge et al. (2004), p. 177. Biermann and Brohm (2005b), p. 293.

216 Cendra (2006), p. 141.

217 The drafters of the GATT explained the word "equivalent" used in this provision with the following example: "If a charge is imposed on perfume because it contains alcohol, the charge to be imposed must take into consideration the value of the alcohol and not the value of the perfume, that is to say the value of the content and not the value of the whole". E/PC/T/TAC/PV/26, page 21, quoted in the *Superfund* case, para. 5.2.7. In the *India – Additional Duties* case, the Appellate Body found that the term "equivalent" calls for a comparative assessment that is both qualitative and quantitative in nature; it also found that the requirement of consistency with Article III:2 must be read together with, and imparts meaning to, the requirement that a charge and internal tax be "equivalent" and that whether a charge is imposed "in excess of" a corresponding internal tax (pursuant to Article III:2) is an integral part of the analysis in determining whether the charge is justified under Article II:2(a). Appellate Body, *India – Additional Import Duties*, paras. 175 and 180.

218 Demaret and Stewardson (1994), pp. 8, 16. Biermann and Brohm (2005b), p. 293. In *Canada – Periodicals*, the Appellate Body confirmed that Article III.2 uses the words "directly or indirectly" in relation to the application of a tax to both imported and like domestic products. Appellate Body, *Canada – Periodicals*, p. 464.

219 Demaret and Stewardson (1994), p. 59.

220 Demaret and Stewardson (1994), p. 18. Pauwelyn (2007), p. 20. Biermann and Brohm (2005b), p. 293.

221 Pursuant to the same line of argument, "directly or indirectly" would relate more to the *manner of application of the tax* to the like imported and domestic products (either directly or indirectly), as opposed to the nature of the tax itself. The Report of the Panel in the GATT case on *Japan – Alcoholic Beverages I* has also been referred to in this respect. The GATT Panel found that the wording "directly or indirectly" implied that, in assessing whether there is tax discrimination, account is to be taken not only of the tax rate "but also of the *taxation methods* (e.g. different kinds of internal taxes, direct taxation of the finished product or indirect taxation by taxing the raw materials used in the product during the various stages of its production) and of the rules for the tax collection (e.g. basis of assessment)" (emphasis added). GATT Panel, *Japan – Alcoholic Beverages I*, para. 5.8. See also Panel Report, *Argentina – Hides and Leather*, para. 11.183. See also Goh (2004), pp. 410, 422.

222 The Superfund Act of 1986, aimed at financing domestic programmes to clean up hazardous waste sites, imposed taxes on petroleum and on chemicals.

223 Hoerner (1998).

224 *Superfund* case, paras. 5.2.4, 5.2.7 and 5.2.10.

225 Goh (2004), pp. 412-413. Pitschas (1995), p. 491. It should be noted, however, that the issue of whether the chemical inputs were physically incorporated into the final product was not examined by the GATT Panel in this case.

226 See GATT Article VI:4. The fact that border tax adjustment on exported products is not countervailable was confirmed by the GATT Panel on *Swedish Anti-Dumping Duties*, which examined the application of Article VI:4 where an anti-dumping scheme applied to products benefiting from an export rebate of duties and charges. The GATT Panel noted that "there was no disagreement between the parties concerned regarding the obligation to take account of legitimate refund of duties and taxes". GATT Panel, *Sweden – AD Duties*, para. 16. See also WTO (1997), para. 62.

227 See GATT Interpretative Ad Note Article XVI and, since 1994, footnote 1 of the SCM Agreement.

228 GATT Working Party (1970), para. 10. It has been argued, however, that the term "applied to" has in its ordinary meaning a narrower scope of operation than the term "borne by". According to this argument, taxes "borne by" would imply that taxes on any inputs or processes on export of the final product could be adjusted. Whereas taxes "applied to" involved a more direct relationship between the tax at issue and the like imported and domestic products being compared. It should also be noted that unlike GATT Article III:2, export-related provisions do not provide for the explicit possibility of taxes being applied "directly or indirectly". See Goh (2004), p. 409; WTO (1997), para. 71; and Chaytor and Cameron (1995), p. 4.

229 GATT Working Party (1970), para. 10.

230 WTO (1997), para. 65.

231 Item (e) reads: "The full or partial exemption remission, or deferral specifically related to exports, of direct taxes [footnote omitted] or social welfare charges paid or payable by industrial or commercial enterprises. [footnote omitted]"

232 Lodefalk and Storey (2005), p. 37.

233 See e.g. Hoerner and Müller (1996), p. 33. More generally see Chaytor and Cameron (1995), p. 6.

234 See e.g. Hoerner and Müller (1996), p. 31. Lodefalk and Storey (2005), p. 38.

235 GATT Working Party (1970), para. 15.

236 However, the Working Party decided not to investigate this matter further, given the scarcity of complaints over the issue at the time of the report. GATT Working Party (1970), para. 15.

237 Hoerner and Müller (1996), p. 33. More generally see Chaytor and Cameron (1995), p. 6.

238 Item (h) reads as follows: "The exemption, remission or deferral of prior-stage cumulative indirect taxes [footnote omitted] on goods and services used in the production of exported products in excess of the exemption, remission or deferral of like prior-stage cumulative indirect taxes on goods or services used in the production of like products when sold for domestic consumption; provided, however, that prior-stage

cumulative indirect taxes may be exempted, remitted or deferred on exported products even when not exempted, remitted or deferred on like products when sold for domestic consumption, if the prior-stage cumulative indirect taxes are levied on inputs that are consumed in the production of the exported product (making normal allowance for waste) [footnote omitted] (...)."

239 PSCI taxes are multi-stage taxes levied each time goods or their components are sold (versus single-stage goods that are levied at one of the stages of supply, i.e. from manufacturing to wholesalers, from wholesalers to retailers or from retailers to consumers). Except if credit is given for the tax paid at each earlier stages, such multi-stage taxes generate multiple taxation, hence their label as "cascade taxes". On the other hand, the value-added tax (VAT) provides for a system of credits, so that at each stage, wholesalers or retailers pay tax on only the increment to value which has taken place since the last transfer and only the final consumer pays tax on the entire value of the good. See Snape and de Souza (2006), p. 11; Hoerner and Müller (1996), pp. 31, 33. Lodefalk and Storey (2005), p. 38.

240 Footnote 61 reads: "Inputs consumed in the production process are inputs physically incorporated, energy, fuels and oil used in the production process and catalysts which are consumed in the course of their use to obtain the exported product."

241 Chaytor and Cameron (1995), p. 6.

242 Pursuant to GATT Article XI, restrictions on the importation or sale of products from other WTO members are prohibited.

243 The main provisions of the Agreement on Technical Barriers to Trade are discussed in Section IV.C.

244 Hufbauer, Charnovitz and Kim (2009), p. 61. Lodefalk and Storey (2005), pp. 41-44; Petsonk (1999), p. 208.

245 Article 1.1 of the SCM Agreement defines a subsidy as a "financial contribution" by a government or public body that confers a "benefit". Article 1.2 of the SCM Agreement provides that only "specific" subsidies fall within the scope of that Agreement.

246 For more information on the key provisions of the SCM Agreement, see below Section IV.B.4.

247 Appellate Body, *US – FSC (Article 21.5 – EC)*, para. 210.

248 Appellate Body, *Korea – Various Measures on Beef*, para. 137.

249 In the GATT context, the 1970 *Working Party on Border Tax Adjustments* suggested some criteria for determining whether products are "like": "the product's end-uses in a given market; consumers' tastes and habits, which change from country to country; the product's properties, nature and quality". GATT Working Party (1970), para. 18. Tariff classification was added as a supplementary element to these criteria by the Appellate Body in Appellate Body Report, *Japan – Alcoholic Beverages II*, p. 114.

250 Appellate Body, *EC – Asbestos*, para. 101.

251 Concerning the likeness analysis in relation to internal *taxes*, the GATT Panel in the *Superfund* case noted that the reason for imposing the tax, i.e. whether the tax was levied to encourage the rational use of environmental resources or for general revenue purposes, was irrelevant. See GATT Panel Report, *US – Superfund*, paras. 5.2.3-5.2.4. Furthermore, in *Japan – Alcoholic Beverages II*, the Appellate Body also found that the policy purpose of a tax measure (the "aim" of a measure) was not relevant for the purpose of Article III:2, first sentence. See Appellate Body, *Japan – Alcoholic Beverages II*, pp. 18-19.

252 See Appellate Body, *EC – Asbestos*, para. 102; Appellate Body, *Japan – Alcoholic Beverages II*, p. 21.

253 Appellate Body, *EC – Asbestos*, para. 102.

254 See e.g. Pauwelyn (2007), at pp. 33-41; Voigt (2008), pp. 61-65; Cendra (2006), pp. 143-145; Werksman (1999), pp. 260-261.

255 See for more details on the case law related to GATT Article XX, WTO (2002).

256 Appellate Body, *US – Gasoline*, p. 22.

257 Appellate Body, *US – Shrimp*, para. 15.

258 GATT Panel, *Thailand – Cigarettes.*

259 Unadopted GATT Panel, *US – Tuna (Mexico)*; unadopted GATT Panel, *US – Tuna (EEC).*

260 Appellate Body, *EC – Asbestos.*

261 Appellate Body, *Brazil – Retreaded Tyres.*

262 GATT Panel, *US – Canadian Tuna.*

263 GATT Panel, *Canada – Herring and Salmon.*

264 *US – Tuna (Mexico)* and *US – Tuna (EEC).*

265 Appellate Body, *US – Shrimp* and Appellate Body, *US – Shrimp (Article 21.5 – Malaysia).*

266 Unadopted GATT Panel, *US – Taxes on Automobiles.*

267 Appellate Body, *US – Gasoline.*

268 Panel, *US – Gasoline*, para. 6.21.

269 Panel, *US – Gasoline*, para. 6.37.

270 See e.g. Meyer-Ohlendorf and Gerstetter (2009), p. 36. Pauwelyn (2007), p. 35.

271 Appellate Body, *US – Shrimp*, para. 133.

272 Pauwelyn (2007), p. 35.

273 Appellate Body, *Brazil – Retreaded Tyres*, para. 178.

274 Appellate Body, *Brazil – Retreaded Tyres*, para. 155.

275 Appellate Body, *Brazil – Retreaded Tyres*, paras. 156-175.

276 Appellate Body, *EC – Asbestos*, para. 172.

277 Appellate Body, *EC – Asbestos*, para. 172.

278 Appellate Body, *US – Shrimp*, para. 141.

279 Appellate Body, *US – Gasoline*, pp. 20-21.

280 Appellate Body, *US – Gasoline*, p. 18.

281 Appellate Body, *US – Gasoline*, p. 19

282 Appellate Body, *US – Shrimp*, para. 138.

283 Appellate Body, *US – Shrimp*, para. 142.

284 Appellate Body, *US – Shrimp*, para. 145.

285 Appellate Body, *Brazil – Retreaded Tyres*, para. 151.

286 Appellate Body, *US – Shrimp*, para. 158.

287 Appellate Body, *Brazil – Retreaded Tyres*, para. 215.

288 Appellate Body, *US – Gasoline*, p. 26.

289 Appellate Body, *US – Shrimp*, para. 166.

290 Appellate Body, *US – Shrimp (Article 21.5 – Malaysia)*, para. 134.

291 Appellate Body, *US – Shrimp (Article 21.5 – Malaysia)*, para. 124.

292 Appellate Body, *US – Shrimp (Article 21.5 – Malaysia)*, para. 134.

293 Appellate Body, *US – Shrimp*, paras. 161-164.

294 Appellate Body, *US – Shrimp*, para. 164.

295 Appellate Body, *US – Shrimp (Article 21.5 – Malaysia)*, para. 144.

296 Appellate Body, *US – Shrimp (Article 21.5 – Malaysia)*, para. 149.

297 Panel, *US – Shrimp (Article 21.5 – Malaysia)*, para. 5.142.

298 IPCC (2007a), Table 4.2, p. 60.

299 Stern (2006), p. 347.

300 See e.g. Stern (2006), pp. 348, 351. Fischer and G. Newell (2007), p. 2. Popp (2006), pp. 311-341. Brewer (2007), p. 3. Wellington et al. (2007), p. 10. IEA (2008a), p. 171.

301 See e.g. IEA (2007b), p. 6. Green (2006), pp. 383-384. Stern (2006), pp. 221-229. Anderson (2006), p. 8.

302 Buck and Verheyen (2001), p. 20.

303 See IEA (1999), p. 10; Saunders and Schneider (2000); Anderson and McKibbin (2000); OECD (2001a), p. 16; Morgan (2007); GTZ (2007); Moltke and McKee eds. (2004); UNEP (2008).

304 GTZ (2007), p. 3. Most recent data indicates that this trend has continued. See GTZ (2009), p. 8.

305 See Government of Pakistan (2006), *Letter of Intent, Memorandum of Economic and Financial Policies, and Technical Memorandum of Understanding*, 20 November 2008, paras. 8 and 9 of Memorandum of Economic and Financial Policies 2008/09-2009/10, at p. 5, at www.finance.gov.pk. Also see Khan, M.Z. (2008), "All fuel subsidies withdrawn", *DAWN*, 20 September 2008.

306 See GTZ (2007), p. 3. See also Nuhu-Koko, A.A. (2008), "Addicted to Fuel and Electricity Subsidies: Getting the Reform Strategies Right", *Nigerian Muse*, 19 July 2008.

307 Stern (2006), p. 350.

308 Fischer and Newell (2007), pp. 2, 21. Stern (2006), p. 365.

309 See OECD/IEA (2004).

310 See Danish Energy Agency at www.energistyrelsen.dk.

311 See the website of the Finnish Funding Agency for Technology and Innovation (Tekes), at www.tekes.fi.

312 See Renewable Energy Sources Act of 25 October 2008, BGBl I S. 2074. For an English translation of the Act, see www.bmu.de. Feed-in tariff legislation has been in place in Germany since the 1991 Electricity Feed-in Act, see IEA (2006b), p. 127.

313 Ministerio de Industria, Turismo y Comercio (2007), "Real Decreto 661/2007, de 25 de mayo, por el que se regula la actividad de producción de energía eléctrica en régimen especial", *Spanish Official Gazette.* For the photovoltaic feed-in tariff, see Ministerio de Industria, Turismo y Comercio (2008), "Real Decreto 1578/2008, de 26 de septiembre, de retribución de la actividad de producción de energía eléctrica mediante tecnología solar fotovoltaica para instalaciones posteriores a la fecha límite de mantenimiento de la retribución del Real Decreto 661/2007, de 25 de mayo, para dicha tecnología", *Spanish Official Gazette.* For a short description in English, see the IEA Climate Change database (2008, last update).

314 See The Climate Group (2007), *Low Carbon Leaders: States and Regions*, 19 p.

315 See Ministry of Innovation, Science, Research and Technology of the German State of North Rhine-Westphalia (2007), *Driving our future. Energy research in North Rhine-Westphalia*, MIWFT, 18 p., at pp. 4-5.

316 The overall objective is a 50 per cent reduction of carbon dioxide by 2050. European Commission (2007), *Fossil Fuel Free Kristianstad, Municipality of Kristianstad, Sweden*, Directorate-General for Energy and Transport, Case Study 254, 5 p.

317 IEA (2008a), p. 184. Gurney et al. (2007), pp. 44-45.

318 See Department for Environment, Food and Rural Affairs (DEFRA) (2006), *United Kingdom's Fourth National Communication under the UNFCCC*, 132 p., at p. 28.

319 See *Valtioneuvoston asetus energiatuen myöntämisen yleisistä ehdoista* (Government Decree on the General Conditions of Granting Energy Aid) of 20 December 2007, at www.finlex.fi. For an overview in English, see the IEA Climate Change database (2008, last update). See also IEA (2004), p. 260.

320 See IEA (2004), p. 309. See also www.kfw-foerderbank.de.

321 See www.sdtc.ca. See also Sustainable Development Technology Canada (2008), *SDTC 2009 Corporate Plan – Executive Summary*, 11 p., at pp. 2, 4.

322 See e.g. Green (2006), pp. 382-384. Zhang and Assunção (2004), p. 362.

323 See e.g. Steenblik (2007).

324 Following Schumpeter's definition of the three stages of technological development, such policies may also be broken down as follows: invention, innovation and diffusion. Invention involves the research and first demonstration of the physical feasibility of a proposed new technology (called research, development and demonstration (R&DD)). Innovation is the stage of first developing and bringing new products or processes to the market, in other words to help them move from the laboratory to commercialization (as many would otherwise end up in the so-called "Valley of Death" due, *inter alia*, to the difficulty of preparing technologies for the market place). And finally, diffusion is the stage of replication and standardization of a technology, and its successful widespread adoption. See Schumpeter (1934). See also Gross and Foxon (2003), p. 119; Brewer (2007), p. 4; Stern (2006), p. 349; Brown et al. (2008).

325 Maurer and Scotchmer (2003), p. 2. Davis, L. and Davis, J. (2004), *How effective are Prizes as incentives to Innovation? Evidence from three 20th century Contests*, Paper presented at DRUID Summer Conference, June 2004, Denmark, 29 p.

326 Newell and Wilson (2005), p. 3.

327 See the website of the Department of Environment and Climate Change of the New South Wales Government at www.environment.nsw.gov.au/grants/ccfund.htm and in particular the Renewable Energy Development Program of the Climate Change Fund.

328 See New Zealand Ministry of Agriculture and Forestry (2008), *Climate Change Research Grants 2007/2008*, available at www.maf.govt.nz/climatechange/slm/grants/research/2007-08/index.htm.

329 See G/SCM/N/95/Kor, 5 May 2004, p. 24.

330 See Newell and Wilson (2005), pp. 3-4; Kalil (2006); Gillingham, Newell and Palmer (2004).

331 See website of the L Prize at www.lightingprize.org.

332 See Australia's Senate (2008), *Answers to Questions on Notice*, Standing Committee on Economics, Resources, Energy and Tourism Portfolio, Additional Estimates 2007-08, 21 February 2008, 4 p., at p. 3. See also IEA Climate Change database (2008, last update).

333 See Australian Government, Department of the Environment, Water, Heritage and the Arts, Greenhouse Gas Abatement Program (GGAP), at www.environment.gov.au. OECD/IEA (2004), p. 125.

334 See e.g. Kutas, Lindberg and Steenblik (2007).

335 A description is available on the website of the Department for Business Enterprise and Regulatory Reform, at www.berr.gov.uk. See also OECD/IEA (2004), p. 637.

336 See US Department of Energy, Energy Efficiency and Renewable Energy, *Montana E85 Laws and Incentives*, at www.eere.energy.gov.

337 See e.g. Gouchoe, Everette and Haynes (2002), p. 3. Clement et al. (2005), p. 4.

338 See "The Renewable Energy Law of the People's Republic of China, adopted at the 14th Session of the Standing Committee of the 10th National People's Congress on 28 February 2005", *Beijing Review* No. 29, 21 July 2005. See also Martinot and Junfeng (2007), p. 15; US National Renewable Energy Laboratory (2004), *Renewable Energy Policy in China: Financial Incentives*, NREL/FS-710-36045, at www.nrel.gov.

339 See Clement et al. (2005), p. 13.

340 Clement et al. (2005), table 7 on p. 13.

341 See the IEA Climate Change database (2008, last update).

342 See the website of SenterNovem, an agency of the Dutch Ministry of Economic Affairs, at www.senternovem.nl. For a description of the VAMIL scheme for accelerated depreciation in English, see also *Case 6: VAMIL and MIA, The Netherlands*, at http://ec.europa.eu/environment/sme.

343 Ringwald (2008), *India Renewable Energy Trends*, Centre for Social Markets Discussion Paper, p. 18.

344 See the website of the United States Database of State Incentives for Renewables & Efficiency (2009) at www.dsireusa.org.

345 See e.g. Ragwitz et al. (2005); Sijm (2002), p. 6; OECD/IEA (2004), p. 87; Ragwitz and Huber (2005).

346 PURPA was amended in 2005 by the Energy Policy Act of 2005, sections 1251 through 1254. See the website of the US Office of Electricity Delivery and Energy Reliability at www.oe.energy.gov. See also OECD/IEA (2004), p. 87. Martinot, Wiser and Hamrin (2005).

347 For the latest version of the Act, see *Renewable Energy Sources Act* of 25 October 2008, BGBl I S. 2074. For an English translation, see www.bmu.de. According to Article 1(2) of the Act, the overall objective is to increase the share of renewable energies in the total electricity supply to at least 30 per cent by the year 2020. See also Butler and Neuhoff (2004), p. 4. Dröge *et al.* (2004), p. 179.

348 Ministerio de Industria, Turismo y Comercio (2007), "Real Decreto 661/2007, de 25 de mayo, por el que se regula la actividad de producción de energía eléctrica en régimen especial", *Spanish Official Gazette*. For the photovoltaic feed-in tariff, see Ministerio de Industria, Turismo y Comercio (2008), "Real Decreto 1578/2008, de 26 de septiembre, de retribución de la actividad de producción de energía eléctrica mediante tecnología solar fotovoltaica para instalaciones posteriores a la fecha límite de mantenimiento de la retribución del Real Decreto 661/2007, de 25 de mayo, para dicha tecnología", *Spanish Official Gazette*. For a short description in English, see the IEA Climate Change database (2008, last update).

349 In Italy, renewable energies are promoted through different price regulation mechanisms, including feed-in tariffs, depending on the source of energy, size of installation, etc. For an overview, see http://res-legal.de/en. See also Castello, S., De Lillo, A. and Guastella, S. (2007), *National Survey Report on PV Power Applications in Italy*, IEA Co-operative Programme on Photovoltaic Power Systems, 19 p., at p. 7; and Tilli, F. et al. (2008), *The Feed in Tariff Scheme in the Italian Case. An Attempt of Removing Barriers for PV Architectural Integration and for Increasing Building Energy Efficiency*, 12 p.

350 The feed-in scheme was created by Article 10 of the Law No. 2000-108 (*Loi No. 2000-108 du 10 février 2000 relative à la modernisation et au développement du service public de l'électricité*, published in the Journal Officiel de la République Française No. 35 of 11 February 2000, p. 2143). For an English translation of the original version of the law, see www.industrie.gouv.fr. For the latest version of the law (in French), see www.legifrance.gouv.fr. For a description of the scheme, see also the website of the Ministry of Ecology, Energy, Sustainable Development and Territorial Planning (in French), at www.industrie.gouv.fr. A description in English is available from http://res-legal.eu/en.

351 See *The Electricity (Feed-In Scheme-Solar Systems) Amendment Act 2008*, available at www.legislation.sa.gov.au. More information on the scheme is available on the website of the Government of South Australia: www.climatechange.sa.gov.au.

352 A list of countries using feed-in tariffs can be found at Renewable Energy Policy Network for the 21st Century (2007), *Renewables 2007: Global Status Report*, 51 p., Table 2 on pp. 23-24.

353 See Ministry of Energy and Mines (2007), *Guidelines to Renewable Energies*, MEM, 92 p. at p. 36 at www.mem-algeria.org. For a summary of the scheme (in French), also see the website of the Electricity and Gas Regulatory Commission: www.creg.gov.dz.

354 Ruangrong, P. (2008), *Thailand's Approach to Promoting Clean Energy in the Electricity Sector*, 5 p., available at http://electricitygovernance.wri.org/files/egi/Thailand.pdf.

355 See "The Renewable Energy Law of the People's Republic of China, adopted at the 14th Session of the Standing Committee of the 10th National People's Congress on 28 February 2005", *Beijing Review* 29, 21 July 2005. Martinot and Junfeng (2007), pp. 14-15.

356 See e.g. Stern (2006), p. 366; Ragwitz et al. (2005), p. 11; IEA (2007b), p. 7; Butler and Neuhoff (2004), p. 24; and Fouquet et al. (2005), pp. 18, 24.

357 See e.g. Ragwitz and Huber (2005), p. 20. Fouquet et al. (2005), p. 26.

358 See e.g. Martinot, Wiser and Hamrin (2005), pp. 12-14.

359 See Database of State Incentives for Renewables and Efficiency, available at www.dsireusa.org.

360 Ontario Ministry of Energy and Infrastructure, *Net Metering in Ontario,* 5 p. at www.energy.gov.on.ca. See the website of BC Hydro, an electricity utility, at www.bchydro.com.

361 See website of the Thai Net Metering Project at http://netmeter.org.

362 See Agredano, J. and Huacuz, J.M. (2007), *PV Technology Status and Prospects in Mexico*, IEA – PVPS Annual Report 2007.

363 OECD/IEA (2004), p. 86.

364 Foxon (2003), p. 41.

365 See New Energy Foundation, "Subsidy Program for Residential PV Systems", available at www.nef.or.jp and OECD/IEA (2004), p. 86.

366 See the website of California Energy Commission, www.energy.ca.gov and Environment California (2006), "The California Solar Initiative: A monumental step to a million solar roofs", *Energy Program News*, 7 March 2006.

367 See ecoACTION, *ecoENERGY Retrofit-Homes*, at www.ecoaction.gc.ca.

368 OECD/IEA (2004), p. 86. World Energy Council (2008), p. 50.

369 See Kreditanstalt für Wiederaufbau (2003), *Das 100.000 Dächer-Solarstrom-Programm: Abschlußbericht*, KfW, at www.kfw.de. See also Agnolucci (2006), p. 3539. The last loan was granted at the end of June 2003. Even though the 100,000 Roofs Programme has ended, KfW, a public bank, still offers loans at preferential conditions for renewable energy projects. Additionally, photovoltaic installations are supported through the feed-in tariff.

370 This is a programme provided by two Indian banking groups in cooperation with UNEP. See UNEP's website at www.unep.fr.

371 UNFCCC (2007a), p. 40.

372 See e.g. Green (2006), p. 385.

373 See e.g. Green (2006), p. 385.

374 WTO (1999), p. 90.

375 Appellate Body Report, *US – Carbon Steel*, para. 73.

376 For a review of environment-related subsidies notifications, see WTO (2008a), pp. 28-56.

377 WTO (1999), p. 92.

378 SCM Article 1. WTO (1999), p. 92.

379 Article 1.1(a)(2) includes any form of income or price support in the sense of Article XVI of GATT 1994, i.e. support which operates directly or indirectly to increase exports of any product from, or reduce imports into, a member's territory.

380 Appellate Body Report, *Canada – Aircraft*, para. 157.

381 SCM Article 2.

382 WTO (1999), p. 93.

383 The SCM Agreement originally contained a third category: non-actionable subsidies. This category existed for five years, ending on 31 December 1999, and was not extended. See SCM Articles 8-9 and 31.

384 See SCM Articles 3-4.

385 See SCM Articles 5-7.

386 SCM Article 5.

387 SCM Article 6.

388 See e.g. Green (2006), at p. 399.

389 Appellate Body Report, *US – Carbon Steel*, para. 73.

390 Appellate Body Report, *US – Carbon Steel*, para. 73. See Part V of the SCM Agreement.

391 See WTO website at www.wto.org.

392 For a discussion of the issue of transfer of technology, see Section I.B.4.

393 TRIPS Article 7.

394 E.g. the Eco-Patent Commons initiative, World Business Council for Sustainable Development (WBCSD), at www.wbcsd.org. See also Taubman, A.S. (2009), "Sharing technology to meet a common challenge, Navigating proposals for patent pools, patent commons and open innovation", *WIPO Magazine* March 2009.

395 UK Intellectual Property Office (2009), "UK 'Green' inventions to get fast-tracked through patent system", Press Release, May 12, 2009.

396 Third World Network (2008), *Brief Note on Technology, IPR and Climate Change*, Bangkok Climate Change Talks Briefing Paper 2.

397 Given the great range of technologies relevant to adaptation and mitigation, the diversity of innovation technology diffusion structures required to meet expected needs, and the emergence of new technologies and new sources of innovation and industrial capacity, including in the developing world, the discussion on the nature, scope and precise costs and benefits of each of these measures is not yet settled.

398 WIPO (2008), *Climate Change and the Intellectual Property System: What Challenges, What Options, What Solutions?*, Version 5.0.

399 Ellis (2007), p. 13.

400 IEA (2008a), p. 73. IEA (2007a), p. 17. See also IEA (2007c). Boot (2009).

401 Stern (2006), p. 378.

402 See the monthly lists of TBT Notifications prepared by WTO, WTO, *Notifications issued during the month of ...*, G/TBT/GEN/N/.... See also Wiel and McMahon (2005). See also the Collaborative Labelling and Appliance Standards Program (CLASP) website, which provides a summary of standards and labelling programmes at www.clasponline.org.

403 Canada's 1992 Energy Efficiency Act, see the website of Natural Resources Canada at www.nrcan.gc.ca.

404 See the website of the US Green Building Council at www.usgbc.org.

405 See www.energyrating.gov.au.

406 See www.energystar.gov.

407 See California's Appliance Efficiency Program, at www.energy.ca.gov.

408 "Agevolazioni nel calcolo dei parametri urbanistici per il miglioramento del comfort ambientale e del risparmio energetico negli edifici", Regione Umbria, Legge Regionale N. 38 Del 20-12-2000, available (in Italian) at www.anit.it.

409 See Section IV.C.4(c) on WTO rules concerning harmonization.

410 See e.g. ISO 13790:2004, Thermal performance of buildings – Calculation of energy use for space heating.

411 See International Standard IEC 61683:1999 on Photovoltaic systems – Power conditioners – Procedure for measuring efficiency.

412 See for instance ISO 9459 on solar heating – domestic water heating systems; ISO 81400-4:2005 on Wind turbines, Part 4: Design and specification of gearboxes.

413 For instance, biodiesel standards in Brazil (ANP No. 42/04) and the United States (ASTM D6751) are applicable for both Fatty Acid Methyl Esters (FAME) and Fatty Acid Ethyl Ester (FAEE), whereas the current European biodiesel standard (EN 14214:2003) is only applicable to FAME. See Tripartite Task Force (2007), *White paper on internationally compatible biofuel standards*, 93 p., at p. 8.

414 Members of the Tripartite Task Force (Brazil, European Union and United States) are experts in the field of biofuels from each region, nominated by the regional standardization institutions and government bodies.

415 Milbrandt, A. and Overend, R.P., (2008), *The Future of Liquid Biofuels for APEC Economies*, APEC Energy Working Group, 102 p., at p. 6.

416 The International Biofuels Forum was launched in March 2007. See UN Department of Public Information (2007), *Press Conference Launching International Biofuels Forum*, New York.

417 For example, ISO Technical Committee TC28/SC7 on liquid biofuels.

418 The Roundtable is an initiative of the Swiss EPFL (École Polytechnique Fédérale de Lausanne) Energy Centre. See http://cgse.epfl.ch.

419 Article 2.8 of the TBT Agreement requires that, wherever appropriate, members shall specify technical regulations based on product requirements in terms of performance, rather than design or descriptive characteristics.

420 For example, under the WTO TBT Agreement, between 2000 and 2008, more than 30 notifications were submitted by WTO members on their draft regulations regarding biofuels. Most proposals were to establish product characteristics – in particular, physical and chemical specifications for biodiesel or ethanol to be used and marketed as fuels. Other proposals had to do with quality requirements for biofuels, definitions and minimum or maximum volumes of biodiesel or ethanol allowed in fuels (e.g. notifications G/TBT/N/THA/179 and 181-2005 from Thailand, G/TBT/N/CRI/57-2006 and 66-2007 from Costa Rica, G/TBT/N/HND/40-2006 and 45-2007 from Honduras, G/TBT/N/GTM 52-2006 and 57-2007 from Guatemala, G/TBT/N/SLV/101-2006 and 107-2007 from El Salvador, G/TBT/N/NIC/82-2006 and 85-2007 from Nicaragua, G/TBT/N/JPN/186-2006 from Japan, and G/TBT/N/NZL/41-2008 from New Zealand).

421 See ANP Act 36/2005 on ethanol and ANP Act 05/2005 on biodiesel.

422 See IS 15464:2004 on anhydrous ethanol for use in the automotive sector, and IS 15607:2005 on biodiesel.

423 See CEN standard prEN 14214 on biodiesel – fatty acid methyl esters (FAME).

424 See e.g. ASTM D6751 for biodiesel.

425 See The Energy Conservation Centre (2008), *Japan Energy Conservation Handbook 2008*, Japan, 134 p., at p. 18. See also Tanaka (2008), p. 11.

426 IPCC (2007e), p. 754.

427 US Environmental Protection Agency (2001), p. 16. Philibert (2003), p. 21; Stern (2006), p. 382.

428 IPCC (2007e), p, 754

429 The category is determined by the relationship between volume and energy consumption. See Directive 96/57/EC of the European Parliament and of the European Council of 3 September 1996 on energy efficiency requirements for household electric refrigerators, freezers and combinations thereof and Framework Directive 2005/32/EC on the setting of ecodesign requirements amending Directive 96/57/EC. The latter now falls under the Framework Directive, of which it has become an implementing measure. The Framework Directive applies to all energy-consuming appliances except vehicles.

430 See www.energyrating.gov.au.

431 See Title 49, United States Code, Subtitle VI. Motor Vehicle and Driver Programs Part C. Information, Standards, and Requirements Chapters 321, 323, 325, 327, 329, and 331 (2006). See website of the National Highway Traffic Safety Administration at www.nhtsa.gov.

432 Stern (2006), p. 382; Wiel and McMahon (2003), p. 1404.

433 The Top Runner Program is prescribed under the "Law Concerning the Rational Use of Energy" (Energy Conservation Law). The types of equipment designated under the Top Runner Program are: passenger vehicles, freight vehicles, air conditioners, electric refrigerators, electric freezers, electric rice cookers, microwave ovens, fluorescent lights, electric toilet seats, TV sets, video cassette recorders, DVD recorders, computers, magnetic disk units, copying machines, space heaters, gas cooking appliances, gas water heaters, oil water heaters, vending machines, transformers. See Ministry of Economy, Trade and Industry (METI), Agency for Natural Resources and Energy, The Energy Conservation Centre (2008), *Top Runner Program: Developing the World's best Energy-Efficient Appliances*, 66 p.

434 Title 49 Code of Federal Regulations (CFR) Parts 523, 531, 533, 534, 536 and 537 (Proposed Rules) published in Federal Register 73:86, May 2008 notified to the WTO in document G/TBT/N/USA/392. See also National Highway Traffic Safety Administration (2008), *Final Environmental Impact Statement Corporate Average Fuel Economy Standards, Passenger Cars and Light Trucks, Model Years 2011-2015*.

435 European Parliament (2008b).

436 Wiel and McMahon (2003), pp. 1404-1405. Stern (2006), p. 386.

437 "Energy Conservation Program for Consumer Products Other Than Automobiles" (42 U.S.C. 62916309). See http://apps1.eere.energy.gov/consumer/ and United States Department of Energy (2008), *Rulemaking Framework for Residential Central Air Conditioners and Heat Pumps*, RIN: 1904AB47, 64 p.

438 Stern (2006), p. 386.

439 Energy-efficiency labels are most commonly found on household appliances, cars, and building. For one survey of the status of energy-efficiency labels and standards in different countries as of September 2004, see Wiel and McMahon (2005), pp. 19-20.

440 Wiel and McMahon (2005), pp. 19-20; See Clasponline for an updated list of the status of energy-efficiency labels and standards across countries: www.clasponline.org.

441 See the Frequently Asked Questions on Appliance Labelling on the website of the Department of Minerals and Energy of the Republic of South Africa at www.dme.gov.za.

442 See G/TBT/Notif.99/498 and G/TBT/Notif.99/498/Add.1 through Add.5. Regulations related to energy-efficiency labelling are available in Spanish at www.puntofocal.gov.ar. An overview in English is available at www.clasponline.org.

443 See G/TBT/N/GHA/2. The Energy Efficiency Standards and Labelling Regulations are available at www.ghanaef.org.

444 More information on the voluntary Energy Efficiency Labelling Scheme is available from the websites of the Sri Lanka Standards Institution at www.slsi.lk and of the Ceylon Electricity Board at www.ceb.lk.

445 See website of the National Agency for Energy Conservation at www.anme.nat.tn. For a more detailed description, see Lihidheb and Waide (2005), *The Tunisian standards and labelling programme*, 16 p.

446 Wiel and McMahon (2005). See also www.clasponline.org.

447 World Energy Council (2008), p. 44.

448 See Australia's Energy Label at www.energyrating.gov.au.

449 See Switzerland's energiEtikette at www.bfe.admin.ch.

450 Canada's EnerGuide Car Labels, see http://oee.nrcan.gc.ca.

451 Wiel and McMahon (2005), pp. 19-20 and p. 58.

452 Soksod, S. and Suwicharcherdchoo, P. (2006), *Rescaling the Energy Label No. 5: 2006 version in Thailand, Appliances Efficiency Improvement Project, Demand Side Implementation Division*, EGAT, 5 p., at p. 2. For an overview of different voluntary labels in Thailand, see www.apec-esis.org.

453 See Indian Bureau of Energy Efficiency (2006), *Energy Efficiency Labels. Details of Scheme for Energy Efficiency Labeling*, Ministry of Power, 15 p., at p. 2. See also the Energy Manager Training website of the Indian Bureau for Energy Efficiency of the Ministry of Power at www.energymanagertraining.com. The programme now covers 11 categories of products on a voluntary basis. For four categories amongst them, the scheme is set to become mandatory, see notifications G/TBT/N/IND/36 and 37 regarding refrigerators and fluorescent lamps, as well as draft regulations published in the Gazette of India of 12 January 2009.

454 The Brazilian Labelling Programme PBE includes both mandatory and voluntary labels, depending on the product. For detailed information including the relevant regulations (in Portuguese), see www.inmetro.gov.br. For an overview in English, see Ministry of Mines and Energy, *Brazilian Labeling Program*, at www.conpet.gov.br. See also G/TBT/N/BRA/197, 256.

455 For more information on the Hong Kong Voluntary Energy Efficiency Labelling Scheme, see the website of the Electrical and Mechanical Services Department at www.emsd.gov.hk. As an example, see the Labelling Scheme for Fax Machines, G/TBT/N/HKG/25.

456 Wiel and McMahon (2003), p. 1403.

457 World Energy Council (2008), p. 43. Wiel and McMahon (2005), pp. 19-20. See also the monthly lists of TBT Notifications prepared by the WTO Secretariat, WTO, *Notifications issued during the month of...*, G/TBT/GEN/N/....

458 See Danish Energy Agency at www.ens.dk.

459 See for the Nordic Swan www.svanen.nu and for the German Blue Angel www.blauer-engel.de.

460 See www.environment.gov.au.

461 Directive 1999/94/EC of the European Parliament and of the European Council of 13 December 1999 relating to the availability of consumer information on fuel economy and CO_2 emissions in respect of the marketing of new passenger cars. This Directive is currently under revision.

462 See Council Directive 92/75/EEC of 22 September 1992 on the indication by labelling and standard product information on the consumption of energy and other resources by household appliances.

463 See www.energyrating.gov.au.

464 See EnerGuide Appliance Label at oee.nrcan.gc.ca.

465 See US Department of Energy, Office of Energy Efficiency and Renewable Energy (EERE) at http://apps1.eere.energy.gov.

466 See for the Nordic Swan http://www.svanen.nu/.

467 See www.blauer-engel.de.

468 See http://ec.europa.eu/environment/ecolabel.

469 See www.carbon-label.co.uk.

470 For instance, the Timberland Company has introduced energy labelling for its footwear, highlighting the energy used in the production process and the proportion of that energy that comes from renewable sources. See www.timberland.com. See also Cortese, A. (2007), "Friend of Nature? Let's see those shoes", *New York Times*, 7 March 2007.

471 For example, Wal-Mart has introduced a "Food Miles Calculator" which allows consumers to calculate the total distance their product has travelled. See http://instoresnow.walmart.com/food-article ektid44214.aspx.

472 See ITC, UNCTAD, UNEP (2007), *Statement on Soil Association Air Freight Consultation*, 17 September 2007, UNCTAD/DITC/TED/MISC/2007/4.

473 Smith, A. et al. (2005), *The Validity of Food Miles as an Indicator of Sustainable Development*, Department for Environment, Food and Rural Affairs, London, 103 p.

474 See for instance Brodt, S. (2007), *Assessment of Energy Use and Greenhouse Gas Emissions in the Food System: A Literature Review*, Agricultural Sustainability Institute, University of California Davis; Annelies Van Hauwermeiren et al. (2007), "Energy Lifecycle Inputs in Food Systems: A Comparison of Local versus Mainstream Cases", Journal of Environmental Policy and Planning, Volume 9:1, pp. 31-51. Saunders, C., Barber, A. and Taylor, G. (2006), *Food Miles – Comparative Energy/Emissions Performance of New Zealand's Agriculture Industry*, Research Report 285, Agribusiness and Economics Research Uni, Lincoln University, 105 p.

475 See Ellis (2007), p. 19. See also CLASP, "Definition of Energy-Efficiency Labels and Standards", *General Information on Standards and Labelling*, at www.clasponline.org. Wiel and McMahon (2005), p. 9.

476 Ellis (2007), p. 19.

477 The Energy Rating Label was first introduced in 1986 in New South Wales and Victoria, and is now mandatory in all states and territories in Australia and in New Zealand. Further details on the Australian Energy Rating labels can be found at www.energyrating.gov.au.

478 See Council Directive 92/75/EEC of 22 September 1992 on the indication by labelling and standard product information of the consumption of energy and other resources by household appliances.

479 See EnerGuide Appliance Label at http://oee.nrcan.gc.ca

480 See the Energy Guide Program at www1.eere.energy.gov

481 For an overview in English, see www.conpet.gov.br.

482 See website of the National Agency for Energy Conservation at www.anme.nat.tn. See also Lihidheb, K. and Waide, P. (2005), *The Tunisian standards and labelling programme*, 16 p.

483 See G/TBT/N/CHN/59. For the text of the China Energy Label regulation in English, see www.energylabel.gov.cn. See also Nan Zhou (2008), *Status of China's Energy Efficiency Standards and Labels for Appliances and International Collaboration*, Ernest Orlando Lawrence Berkeley National Laboratory, 14 p., at p. 11.

484 Soksod and Suwicharcherdchoo (2006), p. 2. Also see http://www.clasponline.org/.

485 Singh, J. and Mulholland, C. (2000), *DSM (demand-side management) in Thailand: A Case Study*, Joint UNDP/World Bank Energy Sector Management Assistance Programme (ESMAP), 15 p., at pp. 3-4. For an overview of different labels in Thailand, see www.apec-esis.org.

486 For more information on Korea's Energy Efficiency Standards & Labeling Program, see www.kemco.or.kr.

487 World Energy Council (2008), p.45.

488 Wiel and McMahon (2005), p. 10.

489 Energy Star, History of Energy Star, www.energystar.gov.

490 International Energy Star partners include: Australia, Canada, the European Union, the European Free Trade Association, Japan, New Zealand, Switzerland and Chinese Taipei. See www.energystar.gov.

491 For more information on the PROCEL label see www.eletrobras.com.

492 For information on the Thai Green Label scheme, see www.tei.or.th/greenlabel.

493 See "China speeds up energy-efficient products certification", *Xinhua News Agency*, 7 August 2008. For an overview of the different Chinese labelling schemes in English, see www.apec-esis.org.

494 Energy Star, www.energystar.gov.

495 Carbon Trust, Carbon Label Footprint, www.carbon-label.co.uk.

496 See ISO/IEC 17000: 2004, para. 4.2.

497 Soksod and Suwicharcherdchoo (2006), p. 2.

498 See e.g. Electrical and Mechanical Services Department (2009), "The Hong Kong Voluntary Energy Efficiency Labelling Scheme for Washing Machines", Hong Kong, 62 p., at p. 16, at www.emsd.gov.hk. The schemes for other products contain similar provisions.

499 ISO/IEC 17000: 2004, para. 4.3.

500 US Green Building Council, LEED, www.usgbc.org.

501 See Energy Star, *Independent Inspection and Testing Helps Make Sure a Home is Energy Efficient*, at www.energystar.gov/.

502 *Directive 2002/91/EC of the European Parliament and of the Council of 16 December 2002 on the energy performance of buildings.*

503 For a definition of certification see ISO/IEC 17000: 2004, para. 5.5.

504 WTO (2006), p. 54.

505 See Natural Resources Canada at www.oee.nrcan.gc.ca.

506 See ISO/IEC 17000: 2004, para. 5.6.

507 WTO (2006), p. 55.

508 See Hong Kong Electrical and Mechanical Services Department (2008), *Code of Practice on Energy Labelling of Products*, at p. 4, www.emsd.gov.hk.

509 See "Energy Conservation Program for Consumer Products; Fluorescent and Incandescent Lamp Test Procedures; Laboratory Accreditation Program" 10 CFR 430.25, *Federal Register*, 29 May 1997, at p. 29223, at www1.eere.energy.gov.

510 WTO (2006), p. 55.

511 See www1.eere.energy.gov. See in particular Petersons, O., Stricklett, K.L. and Hagwood C.R. (2004), "Operating Characteristics of the Proposed Sampling Plans for Testing Distribution Transformers", NIST Technical Note 1456, 25 p. and "Energy Conservation Program for Commercial Equipment: Distribution Transformers Energy Conservation Standards", 10 CFR 431, *Federal Register*, 12 October 2007.

512 For example, under the Montreal Protocol, numerous governments have bans to phase out the use of chlorofluorocarbons (CFCs).

513 See Section III.A.4 on the Montreal Protocol.

514 *Ordinance by the Federal Minister for Agriculture, Forestry, Environment and Water: Management on Bans and Restrictions for Partly Fluorinated and Fully Fluorinated Hydrocarbons and Sulphur Hexafluoride*, BGBl. II Nr. 447/2002. The English version is available at www.bmlfuw.gv.at.

515 See Danish Environmental Protection Agency, *Fact sheet No. 46: Industrial greenhouse gases: HFCs, PFCs and SF_6*, at www.mst.dk. Full text of the *Statutory Order No. 552 of 2 July 2002 on regulations for certain industrial greenhouse gases* (in Danish) is available at www.retsinformation.dk.

516 See Federal Department of the Environment, Transport, Energy and Communications (2003), "Synthetic greenhouse gases under control and better protection of ozone layer", Press Release, 30 April 2003 at www.uvek.admin.ch.

517 See Regulation (EC) No. 842/2006 of 17 May 2006 on certain fluorinated greenhouse gases.

518 Australian Government, Department of the Environment, Water, Heritage and the Arts, *Phase out of incandescent lightbulbs*, at www.environment.gov.au.

519 European Commission (2009), *Commission adopts two regulations to progressively remove from the market non-efficient light bulbs*, Press Release, IP/ 09/411, 18 March 2009.

520 Canada put in place high minimum performance standards for lamps, see Natural Resources Canada, Office of Energy Efficiency (2008), "Canada's Energy Efficiency Regulations. General Service Lamps – New Regulations. Final Bulletin – December 2008", OEE, http://oee.nrcan.gc.ca. For the full text of the regulation, see "Regulations Amending the Energy Efficiency Regulations", SOR/2008-323, *Canada Gazette*, Part II, 142:26, 24 December 2008, p. 2512.

521 The proposed regulation will set high minimum efficiency standards on incandescent lamps, see G/TBT/N/TPKM/64. For the text of the "Proposed draft of the minimum energy efficiency requirements of Incandescent lamps for general service", see www.bsmi.gov.tw. Also see "Taiwan Switches On 5-year Green Plan to Ban Incandescent Lights", CENS, 7 November 2008, www.cens.com.

522 See G/TBT/N/ARG/246. The full text of Ley No 26.473 is available at www.puntofocal.gov.ar. See also Greenpeace, *Argentina to Ban the Bulb*, 14 March 2008.

523 Meyers, McMahon and McNeil (2005), p. 2.

524 Winters Lynch (1994), p. 5.

525 See e.g. Geller *et al.* (2006).

526 Wiel and McMahon (2003), p. 1408. Geller *et al.* (2006), pp. 563, 568-570. IEA (2000), p. 107. Colombier and Menanteau (1997). See also the California Energy Commission's website at www.energy.ca.gov.

527 Meyers, McMahon and McNeil (2005), p. 33.

528 Winters Lynch (1994), p. 5.

529 OECD (1997), p. 70.

530 OECD (2008c), p. 11.

531 See OECD (2008c), p. 29. OECD (1997), p. 48. See also www.svanen.nu.

532 Banerjee and Solomon (2003), p. 115.

533 Huh (1999). Banerjee and Solomon (2003), p. 119. Wiel and McMahon (2003), p. 1403.

534 Wiel and McMahon (2005).

535 Faiz, Weaver and Walsh (1996), p. 22.

536 In the *EC – Asbestos* case, the Appellate Body indicated that not all internal measures covered by Article III:4 of the GATT 1994 "affecting" the "sale, offering for sale, purchase, transportation, distribution or use" of a product are necessarily "technical regulations" under the TBT Agreement. Appellate Body Report, *EC – Asbestos*, para. 77.

537 For a detailed explanation of Article XX, see WTO (2002).

538 A technical regulation is defined in TBT Annex 1, Paragraph 1 as a: "Document which lays down product characteristics or their related processes and production methods, including the applicable administrative provisions, with which compliance is mandatory. It may also include or deal exclusively with terminology, symbols, packaging, marking or labelling requirements as they apply to a product, process or production method". In addition, Annex 1, Paragraph 1 provides the following examples of requirements which can be included in a technical regulation: terminology requirements; symbol requirements; packaging requirements; marking requirements; and labelling requirements.

539 A standard is defined in TBT Annex 1, Paragraph 2 as a: "Document approved by a recognized body, that provides, for common and repeated use, rules, guidelines or characteristics for products or related processes

and production methods, with which compliance is not mandatory. It may also include or deal exclusively with terminology, symbols, packaging, marking or labelling requirements as they apply to a product, process or production method".

540 A conformity assessment procedure is defined in TBT Annex 1, Paragraph 3 as: "Any procedure used, directly or indirectly, to determine that relevant requirements in technical regulations or standards are fulfilled". The Explanatory note of Annex 1, Paragraph 3 provides a non-exhaustive list of conformity assessment procedures which include: procedures for sampling, testing and inspection; evaluation, verification and assurance of conformity; and registration, accreditation and approval.

541 TBT Article 1.3.

542 Pursuant to the General interpretative note to Annex 1A, if there is conflict between a provision of the GATT 1994 and a provision of another agreement contained in Annex 1A of the WTO Agreement, e.g. the TBT Agreement, the provision of the other agreement shall prevail to the extent of the conflict. See Appellate Body, *Brazil – Desiccated Coconut*, p. 16.

543 The relevant provisions for mandatory requirements are Articles 2 and 3 while Article 4 and Annex 3 are relevant to voluntary standards. For conformity assessment procedures, key provisions are Articles 5 to 9.

544 See Article 4 and Annex 3 of the TBT Agreement.

545 TBT Annex 3, Paragraph B.

546 Pursuant to TBT Annex 1, Paragraph 8, a non-governmental body is a "[b]ody other than a central government body or a local government body, including a non-governmental body which has legal power to enforce a technical regulation". See e.g. Appleton (2009), p. 13.

547 In addition, TBT Annex 1.1 provides the following examples of requirements which can be included in a technical regulation: terminology, symbols, packaging, marking or labelling requirements as they apply to a product, process or production method.

548 Appellate Body, *EC – Sardines*, para. 180.

549 Appellate Body, *EC – Asbestos*, para. 67.

550 Annex 1, paras. 1 and 2. Pursuant to Annex 1.2, a standard is a "[d]ocument approved by a recognized body, that provides, for common and repeated use, rules, guidelines or characteristics for products or related processes and production methods, with which compliance is not mandatory. It may also include or deal exclusively with terminology, symbols, packaging, marking or labelling requirements as they apply to a product, process or production method".

551 In response to a request of the Committee on Trade and Environment in 1995, the WTO prepared a note on the negotiating history – covering both the Tokyo and the Uruguay Round negotiations – which included a discussion on the coverage of the TBT Agreement relating to processes and production methods unrelated to product characteristics. See WTO (1995), pp. 37-54.

552 For a discussion of the non-product related PPM issue, see e.g. Waide and Bernasconi-Osterwalder (2008), p. 8. Appleton (2009), pp. 6-7. Verrill (2008), p. 47.

553 See TBT Articles 2.1 (for technical regulations), 5.1.1 (for conformity assessment procedures) and Annex 3.D (for standards).

554 The non-discrimination principle and the related terms "like products" and "no less favourable treatment than" have not been tested in dispute settlement proceedings in the TBT context. For more information on the like product concept under the GATT, see Section IV.I.A.

555 See TBT Articles 2.2 (for technical regulations), 5.1.2 (for conformity assessment procedures) and Annex 3.E (for standards).

556 See TBT Article 2.2.

557 TBT Article 2.2.

558 TBT Article 5.1.2.

559 See Section IV.A.3(b)(ii) on the necessity test with Article XX.

560 Unadopted GATT panel, *US – Automobiles*, para. 2.2.

561 Unadopted GATT panel, *US – Automobiles*, para. 2.5.

562 Unadopted GATT panel, *US – Automobiles*, paras. 2.15-2.16.

563 The national treatment principle as contained in GATT Article III:2. See unadopted GATT panel, *US – Automobiles*, paras. 5.16, 5.37.

564 As contained in GATT Article III:4.

565 Unadopted GATT panel, *US – Automobiles*, para. 5.55.

566 For a discussion on this see Assunção and Zhang (2002).

567 In the SPS Agreement, harmonization is defined as "The establishment, recognition and application of common sanitary and phytosanitary measures by different Members" (Annex A.2).

568 TBT Article 2.7.

569 TBT Article 6.3.

570 TBT Article 2.4 (for technical regulations), 5.4 (for conformity assessment procedures) and Annex 3.F (for standards). Concerning conformity assessment procedures, Article 5.4 reads "In cases where a positive assurance is required that products conform with technical regulations or standards, and relevant guides or recommendations issued by international standardizing bodies exist or their completion is imminent, Members shall ensure that central government bodies use them, or the relevant parts of them, as a basis for their conformity assessment procedures, except where, as duly explained upon request, such guides or recommendations or relevant parts are inappropriate for the Members concerned, for, *inter alia*, such reasons as: national security requirements; the prevention of deceptive practices; protection of human health or safety, animal or plant life or health, or the environment; fundamental climatic or other geographical factors; fundamental technological or infrastructural problems."

571 The *EC – Sardines* case is very informative concerning the interpretation of this requirement. *EC – Sardines*, Panel and Appellate Body Reports.

572 TBT Article 2.5.

573 TBT Article 2.6.

574 See "Decision of the Committee on principles for the development of international standards, guides and recommendations with relation to Articles 2, 5 and Annex 3 of the Agreement" contained in G/TBT/9.

575 See TBT Articles 2 and 5.

576 G/TBT/13, para. 16.

577 TBT Article 13.1.

578 G/TBT/N/BRA/240, 17 April 2007

579 G/TBT/N/EEC/194, 30 April 2008.

580 G/TBT/N/SGP/5, 15 August 2008. See also European Parliament (2008b).

581 G/TBT/N/CHN/330, G/TBT/N/CHN/331, G/TBT/N/CHN/332, 29 January 2008.

582 See TBT Article 11.

583 This last obligation is only relevant to WTO members which are members or participants of international or regional systems for conformity assessment. See Articles 11.2, 4, 5 and 6.

584 See e.g. European Communities (2008), *Technical Assistance Activities in the TBT Field (European Commission and EU Member States funded. Active Projects in 2006-2007)*, G/TBT/W/303.

Conclusions

The main purpose of this Report has been to provide the reader with an understanding of the debate on the linkages between trade and climate change. The material reviewed shows that trade intersects with climate change in a multitude of ways. In part, this is due to the innumerable implications that climate change may have in terms of its potential impacts and the profound regulatory and economic changes that will be required to mitigate and adapt to these impacts.

Moreover, the trade and climate change debate is taking place in the context of the current financial and economic crisis, making action on climate change even more challenging, and the need for vigilance against trade protectionism more critical. These multiple challenges emphasize that the world cannot continue with "business as usual". There is a profound need for a successful conclusion to the current negotiations on both climate change and trade opening.

Most importantly, the debate on trade and climate change is taking place against the backdrop of vital multilateral climate change negotiations, which are due to come to a conclusion at the 15th Conference of the Parties to the UNFCCC meeting in December 2009 in Copenhagen, Denmark. Addressing climate change represents one of the most urgent challenges of our time, and requires concerted action at both the national and the international level. A multilateral agreement with binding commitments establishing the framework for reducing greenhouse gas emissions for post-2012 and beyond should be the main instrument for addressing climate change.

As the scientific literature on climate change illustrates, greenhouse gas emissions generated from human activities have resulted in global warming. This trend is projected to continue unless there are significant changes to current laws, policies and actions. Most sectors of the global economy are likely to be affected by climate change, and this will often have implications for trade.

Furthermore, many of the sectors most affected, such as agriculture, forestry and fisheries, are critical for developing countries. Climate change is likely to alter the comparative advantage of these countries in such sectors, and thereby alter the pattern of international trade. Moreover, climate change is expected to have an impact on trade infrastructure and trade transportation routes. More studies quantifying the impact of climate change on trade are needed.

Economists have developed an analytical framework that is useful in conceptualizing how trade opening impacts on greenhouse gas emissions. On the one hand, the literature indicates that more open trade is likely to increase CO_2 emissions as a result of increased economic activity (the scale effect). On the other hand, trade opening could facilitate the adoption of technologies that reduce the emission-intensity of goods and their production process (the technique effect) and lead to a change in the mix of production from energy-intensive to less energy-intensive sectors if it is where it has a comparative advantage (the composition effect).

Although most studies to date have found that the scale effect tends to outweigh the technique and composition effects in terms of CO_2 emissions, it remains difficult to determine in advance the magnitude of each of these three effects, and therefore estimating the overall impact of trade on greenhouse gas emissions can be challenging. More *ex post* studies in this area would be helpful to fine-tune the analytical framework.

As noted in this Report, international trade involves emissions of greenhouse gases through the transportation of goods. However, most transportation is through maritime transport, which accounts for a relatively small share of the greenhouse gas emissions of the transport sector, and in terms of some indicators, is the most energy-efficient form of transport in terms of greenhouse gas emissions.

This Report identifies a few key areas where technology has the potential to significantly reduce greenhouse gas emissions. For example, there is scope for energy-efficient technologies in transport, buildings and industry, and for production to switch to zero- or low-carbon energy technologies. International trade can serve as a conduit for diffusing these technologies which mitigate climate change.

A successful conclusion of WTO negotiations on opening markets to environmental goods and services will help improve access to climate-friendly goods and technologies. However, more research is needed on how trade and trade opening contribute to the development and diffusion of climate-friendly technology.

The review of national mitigation and adaptation measures, provided in the last part of the Report, illustrates the wide range of policy measures available to governments to help reduce greenhouse gas emissions. It also highlights the impact that this complex web of measures might have on international trade and the multilateral trading system.

The measures reviewed range from traditional regulatory instruments to economic incentives and financial measures. For instance, the Report provides ample evidence that in recent years there has been a proliferation of technical requirements (including voluntary standards and labelling schemes) related to climate-friendly goods and energy efficiency. Likewise, the number of financial support programmes, including support for the deployment of renewable sources of energy, has also increased recently. WTO bodies provide an important forum to debate policy measures: the Committee on Trade and Environment, for example, could discuss, among others, trade-related measures that could help support climate change mitigation and adaptation or to what extent trade is affected by requirements for emissions reduction and energy efficiency.

Price-based mechanisms, such as a carbon tax on fossil fuels or a tax on energy, have been employed in several countries over the past two decades as a means of internalizing the environmental cost of greenhouse gas emissions. More recently, attention has focused on emission trading schemes. These involve fixing a cap on total emission levels, translating this into allowances to cover emissions, and creating a market to trade these allowances at a price determined by the market. More empirical work on the economic implications and environmental effectiveness of emission trading schemes would be useful.

There is considerable debate on the extent to which certain industrial sectors may be economically affected by carbon-constraining domestic policies, and in particular, by emission trading schemes. Policies aimed at preventing carbon leakage (i.e. the risk that energy-intensive industries will simply relocate to countries with less rigid emission regulations) and at protecting competitiveness in these sectors are also under discussion.

Government policies range from exemptions from participation in emission trading schemes to the use of border trade measures. The debate on the potential use of border measures has highlighted the formidable difficulties involved in applying such measures. These include the challenge of precisely assessing the quantity of CO_2 emitted during a product's production, which may depend on the company and the country, and the difficulty of measuring the economic impact of an emission trading scheme on a particular industry. Further research on methodologies to address these difficulties could be useful to policy-makers.

There are a vast number of views expressed by academics, policy-makers, and various stakeholders on how trade is affected by measures to mitigate climate change, and on the extent to which these measures are consistent with WTO rules. A number of GATT and WTO rules deal specifically with many of the economic and regulatory instruments used in a number of countries. However, the relevance of WTO rules to climate change mitigation policies, as well as the implications for trade and the environmental effectiveness of these measures, will very much depend on how these policies are designed and the specific conditions for implementing them.

Bibliography

Aaheim, A.H. and Schjolden, A. (2004), "An approach to utilise climate change impacts studies in national assessments", *Global Environmental Change* 14, pp. 147-160.

ABI (Association of British Insurers) (2004), *A Changing Climate for Insurance – A Summary Report for Chief Executives and Policymakers*, London, 20 p.

Acemoglu, D. (2002), "Technical Change, Inequality, and the Labor Market", *Journal of Economic Literature* 40:1, pp. 7-72.

Acharya, R.C. and Keller, W. (2007), "Technology Transfer through Imports", *CEPR Discussion Paper* 6296, CEPR, London.

ACIA (Arctic Climate Impact Assessment) (2005), *Arctic Climate Impact Assessment*, Cambridge University Press, Cambridge.

ADB (Asian Development Bank) (2005), *Climate Proofing – A Risk-based Approach to Adaptation*, Pacific Studies Series, Asian Development Bank, The Philippines.

Adger, W.N., Agrawala, S., Mirza, M.M.Q., Conde, C., O'Brien, K., Pulhin, J., Pulwarty, R., Smit, B. and Takahashi, K. (2007), "Assessment of adaptation practices, options, constraints and capacity", in Parry, M.L., Canziani, O.F., Palutikof, J.P., van der Linden, P.J. and Hanson, C.E., (eds.), *Climate Change 2007: Impacts, Adaptation and Vulnerability. Contribution of Working Group II to the Fourth Assessment Report of the Intergovernmental Panel on Climate Change,* Cambridge University Press, Cambridge, pp. 717-743.

Aghion, P., Bloom, N., Blundell, R., Griffith, R. and Howitt, P. (2005), "Competition and Innovation: An Inverted-U Relationship", *Quarterly Journal of Economics* 120:2, pp. 701-728.

Agnolucci, P. (2004), "Ex-post valuations of CO_2-based taxes: a survey", *Tyndall Center, Working Paper* 52, 57 p.

Agnolucci, P. (2006), "Use of economic instruments in the German renewable electricity policy", *Energy Policy* 34, pp. 3538-3548.

Agrawala, S. and Fankhauser, S., (eds.) (2008), *Economic Aspects of Adaptation to Climate Change: Costs, Benefits, and Policy Instruments*, OECD, Paris.

Åhman, M. (2007), *EU Emissions Trading Scheme: contentious issues*, Swedish Environmental Research Institute, Prepared for the Energy Policy Advisory Group of the European Commission, 6 p.

AIACC (Assessments of Impacts and Adaptations to Climate Change) (2003-2007), Working papers and publications available at www.aiaccproject.org/publications_reports/Pub_Reports.html.

Alavi, R. (2007), "An Overview of Key Markets, Tariffs and Non-tariff Measures on Asian Exports of Select Environmental Goods", *ICTSD Programme on Trade and Environment, Issue Paper* 4, 36 p.

Alcamo, J., Moreno, J.M., Nováky, B., Bindi, M., Corobov, M., Devoy, R.J.N., Giannakopoulos, C., Martin, E., Olesen, J.E., and Shvidenko, A. (2007), "Europe", in Parry, M.L., Canziani, O.F., Palutikof, J.P., van der Linden, P.J. and Hanson, C.E., (eds.), *Climate Change 2007: Impacts, Adaptation and Vulnerability. Contribution of Working Group II to the Fourth Assessment Report of the Intergovernmental Panel on Climate Change*, Cambridge University Press, Cambridge, pp. 541-580.

Aldy, J.E. (2005), "An Environmental Kuznets Curve Analysis of U.S. State-Level Carbon Dioxide Emissions", *Journal of Environment and Development* 14:1, pp. 48-72.

Aldy, J.E., Baron, R. and Tubiana, L. (2003), "Addressing cost. The political economy of climate change", in Aldy, J.E., Ashton, J., Baron, R., Bodansky, R., Charnovitz, S., Diringer, E., Heller T. C., Pershing, J., Shukla P.R., Tubiana, L., Tudela, F. and Wang, X., *Beyond Kyoto. Advancing the international effort against climate change*, Pew Centre of Global Climate Change, Arlington, VA, 170 p.

Alexander, L.V., Zhang, X., Peterson, T. C., Caesar, J., Gleason, B., Klein Tank, A.M.G., Haylock, M., Collins, D., Trewin, B., Rahim, F., Tagipour, A., Kumar Kolli, R., Revadekar, J.V., Griffiths, G., Vincent, L., Stephenson, D. B., Burn, J., Aguilar, E., Brunet, M., Taylor, M., New, M., Zhai, P., Rusticucci, M. and Luis Vazquez Aguirre J. (2006), "Global observed changes in daily climate extremes of temperature and precipitation", *Journal of Geophysical Research* 111, D05109.

Allan, R.P. and Soden, B.J. (2008), "Atmospheric Warming and the Amplification of Precipitation Extremes", *Science Express* 321:5895, pp. 1481-1484.

Andersen, S.O., Sarma, K.M. and Taddonio, K. (2007), *Technology Transfer for the Ozone Layer: Lessons for Climate Change*, Earthscan Publications, London.

Anderson, D. (2006), *Costs and Finance of Abating Carbon Emissions in the Energy Sector*, Imperial College, London, 63 p.

Anderson, K. and McKibbin, W.J. (2000), "Reducing coal subsidies and trade barriers: their contribution to greenhouse gas abatement", *Environment and Development Economics* 5, pp. 457-481.

Andreoni, J. and Levinson, A. (2001), "The Simple Analytics of the Environmental Kuznets Curve", *Journal of Public Economics* 80:2, pp. 269-286.

Anisimov, O.A., Vaughan, D.G., Callaghan, T.V., Furgal, C., Marchant, H., Prowse, T.D., Vilhjálmsson, H. and Walsh, J.E. (2007), "Polar regions (Arctic and Antarctic)", in Parry, M.L.,

Canziani, O.F., Palutikof, J.P., van der Linden, P.J. and Hanson, C.E., (eds.), *Climate Change 2007: Impacts, Adaptation and Vulnerability. Contribution of Working Group II to the Fourth Assessment Report of the Intergovernmental Panel on Climate Change*, Cambridge University Press, Cambridge, pp. 653-685.

Antweiller, W., Copeland, B.R. and Taylor, M.S. (2001) "Is Free Trade Good for the Environment?" *American Economic Review* 91:4, pp. 877-908.

Appleton, A.E. (2009), "Private Climate Change Standards and Labelling Schemes under the WTO Agreement on Technical Barriers to Trade", in Cottier, T., Nartova, O. and Bigdeli, S., (eds.), *International Trade Regulation and the Mitigation of Climate Change, 2007 World Trade Forum, World Trade Institute*, Cambridge University Press, forthcoming 2009, 16 p.

Archibugi, D. and Coco, A. (2005), "Measuring technological capabilities at the country level: A survey and a menu for choice", *Research Policy* 34:2, pp. 175-194.

Arimura, T.H. (2002), "An empirical study of the SO_2 allowance market: effects of PUC regulations", *Journal of Environmental Economics and Management* 44, pp. 271-289.

Arnell, N.W. (2004), "Climate change and global water resources: SRES emissions and socio-economic scenarios", *Global Environmental Change* 14, pp. 13-52.

Assunção, L. and Zhang, Z. (2002), *Domestic Climate Policies and the WTO*, Munich Personal RePEc Archive, 29 p.

Aulisi A., Farrell, A., Pershing, J. and Vandeveer, S. (2005), *Greenhouse Gas Emissions Trading in U.S. States – Observations and Lessons from the OTC NOx Budget Program*, World Resources Institute, Washington, DC, 36 p.

Australia (2008), *Carbon Pollution Reduction Scheme: Australia's Low Pollution Future*, White Paper.

Autor, D.H., Katz, L.F. and Kearney, M.S. (2008), "Trends in U.S. Wage Inequality: Revising the Revisionists", *Review of Economics and Statistics* 90:2, pp. 300-23.

Baldwin, R.E. (2000), "Trade and Growth: Still Disagreement about the Relationships", *Economics Department Working Paper* 264, OECD, Paris.

Banerjee, A. and Solomon, B.D. (2003), "Ecolabeling for energy efficiency and sustainability: a meta evaluation of US programs", *Energy Policy* 31, pp. 109-123.

Bapna, M. and McGray, H., (Forthcoming), *Financing adaptation: Opportunities for innovation. Forthcoming in the book: Climate Change and Global Poverty: A Billion Lives in the Balance?*, Brookings Institution Press, Washington, DC.

Baranzini, A., Goldemberg, J. and Speck, S. (2000), "Survey – A future for carbon taxes", *Ecological Economics* 32, pp. 395-412

Barker, T., Bashmakov, I., Alharthi, A., Amann, M., Cifuentes, L., Drexhage, J., Duan, M., Edenhofer, O., Flannery, B., Grubb, M., Hoogwijk, M., Ibitoye, F.I., Jepma, C.J., Pizer, W.A. and Yamaji, K. (2007), "Mitigation from a cross-sectoral perspective", in Metz, B., Davidson, O.R., Bosch, P.R., Dave, R. and Meyer, L.A. (eds.), *Climate Change 2007: Mitigation. Contribution of Working Group III to the Fourth Assessment Report of the Intergovernmental Panel on Climate Change*, Cambridge University Press, Cambridge and New York, NY.

Baron, R. (1997), "Economic/Fiscal Instruments: Taxation (i.e. Carbon/Energy)", Annex I Expert Group on the UNFCCC, *OECD Working Paper* 4, OCDE/GD(97)188, 94 p.

Baron, R. and Bygrave, S. (2002), *Towards International Emissions Trading: Design Implications for Linkages*, OECD/IEA Information Paper, 50 p.

Baron, R. and ECON-Energy (1997), "Economic/fiscal instruments: competitiveness issues related to carbon/energy taxation", Annex I Expert Group on the UNFCCC, *Working Paper* 14, OECD/IEA, 65 p.

Baron, R., Reinaud, J., Genasci M. and Philibert, C. (2007), *Sectoral approaches to greenhouse gas mitigation: exploring issues for heavy industries*, IEA Information Paper, OECD/IEA, 76 p.

Barreto, L. and Klaassen, G. (2004), "Emissions Trading and the Role of Learning-by-doing Spillovers in the 'Bottom-up' Energy-Systems ERIS Model", *International Journal of Energy Technology and Policy* 2:1-2, pp. 70-95.

Barrett, S. (1994), "Self-enforcing International Environmental Agreements", *Oxford Economic Papers* 46, pp. 878-894.

Barrett, S. (1997), "The Strategy of Trade Sanctions in International Environmental Agreements", *Resource and Energy Economics* 19:4, pp. 345-361.

Barton, J. H. (2007), *Intellectual Property and Access to Clean Energy Technologies in Developing Countries. An Analysis of Solar Photovoltaic, Biofuel and Wind Technologies*, ICTSD Programme on Trade and Environment, 35 p.

Baumert, K.A., Herzog, T. and Pershing, J. (2005), *Navigating the Numbers Greenhouse Gas Data and International Climate Policy*, World Resources Institute, USA.

Baumol, W.J. (1972), "On Taxation and the Control of Externalities", *American Economic Review*, pp. 307-322.

Baumol, W.J. and Oates, W.E. (1971), "The Use of Standards and Prices for Protection of the Environment", *Swedish Journal of Economics* 73, pp. 42-54.

Bell, M. (1997), "Technology Transfer to Transition Countries: Are there Lessons from the Experience of the Post-war Industrialising Countries?", in Dyker, D.A. (ed.), *The technology of transition*, Central European University Press, Budapest, pp. 63-94.

Bell, M. and Pavitt, K. (1993), "Technological accumulation and industrial growth: Contrasts between developed and developing countries", *Industrial and Corporate Change* 2:2, pp. 157-200.

Bennett, D. (2002), *Innovative Technology Transfer Framework Linked to Trade for UNIDO Action*, United Nations Industrial Development Organization (UNIDO), Vienna, 54 p.

Bernstein, L., Roy, J., Delhotal, K.C., Harnisch, J., Matsuhashi, R., Price, L., Tanaka, K., Worrell, E., Yamba, F. and Fengqi, Z. (2007), "Industry", in Metz, B., Davidson, O.R., Bosch, P.R., Dave, R., and Meyer, L.A. (eds.), *Climate Change 2007: Mitigation. Contribution of Working Group III to the Fourth Assessment Report of the Intergovernmental Panel on Climate Change,* Cambridge University Press, Cambridge and New York, NY.

Betz, R. and Stato, M. (2006), "Emissions trading: lessons learnt from the 1st phase of the EU-ETS and prospects for the 2nd phase", *Climate Policy* 6, pp. 351-359.

Bhagwati, J. and Mavroidis, P.C. (2007), "Is action against US exports for failure to sign Kyoto Protocol WTO-legal?", *World Trade Review* 6:2, pp. 299-310.

Biermann, F., Böhm, F., Brohm, R., Dröge, S. and Trabol, H (2003), *The Polluter Pays Principle under WTO Law: The Case of National Energy Policy Instruments*, Federal Ministry of the Environment, Nature Conservation and Nuclear Safety, Research Report, 81 p.

Biermann, F. and Brohm, R. (2005a), "Border Adjustments on Energy Taxes: A Possible Tool for European Policymakers in Implementing the Kyoto Protocol?", *Vierteljahrshefte zur Wirtschaftsforschung* 74:2, pp. 249-258.

Biermann, F. and Brohm, R. (2005b), "Implementing the Kyoto Protocol without the USA: the strategic role of energy tax adjustments at the border", *Climate Policy* 4, pp. 289-302.

Bijker, W., Hughes, T.P. and Pinch, T. (eds.) (1989), *The Social Construction of Technological Systems: New Directions in the Sociology and History of Technology*, MIT Press, Cambridge, MA.

BioGlossary (accessed May 2009). Available at www.everythingbio.com/glos/index.php.

Boemare, C. and Quirion P. (2002), "Implementing Greenhouse Gas Trading in Europe: Lessons from Economic Theory and International Experiences", *FEEM Working Paper* 35, 25 p.

Bohm, P. (2003), "Allocating Allowances in Greenhouse Gas Emissions Trading", *Emissions Trading Policy Briefs* 2, 16 p.

Boko, M., Niang, I., Nyong, A., Vogel, C., Githeko, A., Medany, M., Osman-Elasha, B., Tabo, R. and Yanda, P. (2007), "Africa", in Parry, M.L., Canziani, O.F., Palutikof, J.P., van der Linden, P.J. and Hanson, C.E. (eds.), *Climate Change 2007: Impacts, Adaptation and Vulnerability. Contribution of Working Group II to the Fourth Assessment Report of the Intergovernmental Panel on Climate Change*, Cambridge University Press, Cambridge, pp. 433-467.

Bony, S., Dufresne, J.L., Colman, R., Kattsov, V.M., Allan, R.P., Bretherton C.S., Hall, A., Hallegatte, S., Holland, M.M., Ingram, W., Randall, D.A., Soden, B.J., Tselioudis, G., Webb, M.J. (2006), "How well do we understand and evaluate climate change feedback processes?", *Journal of Climate* 19, pp. 3445-3482.

Boom, J.T. and Nentjes, A. (2003), "Alternative Design Options for Emissions Trading: A Survey and Assessment of the Literature", in Faure, M., Gupta, J. and Netjes A. (eds.), *Climate change and the Kyoto protocol: The Role of Institutions and Instruments to Control Global Change*, Edward Elgar Publishing, Cheltenham, 361 p., pp. 45-67.

Boot, P. (2009), *The overriding importance of energy efficiency: global trends and needs*, presentation at the Joint Workshop of the IEA/ISO/IEC on International Standards to Promote Energy Efficiency and Reduce Carbon Emissions.

Borjas, G.J., Freeman, B., Katz, L.F., DiNardo, J., and Abowd, J.M. (1997), "How Much Do Immigration and Trade Affect Labor Market Outcomes?", *Brookings Papers on Economic Activity* 1997:1, pp. 1-90.

Bound, J. and Johnson, G. (1992), "Changes in the Structure of Wages in the 1980s: An Evaluation of Alternative Explanations", *American Economic Review* 82:3, pp. 371-92.

Brewer, T.L. (2007), *The technology agenda for international climate change policy: A taxonomy for structuring analyses and negotiations*, Background paper for European Climate Platform seminar on "Strategic aspects of technology for the UNFCCC and climate change debate: The Post-Bali technology agenda", 8 p.

Brooks, N. and Adger, W.N. (2005), "Assessing and enhancing adaptive capacity", in Lim, B., Spanger-Siegfried, E., Burton, I., Malone, E.L. and Huq, S. (eds.), *Adaptation Policy Frameworks for Climate Change*, Cambridge University Press, New York, NY, pp. 165-182.

Brown, M.A., Chandler, J., Lapsa, M.V. and Sovacool, B.K. (2008), *Carbon Lock-In: Barriers to Deploying Climate Change Mitigation Technologies*, Oak Ridge National Laboratory, ORNL/TM-2007/124, 153 p.

Buck, M. and Verheyen, R. (2001), *International Trade Law and Climate Change – A Positive Way Forward*, FES-Analyse Ökologische Marktwirtschaft, 43 p.

Bui, L. (1993), *Studies in Trade and Transboundary Externalities*, PhD Dissertation, MIT, Cambridge, MA, 127 p.

Bui, L. (1998), "Gains from Trade and Strategic Interaction: Equilibrium Acid Rain Abatement in the Eastern United States and Canada", *American Economic Review* 88:4, pp. 984-1001.

Bundesamt für Energie Schweiz (2007), *Erfahrungen mit Energiesteuern in Europa: Lehren für die Schweiz*, 173 p.

Burniaux, J. and Château, J. (2008), "An Overview of the OECD ENV-Linkages Model", *OECD Economics Department Working Papers* 653, OECD Publishing, 27 p.

Burton, I., Diringer, E. and Smith, J. (2006), *Adaptation to Climate Change: International Policy Options*, Pew Centre on Global Climate Change, Arlington, VA, 28 p.

Butler, L. and Neuhoff, K. (2004), "Comparison of Feed in Tariff, Quota and Auction Mechanisms to Support Wind Power Development", *MIT Institute Working Paper* 70, Cambridge, MA, 35 p.

Canada (2001), *Framework for Conducting Environmental Assessments of Trade Negotiations*, Canadian Department of Foreign Affairs and International Trade.

Canada (2007), *Regulatory Framework for Air Emissions*, Ministry of Environment, 38 p.

Canada (2008), *Turning the Corner: Taking Action to Fight Climate Change*, 8 p.

Canadell, J.G., Le Quéré, C., Raupach, M.R., Field, C.B., Buitehuis, E.T., Ciais, P., Conway, T.J., Gillett, N.P., Houghton, R.A. and Marland, G. (2007), "Contributions to accelerating atmospheric CO_2 growth from economic activity, carbon intensity and efficiency of natural sinks", *Proceedings of the National Academy of Sciences* 104:47, pp. 18866-18870.

Capoor, K. and Ambrosi, P. (2007), *State and Trends of the Carbon Market 2007*, World Bank, Washington, DC, 45 p.

Carbon Trust (2004), *The European Emissions Trading Scheme: Implications for Industrial Competitiveness*, London, 31 p.

CDIAC (Carbon Dioxide Information Analysis Center) (2009). Available at http://cdiac.ornl.gov.

Cebon, M. (2003), *The Australia-US Free Trade Agreement: An Environmental Impact Assessment*. Available at www.ozprospect.org/pubs/FTA.pdf.

CEC (1999a), *Issue Study 1. Maize in Mexico: Some Environmental Implications of the North American Free Trade Agreement (NAFTA)*. Available at www.cec.org/files/pdf/ECONOMY/engfeed_EN.pdf.

CEC(1999b), *Issue Study 2. Feedlot Production of Cattle in the United States and Canada: Some Environmental Implications of the North American Free Trade Agreement (NAFTA)*. Available at www.cec.org/files/pdf/ECONOMY/engfeed_EN.pdf.

CEC (1999c), *Issue Study 3. Electricity in North America: Some Environmental Implications of the North American Free Trade Agreement (NAFTA)*. Available at www.cec.org/files/pdf/ECONOMY/engelect_EN.pdf.

CEC (2002), *The Environmental Effects of Free Trade Papers Presented at the North American Symposium on Assessing the Linkages between Trade and Environment*. Available at www.cec.org/files/pdf/ECONOMY/symposium-e.pdf.

Cendra, J. de (2006), "Can Emissions Trading Schemes be Coupled with Border Tax Adjustments? An Analysis vis-à-vis WTO Law", *Review of European Community & International Environmental Law* 15:2, pp. 131-145.

Chandra, A. and Zulkieflimansyah (2003), "The dynamic of technological accumulation at the microeconomic level: lessons from Indonesia - a case study", *Asia Pacific Management Review* 8:3, pp. 365-407.

Chapman, L. (2007), "Transport and Climate Change: A Review", *Journal of Transport Geography* 15, pp. 354-367.

Charnovitz, S. (2003), "Trade and Climate: Potential Conflicts and Synergies", in Aldy, J.E., Ashton, J., Baron, R., Bodansky, R., Charnovitz, S., Diringer, E., Heller T. C., Pershing, J., Shukla P.R., Tubiana, L., Tudela, F., and Wang, X., *Beyond Kyoto. Advancing the international effort against climate change*, Pew Centre of Global Climate Change, Arlington, VA, pp. 141-170.

Chasek, P.S., Downie, D.L. and Brown, J.W. (2006), *Global Environmental Politics*, 4th edition, Westview Press, Cambridge.

Chaytor, B. and Cameron, J. (1995), *Taxes for Environmental Purposes: The Scope for Border Tax Adjustment under WTO Rules*, World Wildlife Fund, Gland, 17 p.

Chen, M. (1996), *Managing International Technology Transfer*, Van Nostrand Reinhold Company, New York, NY, 256 p.

Christensen, J.H., Hewitson, B., Busuioc, A., Chen, A., Gao, X., Held, I., Jones, R., Kolli, R.K., Kwon, W.-T., Laprise, R., Magaña Rueda, V., Mearns, L., Menéndez, C.G. , Räisänen, J., Rinke, A., Sarr, A. and Whetton, P. (2007), "Regional Climate Projections", in Solomon, S., Qin, D., Manning, M., Chen, Z., Marquis, M., Averyt, K.B., Tignor, M. and Miller, H.L. (eds.), *Climate Change 2007: The Physical Science Basis. Contribution of Working Group I to the Fourth Assessment Report of the Intergovernmental Panel on Climate Change*, Cambridge University Press, Cambridge, UK and New York, NY.

Claro, E. and Lucas, N. (2007), "Environmental goods: trade flows, policy considerations and negotiating strategies", in ICTSD, *Trade in Environmental Goods and Services and Sustainable Development, Domestic Considerations and Strategies for WTO negotiations*, Policy Discussion Paper, pp. 32-60.

Clémençon, R. (2008), "The Bali Road Map: A First Step on the Difficult Journey to a Post-Kyoto Protocol Agreement", *The Journal of Environment and Development* 17:1, pp. 70-94.

Clement, D., Lehman, M., Hamrin, J. and Wiser, R. (2005), *International Tax Incentives for Renewable Energy: Lessons for Public Policy*, prepared for Energy Foundation China Sustainable Energy Program, Centre for Resource Solutions, 27 p.

Cline, W.R. (2007), *Global Warming and Agriculture: Impact Estimates by Country*, Peterson Institute for International Economics, Washington, DC.

Coase, R. (1960), "The Problem of Social Cost", *The Journal of Law and Economics* 3, pp. 1-44.

Coe, D.T. and Helpman, R. (1995), "International R&D Spillovers", *European Economic Review* 39:5, pp. 859-887.

Coe, D.T., Helpman, E. and Hoffmaister, A. (1997), "North-South R&D Spillovers", *Economic Journal* 107, pp. 134-149.

Cole, M.A. and Elliott, R.J.R. (2003a), "Determining the Trade–Environment Composition Effect: The Role of Capital, Labor and Environmental Regulations", *Journal of Environmental Economics and Management* 46:3, pp. 363-383.

Cole, M.A. and Elliott, R.J.R. (2003b), "Do environmental regulations influence trade patterns? Testing old and new trade theories", *The World Economy* 26:8, pp. 1163-1186.

Colombier, M. and Menanteau, P. (1997), "From energy labelling to performance standards: some methods of stimulating technical change to obtain greater energy efficiency", *Energy Policy* 25:4, pp. 425-434.

Confalonieri, U., Menne, B., Akhtar, R., Ebi, K.L., Hauengue, M., Kovats, R.S., Revich, B. and Woodward, A. (2007), "Human health", in Parry, M.L., Canziani, O.F., Palutikof, J.P., van der Linden, P.J. and Hanson, C.E. (eds.), *Climate Change 2007: Impacts, Adaptation and Vulnerability. Contribution of Working Group II to the Fourth Assessment Report of the Intergovernmental Panel on Climate Change*, Cambridge University Press, Cambridge, pp. 391-431.

Convery, F. (2003), "Issues in Emissions Trading – an Introduction", *Emissions Trading Policy Briefs*, 12 p.

Copeland, B.R. and Taylor, M.S. (2003), *Trade and the Environment*, Princeton University Press, Princeton and Oxford.

Copeland, B.R. and Taylor, M.S. (2004), "Trade, Growth and the Environment", *Journal of Economic Literature* 46:1, pp. 7-71.

Copenhagen Economics and IPR Company (2009), *Are IPR a barrier to the transfer of climate change technology?*, Report commissioned by the European Commission (DG Trade), 55 p.

Cosbey, A. (2007), "Unpacking the Wonder Tool: Border Charges in Support of Climate Change", *Bridges* 11:7, ICTSD.

Cosbey, A. (2008), *Border Carbon Adjustment*, Trade and Climate Change Seminar, Copenhagen June 2008, IISD, German Marshall Fund of the United States, 8 p.

Cosbey, A. and Tarasofsky, R. (2007), *Climate Change, Competitiveness and Trade*, Chatham House Report, 32 p.

Cressey, D. (2007), "Arctic melt opens Northwest passage", *Nature* 449.

Cruz, R.V., Harasawa, H., Lal, M., Wu, S., Anokhin, Y., Punsalmaa, B., Honda, Y., Jafari, M., Li, C. and Huu Ninh, N. (2007), "Asia", in Parry, M.L., Canziani, O.F., Palutikof, J.P., van der Linden, P.J. and Hanson, C.E. (eds.), *Climate Change 2007: Impacts, Adaptation and Vulnerability. Contribution of Working Group II to the Fourth Assessment Report of the Intergovernmental Panel on Climate Change*, Cambridge University Press, Cambridge, pp. 469-506.

CTI (Climate Technology Initiative) (2001), *DRAFT. Methods for Climate Change Technology Transfer Needs* 1/7:08. Available at CTI. http://www.climatetech.net/pdf/Ccmethod.pdf.

Dales, J. (1968), *Pollution, Property and Prices. An Essay in Policy-Making and Economics*, University of Toronto Press.

Danish, W.D. (2007), "The International Regime", in Gerrard, M.B. (ed.), *Global Climate Change and U.S. Law*, American Bar Association, Chicago, IL, 754 p.

Deardorff, A.V. (2006), *Terms of Trade. Glossary of International Economics*, World Scientific, 383 p.

Dechezleprêtre, A., Glachant, M., Hascic, I., Johnstone, N. and Ménière, Y. (2008), *Invention and Transfer of Climate Change Mitigation Technologies on a Global Scale: A Study Drawing on Patent Data*, CERNA Research Programme on Technology Transfer and Climate Change, Final Report, 49 p.

Demailly, D. and Quirion, P. (2006), "CO_2 abatement, competitiveness and leakage in the European cement industry under the EU ETS: grandfathering versus output-based allocation", *Climate Policy* 6, pp. 93-113.

Demaret, P. and Stewardson, R. (1994), "Border tax adjustments under GATT and EC law, and general implications for environmental taxes", *Journal of World Trade* 28, pp. 5-66.

Dinan, T. (2007), *Trade-offs in Allocating Allowances for CO_2 Emissions*, Congressional Budget Office, Economic and Budget Issue Brief, 8 p.

Doelle, M. (2004), "Climate Change and the WTO: Opportunities to Motivate State Action on Climate Change through the World Trade Organization", *RECIEL* 13:1, pp. 85-103.

Dollar, D. (1992), "Outward-oriented Developing Economies Really Do Grow More Rapidly: Evidence from 95 LDCs, 1976-1985", *Economic Development and Cultural Change* 40:3, pp. 523-544.

Dröge, S., Trabold, H., Biermann, F., Böhm, F. and Brohm, R. (2004), "National climate change policies and WTO law: a case study of Germany's new policies", *World Trade Review* 3:2, pp. 161-187.

Dutrénit, G. (2004), "Building Technological Capabilities in Latecomer Firms: A Review Essay", *Science Technology & Society* 9:2, pp. 209-241.

Easterling, W., Hurd, B. and Smith J. (2004), *Coping with Global Climate Change: The Role of Adaptation in the United States*, Pew Center on Global Climate Change, Arlington, VA.

Easterling, W.E., Aggarwal, P.K., Batima, P., Brander, K.M., Erda, L., Howden, S.M., Kirilenko, A., Morton, J., Soussana, J.- F., Schmidhuber, J. and Tubiello, F.N. (2007), "Food, fibre and forest products", in Parry, M.L., Canziani, O.F., Palutikof, J.P., van der Linden, P.J. and Hanson, C.E. (eds.), *Climate Change 2007: Impacts, Adaptation and Vulnerability. Contribution of Working Group II to the Fourth Assessment Report of the Intergovernmental Panel on Climate Change*, Cambridge University Press, Cambridge, pp. 273-313.

Eaton, J. and Kortum, S. (2001), "Trade in Capital Goods", *European Economic Review* 45:7, pp. 1195-1235.

Ederington, J. and Minier, J. (2003), "Is environmental policy a secondary trade barrier? An empirical analysis", *Canadian Journal of Economics* 36:1, pp. 137-154.

Edquist, C. and Edquist, O. (1979), "Social Carriers of Techniques for Development", *Journal of Peace Research* 16:4, pp. 313-331.

Edwards, S. (1998), "Openness, Productivity and Growth: What Do We Really Know?", *Economic Journal* 108:1, pp. 383- 398.

EIA (Energy Information Administration) (2007), *International Energy Annual 2005*. Available at www.eia.doe.gov/iea.

EIA (2008), *International Energy Outlook 2008*, Energy Information Administration, Office of Integrated Analysis and Forecasting, U.S. Department of Energy, Washington, DC. Available at www.eia.doe.gov/oiaf/ieo/pdf/0484(2008).pdf.

Ekins, P. and Barker, T. (2002), "Carbon taxes and carbon emissions trading", in Hanley, N. and Roberts, C. (eds.), *Issues in Environmental Economics*, Blackwell Publishing, pp. 75-126.

Ellerman, A.D. and Joskow, P.L. (2008), *The European Union's Emissions Trading System in Perspective*, Pew Center on Global Climate Change, 51 p.

Ellis, J. and Tirpak, D. (2006), *Linking GHG emission trading schemes and markets*, OECD and IEA information paper, 33 p.

Ellis, M. (2007), *Experience with energy efficiency regulations for electrical equipment*, IEA Information Paper, OECD/IEA, 103 p.

Emori, S. and Brown, S.J. (2005), "Dynamic and thermodynamic changes in mean and extreme precipitation under changed climate", *Geophysical Research Letters* 32, L17706, doi:10.1029/2005GL023272.

Enkvist, P., Nauclér, T. and Rosander, J. (2007), "A cost curve for greenhouse gas reduction", *The McKinsey Quarterly* 1, McKinsey & Company.

Eriksen, S.H. and Kelly, P.M. (2007), "Developing credible vulnerability indicators for climate adaptation policy assessment", *Mitigation and Adaptation Strategies for Global Change* 12, pp. 495-524.

Estevadeordal, A., Shearer, M., and Suominen, K. (forthcoming), "Market Access Provisions in Regional Trade Agreements", in Estevadeordal, A., Suominen, K., and Teh, R. (eds.), *Regional Rules in the Global Trading System*, Cambridge University Press, Cambridge.

European Commission (2008), *Questions and Answers on the revised EU Emissions Trading System*, MEMO/08/796.

European Environment Agency (2005), "Market-based instruments for environmental policy in Europe", *EEA Technical Report* 8/2005, Copenhagen, 155 p.

European Parliament (2008a), "European Parliament legislative resolution of 17 December 2008 on the proposal for a directive of the European Parliament and of the Council amending Directive 2003/87/EC so as to improve and extend the greenhouse gas emission allowance trading system of the Community".

European Parliament (2008b), "Position of the European Parliament adopted at first reading on 17 December 2008 with a view to the adoption of Regulation (EC) No. ../2009 of the European Parliament and of the Council setting emission performance standards for new passenger cars as part of the Community's integrated approach to reduce CO_2 emissions from light-duty vehicles."

Eurostat (2003), *Energy taxes in the Nordic countries – does the polluter pay?*, National Statistical Offices in Norway, Sweden, Finland and Denmark, 43 p.

Faiz, A., Weaver, C.S. and Walsh, M.P. (1996), *Air Pollution from Motor Vehicles: Standards and Technologies for Controlling Emissions*, World Bank Publications, Washington, 246 p.

Feenstra, R.C. and Hanson, G.H. (1999), "The Impact of Outsourcing and High-Technology Capital on Wages: Estimates for the United States, 1979-1990", *Quarterly Journal of Economics* 114:3, pp. 907-40.

Field, C.B., Mortsch, L.D., Brklacich, M., Forbes, D.L., Kovacs, P., Patz, J.A., Running, S.W. and Scott, M.J. (2007), "North America", in Parry, M.L., Canziani, O.F., Palutikof, J.P., van der Linden, P.J. and Hanson, C.E. (eds.), *Climate Change 2007: Impacts, Adaptation and Vulnerability. Contribution of Working Group II to the Fourth Assessment Report of the Intergovernmental Panel on Climate Change*, Cambridge University Press, Cambridge, pp. 617-652.

Fisher, B.S., Nakicenovic, N., Alfsen, K., Corfee Morlot, J., de la Chesnaye, F., Hourcade, J.-Ch., Jiang, K., Kainuma, M., La Rovere, E., Matysek, A., Rana, A., Riahi, K., Richels, R., Rose, S., van Vuuren, D. and Warren, R. (2007), "Issues related to mitigation in the long term context", in Metz, B., Davidson, O.R., Bosch, P.R., Dave, R. and Meyer, L.A. (eds.), *Climate Change 2007: Mitigation. Contribution of Working Group III to the Fourth Assessment Report of the Inter-governmental Panel on Climate Change*, Cambridge University Press, Cambridge, pp. 169-250.

Fischer, C. (2003), *Combining Rate-Based and Cap-and-Trade Emissions Policies*, Resources for the Future, Discussion Paper, 23 p.

Fischer, C. and Newell, R.G., (2007), *Environmental and Technology Policies for Climate Mitigation*, Resources for the Future, Discussion Paper, 52 p.

Fischer, G., Shah, M., Tubiello, F.N. and van Velhuizen, H. (2005), "Socio-economic and climate change impacts on agriculture: an integrated assessment 1990 – 2080", *Philosophical Transactions of the Royal Society* 360, pp. 2067-2083.

Forster, P., Ramaswamy,vV., Artaxo, P., Berntsen, T., Betts, R., Fahey, D.W., Haywood, J., Lean, J., Lowe, D.C., Myhre, G., Nganga, J., Prinn, R., Raga, G., Schulz, M. and Van Dorland, R. (2007), "Changes in Atmospheric Constituents and in Radiative Forcing", in Solomon, S., Qin, D., Manning, M., Chen, Z., Marquis, M., Averyt, K.B., Tignor, M. and Miller, H.L. (eds.), *Climate Change 2007: The Physical Science Basis. Contribution of Working Group I to the Fourth Assessment Report of the Intergovernmental Panel on Climate Change*, Cambridge University Press, Cambridge, UK and New York, NY.

Fouquet, D., Grotz, C., Sawin, J. and Vassilakos, N. (2005), *Reflections on a possible unified EU financial support scheme for renewable energy systems (RES): a comparison of minimum-price and quota systems and an analysis of market conditions*, European Renewable Energies Federation and Worldwatch Institute, Brussels and Washington, DC, 26 p.

Foxon, T.J. (2003), *Inducing innovation for a low-carbon future: drivers, barriers and policies*, A report for The Carbon Trust, 55 p.

Frankel, J. and Rose, A. (2005), "Is Trade Good or Bad for the Environment? Sorting Out the Causality", *Review of Economics and Statistics* 87:1, pp. 85-91.

Frei, C. and Schär. C. (2001), "Detection of probability of trends in rare events: Theory and application to heavy precipitation in the Alpine region", *Journal of Climate* 14, pp. 1568-1584.

Garnaut, R. (2008), *The Garnaut climate change review*, Cambridge University Press, Cambridge, 680 p.

GATT (General Agreement on Tariffs and Trade) Working Party (1970), *Border tax adjustments,* Report adopted on 2 December 1970, L/3464, BISD 18S/97-109.

Geller, H., Harrington, P., Rosenfeld, A.H., Tanishima, S. and Unander, F. (2006), "Policies for increasing energy efficiency: Thirty years of experience in OECD countries", *Energy Policy* 34, pp. 556-573.

Genasci, M. (2008), "Border Tax Adjustments and Emissions Trading: The Implications of International Trade Law for Policy Design", *Carbon and Climate Law Review* 1.

Gillingham, K., Newell, R. and Palmer, K. (2004), *Retrospective examination of demand-side energy efficiency policies*, Resources for the Future, Discussion Paper 04-19 REV, 97 p.

Globerman, S., Kokko, A. and Sjöholm, F. (2000), "Technology Sourcing in Swedish MNEs and SMEs: Evidence from Patent Data", *Kyklos* 53:1, pp. 17-38.

Goh, G. (2004), "The World Trade Organization, Kyoto and Energy Tax Adjustments at the Border", *Journal of World Trade* 38:3, pp. 395-423.

Goldberg, P.K. and Pavcnik, N. (2004), "Trade, Inequality and Poverty: What Do We Know? Evidence from Recent Trade Liberalization Episodes in Developing Countries", in Collins, S.M. and Graham, C. (eds.), *Brookings Trade Forum 2004*, Brookings Institution Press, Washington, DC, pp. 223-69.

Goldberg, P.K. and Pavcnik, N. (2005), "Trade, Wages, and the Political Economy of Trade Protection: Evidence from the Colombian Trade Reforms", *Journal of International Economics* 66:1, pp. 75-105.

Goldberg, P.K. and Pavcnik, N. (2007), "Distributional Effects of Globalization in Developing Countries", *Journal of Economic Literature* 45:1, pp. 39-82.

Gouchoe, S., Everette, V. and Haynes, R. (2002), *Case studies on the Effectiveness of State Financial Incentives for Renewable Energy*, National Renewable Energy Laboratory, Subcontractor Report, NREL/SR-620-32819.

Goulder, L.H. and Schneider, S.L. (1999) "Induced Technological Change and the Attractiveness of CO_2 Emissions Abatement Policies", *Resource and Energy Economics* 21, pp. 211-253.

Green, A. (2006), "Trade rules and climate change subsidies", *World Trade Review* 5:3, pp. 377-414.

Grether, J. M., Mathys, N. A. and de Melo, J. (2007), "Trade, Technique and Composition Effects: What is Behind the Fall in World-Wide SO2 Emissions 1990-2000?", *Fondazione Eni Enrico Mattei Nota Di Lavoro* 93.

Gross, R. and Foxon, T. (2003), "Policy support for innovation to secure improvements in resource productivity", *International Journal of Environmental Technology and Management* 3:2.

Grossman, G.M. and Helpman, E. (1991), *Innovation and Growth in the Global Economy*, MIT Press, Cambridge, MA, 375 p.

Grossman, G.M. and Krueger, A.B. (1993), "Environmental Impacts of a North American Free Trade Agreement", in Garber, P.M. (ed.), *The US-Mexico Free Trade Agreement*, MIT Press, Cambridge, MA, pp. 13-56.

GTZ (Gesellschaft für Technische Zusammenarbeit) (2007), *International Fuel Prices 2007*, Federal Energy Ministry for Economic Cooperation and Development, Bonn, 101 p.

GTZ (Gesellschaft für Technische Zusammenarbeit) (2009), *International Fuel Prices 6th Edition – Data Preview*, 11 p.

Gupta, S., Tirpak, D.A., Burger, N., Gupta, J., Höhne, N., Boncheva, A.I., Kanoan, G.M., Kolstad, C., Kruger, J.A., Michaelowa, A., Murase, S., Pershing, J., Saijo, T. and Sari, A. (2007), "Policies, Instruments and Co-operative Arrangements", in Metz, B., Davidson, O.R., Bosch, P.R., Dave, R. and Meyer, L.A. (eds.), *Climate Change 2007: Mitigation. Contribution of Working Group III to the Fourth Assessment Report of the Intergovernmental Panel on Climate Change*, Cambridge University Press, Cambridge and New York, NY.

Gurney, A., Ford, M., Low, K., Tulloh, C., Jakeman, G. and Gunasekera, D. (2007), *Technology.* "Toward a low emissions future", *Australian Bureau of Agricultural and Resource Economics, ABARE Research Report* 07:16, 131 p.

Hagedoorn, J. (1990), "Organizational modes of inter–firm cooperation and technology transfer". *Technovation* 10:1, pp. 17-30.

Haites, E., Duan, M. and Seres, S. (2006), "Technology transfer by CDM projects", *Climate Policy* 6:3, pp. 327-344.

Hansen, U.E. (2008), "Technology and knowledge transfer from Annex 1 countries to Non Annex 1 countries under the Kyoto Protocol's Clean Development Mechanism (CDM) – An empirical case study of CDM projects implemented in Malaysia", *CD4CDM, Working Paper No. 5*, UNEP Risoe Centre.

Hanson, G. and Harrison, A. (1999), "Trade and Wage Inequality in Mexico", *Industrial and Labor Relations Review* 52.2, pp. 271-88.

Harris, M.N., Kónya, L. and Mátyás, L. (2002), "Modelling the Impact of Environmental Regulations on Bilateral Trade Flows: OECD, 1990-96", *The World Economy* 25:3, pp. 387-405.

Harrison, A. and Hanson, G. (1999), "Who Gains from Trade Reform? Some Remaining Puzzles", *Journal of Development Economics* 59:1, pp. 125-54.

Harvey, I. (2008), *Intellectual Property Rights, The Catalyst to Deliver Low Carbon Technologies, Breaking the Climate Deadlock*, Briefing Paper, The Climate Group, 17 p.

Haskel, J. and Slaughter, M.J. (2002), "Does The Sector Bias of Skill-biased Technical Change Explain Changing Skill Premia?", *European Economic Review* 46:10, pp. 1757-83.

Hayashi, F. (2000), *Econometrics*, Princeton University Press, Princeton, NJ.

Helpman, E. (1997), "R&D and Productivity: the International Connection", *National Bureau of Economic Research (NBER) Working Paper* 6101, Cambridge, Massachusetts.

Hennessy, K., Fitzharris, B., Bates, B.C., Harvey, N., Howden, S.M., Hughes, L., Salinger J. and Warrick, R. (2007), "Australia and New Zealand", in Parry, M.L., Canziani, O.F., Palutikof, J.P., van der Linden, J.P. and Hanson, C.E. (eds.), *Climate Change 2007: Impacts, Adaptation and Vulnerability. Contribution of Working Group II to the Fourth Assessment Report of the Intergovernmental Panel on Climate Change,* Cambridge University Press, Cambridge, pp. 507-540.

Hertel, T. and Randhir, T. (2000), "Trade Liberalization as a Vehicle for Adapting to Global Warming", *Agriculture and Resource Economics Review* 29:2, pp. 1-14.

Hoekman, B. and Javorcik, B.S. (eds.) (2006), *Global Integration and Technology Transfer*, Palgrave Macmillan, New York, NY.

Hoerner A. (1998), *The role of Border Tax Adjustments in Environmental Taxation: Theory and US Experience*, Working Paper, Presented at the International Workshop on Market Based Instruments and International Trade of the Institute for Environmental Studies, Amsterdam.

Hoerner, J.A. and Müller, F. (1996), *Carbon taxes for climate protection in a competitive world*, A paper prepared for the Swiss Federal Office for Foreign Economic Affairs by the Environmental Tax Program of the Center for Global Change, University of Maryland College Park, 47 p.

Holt, C., Shobe, W., Burtraw, D., Palmer, K. and Goeree, J. (2007), *Auction design for selling CO_2 emission allowances under the Regional Greenhouse Gas Initiative*, Final Report, RGGI, 130 p.

Holz-Eakin, D., and Selden, T.M. (1995), "Stoking the Fires? CO_2 Emissions and Economic Growth", *Journal of Public Economics* 57:1, pp. 85-101.

Hourcade, J.-C., Demailly, D., Neuhoff, K. and Sato, M. (2007), *Differentiation and Dynamics of EU ETS Industrial Competitiveness Impacts*, Climate Strategies, 108 p.

Houser, T., Bradley, R., Childs, B., Werksman, J. and Heilmayr, R. (2008), *Levelling the Carbon Playing Field. International Competition and US Climate Policy Design,* Peterson Institute for International Economics and World Resources Institute, Washington DC, 95 p.

Howse, R. and Bork, P.B. van (2006), "Options for Liberalising Trade in Environmental Goods in the Doha Round", *ICTSD Programme on Trade and Environment* 2, 32 p.

Huang, W.M., Lee, G.W.M. and Wu, C.C. (2008), "GHG Emissions, GDP Growth and the Kyoto Protocol: A Revisit of Environmental Kuznets Curve Hypothesis", *Energy Policy* 36, pp. 239-247.

Huh, K. (1999), "Initial Experiences with Energy Labelling Programmes: Evaluating the Effectiveness of Energy Labelling", *Compendium on Energy Conservation Legislation in Countries of the Asia and Pacific Region*, UNESCAP.

Hummels, D. (2007), "Transportation Costs and International Trade in the Second Era of Globalization", *Journal of Economic Perspectives* 21:3, pp. 131-154.

Hunter, D., Salzman, J. and Zaelke, D. (2002), *International Environmental Law and Policy*, Foundation Press, New York, NY.

Hutchison, C. (2006), "Does TRIPS facilitate or impede Climate Change Technology Transfer into Developing Countries?", *Law & Technology Journal* 3, University of Ottawa, pp. 517-537.

IATA (International Air Transport Association) (2007), *World Air Transport Statistics*, IATA Geneva.

ICTSD (International Centre for Trade and Sustainable Development) (2008a), *Climate Change, Technology Transfer and Intellectual Property Rights*, Copenhagen Economics, 11 p.

ICTSD (2008b), *Liberalization of Trade in Environmental Goods for Climate Change Mitigation: The Sustainable Development Context*, Publication prepared for the Seminar on Trade and Climate Change, Copenhagen, 8 p.

IEA (International Energy Agency) (1999), *World Energy Outlook Insights, Looking at Energy Subsidies: Getting the Prices Right*, 224 p.

IEA (2000), *Energy Labels and Standards*, OECD/IEA, 195 p.

IEA (2001), *International Emission Trading: From Concept to Reality*, 159 p.

IEA (2004), *Renewable Energy: Market and Policy Trends in IEA Countries*, IEA/OECD, 668 p.

IEA (2006a), *Energy Technology Perspectives 2006 – Scenarios & Strategies to 2050, In support of the G8 Plan of Action*, OECD/IEA, Paris.

IEA (2006b), *Wind Energy Annual Report 2006*, 271 p.

IEA (2006c), *World Energy Outlook 2006*, IEA, Paris.

IEA (2007), *CO_2 Emissions from Fuel Combustion: 1971-2005*, IEA, Paris.

IEA (2007a), *Energy Use in the New Millennium*, OECD/IEA, 165 p.

IEA (2007b), *Renewables in global energy supply*, IEA Fact Sheet, 28 p.

IEA (2007c), *Tracking Industrial Energy Efficiency and CO_2 Emissions, Energy Indicators*, OECD/IEA, 321 p.

IEA (2008a), *Energy Technology Perspectives 2008 – Scenarios and Strategies to 2050*, 650 p.

IEA (2008b), *World Energy Outlook 2008*, IEA, Paris.

IEA Climate Change database (2008, last update), *Addressing Climate Change Policies and Measures Database*. Available at www.iea.org/textbase/pm/?mode=cc.

IMF (International Monetary Fund) (2008), *The Fiscal Implications of Climate Change*, Fiscal Affairs Department, 40 p.

IMO (International Maritime Organization) (2007), *International Shipping and World Trade: Facts and Figures*. Available at www.imo.org/includes/blastDataOnly.asp/data_id%3D23754/InternationalShippingandWorldTrade-factsandfigures.pdf.

IMO (2008), *Prevention of Air Pollution from Ships: Updated 2000 Study on Greenhouse Gas Emissions from Ships*, Phase 1 Report. MEPC 58/INF.6, International Maritime Organization, London.

IFA (International Fertilizer Industry Association) (2007), *Fertilizer consumption statistics*. Available at www.fertilizer.org/ifa/statistics.asp.

IPCC (Intergovernmental Panel on Climate Change) (1990), *Climate Change 1990: The IPCC Impacts Assessment. Contribution of Working Group II to the First Assessment Report of the Intergovernmental Panel on Climate Change*, Tegart, W.J.McG., Sheldon, G.W. and Griffiths, D.C. (eds.), Australian Government Publishing Service, Canberra.

IPCC (1995), *Climate Change 1995: Impacts, Adaptations and Mitigation of Climate Change. Contribution of Working Group II to the Second Assessment Report of the Intergovernmental Panel on Climate Change*, Watson, R.T., Zinyowera, M.C., Moss, R.H. and Dokken, D.J. (eds.), Cambridge University Press, Cambridge and New York, NY.

IPCC (2000a), *Emissions Scenarios. A special report of the International Panel on Climate Change (IPCC) Working Group III*, Cambridge University Press, Cambridge.

IPCC (2000b), *Methodological and technological issues in technology transfer. A special report of the International Panel on Climate Change (IPCC) Working Group III*, Cambridge University Press, Cambridge.

IPCC (2001a), *Climate Change 2001: Impacts, Adaptations and Vulnerability of Climate Change. Contribution of Working Group II to the Third Assessment Report of the Intergovernmental Panel on Climate Change*, McCarthy, J.J., Canziani, O.F., Leary, N.A., Dokken, D.J., and White, K.S. (eds.), Cambridge University Press, Cambridge and New York, NY, 1000 p.

IPCC (2001b), *Climate Change 2001: Synthesis Report. A Contribution of Working Groups I, II, and III to the Third Assessment Report of the Integovernmental Panel on Climate Change*, Watson, R.T. and the Core Writing Team (eds.), Cambridge University Press, Cambridge and New York, NY, 398 p.

IPCC (2007a), *Climate Change 2007: Synthesis Report. Contribution of Working Groups I, II and III to the Fourth Assessment Report of the Intergovernmental Panel on Climate Change*, Core Writing Team, Pachauri, R.K and Reisinger, A. (eds.), IPCC, Geneva, 104 p.

IPCC (2007b), *Glossary of terms used in the IPCC Fourth Assessment Report. Working Groups I, II and III*. Available at www.ipcc.ch/glossary/index.htm.

IPCC (2007c), "Summary for Policymakers", in Solomon, S., Qin, D., Manning, M., Chen, Z., Marquis, M., Averyt, K.B., Tignor, M. and Miller, H.L. (eds.), *Climate Change 2007:*

The Physical Science Basis. Contribution of Working Group I to the Fourth Assessment Report of the Intergovernmental Panel on Climate Change, Cambridge University Press, Cambridge and New York, NY.

IPCC (2007d), "Summary for Policymakers", in Parry, M.L., Canziani, O.F., Palutikof, J.P., van der Linden, P.J. and Hanson, C.E. (eds.), *Climate Change 2007: Impacts, Adaptation and Vulnerability. Contribution of Working Group II to the Fourth Assessment Report of the Intergovernmental Panel on Climate Change*, Cambridge University Press, Cambridge, 7-22.

IPCC (2007e), *Climate Change 2007: Mitigation. Contribution of Working Group III to the Fourth Assessment Report of the Intergovernmental Panel on Climate Change*, Metz, B., Davidson, O.R., Bosch, P.R., Dave R., Meyer L.A. (eds..), Cambridge University Press, Cambridge and New York, NY.

IPCC (2007f), "Summary for Policymakers", in Metz, B., Davidson, O.R., Bosch, P.R., Dave, R., Meyer, L.A. (eds.), *Climate Change 2007: Mitigation. Contribution of Working Group III to the Fourth Assessment Report of the Intergovernmental Panel on Climate Change*, Cambridge University Press, Cambridge and New York, NY.

Ismer, R. and Neuhoff, K. (2007), "Border Tax Adjustments: A Feasible Way to Address Non participation in Emission Trading", *Cambridge Working Papers, CMI Working Paper* 36, 42 p.

Jacot, J.H. (1997), "A general taxonomic approach to technology policy", in Dyker, D.A. (ed.), *The technology of transition*, Central European University Press, Budapest, pp. 20-28.

Jaffe, A.B., Peterson, S.R., Portney, P.R. and Stavins, R.N. (1995), "Environmental Regulation and the Competitiveness of U.S. Manufacturing: What Does the Evidence Tell Us?", *Journal of Economic Literature* 33, pp. 132-163.

Janzen, B.G. (2008), "International Trade Law and the 'Carbon Leakage' Problem: Are Unilateral U.S. Import Restrictions the Solution?", *Sustainable Development Law and Policy* Winter, pp. 22-26.

Jha, V. (2008a), *EGS and Climate Change: A Reality Check*, PowerPoint presentation at UNEP Workshop on Post Bali: A Dialogue on Trade, Climate Change and Development. Available at www.unep.ch/etb/events/2008TradeClimateChangeMtg11Feb.php.

Jha, V. (2008b), "Environmental Priorities and Trade Policy for Environmental Goods: A Reality Check", *ICTSD Programme on Trade and Environment, Issue Paper* 7, 73 p.

Jones, L.E. and Manuelli, R.E. (1995), "A Positive Model of Growth and Pollution Controls", *National Bureau of Economic Research, Working Paper* 5205.

Jones, R.N. and Preston, B.L. (2006), *Climate Change Impacts, Risk and the Benefits of Mitigation*, A report for the Energy Futures Forum, CSIRO.

Juhn, C., Murphy, K.M. and Pierce, B. (1993), "Wage Inequality and the Rise in Returns to Skill", *Journal of Political Economy* 101:3, pp. 410-42.

Kahn Ribeiro, S., Kobayashi, S., Beuthe, M., Gasca, J., Greene, D., Lee, D.S., Muromachi, Y., Newton, P.J., Plotkin, S., Sperling, D., Wit, R., and Zhou, P.J. (2007), "Transport and Its Infrastructure", in Metz, B., Davidson, O.R., Bosch, P.R., Dave, R. and Meyer, L.A. (eds.), *Climate Change 2007: Mitigation. Contribution of Working Group III to the Fourth Assessment Report of the Intergovernmental Panel on Climate Change*, Cambridge University Press, Cambridge and New York, pp. 323-385.

Kaniaru, D. (ed.) (2007), *The Montreal Protocol: Celebrating 20 Years of Environmental Progress: Ozone Layer and Climate*, UNEP/Earthprint, London, 359 p.

Kalil, T. (2006), "Prizes for Technological Innovation", *The Hamilton Project Discussion Paper 2006-08*, The Brookings Institution, 29 p.

Keller, W. (2004), "International Technology Diffusion", *Journal of Economic Perspectives* 42, pp. 752-782.

Keller, W. (2007), "Transfer of Technology", in Blume, L. and Durlauf, S. (eds.), *New Palgrave Dictionary of Economics*, 2nd edition, MacMillan.

Kelly, D.L. (1997), *On Kuznets Curves Arising from Stock Externalities*, Department of Economics Working Paper, University of California, Santa Barbara, CA.

Kennett, M. (2005), "Environmental Goods and Services. A Synthesis of Country Studies", *OECD Trade and Environment, Working Paper* 3, 27 p.

Kirkpatrick, C., Lee, N., Curran, J., Franklyn, J., George, C. and Nomura, H. (2002), *Further Development of the Methodology for a Sustainability Impact Assessment of Proposed WTO Negotiations*, Final Report to the European Commission Manchester: Institute for Development Policy and Management, University of Manchester.

Klein, R.J.T., Huq, S., Denton, F., Downing, T.E., Richels, R.G., Robinson, J.B. and Toth, F.L. (2007), "Inter-relationships between adaptation and mitigation", in Parry, M.L., Canziani, O.F., Palutikof, J.P., van der Linden, P.J. and Hanson, C.E. (eds.), *Climate Change 2007: Impacts, Adaptation and Vulnerability. Contribution of Working Group II to the Fourth Assessment Report of the Intergovernmental Panel on Climate Change*, Cambridge University Press, Cambridge, pp. 745-777.

Klein Tank, A.M.G. and Können, G.P. (2003), "Trends in indices of daily temperature and precipitation extremes in Europe, 1946–1999", *Journal of Climate* 16, pp. 3665-3680.

Klepper, G. and Peterson, S. (2003), "International Trade and Competitiveness Effects", *Emissions Trading Policy Briefs* 6, CATEP Project, Environmental Institute, 16 p.

Kollmuss, A., Zink, H. and Polycarp, C. (2008), *Making Sense of the Voluntary Carbon Market: A Comparison of Carbon Offset Standards*, WWF, Stockholm Environment Institute and Tricorona, 105 p.

Kolstad, C.D. (2000), *Environmental Economics*, Oxford University Press, New York/Oxford, 400 p.

Kraemer, R.A., Hinterberger, F. and Tarasofsky, R. (2007), *What contribution can trade policy make towards combating climate change?*, Policy Department External Policies, European Parliament, Brussels.

Krämer, L. (2002), *Casebook on EU Environmental Law*, Hart Publishing, Oxford, 440 p.

Krugman, P. (1994), "Competitiveness: A dangerous obsession", *Foreign Affairs* 73:2, pp. 28-44.

Part I

Part II

Part III

Part IV

Kuada, J. (ed.) (2003), *Culture and Technological Transformation in the South: Transfer or Local Innovation*, Samfundslitteratur, Copenhagen.

Kumar, V., Kumar, U. and Persaud, A. (1999), "Building technological Capability Through Importing technology: The Case of Indonesian Manufacturing Industry", *Journal of Technology Transfer* 24:1, pp. 81-96.

Kundzewicz, Z.W., Mata, L.J., Arnell, N.W., Döll, P., Kabat, P., Jiménez, B., Miller, K.A., Oki, T., Sen, Z. and Shiklomanov, I.A. (2007), "Freshwater resources and their management", in Parry, M.L., Canziani, O.F., Palutikof, J.P., van der Linden, P.J. and Hanson, C.E. (eds.), *Climate Change 2007: Impacts, Adaptation and Vulnerability. Contribution of Working Group II to the Fourth Assessment Report of the Intergovernmental Panel on Climate Change*, Cambridge University Press, Cambridge, pp. 173-210.

Kutas, G., Lindberg, C. and Steenblik, R. (2007), *Biofuel – At What Cost?, Government Support for ethanol and biodiesel in the EU*, International Institute for Sustainable Development, 104 p.

Kypreos, S. and Bahn, O. (2003), "A MERGE model with Endogenous Technological Progress", *Environmental Modeling and Assessment* 8:3, pp. 249-259.

Le Quéré, C., Rödenbeck, C., Buitenhuis, E.T., Conway, T.J., Langenfelds, R., Gomez, A., Labuschagne, C., Ramonet, M., Nakazawa, T., Metzl, N., Gillett, N. and Heimann, M. (2007), "Saturation of the Southern Ocean CO_2 Sink Due to Recent Climate Change", *Science* 316:5832, pp. 1735-1738.

Le Treut, H., Somerville, R., Cubasch, U., Ding, Y., Mauritzen, C., Mokssit, A., Peterson, T. and Prather, M. (2007), "Historical Overview of Climate Change", in Solomon, S., Qin, D., Manning, M., Chen, Z., Marquis, M., Averyt, K.B., Tignor, M. and Miller, H.L. (eds.), *Climate Change 2007: The Physical Science Basis. Contribution of Working Group I to the Fourth Assessment Report of the Intergovernmental Panel on Climate Change*, Cambridge University Press, Cambridge and New York, NY.

Lemke, P., Ren, J., Alley, R.B., Allison, I., Carrasco, J., Flato, G., Fujii, Y., Kaser, G., Mote, P., Thomas, R.H. and Zhang, T. (2007) "Observations: Changes in Snow, Ice and Frozen Ground", in Solomon, S., Qin, D., Manning, M., Chen, Z., Marquis, M., Averyt, K.B., Tignor, M. and Miller, H.L. (eds.), *Climate Change 2007: The Physical Science Basis. Contribution of Working Group I to the Fourth Assessment Report of the Intergovernmental Panel on Climate Change*, Cambridge University Press, Cambridge and New York, NY.

Levin, K. and Pershing, J. (2008), *Climate Science 2007. Major New Discoveries*, WRI Issue Brief, World Resources Institute, Washington, DC.

Levin, M. (1997), "Technology transfer is organizational development: An investigation into the relationship between technology transfer and organizational change", *International Journal of Technology Management* 14:2-4, pp. 297-308.

Levine, M., Ürge-Vorsatz, D., Blok, K., Geng, L., Harvey, D., Lang, S., Levermore, G., Mongameli Mehlwana, A., Mirasgedis, S., Novikova, A., Rilling, J., Yoshino, H. (2007), "Residential and commercial buildings", in, Metz, B., Davidson, O.R., Bosch, P.R., Dave, R. and Meyer, L.A. (eds.), *Climate Change 2007: Mitigation. Contribution of Working Group III to the Fourth Assessment Report of the Intergovernmental Panel on Climate Change*, Cambridge University Press, Cambridge and New York, NY.

Levitus, S., Antonov, J.I. and Boyer, T.P. (2005), "Warming of the World Ocean, 1955-2003", *Geophysical Research Letters* 32:L02604.

Littleton, M. (2008), "The TRIPS Agreement and Transfer of Climate-Change-Related Technologies to Developing Countries", *UNDESA Working Paper* 71, ST/ESA/2008/DWP/71, 44 p.

Lodefalk, M. and Storey, M. (2005), "Climate Measures and WTO Rules on Subsidies", *Journal of World Trade* 39:1, pp. 23-44.

López, A. (2009), "Innovation and Appropriability, Empirical Evidence and Research Agenda", in World Intellectual Property Organization (WIPO), *The Economics of Intellectual Property, Suggestions for Further Research in Developing Countries and Countries with Economies in Transition*, pp.1-40.

Maddison, A. (2001), *The World Economy: A Millennial Perspective*, OECD, Paris.

Magrin, G., Gay García, C., Cruz Choque, D., Giménez, J.C., Moreno, A.R., Nagy, G.J., Nobre, C. and Villamizar, A. (2007), "Latin America", in Parry, M.L., Canziani, O.F., Palutikof, J.P., van der Linden, P.J. and Hanson C.E. (eds.), *Climate Change 2007: Impacts, Adaptation and Vulnerability. Contribution of Working Group II to the Fourth Assessment Report of the Intergovernmental Panel on Climate Change*, Cambridge University Press, Cambridge, pp. 581-615.

Managi, S. (2004), "Trade Liberalization and the Environment: Carbon Dioxide for 1960-1999", *Economics Bulletin* 17:1, pp. 1-5.

Managi, S., Hibiki, A. and Tsurumi, T. (2008), "Does Trade Liberalization Reduce Pollution Emissions, *Research Institute of Economy, Trade and Industry (RIETI) Discussion Paper Series* 08-E-013.

Markusen, J.R. (1975a), "Cooperative Control of International Pollution and Common Property Resources", *Quarterly Journal of Economics* 89:4, pp. 618-632.

Markusen, J.R. (1975b), "International Externalities and Optimal Tax Structures", *Journal of International Economics* 5, pp. 15-29.

Marland, G., Boden, T.A. and Andres, R.J. (2007), "Global, Regional, and National CO_2 Emissions", in *Trends: A Compendium of Data on Global Change*, Carbon Dioxide Information Analysis Center, Oak Ridge National Laboratory, US Department of Energy, Oak Ridge, TN.

Martinot, E. and Junfeng, L. (2007), *Powering China's Development*, Worldwatch Institute Special Report, 50 p.

Martinot, E., Sinton, J.E. and Haddad, B.M. (1997), "International technology transfer for climate change mitigation and the cases of Russia and China", *Annual Review of Energy and the Environment* 22, pp. 357-401.

Martinot, E., Wiser, R. and Hamrin, J. (2005), *Renewable Energy Policies and Markets in the United States*, Center for Resources Solutions of San Francisco, 27 p.

Maskus, K.E. (2005), "The Role of Intellectual Property Rights in Encouraging Foreign Direct Investment and Technology Transfer", in Fink, C. and Maskus, K.E. (eds.), *Intellectual Property and Development. Lessons from Recent Economic Research*, Oxford University Press, New York, NY, pp. 41-75.

Maurer, S.M. and Scotchmer S. (2003), "Procuring knowledge", *NBER Working Paper* 99303, 39 p.

McCarney, G. and Adamowicz, V. (2005), *The Effects of Trade Liberalization on the Environment: An Empirical Study*, selected paper prepared for presentation at the Canadian Agricultural Economics Society Annual Meeting 6-8 July, San Francisco, California.

McGregor, P.G., Swales, K.K. and Turner, K. (2008), "The CO_2 'Trade Balance' Between Scotland and the Rest of the UK: Performing a Multi-Region Environmental Input-Output Analysis with Limited Data", *Ecological Economics* 66:4, pp. 662-673.

McKibben, W.J. and Wilcoxen, P.J. (2004), "Climate Policy and Uncertainty: the Roles of Adaptation Versus Mitigation", Brookings Discussion Papers in *International Economics* 161.

McKinsey (2009), *Pathways to a low-carbon economy*, McKinsey & Company, New York, NY.

McMichael, A.J., Campbell-Lendrum, D., Kovats, S., Edwards, S., Wilkinson, P., Wilson, T., Nicholls, R., Hales, S., Tanser, F., Le Sueur, D., Schlesinger, M. and Andronova, N. (2004), "Global climate change", in Ezzati, M., Lopez, A.D., Rodgers, A. and Murray, C.J.L., *Comparative Quantification of Health Risks: Global and Regional Burden of Disease due to Selected Risk Factors*, World Health Organization, Geneva.

Meehl, G.A., Stocker, T.F., Collins, W.D., Friedlingstein, P., Gaye, A.T., Gregory, J.M., Kitoh, A., Knutti, R., Murphy, J.M., Noda, A., Raper, S.C.B., Watterson, I.G., Weaver, A.J. and Zhao, Z.-C. (2007), "Global Climate Projections", in Solomon, S., Qin, D., Manning, M., Chen, Z., Marquis, M., Averyt, K.B., Tignor, M. and Miller, H.L. (eds.), *Climate Change 2007: The Physical Science Basis. Contribution of Working Group I to the Fourth Assessment Report of the Intergovernmental Panel on Climate Change*, Cambridge University Press, Cambridge and New York, NY.

Meidinger, E. (1985), "On Explaining the Development of 'Emissions Trading' in U.S. Air Pollution Regulation", *Law & Policy* 7:4, pp. 457-489.

Mendelsohn, R., Morrison, W., Schlesinger, M.E. and Andronova, N.G. (2000), "Country-specific market impacts of climate change", *Climatic Change* 45, pp. 553-569.

Menne, B. and Ebi, K.L. (eds.) (2006), *Climate Change and Adaptation Strategies for Human Health*, Steinkopff Verlag Darmstadt.

Metcalfe, J.S. (1995), "Technology systems and technology policy in an evolutionary framework", *Cambridge Journal of Economics* 19:1, pp. 25-46.

Meyer-Ohlendorf, N. and Gerstetter, C. (2009), "Trade and Climate Change. Triggers or Barriers for Climate Friendly Technology Transfer and Development?", *Dialogue on Globalization, Occasional Papers* 41, 42 p.

Meyers, S., McMahon, J. and McNeil, M. (2005), "Realized and Prospective Impacts of US Energy Efficiency Standards for Residential Appliances", 2004 Update, *Lawrence Berkeley National Laboratory* 56417, Environmental Energy Technologies Division, 39 p.

Mimura, N., Nurse, L., McLean, R.F., Agard, J., Briguglio, L., Lefale, P., Payet, R. and Sem, G. (2007), "Small islands", in Parry, M.L., Canziani, O.F., Palutikof, J.P., van der Linden, P.J. and Hanson, C.E. (eds.), *Climate Change 2007: Impacts, Adaptation and Vulnerability. Contribution of Working Group II to the Fourth Assessment Report of the Intergovernmental Panel on Climate Change*, Cambridge University Press, Cambridge, pp. 687-716.

Missfeldt, F. and Hauff, J. (2004), "The role of economic instruments", in Owen, A.D. and Hanlex, N., (eds.), *The Economics of Climate Change*, Routledge, New York, NY, pp. 115-146.

Moltke A. von, McKee, C. (eds.) (2004), *Energy Subsidies: Lessons Learned in Assessing their Impact and Designing Policy Reforms*, Greenleaf Publishing, Sheffield, 175 p.

Moomaw, W.R. and Unruh, G.C. (1997), "Are Environmental Kuznets Curves Misleading Us? The Case of CO_2 Emissions", *Environment and Development Economics* 2:4, pp. 451-463.

Morgan, T. (2007), *Energy Subsidies. Their Magnitude, How they Affect Energy Investment and Greenhouse Gas Emissions, and Prospects for Reform*, Report to the UNFCCC Secretariat, 25 p.

Morgenstern, R.D., Aldy, J.E., Herrnstadt, E.M., Ho, M. and Pizer, W.A. (2007), "Competitiveness Impacts of Carbon Dioxide Pricing Policies on Manufacturing", in Kopp, R.J. and Pizer, W.A., *Assessing U.S. Climate Policy Options. A report summarizing work at RFF as part of the inter-industry U.S. Climate Policy Forum*, Resources for the Future, 203 p.

Mote, T.L. (2007), "Greenland surface melt trends 1973 – 2007: Evidence of a large increase in 2007", *Geophysical Research Letters* 34, L22507.

Muller. G and Hoerner, A (1997), *Using A Border Adjustment To Take The Lead On Climate Change Without Encouraging Runaway Shops*.

Mytelka, L. (2007), "Technology Transfer Issues in Environmental Goods and Services. An illustrative Analysis of Sectors Relevant to Air–pollution and renewable Energy", *ICTSD Trade and Environment Series Issue Paper* 6, International Centre for Trade and Sustainable Development, Geneva. Available at http://ictsd.net/downloads/2008/04/2007-04-lmytelka.pdf.

NASA (National Aeronautics and Space Administration) (2007), *Record Arctic Sea Ice Loss in 2007*. Available at http://earthobservatory.nasa.gov/Newsroom/NewImages/Images/arctic_ams_2007259.jpg.

Neelin, J.D., Münnich, M., Su, H., Meyerson, J.E. and Holloway, C.E. (2006), Tropical drying trends in global warming models and observations, *Proceedings of the National Academy of Sciences of the USA* 103, pp. 6110-6115.

Newell, R.G. and Wilson, N.E. (2005), "Technology Prizes for Climate Change Mitigation", *Resources for the Future (RFF), Discussion Paper 05-33*, 46 p.

Newman, J. (2005), *Policies to Reduce Greenhouse Gas Emissions in Industry: Implications for Steel*, OECD, SG/STEEL(2005)2, 27 p.

Ngheim, S.V., Rigor, I.G., Perovich, D.K., Clemente-Colón, P., Weatherly, J.W. and Neumann, G. (2007), "Rapid Reduction of Arctic Perennial Sea Ice", *Geophysical Research Letters* 34.

Nicholls, R.J., Wong, P.P., Burkett, V.R., Codignotto, J.O., Hay, J.E., McLean, R.F., Ragoonaden, S. and Woodroffe, C.D. (2007), "Coastal systems and low-lying areas", in Parry, M.L., Canziani, O.F., Palutikof, J.P., van der Linden, P.J. and Hanson, C.E. (eds.), *Climate Change 2007: Impacts, Adaptation and Vulnerability. Contribution of Working Group II to the Fourth Assessment Report of the Intergovernmental Panel on Climate Change*, Cambridge University Press, Cambridge, pp. 315-356.

NOAA (National Oceanic and Atmospheric Administration) (2007), *Climate of 2007 – in historical perspective*, Annual report, National Climatic Data Center, NOAA. Available at www.ncdc.noaa.gov/oa/climate/research/2007/ann/ann07.html

Nordhaus, W.D. (1997), *Climate Allowances Protocol (CAP): Comparison of Alternative Global Tradeable Emissions Regimes*, Paper presented to the NBER/Yale Workshop on International Environmental Economics, Snowmass, CO.

NOVA Science in the News (2009), *Glossary. Enhanced Greenhouse Effect – A Hot International Topic*, Australian Academy of Science. Available at www.science.org.au/nova/016/016glo.htm.

Nyong, A. (2008), "Climate Change Impacts in the Developing World: Implications for Sustainable Development", chapter forthcoming in *Development in the Balance: How Will the World's Poor Cope with Climate Change?*, Brookings Institution Press, Washington, DC.

OECD (Organisation for Economic Co-operation and Development) (1994), *Methodologies for Trade and Environmental Reviews*, OECD, Paris.

OECD (1997), *Eco-labelling: Actual Effects of Selected Programs*, OECD/GD(97)105, 81 p.

OECD (1999), *The Environmental Goods and Services Industry: Manual for Data Collection and Analysis*, OECD, Paris.

OECD (2001a), *Environmental Effects of Liberalizing Fossil Fuels Trade: Results from the OECD Green Model*, COM/TD/ENV(2000)38/FINAL, 35 p.

OECD (2001b), *Environmental Goods and Services. The Benefits of further global trade liberalization*, OECD, Paris, 114 p.

OECD (2001c), *Environmentally Related Taxes in OECD Countries, Issues and Strategies*, OECD, Paris, 142 p.

OECD (2004), *Current International Shipping Market Trends – Community Maritime Policy and Legislative Initiatives*, A paper presented at the OECD Workshop on Maritime Transport, OECD, Paris.

OECD (2005), *Trade that Benefits the Environment and Development: Opening Markets for Environmental Goods and Services*, OECD, Paris.

OECD (2006a), *Decoupling the Environmental Impacts of Transport from Economic Growth*, OECD, Paris.

OECD (2006b), *The Political Economy of Environmentally related Taxes*, OECD, Paris, 199 p.

OECD (2008a), *Climate Change Mitigation: What do we do?*, OECD, Paris.

OECD (2008b), *OECD Environmental Outlook to 2030*, OECD, Paris, 517 p.

OECD (2008c), *Promoting Sustainable Consumption: Good practices in OECD countries*, 59 p.

OECD-IEA (1997), *Questions and answers on emission trading among Annex I countries*, Information paper, 15 p.

Pacala, S. and Socolow, R. (2004), "Stabilization wedges: Solving the climate problem for the next 50 years with current technologies" in *Science* 305:5686, pp. 968-972. Supporting Online Material available at http://carbonsequestration.us/Papers-presentations/htm/Pacala-Socolow-ScienceMag-Aug2004.pdf.

Pachauri, R. (2007), *Conference of the Parties to the UNFCCC serving as the meeting of the Parties to the Kyoto Protocol (COP/MOP), Opening Ceremony 12 December 2007* – WMO/UNEP Intergovernmental Panel on Climate Change, Mr Rajendra Pachauri, Chairman (video presentation). Available at www.un.org/webcast/unfccc/2007/index.asp?go=09071212.

Parker, L. (2008), *"Carbon leakage" and Trade: Issues and Approaches*, Congressional Research Service, Report R40100, 40 p.

Parry, M.L., Canziani, O.F., Palutikof, J.P. and Co-authors (2007), "Technical Summary", in Parry, M.L., Canziani, O.F., Palutikof, J.P., van der Linden, P.J. and Hanson, C.E. (eds.), *Climate Change 2007: Impacts, Adaptation and Vulnerability. Contribution of Working Group II to the Fourth Assessment Report of the Intergovernmental Panel on Climate Change*, Cambridge University Press, Cambridge, pp. 23-78.

Pauwelyn, J. (2007), *US Federal Climate Policy and competitiveness Concerns: The Limits and Options of International Trade Law*, Nicholas Institute for Environmental Policy Solutions, Duke University, Working Paper, 44 p.

Peretto, P.F. (2003), "Endogenous Market Structure and the Growth and Welfare Effects of Economic Integration", *Journal of International Economics* 60:1, pp. 177-201.

Perkins, R. (2003), "Environmental leapfrogging in developing countries: A critical assessment and reconstruction", *Natural Resources Forum* 27:3, pp. 177-188.

Peters, G.P. and Hertwich, E.G. (2008a), "CO_2 Embodied in International Trade with Implications for Global Climate Policy", *Environmental Science & Technology* 42:5, pp. 1401-1407.

Peters, G.P. and Hertwich, E.G. (2008b), "Post-Kyoto Greenhouse Gas Inventories: Production Versus Consumption", *Climatic Change* 86, pp. 51-66.

Petersen, S. (2007), "Greenhouse gas mitigation in developing countries through technology transfer?: a survey of empirical evidence", *Mitigation and Adaptation Strategies for Global Change* 13:3, pp. 282-305.

Peterson, S. (2003), *Monitoring, Accounting and Enforcement in Emission Trading Regimes*, OECD, CCNM/GF/SD/ENV(2003)5/FINAL, 21 p.

Philibert, C. (2003), *Technology, Innovation, Development and Diffusion*, OECD and IEA Information Paper, COM/ENV/EPOC/IEA/SLT(2003)4, 48 p.

Philibert, C. (2006a), *Barriers to Technology Diffusion: The Case of Solar Thermal Technologies*, OECD/IEA, COM/ENV/EPOC/IEA/SLT(2006)9, 28 p.

Philibert, C. (2006b), *Certainty versus Ambition, Economic Efficiency in Mitigating Climate Change*, IEA/OECD, Report Number LTO/2006/03, 39 p.

Philibert, C. and Reinaud, J. (2004), *Emissions Trading: Taking stock and looking forward*, OECD-IEA, COM/ENV/EPOC/IEA/SLT(2004)/3, 44 p.

Pielke Jr, R., Wigley, T. and Green, C. (2008), "Dangerous assumptions", *Nature* 452, pp. 531-532.

Pitschas, C. (1995), "GATT/WTO Rules for Border Tax Adjustments and the Proposed European Directive Introducing a Tax on Carbon Dioxide Emissions and Energy", *Georgia Journal of International and Comparative Law* 24, pp. 479-500.

Pizer, W. (1999), "Choosing price or quantity controls for greenhouse gases", *Resources for the Future, Climate Issues Brief* 17, 12 p.

Pizer, W.A. (2007), "Scope and Point of Regulation for Pricing Policies to Reduce Fossil-Fuel CO_2 Emissions", in Kopp, R.J. and Pizer, W.A., *Assessing U.S. Climate Policy options. A report summarizing work at RFF as part of the inter-industry U.S. Climate Policy Forum*, 203 p.

Planistat-Luxembourg (2002), *Sustainable Impact Assessment (SIA) of the Trade Aspects of Negotiations for an Association Agreement between the European Communities and Chile.* Available at http://trade.ec.europa.eu/doclib/docs/2006/september/tradoc_112388.pdf.

Popp, D. (2006), "R&D Subsidies and Climate Policy: Is there a 'Free Lunch'?", *Climatic Change* 77:3-4, pp. 311-341.

Porter, M. and van der Linde, C. (1995), "Toward A New Conception of the Environment-Competitiveness Relationship", *Journal of Economic Perspectives* 9:4, pp. 97-118.

Ragwitz, M., Resch, G., Faber, T. and Huber, C. (2005), *Monitoring and evaluation of policy instruments to support renewable electricity in EU Member States*, Fraunhofer Institute Systems and Innovation Research, 39 p.

Ragwitz, R. and Huber, C. (2005), *Feed-in systems in Germany and Spain, and a comparison*, Frauenhofer Institute for Systems and Innovation research, 27 p.

Rahmstorf, S., Cazenave, A., Church, J., Hansen, J., Keeling, R., Parker, D. and Somerville, R. (2007), "Recent climate observations compared to projections", *Science* 316.

Ramanathan, K. (1994), "The polytrophic components of manufacturing technology", *Technological Forecasting and Social Change* 46:3, pp. 221-258.

Raupach, M.R., Marland, G., Ciais, P., Le Quéré, C. and Field, C.B. (2007), Global and regional drivers of accelerating CO_2 emissions, *Proceedings of the National Academy of Sciences* 104:24, pp. 10288-10293.

Reddy, N.M. and Zhao, L. (1990), "International technology transfer: A review", *Research Policy* 19:4, pp. 285-307.

Reilly, J. and Hohmann, N. (1993), "Climate Change and Agriculture: The Role of International Trade", *American Economic Review Papers and Proceedings* 83:2, pp. 306-323.

Reinaud, J. (2005), *Industrial competitiveness under the European Union Emissions Trading Scheme*, IEA information paper, 91 p.

Reinaud, J. (2008a), *Climate Policy and Carbon Leakage, Impacts of the European Emissions Trading Scheme on Aluminium*, IEA Information Paper, OECD/IEA, 43 p.

Reinaud, J. (2008b), *Issues behind Competitiveness and Carbon Leakages, Focus on Heavy Industry*, IEA Information Paper, OECD/IEA, 120 p.

Reinaud, J. and Philibert, C. (2007), *Emissions trading: trends and prospects*, OECD/IEA, 42 p.

Rich, D. (2004), "Climate Change, Carbon Taxes and International trade: An Analysis of the Emerging Conflict between the Kyoto Protocol and the WTO", *Environmental Economics and Policy, Globalization and the Natural Environment, Course* 131, Berkley Institute of the Environment, 14 p.

Richels, R.G., Tol, R.S.J. and Yohe, G.W. (2008), "Future scenarios for emissions need continual adjustment", *Nature* 453:155.

Rip, A. and Kemp, R. (1998), "Technological Change", in Rayner, S. and Malone, E.L. (eds.), *Human Choice and Climate Change* 2, Resources and Technology, Batelle Press, Washington, DC, pp. 327-400.

Rivera-Batiz, L.A. and Romer, P. (1991), "Economic Integration and Endogenous Growth", Quarterly *Journal of Economics* 106:2, pp. 531-555.

Roberts, J.T. and Grimes, P.E. (1997), "Carbon Intensity and Economic Development 1962-91: A Brief Exploration of the Environmental Kuznets Curve", *World Development* 25:2, pp. 191-198.

Rodriguez, F. and Rodrik, D. (1999), "Trade Policy and Economic Growth: A Skeptic's Guide to the Cross-National Evidence", *NBER Working Paper* 7081, NBER, Cambridge, MA.

Rogner, H.-H., Zhou, D., Bradley, R.. Crabbé, P., Edenhofer, O., Hare, B., Kuijpers, L. and Yamaguchi, M. (2007), "Introduction", in Metz, B., Davidson, O.R., Bosch, P.R., Dave, R. and Meyer, L.A. (eds.), *Climate Change 2007: Mitigation. Contribution of Working Group III to the Fourth Assessment Report of the Intergovernmental Panel on Climate Change*, Cambridge University Press, Cambridge and New York, NY.

Romer, P. (1986), "Increasing Returns and Long Run Growth", *Journal of Political Economy* 94, pp. 1002-1037.

Romer, P. (1990), "Endogenous Technological Change" *Journal of Political Economy* 98, S71-S102.

Rosenberg, N. (1982), *Inside the Black Box: Technology and Economics*, Cambridge University Press, Cambridge.

Rosenzweig, C., Casassa, G., Karoly, D.J., Imeson, A., Liu, C., Menzel, A., Rawlins, S., Root, T.L., Seguin, B. and Tryjanowski, P. (2007), "Assessment of observed changes and responses in natural and managed systems" in Parry, M.L., Canziani, O.F., Palutikof, J.P., van der Linden, P.J. and Hanson, C.E. (eds.), *Climate Change 2007: Impacts, Adaptation and Vulnerability. Contribution of Working Group II to the Fourth Assessment Report of the Intergovernmental Panel on Climate Change*, Cambridge University Press, Cambridge, pp. 79-131.

Rosenzweig, C., Karoly, D., Vicarelli M., Neofotis, P., Qigang Wu, Casassa, G., Menzel, A., Root, T.L., Estrella, N., Seguin, B., Tryjanowski, P., Chunzhen Liu, Rawlins, S. and Imeson, A. (2008), "Attributing physical and biological impacts to anthropogenic climate change", *Nature* 453, pp. 353-357.

Rosenzweig, C., Parry, M., Frohberg, K. and Fisher, G. (1993), *Climate Change and World Food Supply*, Oxford: Environmental Change Unit, University of Oxford.

Rounsevell, M.D.A, Reginster, I., Araújo, M.B., Carter, T.R., Dendoncker, N., Ewert, F., House, J.I., Kankaanpää, S., Leemans, R., Metzger, M.J., Schmit, C., Smith, P. and Tuck, G. (2006), "A coherent set of future land use change scenarios for Europe", *Agriculture Ecosystems and Environment* 114, pp. 57-68.

Rowell, D.P., and Jones, R.G. (2006), Causes and uncertainty of future summer drying over Europe, *Climate Dynamics* 27, pp. 281-299.

Sachs, J.D. and Warner, A. (1995), "Economic Reform and the Process of Global Integration", *Brookings Papers on Economic Activity* 1995:1, pp. 1-95.

Saddler H., Muller, F. and Cuevas, C. (2006), "Competitiveness and Carbon Pricing. Border adjustments for greenhouse policies", *The Australia Institute, Discussion Paper* 86, 53 p.

Sagafi-Nejad, T. (1991), "International Technology Transfer Literature: Advances in theory, empirical research, and policy", in Robinson, R.D., *The International Communication of Technology: A Book of Readings*, Taylor and Francis, Oxford.

Sanchez-Choliz, J. and Duarte, R. (2004), "CO_2 Emissions Embodied in International Trade: Evidence for Spain", *Energy Policy* 32:18, pp. 1999-2005.

Saunders, S. and Schneider, K. (2000), *Removing Energy Subsidies in Developing and Transition Economies*, ABARE, Conference Paper presented at 23rd Annual IAEE International Conference, Sydney, 21 p.

SBSTA (Subsidiary Body for Scientific and Technological Advice) (2007), *Synthesis report on technologies for adaptation identified in the submissions from Parties and relevant organizations*, United Nations Office at Geneva. Available at http://unfccc.int/resource/docs/2007/sbsta/eng/06.pdf.

Schumpeter, J.A. (1934), *The Theory of Economic Development*, Harvard University Press.

Schuster, U. and Watson, A.J. (2007), "A variable and decreasing sink for atmospheric CO_2 in the North Atlantic", *Journal of Geophysical Research* 112, C11006.

Sewell, W.R.D. (1969), "Review of Pollution, Property & Prices: An Essay in Policy-Making and Economics by J.H. Dales", *Canadian Journal of Political Science* 2:3, pp. 386-387.

Shafik, N. (1994), "Economic Development and Environmental Quality: An Econometric Analysis", *Oxford Economic Papers* 46, pp. 757-773.

Sharif, M.N. (1994), "Integrating business and technology strategies in developing countries", *Technological Forecasting and Social Change* 45:2, pp.151-167.

Shui, B. and Harriss, R.C. (2006), "The Role of CO_2 Embodiment in US-China Trade", *Energy Policy* 34:18, pp. 4063-4068.

SIA-EMFTA Consortium (The European Union's Sustainability Impact Assessment Study of the EuroMediterranean Free Trade Area) (2007), *Sustainability Impact Assessment of the Euro-Mediterranean Free Trade Area*. Available at http://trade.ec.europa.eu/doclib/docs/2006/november/tradoc_131340.pdf.

Sijm, J.P.M. (2002), *The performance of feed-in-tariffs to promote renewable electricity in European countries*, Energy Research Centre of the Netherlands (ECN-C-02-083), 18 p.

Sijm, J.P.M., Kuik, O.J., Patel, M., Oikonomou, V., Worrell, E., Lako, P., Annevelink, E., Nabuurs, G.J. and Elbersen, H.W. (2004), *Spillovers of Climate Policy: An Assessment of the Incidence of Carbon Leakage and Induced Technological Change due to CO_2 Abatement Measures*, ECN, Bilthoven.

Sindico, F. (2008), "The EU and Carbon Leakage: How to Reconcile Border Adjustments with the WTO? ", *European Energy and Environmental Law Review* 17:6, pp. 328-340.

Sinner, J. (2002), *Addressing Competitiveness Impacts of Climate Change Policies*, A Report to New Zealand's Ministry of Economic Development, 37 p.

Smit, B. and Wandel, J. (2006), "Adaptation, adaptive capacity and vulnerability", *Global Environmental Change* 16, pp. 282-292.

Smith, J.U., Smith, P., Wattenbach, M., Zaehle, S., Hiederer, R., Jones, R.J.A., Montanarella, L., Rounsevell, M.D.A., Reginster, I. and Ewert, F. (2005), "Projected changes in mineral soil carbon of European croplands and grasslands, 1990-2080", *Global Change Biology* 11, pp. 2141-2152.

Smith, P., Martino, D., Cai, Z., Gwary, D., Janzen, H., Kumar, P., McCarl, B., Ogle, S., O'Mara, F., Rice, C., Scholes and B., Sirotenko, O. (2007), "Agriculture", in Metz, B., Davidson, O.R., Bosch, P.R., Dave, R. and Meyer, L.A. (eds.), *Climate Change 2007: Mitigation. Contribution of Working Group III to the Fourth Assessment Report of the Intergovernmental Panel on Climate Change*, Cambridge University Press, Cambridge and New York, NY.

Snape, J. and Souza, J. de (2006), *Environmental taxation law. Policy, contexts and practice*, Ashgate, 648 p.

Soksod, S. and Suwicharcherdchoo, P. (2006), *Rescaling the Energy Label No. 5: 2006 version in Thailand*, Appliances Efficiency Improvement Project, Demand Side Implementation Division, EGAT, 5 p. Available at http://e-nett.sut.ac.th/pdf%5CENETT49-139.pdf.

Solow, R.M. (1956), "A Contribution to the Theory of Economic Growth", *Quarterly Journal of Economics* 70:1, pp. 65-94.

Steenblik, R. (2005), "Liberalisation of Trade in Renewable-Energy Products and Associated Goods: Charcoal, Solar Photovoltaic Systems, and Wind Pumps and Turbines", *OECD Trade and Environment, Working Paper* 7, 40 p.

Steenblik, R. (2006), "Liberalisation of Trade in Renewable-Energy Products and Associated Goods: Biodiesel, Solar Thermal and Geothermal Energy", *Working Paper* 1, OECD Trade and Environment, 26 p.

Steenblik, R. (2007), *Biofuels – At What Cost? Government support for ethanol and biodiesel in selected OECD countries. A synthesis of reports addressing subsidies for biofuels in Australia, Canada, the European Union, Switzerland and the United States*, The Global

Subsidies Initiative (GSI) of the International Institute for Sustainable Development (IISD), 72 p.

Steenblik, R. and Matsuoka, T. (2008), *Facilitating trade in selected climate change-mitigation technologies in the electricity generation and heavy-industry sectors*, COM/TAD/ENV/JWPTE(2008)28, 79 p.

Stefano, C. (2008), "Assessing the EU-ETS Effectiveness in Reaching the Kyoto Target: An Analysis of the Cap Stringency", *Rotterdam Institute of Law and Economics, Working Paper Series* 2008/14, 32 p.

Stephens, G.L. (2005), Cloud feedbacks in the climate system: a critical review, *Journal of Climate* 18, pp. 237-273.

Stern, N. (2006), *The Economics of Climate Change: The Stern Review*, Cambridge University Press, Cambridge, 308 p.

Stiglitz, J.E. (2006), "A New Agenda for Global Warming", *Economists' Voice*, Berkeley Electronic Press.

Stiglitz, J.E. (2007), *Making Globalization Work*, Penguin Books, 384 p.

Stokey, N.L. (1998), "Are there Limits to Growth?", *International Economic Review* 39:1, pp. 1-31.

Suri, V. and Chapman, D. (1998), "Economic Growth, Trade and Energy: Implications For the Environmental Kuznets Curve", *Ecological Economics* 25:2, pp. 195-208.

Tanaka, K. (2008), *Assessing Measures of Energy Efficiency Performance and Their Application in Industry*, IEA Information Paper, OECD/IEA, 40 p.

Thomas, C.D., Cameron, A., Green, R.E., Bakkenes, M., Beaumont, L.J., Collingham, Y,C., Erasmus, B.F.N., de Siqueira, M.F., Grainger, A., Hannah, L., Hughes, L., Huntley, B., Jaarsveld, A.S. van, Midgley, G.F., Miles, L., Ortega-Huerta, M.A., Townsend Peterson, A., Phillips O.L. and Williams, S.E. (2004), "Extinction risk from climate change", *Nature* 427, pp. 145-147.

Thompson, L.G., Mosley-Thompson, E., Davis, M.E., Henderson, K.A., Brecher, H.H., Zagorodnov, V.V., Mashiotta, T.A., Lin, P.N., Mikhalenko, V.N., Hardy, D.R. and Beer, J. (2002), "Kilimanjaro ice core records: evidence of Holocene change in tropical Africa", *Science* 298, pp. 589-593.

Thorne, S. (2008), "Towards a framework of clean energy technology receptivity", *Energy Policy* 36:8, pp. 2831-2838.

Thuiller, W., Broennimann, O., Hughes, G., Alkemade, J.R.M., Midgley, G.F. and Corsi, F. (2006), "Vulnerability of African mammals to anthropogenic climate change under conservative land transformation assumptions", *Global Change Biology* 12, pp. 424-440.

Tietenberg, T. (1998), "Tradable Permits and the Control of Air Pollution-Lessons from the United States", *Zeitschrift für Angewandte Umweltforschung, Sonderheft* 9, pp. 11-31.

Tietenberg, T. (2002), "Lessons from using transferable permits to control air pollution in the United States", in Van den Bergh J.C.J.M. (ed.), *Handbook of environmental and resource economics*, 1328 p.

Tietenberg, T. (2006), *Emissions Trading. Principles and Practice*, Second Edition, 230 p.

Tol, R.S.J, Bohn, M., Downing, T.E., Guillerminet, M., Hizsnyik, E., Kasperson, R., Lonsdale, K., Mays, C., Nicholls, R.J., Olsthoorn, A.A., Pfeifle, G., Poumadere, M, Toth, F.L., Vafeidis, N., van derWerff, P.E. and Yetkiner, I.H. (2006), "Adaptation to five metres of sea level rise", *Journal of Risk Research* 9:5, pp. 467-482.

Tol, R.S.J. (2002), "Estimates of the damage costs of climate change. Part 1: benchmark estimates", *Environmental and Resource Economics* 21, pp. 47-73.

Torras, M. and Boyce, J. (1998), "Income, Inequality and Pollution", *Ecological Economics* 25:2, pp. 147-160.

Trenberth, K.E., Jones, P.D., Ambenje, P., Bojariu, R., Easterling, D., Klein Tank, A., Parker, D., Rahimzadeh, F., Renwick, J.A., Rusticucci, M., Soden, B. and Zhai, P. (2007), "Observations: Surface and Atmospheric Climate Change", in Solomon, S., Qin, D., Manning, M., Chen, Z., Marquis, M., Averyt, K.B., Tignorm, M. and Miller, H.L. (eds.), *Climate Change 2007: The Physical Science Basis*, Contribution of Working Group I to the Fourth Assessment Report of the Intergovernmental Panel on Climate Change, Cambridge University Press, Cambridge and New York, NY.

Tsigas, M.E., Friswold, G.B. and Kuhn, B. (1997), "Global Climate Change and Agriculture" in Hertel, T.W. (ed.), *Global Trade Analysis: Modeling and Applications*, Cambridge University Press, New York.

Turner, B.L., Kasperson, R.E., Matson, P.A., McCarthy, J.J., Corell, R.W., Christensen, L., Eckley, N., Kasperson, J.X., Luers, A., Martello, M.L., Polsky, C., Pulsipher, A. and Schiller, A. (2003), "A framework for vulnerability analysis in sustainability science", *Proceedings of the National Academy of Sciences USA* 100, pp. 8074-8079.

UNCTAD (United Nations Conference on Trade and Development) (2007a), *Review of Maritime Transport 2007*, UNCTAD, Geneva.

UNCTAD (2007b), *UNCTAD Transport Newsletter* 38, UNCTAD, Geneva.

UNEP (United Nations Environment Programme) (2001), *Reference Manual for the Integrated Assessment of Trade-Related Policies*, UNEP, New York and Geneva.

UNEP (2002), *An emerging market for the environment: A guide to Emission Trading*, 40 p.

UNEP (2007a), *Global Outlook for Snow and Ice*, Editing and production by UNEP/GRID-Arendal. Available at www.unep.org/geo/geo_ice/.

UNEP (2007b), *Global Environment Outlook – GEO4: Environment for Development*, UNEP, New York and Geneva, 540 p.

UNEP (2008), *Reforming Energy Subsidies, Opportunities to Contribute to the Climate Change Agenda*, 32 p.

UNEP/GRID-Arendal (2008), *Atmospheric concentrations of carbon dioxide (CO_2) - Mauna Loa or Keeling curve*. Available at http://maps.grida.no/go/graphic/atmospheric-concentrations-of-carbon-dioxide-co2-mauna-loa-or-keeling-curve and based on data from NOAA Earth System Research Laboratory, accessed 8 November 2007 at www.esrl.noaa.gov/gmd/ccgg/trends/co2_data_mlo.html.

UNEP-UNCTAD (2002), *An emerging market for the environment: a Guide to emissions trading*, 40 p.

UNFCCC (United Nations Framework Convention on Climate Change) (1998), *Kyoto Protocol to the United Nations Framework Convention on climate change*. Available at http://unfccc.int/resource/docs/convkp/kpeng.pdf.

UNFCCC (2006), *Technologies for adaptation to climate change*, produced by the Adaptation, Technology and Science Programme of the UNFCCC Secretariat, Bonn.

UNFCCC (2007a), *Climate Change – Impacts Vulnerabilities and Adaptation in Developing Countries*, 60 p.

UNFCCC (2007b), *Technologies for adaptation to the adverse effects of climate change*. Available at www.rtcc.org/2007/html/dev_adaptation_unfccc.html.

UNFCCC (2008), *Report of the Conference of the Parties on its thirteenth session*, held in Bali from 3 to 15 December 2007, Addendum Part Two: Action taken by the Conference of the Parties at its thirteenth session, UNFCCC, Climate Change Secretariat, Bonn. Available at http://unfccc.int/resource/docs/2007/cop13/eng/06a01.pdf#page=3. (8/8–08).

United Nations (1997), "Glossary of Environment Statistics", *Studies in Methods, Series F, No. 67*, New York.

University of Manchester (2007), *Update of the Overall Preliminary Trade SIA EU-MERCOSUR Final Report, unpublished manuscript*. Available at http://www.sia-trade.org/mercosur/phase1/OVERALL_FINAL__REVISEDNOVEMBER.pdf

US Committee on Energy and Commerce (2007), *Climate Change Legislation Design White Paper: Scope of a Cap-and-Trade Program*, 22 p.

US Committee on Energy and Commerce (2008), *Climate Change Legislation Design White Paper: Competitiveness Concerns/Engaging Developing Countries*, 16 p.

US Environmental Protection Agency (2001), *The United States Experience with Economic Incentives for Protecting the Environment*, EPA-240-R-01-001, 230 p.

US Environmental Protection Agency (2003), *Tools of the Trade: A Guide to Designing and Operating a Cap and Trade Programme for Pollution Control*, EPA-W430-B-03-002, 78 p.

US Environmental Protection Agency (2007), *Inventory of U.S. Greenhouse gas Emissions and Sinks: 1990-2005, Annex 2: Methodology and Data for Estimating CO_2 Emissions from Fossil Fuel Combustion*, EPA-430-R-07-002, 393 p.

US Trade Representative (2000) *Guidelines for Implementation of Executive Order 13141: Environmental Review of Trade Agreements*. www.ustr.gov/sites/default/files/guidelines%20for%2013141.pdf

Valverde, L.J. and Andrews, M.W. (2006), *Global Climate Change and Extreme Weather: An Exploration of Scientific Uncertainty and the Economics of Insurance*, Insurance Information Institute, New York, NY, 51 p.

Velders, G.J.M., Andersen, S.O., Daniel, J.S., Fahey, D.W., and McFarland, M. (2007a), "Climate Benefits of an Accelerated HCFC Phase-out: Addendum", in Kaniaru, D. (ed.), *The Montreal Protocol: Celebrating 20 Years of Environmental Progress: Ozone Layer and Climate*, UNEP/Earthprint, London, 359 p.

Velders G.J.M., Andersen S.O., Daniel J.S., Fahey D.W., and McFarland M. (2007b), "The Importance of the Montreal Protocol in Protecting Climate", *Proceedings of the National Academy of Science of the USA* 104:12, pp. 4814-4819.

Verburg, R., Woltjer, G., Tabeau, A., Eickhout, B. and Stehfest, E. (2008), *Agricultural Trade Liberalisation and Greenhouse Gas Emissions: A simulation Study Using the GTAP-IMAGE Modelling Framework*, LEI, The Hague.

Verrill, C.O. Jr. (2008), "Maximum, Carbon Intensity Limitations and the Agreement on Technical Barriers to Trade", *Carbon and Climate Law Review* 1/2008, pp. 43-53.

Voigt, C. (2008), "WTO Law and International Emissions Trading: Is there Potential for Conflict?", *Carbon and Climate Law Review* 1, pp. 54-66.

Waide, P. and Bernasconi-Osterwalder, N. (2008), *Standards, Labelling and Certification*, Trade and Climate Change Seminar, 18-20 June 2008, Copenhagen, GMF/IISD, Background Paper, 11 p.

Webb, M.J., Senior, C.A., Sexton, D.M.H., Ingram, W.J., Williams, K.D., Ringer, M.A., McAvaney, B.J., Colman, R., Soden, B.J., Gudgel, R., Knutson, T., Emori, S., Ogura, T., Tsushima, Y., Andronova, N., Li,vB., Musat, I., Bony, S. and Taylor, K.E. (2006), "On the contribution of local feedback mechanisms to the range of climate sensitivity in two GCM ensembles", *Climate Dynamics* 27, pp. 17-38.

Weber, C.L., Peters, G.P., Guan, D. and Hubacek, K. (2008), "The Contribution of Chinese Exports to Climate Change", *Energy Policy* 36, pp. 3572-3577.

WEC (World Energy Council) (2008), *Energy Efficiency Policies around the World: Review and Evaluation*, 117 p.

Wellington, F., Bradley, R., Childs Staley, B., Rigdon, C. and Pershing, J. (2007), *Scaling Up: Global Technology Deployment to Stabilize Emissions*, World Resources Institute, 20 p.

Werksman, J. (1999), "Greenhouse Gas Emissions Trading and the WTO", *Review of European Community and International Environmental Law* 8:3, pp. 251-264.

WHO (World Health Organization) (2000), "Vegetation Fires", *Fact Sheet No. 254*, 3 p. Available at www.who.int/mediacentre/factsheets/fs254/en/index.html.

Wiedmann, T., Wood, R., Lenzen, M., Minx, J., Guan, D. and Barrett, J. (2007), *Development of an Embedded Carbon Emissions Indicator – Producing a Time Series of Input-Output Tables and Embedded Carbon Dioxide Emissions for the UK by Using a MRIO Data Optimisation System*, Report to the UK Department for Environment, Food and Rural Affairs by Stockholm Environment Institute at the University of York and Centre for Integrated Sustainability Analysis at the University.

Wiel, S. and McMahon, J. (2003), "Governments should implement energy-efficiency standards and labels – cautiously", *Energy Policy* 31, pp. 1403-1415.

Wiel, S. and McMahon, J.E. (2005), *Energy Efficiency Labels and Standards: A Guidebook for Appliances, Equipment, and Lighting*, Collaborative Labeling and Appliance Standards Program, Washington, DC, 300 p.

Wilbanks, T.J. and Sathaye, J. (2003), "Integrating mitigation and adaptation as possible responses to global climate change", *Environment* 45:5, pp. 28-38.

Wilbanks, T.J., Romero Lankao, P., Bao, M., Berkhout, F., Cairncross, S., Ceron, J.-P., Kapshe, M., Muir-Wood, R. and Zapata-Marti, R. (2007a), "Industry, settlement and society" in Parry, M.L., Canziani, O.F., Palutikof, J.P., van der Linden, P.J. and Hanson, C.E. (eds.), *Climate Change 2007: Impacts, Adaptation and Vulnerability. Contribution of Working Group II to the Fourth Assessment Report of the Intergovernmental Panel on Climate Change*, Cambridge University Press, Cambridge, pp. 357-390.

Wilbanks, T.J., Leiby, P., Perlack, R., Ensminger, T.J. and Wright, S.B. (2007b), *Toward an integrated analysis of mitigation and adaptation: some preliminary findings, Mitigation and Adaptation Strategies for Global Change* 12, pp. 713-725.

Wilkins, G. (2002), *Technology Transfer for Renewable Energy. Overcoming barriers in Developing Countries*, The Royal Institute of International Affairs, Earthscan Publications, London, 237 p.

Willis, J.K., Roemmich, D., and Cornuelle, B. (2004), "Interannual variability in upper-ocean heat content, temperature and thermosteric expansion on global scales", *Journal of Geophysical Research* 109, C12036.

Winters Lynch, J. (1994), *Determinants of Effectiveness for Environmental Certification and Labelling Programs*, US EPA, Washington DC, 98 p.

Wood, A. (1999), "Openness and Wage Inequality in Developing Countries: The Latin American Challenge to East Asian Conventional Wisdom" in Baldwin, R., Cohen, D., Sapir, A. and Venables, A. (eds.), *Market Integration, Regionalism and the Global Economy*, Cambridge University Press, Cambridge, New York and Melbourne, pp. 153-181.

World Bank (1992), *The World Bank Development Report 1992: Development and the Environment*, The World Bank, Washington, DC.

World Bank (2008a), *Development and Climate Change. A Strategic Framework for the World Bank Group*, Consultation Draft, August 2008. Available at http://siteresources.worldbank.org/EXTCC/Resources/407863-1219339233881/DevelopmentandClimateChange.pdf.

World Bank (2008b), *International trade and climate change*, The World Bank, Washington DC, 144 p.

WRI (World Resources Institute) (2009), *Climate Analysis Indicators Tool (CAIT) Version 6.0.* Washington, DC. Available at http://cait.wri.org/.

Worrell, E., Berkel, R.V., Fengqi, Z., Menke, C., Schaeffer, R. and Williams, R.O. (2001), "Technology transfer of energy efficient technologies in industry: a review of trends and policy issues", *Energy Policy* 29:1, pp. 29-43.

WTO (World Trade Organization) (1995), *Negotiating History of the Coverage of the Agreement on TBT with Regard to Labelling Requirements, Voluntary Standards, and Processes and Production Methods Unrelated to Product Characteristics*, G/TBT/W/11, Note by the Secretariat, 54 p.

WTO (1997), *Taxes and Charges for Environmental Purposes – Border Tax Adjustment*, WT/CTE/W/47, Note by the Secretariat, 24 p.

WTO (1999), *Guide to the Uruguay Round Agreements*, Kluwer Law International, The Hague, London, Boston, WTO Secretariat, 285 p.

WTO (2002), *GATT/WTO Dispute Settlement Practice Relating to GATT Article XX, Paragraphs (b), (d) and (g)*, WT/CTE/W/203, Note by the Secretariat, 48 p.

WTO (2006), *A Handbook on the TBT Agreement*, WTO Secretariat, Geneva, 187 p.

WTO (2007), *List of Environmental Reviews*, WT/CTE/W/245, Note by the Secretariat, 21 p.

WTO (2008a), *Environmental database for 2005*, WT/CTE/EDB/5, Note by the Secretariat, 97 p.

WTO (2008b), *International Trade Statistics 2008*, WTO, Geneva, 255 p.

WTO (2008c), *World Trade Report 2008: Trade in a Globalizing World*, WTO, Geneva, 178 p.

Xu, B. and Wang, J. (1999), "Capital Goods Trade and R&D Spillovers in the OECD", *Canadian Journal of Economics* 32, pp. 1258-1274.

Xu, X. (2000), "International Trade and environmental regulation: time series evidence and cross section test", *Environmental and Resource Economics* 17:3, pp. 233-257.

Yohe, G. and Tol, R.S.J. (2002), "Indicators for social and economic coping capacity – moving toward a working definition of adaptive capacity", *Global Environmental Change* 12, pp. 25-40.

Zhang, Z. (1998), "Greenhouse Gas Emissions Trading and the World Trading System", *Journal of World Trade* 32:5, pp. 219-239.

Zhang, Z. and Assunção, L. (2004), "Domestic Climate Policies and the WTO", *The World Economy* 27:3, pp. 359-386.

Zhang,vZ. and Baranzini A. (2004), "What do we know about carbon taxes? An inquiry into their impacts on competitiveness and distribution of income", *Energy Policy* 32, pp. 507-518.

GATT and WTO Case Law

GATT Panel Report, *Canada – Measures Affecting Exports of Unprocessed Herring and Salmon* ("*Canada – Herring and Salmon*"), L/6268, adopted 22 March 1988, BISD 35S/98.

GATT Panel Report, *Japan – Customs Duties, Taxes and Labelling Practices on Imported Wines and Alcoholic Beverages* ("*Japan – Alcoholic Beverages I*"), L/6216, adopted 10 November 1987, BISD 34S/83.

GATT Panel Report, *Swedish Anti-Dumping Duties* ("*Sweden – AD Duties*"), L/328, adopted 26 February 1955, BISD 3S/81.

GATT Panel Report, *Thailand – Restrictions on Importation of and Internal Taxes on Cigarettes* ("*Thailand – Cigarettes*"), DS10/R, adopted 7 November 1990, BISD 37S/200.

GATT Panel Report, *United States – Prohibition of Imports of Tuna and Tuna Products from Canada* ("*US – Canadian Tuna*"), L/5198, adopted 22 February 1982, BISD 29S/91.

GATT Panel Report, *United States Tax Legislation (DISC)* ("*US – DISC*"), L/4422, adopted 7 December 1981, BISD 23S/98.

GATT Panel Report, *United States – Taxes on Petroleum and Certain Imported Substances* ("*US – Superfund*"), L/6175, adopted 17 June 1987, BISD 34S/136.

GATT Panel Report, *United States – Taxes on Automobiles* ("*US – Taxes on Automobiles*"), DS31/R, 11 October 1994, unadopted.

GATT Panel Report, *United States – Restrictions on Imports of Tuna* ("*US – Tuna (EEC)*"), DS29/R, 16 June 1994, unadopted.

GATT Panel Report, *United States – Restrictions on Imports of Tuna* ("*US – Tuna (Mexico)*"), DS21/R, 3 September 1991, unadopted, BISD 39S/155.

WTO Panel Report, *Argentina – Measures Affecting the Export of Bovine Hides and Import of Finished Leather* ("*Argentina – Hides and Leather*"), WT/DS155/R and Corr.1, adopted 16 February 2001, DSR 2001:V, 1779.

WTO Appellate Body Report, *Brazil – Measures Affecting Desiccated Coconut* ("*Brazil – Desiccated Coconut*"), WT/DS22/AB/R, adopted 20 March 1997, DSR 1997:I, 167.

WTO Appellate Body Report, *Brazil – Measures Affecting Imports of Retreaded Tyres* ("*Brazil – Retreaded Tyres*"), WT/DS332/AB/R, adopted 17 December 2007.

WTO Appellate Body Report, *Canada – Measures Affecting the Export of Civilian Aircraft* ("*Canada – Aircraft*"), WT/DS70/AB/R, adopted 20 August 1999, DSR 1999:III, 1377.

WTO Appellate Body Report, *Canada – Certain Measures Concerning Periodicals* ("*Canada – Periodicals*"), WT/DS31/AB/R, adopted 30 July 1997, DSR 1997:I, 449.

WTO Appellate Body Reports, *China – Measures Affecting Imports of Automobile Parts* ("*China – Auto Parts*"), WT/DS339/AB/R, WT/DS340/AB/R, WT/DS342/AB/R, adopted 12 January 2009.

WTO Appellate Body Report, *European Communities – Measures Affecting Asbestos and Asbestos-Containing Products* ("*EC – Asbestos*"), WT/DS135/AB/R, adopted 5 April 2001, DSR 2001:VII, 3243.

WTO Appellate Body Report, *European Communities – Trade Description of Sardines* ("*EC – Sardines*"), WT/DS231/AB/R, adopted 23 October 2002, DSR 2002:VIII, 3359.

WTO Appellate Body Report, *India – Additional and Extra-Additional Duties on Imports from the United States* ("*India – Additional Import Duties*"), WT/DS360/AB/R, adopted 17 November 2008.

WTO Appellate Body Report, *Japan – Taxes on Alcoholic Beverages* ("*Japan – Alcoholic Beverages II*"), WT/DS8/AB/R, WT/DS10/AB/R, WT/DS11/AB/R, adopted 1 November 1996, DSR 1996:I, 97.

WTO Appellate Body Report, *Korea – Measures Affecting Imports of Fresh, Chilled and Frozen Beef* ("*Korea – Various Measures on Beef*"), WT/DS161/AB/R, WT/DS169/AB/R, adopted 10 January 2001, DSR 2001:I, 5.

WTO Appellate Body Report, *United States – Countervailing Duties on Certain Corrosion-Resistant Carbon Steel Flat Products from Germany* ("*US – Carbon Steel*"), WT/DS213/AB/R and Corr.1, adopted 19 December 2002, DSR 2002:IX, 3779.

WTO Appellate Body Report, *United States – Tax Treatment for "Foreign Sales Corporations" – Recourse to Article 21.5 of the DSU by the European Communities* ("*US – FSC (Article 21.5 – EC)*"), WT/DS108/AB/RW, adopted 29 January 2002, DSR 2002:I, 55.

WTO Appellate Body Report, *United States – Standards for Reformulated and Conventional Gasoline* ("*US – Gasoline*"), WT/DS2/AB/R, adopted 20 May 1996, DSR 1996:I, 3.

WTO Appellate Body Report, *United States – Import Prohibition of Certain Shrimp and Shrimp Products* ("*US – Shrimp*"), WT/DS58/AB/R, adopted 6 November 1998, DSR 1998:VII, 2755.

WTO Appellate Body Report, *United States – Import Prohibition of Certain Shrimp and Shrimp Products – Recourse to Article 21.5 of the DSU by Malaysia* ("*US – Shrimp (Article 21.5 – Malaysia)*"), WT/DS58/AB/RW, adopted 21 November 2001, DSR 2001:XIII, 6481.

Abbreviations and symbols

BTA	Border tax adjustment
CDM	Clean Development Mechanism
CH_4	Methane
CO_2	Carbon dioxide
CO_2-eq	Carbon dioxide equivalent
COP	Conference of the Parties
CTE	Committee on Trade and Environment
EC	European Community
EIA	US Energy Information Administration
ETS	Emission trading scheme
EU	European Union
EU-ETS	European Union Emission Trading Scheme
GATS	General Agreement on Trade in Services
GATT	General Agreement on Tariffs and Trade
GCMs	General Circulation Models
GDP	Gross Domestic Product
GHG	Greenhouse Gas
$GtCO_2$-eq	Giga tonnes of carbon dioxide equivalent
GWP	Global Warming Potential
HCFC	Hydrochlorofluorocarbon
HFCs	Hydrofluorocarbon
HS	Harmonized Commodity Description and Coding System
IEA	International Energy Agency
IMO	International Maritime Organization
IPCC	Intergovernmental Panel on Climate Change
IPRs	Intellectual property rights
ISO	International Organization for Standardization
MEA	Multilateral Environmental Agreement
MERCOSUR	Southern Common Market
N_2O	Nitrous oxide
NAFTA	North American Free Trade Agreement
ODS	Ozone Depleting Substances
OECD	Organisation for Economic Co-operation and Development
PFCs	Perfluorocarbons
ppm	parts per million
PPMs	Processes and production methods
R&D	Research and Development
RTA	Regional Trade Agreement
SCM Agreement	Agreement on Subsidies and Countervailing Measures
SF_6	Sulphur hexafluoride
SRES	Special Report on Emission Scenarios
TBT	Technical barriers to trade
UNFCCC	United Nations Framework Convention on Climate Change
US$	US dollar

Full table of contents